GUIDE TO
California Planning

GUIDE TO
California Planning

THIRD EDITION

William Fulton
Paul Shigley

GUIDE TO
California Planning

ISBN-10: 0-923956-45-X
ISBN-13: 978-0-923956-45-5

IMPORTANT NOTICE

Before you rely on the information in this
book, please be sure you have the latest
edition and are aware that some changes
in statutes or case law may have gone
into effect since the date of publication.
The book, moreover, provides general
information about the law. Readers
should consult an attorney before relying
on the representations found herein.

September 2005

Solano Press Books
P.O. Box 773 • Point Arena, California 95468
tel (800) 931-9373 • fax (707) 884-4109
email spbooks@solano.com
Internet www.solano.com

Printed in the United States of America
10 9 8 7 6 5 4

The Book at a Glance

Contents

Part One ▪ The California Landscape

Part Two ▪ The Local Planning Process

Contents

Contents

Contents

Contents

Contents
Short Articles

Contents
Short Articles

Preface

When I sat down to write the first edition of *Guide to California Planning,* I used to have to coax my daughter to sleep in her crib in order to get some peace and quiet to get the job done. As the third edition goes to press, she is in high school–voluble, articulate, and full of ideas about the future of California's cities and natural landscapes.

Which means that this book has been around for a long time–long enough to see several governors come and go, to say nothing of planning fads, real estate cycles, and Internet bubbles. (I actually typed part of the first edition on a typewriter.)

California has changed much during this time. The state's population has increased by more than 6 million people with no sign of slowing down. The demographic shift during that time has been particularly dramatic, creating the first truly multi-racial, multi-ethnic state. Home prices have more than doubled and are now the highest in the country. The state is increasingly expensive, crowded, and urban in a way that was unimaginable at the time this book was first written.

If, as a reader, you notice my co-author Paul Shigley and I struggling to convey the essence of this intensely urban society in this third edition, it shouldn't be surprising. The entire planning profession in California is struggling too–to apply procedures and principles dating back to the suburban era of the 1960s and '70s to a very different state in the 21st century. The third edition stands as a portrait of a state in flux.

Nevertheless, it is our hope that the changes and updates that we have made in this edition will be valuable to all readers. When the first edition of the *Guide* was published, we were surprised that it received an overwhelming reception and unexpected popularity in academic quarters. Warren Jones, founder of Solano Press Books, came to me in 1987 with the idea of writing for an audience of professionals and citizens—practicing planners and consultants, land use lawyers, newly appointed planning commissioners, angry citizen activists. Quickly, however, the *Guide* became a staple in planning classrooms throughout the state. This bonus has continued to pay dividends by keeping me in touch with both professors and students who have used the book over the years. Almost weekly, I am both flattered and horrified when some gray-haired, middle-aged planning director comes up to tell me that he or she used this book as an undergraduate.

In crafting the third edition, Paul and I focused mostly on reshaping the last hundred pages of the book—the descriptions of urban development and natural resource protection that have become increasingly important in the last decade. We devoted considerable attention to smart growth and infill housing, which have emerged only since 2000 as the major topic of conversation among planners in the state. We have also expanded the natural resource section to hint at the next generation of issues—stormwater runoff, nonpoint source pollution, total maximum daily load, and a whole of host of emerging acronyms that will bring natural resource protection more deeply into the planning and replanning of urban areas in the 21st century.

So, as you can see, even after all this time, understanding how planning works in California is still a struggle for us. But we hope that we have articulated the trends and processes clearly enough in this book that it won't be a struggle for you.

> — William Fulton
> Ventura, California
> August 2005

Acknowledgments

It is never easy to fit the task of writing a book into a typical busy life. You can plan, schedule, and anticipate, but once you get into it, you never know how long it is going to take or what else you are going to have to sacrifice to get it done. In this sense every book is a small miracle produced by lots of people.

The Third Edition of *Guide to California Planning* is mostly a testament to the skill and persistence of my colleague Paul Shigley, the editor of *California Planning & Development Report*. When Paul agreed in late 2003 to take the lead in the revisions for the new edition, I don't think he really knew what he was getting into. But the results speak for themselves. I have never met another journalist capable of understanding and articulating the process of land use planning as well as Paul does, and his knowledge of central and northern California more than counterbalances my southern, coastal-centric perspective. Our collaboration is a joy to me, and this edition probably would not exist without him.

It would take an entire book to thank everyone who has helped with the effort of *Guide to California Planning* over the last 15 years, but I will name a few. Over the last six years, my colleagues at Solimar Research Group have provided all kinds of assistance for which I am grateful. These include Ryan Aubry, Karin Garite, Alicia Harrison, Erik Kancler, Mary Molina, Peter Sezzi, Susan Weaver, and Chris Williamson. Aaron Engstrom in particular made an important contribution in getting the book out the door. As always I am grateful to my students in the UC Davis Extension Land Use and Natural Resources Certificate Program. These mid-career professionals—several hundred of them over the past 15 years—have served as a kind of intelligence-gathering system helping me stay in touch with what's going on in the world of planning practice. Most recently, Dowell Myers and others at the School of Policy, Planning, and Development at the University of Southern California have provided me with a rewarding academic home, and Dowell himself has served as a source of insight and inspiration on the state's ongoing demographic changes. Vicki Torf provided support, inspiration, and a lot of hard work on the *Guide* for many years and without her this book probably never would have been finished in the first place. And our daughter Sara Torf-Fulton is full of energy, enthusiasm, and ideas about cities. For that I am grateful, and for her I am more than happy to keep pushing to use good planning to shape a better future for the next generation of Californians.

— William Fulton
Ventura, California
August 2005

In 1986, only a few weeks into in my professional journalism career, I attended my first land use hearing. It was an informal gathering conducted by a Sacramento County supervisor concerning a proposed strip mall in the then-unincorporated community of Citrus Heights. At the time, I knew nothing about land use planning. As I persisted as a newspaper reporter, though, I gained an appreciation for—and even a level of expertise in—planning, regulatory schemes, and real estate development.

By far the most important people in my on-the-job education in planning were, naturally, planners. Over the years, I have spent untold hours interviewing and talking informally with professional planners. The vast majority of these planners have been exceedingly patient as they explained not only particular development proposals, but the regulatory and political systems within which they work. Among the planners who were most helpful during my 12 years in the newspaper business were Richard Spitler, Andrew Cassano, Tom Parilo, Denis Cook, Sharon Boivin, David Shpak, Pat Norman, Kent Manuel, and Mike Mitchell.

Any understanding of planning in California also requires a grasp of how local government is organized and funded. Among the public officials who assisted me in this area were Gene Albaugh,

Gene Haroldsen, Beryl Robinson Jr., Wes Peters, Mike Warren, Dan Landon, Jan Hagel, Jim Curtis, and Cathy Thompson.

In 1999, I made the move from newspapers to *California Planning & Development Report*, where I have had the opportunity to write about land use full-time and at a much deeper level. My education has continued thanks to planners, attorneys, developers, and other professionals in the field, as well as a variety of public policy experts. At the top of my list are Peter Detwiler, Fred Silva, Randy Kanouse, Clyde McDonald, Daniel Carrigg, Susan Brandt-Hawley, James Moose, Dan Curtin, Steve Kostka, Larry Mintier, Ted James, Jeff Loux, and the late Jim Roddy.

Of course, sometimes your best sources are close at hand. While at CP&DR, I have had the good fortune to work with Publisher William Fulton, Contributing Editors Morris Newman, John Krist, and Kenneth Jost, and former columnist Stephen Svete—all of whom have been around the land use business in one form or another for longer than I have. Thanks, gentlemen, for treating a small-town newspaper reporter as a peer.

Finally, I thank my wife, Dana. A longtime public servant, she has taught me much of what I know about local government finance, management, and accounting. Plus, she never tires of my after-work stories about the intricacies of CEQA or the latest downtown plan for an inner-ring suburb. Thanks, Sweetie.

       — Paul Shigley
       Centerville, California
       August 2005

About the Authors

William Fulton is President of Solimar Research Group (www.solimar.org) and a Senior Scholar at the School of Policy, Planning, and Development at the University of Southern California. Mr. Fulton founded *California Planning & Development Report* in 1986 and wrote the first two editions of *Guide to California Planning*, published in 1991 and 1999. He has written several other books, including *The Reluctant Metropolis: The Politics of Urban Growth in Los Angeles* (1997) and *The Regional City: Planning for the End of Sprawl*, co-authored with Peter Calthorpe (2001). His recent work at Solimar has focused on infill development policies in land-constrained communities. A graduate of the UCLA Graduate School of Architecture and Urban Planning, Mr. Fulton lives in Ventura, California with his daughter, Sara Torf-Fulton. He was elected to the Ventura City Council in 2003.

Paul Shigley has been the Editor of *California Planning & Development Report* (www.cp-dr.com) since 1999. Prior to joining *CP&DR*, he was a newspaper reporter and editor in Northern California for 12 years, during which time he covered everything from county fair pig judging to government land use policy. More recently, his work has appeared in *Governing* and *Planning* magazines, and on the op-ed pages *of The Washington Post, the Los Angeles Times, the Sacramento Bee,* and *the Bakersfield Californian*. A graduate of California State University, Sacramento, he and his wife, Dana, live in the Shasta County community of Centerville.

Part One

The California Landscape

Chapter 1

Introduction: How Planning in California Really Works

For more than a century and a half, the story of California has been the story of growth. From a standing start at statehood in 1850, the Golden State has accumulated some 37 million residents today. That's a Texas and a half, or New York doubled. It's more than Canada or Colombia, and more than the other 10 Western states combined. Just since the beginning of World War II—that is, since the beginning of California's modern industrial era—the state's population has grown by some 30 million residents, or 1,300 new residents every day. In other words, California has added half a million people per year every year for the past 65 years—a level of sustained population growth virtually unsurpassed in the history of the industrialized world.

Just since the beginning of World War II, California's population has grown by some 30 million residents, or 1,300 new residents every day.

Even though the state's population growth fluctuates depending on economic conditions, the underlying upward trend doesn't change much. During the first half of the 1990s, California was in a deep economic recession. Yet population continued to bound upward by some 300,000 to 400,000 persons per year. When the economy bounced back, so did population growth—quickly reaching a level approaching 600,000 persons per year. So many of these new residents were children that California's school officials estimated that the state should be building one elementary school classroom every single day to keep up.

All these people do a lot of things and consume a lot of land, and here too the numbers are staggering. Today, California still has more than 17 million jobs. The state also has 32 million registered cars and trucks—an increase of 10 million just since 1990, which incidentally was the last time the state gas tax was increased. (As if to

Despite the recession of the early 1990s, California still has more than 17 million jobs.

California's Profile

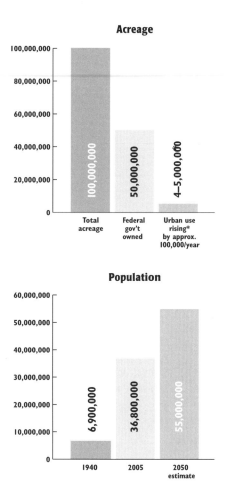

Acreage

Total acreage	Federal gov't owned	Urban use rising* by approx. 100,000/year
100,000,000	50,000,000	4–5,000,000

Population

1940	2005	2050 estimate
6,900,000	36,800,000	55,000,000

Jobs/Registered Cars

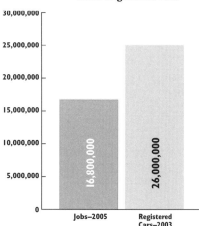

Jobs–2005	Registered Cars–2003
16,800,000	26,000,000

confirm all those stereotypes about California being the ultimate car-oriented society, the state actually has more registered vehicles than licensed drivers.)

The sprawling metropolitan areas being created by this large and dynamic society have been well documented. Most people go to work close to where they live, but these new communities are dotted all across the California landscape, sometimes seemingly at random. And the long-distance commuting that does take place has assumed a metaphorical significance in the California culture.

Riverside County seeks to lure jobs inside its borders so commuters will stop driving 50 or 60 miles to Orange County for work. Modesto, 100 miles inland, sometimes insists that it is part of the Bay Area. San Diegans joke that the Marines at Camp Pendleton are there to protect them from Los Angeles. Currently, between 4 million and 5 million acres of California land is devoted to urban use, and that figure is rising by more than 100,000 acres per year. (Altogether the state has about 100 million acres of land inside its boundaries, half of it owned by the federal government.)

And despite the sheer magnitude of the numbers, this growth dynamic is expected to continue. Global economic and demographic forces still favor California and appear likely to push growth into the state for another couple of generations at least. State demographers recently predicted that California's population will increase to more than 54 million by 2050—and that was a decrease from the last estimate! Even if this prediction proves to be an overestimate, there is little doubt that the population will continue to rise measurably in the decades ahead, along with the human activity that goes with it.

Around this culture of growth, California has built up a huge infrastructure of urban and environmental planning. In virtually every community, large or small, local politics revolves around the question of growth—how to accommodate it, how to shape it, and often how to repel it. A cadre of planners, biologists, lawyers, engineers, and other specialists troll the state looking for clients (developers, cities, counties, school districts, homeowner groups, and others) who will hire them to assist in the process. Through technical analyses, public hearings, litigation, and a thousand other techniques, all these players engage in a constant public debate about what gets built where.

For decades, this planning infrastructure has revolved around the single question of how to consume more undeveloped land— where to build the highways, where to build the houses, which farmland to chew up, how to save wetlands and other environmentally sensitive areas. With the state growing so rapidly, the underlying assumption was that each person, each car, and each job added to the state's inventory required urban California to encroach more deeply into farmland and nature. All the state's planning processes still reflect this bias—the general plan system, analysis under the California Environmental Quality Act (CEQA), and especially the state's sophisticated system of subdivision regulations. Throughout the state, planning is at least partly the task of imagining what a community will be like at "buildout," that misty moment in the future when all land has finally been consumed and everyone is settled into a tidy new neighborhood.

CEQA = California Environmental Quality Act

Yet over the last decade, growth in California has taken on a fundamentally different character. For the first time in history, the state is growing more from within than from without. And for the first time in memory, that growth has as much to do with the volatile recycling of urban neighborhoods as with the consumption of raw land.

For the first time in history, the state is growing more from within than from without. And for the first time in memory, that growth has as much to do with the volatile recycling of urban neighborhoods as with the consumption of raw land.

Even as late as 1970, the state was mostly a non-Hispanic white (78 percent) middle-class suburban society, increasingly concerned with protecting the environment and quality of life people had worked so hard to attain. These Californians, or their parents, came from other parts of the United States. To them, planning was the process of managing the arrival of other middle-class migrants from the East and Midwest into the new suburbs being constructed all over the state.

Today, California's growth is driven largely by immigration from Latin America and Asia—and even more important, by the large families born to those immigrants once they are here. More than half a million babies are now born each year in California. The state best known as the "end of the rainbow," luring immigrants from all over the country and all over the world, is now producing most of its residents from within.

Today, California's growth is driven largely by immigration from Latin America and Asia—and even more important, by the large families born to those immigrants once they are here.

As others have documented extensively, this "new" California is not only increasingly native-born, but also increasingly diverse. Today non-Hispanic whites represent less than half the population, with Latinos making up about a third; by 2010, these numbers will be about even. Asians' numbers are growing even faster in percentage terms, constituting another 11 percent. (African Americans have remained constant at about 7 percent.) In recent years, population growth has led not so much to wholesale destruction of the natural landscape for new suburbs, though that still happens, but to a radical alteration of existing urban neighborhoods, as extended families buy larger homes and poor families double up or live in garages.

Redevelopment, infill, high-density, mixed use—these are the phrases that dominate California planning today, and they reflect the state's changing circumstances.

Development still occurs on the urban fringe, especially in the Central Valley and the Inland Empire, which have emerged as the new suburban frontier. But in most parts of the state, the nature of urban growth has changed dramatically since this book was first published in 1991. California today is a far more racially mixed and working-class state than it was 30 years ago. The old suburban frontiers like Orange County and Silicon Valley have matured into urban areas—diverse, thriving, and running out of land. Redevelopment, infill, high-density, mixed use—these are the phrases that dominate California planning today, and they reflect the state's changing circumstances. California today is a mature, expensive, crowded urban place.

Yet the planning system described in this book remains largely unchanged from the 1960s and '70s, when it was created and put into place. The system still assumes, by and large, that California is a suburbanizing state dominated by the conversion of raw land to the first generation of suburban development. In the past decade, the system has lurched slightly toward today's urban reality, but with great difficulty.

As we move deeper into the 21st century, we are faced with the task of adapting a cumbersome structure oriented toward suburbia so that we may cope with a very different society.

As we move deeper into the 21st century, we are faced with the task of adapting a cumbersome structure oriented toward suburbia so that we may cope with a very different society. Regulating the subdivision of land will, no doubt, remain an important activity. California continues to have a big market for new houses, new offices, and new stores, as well as a huge cadre of real estate developers looking for projects. But over time the build-out scenario will become relatively less important compared with the question of what happens when a supposedly built-out neighborhood suddenly starts growing and changing in ways the original planners never anticipated.

It is impossible from this vantage point to guess how this more volatile, urban-oriented future will play out for planning in California. Most of the planning expertise in the state—and most of the technical tools the planners use—is oriented toward measuring and regulating the first generation of a community's growth. It is even hard to determine how to revise a book like this in the face of these changes; as will be obvious to any reader, this book is still necessarily tied in some ways to the old, land-oriented way of approaching planning in California. But there is no question that, in the long run, planning will have to adapt to the notion that California is a more mature society nowadays, with a different set of needs than ever before.

There is no question that, in the long run, planning will have to adapt to the notion that California is a more mature society nowadays, with a different set of needs than ever before.

What Planning Is

Throughout this book, the word "planning" will be used to encompass the broad range of activities usually lumped together under the terms "urban planning" and "regional planning," including housing policy and environmental planning. In most instances, however, this term will refer specifically to land use planning. A good working definition of land use planning as the term is used in this book would be:

> The process by which public agencies—mostly govern-ments—determine the intensity and geographical arrangements of various land uses in a community.

Land use planning is the process by which public agencies—mostly local governments—determine the intensity and geographical arrangements of various land uses in a community.

Put more simply, planning is the process by which our society decides what gets built where.

At various times in its history, planning has also sought to encompass a broad range of social policy and economic development issues. This book's definition of the word "planning" does not include these activities directly. They are dealt with only indirectly, when the way land is used and distributed within a community affects people's social and economic circumstances.

Planning occurs in a variety of settings—urban, suburban, rural, and even regional. There is the planning of mature cities, which has two aspects: the recycling of older neighborhoods and business districts into denser communities, which often raises questions of how to concentrate development in one area in order to protect another; and attempts to revive ailing inner city neighborhoods, which often involves luring new development to areas perceived as risky. There is the re-planning of older suburbs, which now must accommodate more housing and economic activity even though they have run out of land. There is the planning of fast-growing suburban areas developing for the first time—places such as Riverside County—which often raises questions of infrastructure finance, site planning, traffic flow, and protection of open space. (This type of planning is often conducted by the smaller cities—those with populations of up to 100,000—that govern most suburban areas in California.) There is the planning of small towns and rural areas, which often focuses on preservation of historic buildings and farmland, as well as economic development. And then there is planning at the regional level—assuring that each region has a good mixture of jobs, housing, transportation options, and other land uses required for communities to function.

This book will focus, at one time or another, on all these different types of planning, but with more emphasis on some than on others. As originally written in 1991, *Guide to California Planning* dealt mostly with emerging suburban areas because that's where most of the state's planning effort was concentrated. But since the nature of California's growth patterns is changing, in the future more attention will be focused on city neighborhoods and mature older suburbs, as well as newly developing areas on the metropolitan fringe.

This edition does incorporate more information about redevelopment, "smart growth" and "New Urbanism," and other issues associated with growth and planning of existing urban areas. And, of course, both mature and emerging communities deal with the same set of planning laws and processes that will be described in this book. To a considerable degree however, the book will continue to focus on the traditional definition of planning as managing the conversion of natural or farm areas to urban use. In part, this is simply because the book necessarily reflects the prevailing biases of the system that it purports to explain.

Even within this somewhat narrow definition, however, the concept of planning covers a lot of ground. In general, it is fair to say that the process includes five interrelated activities:

- **Design.** The physical layout of a community or a specific development project, including site planning and urban design.
- **Laws and regulation.** The shaping and application of state laws and local regulations to a particular planning process or to a specific development project.
- **Environmental analysis.** The task of assessing the impact of any given plan or development project on the state's environment, an analysis that can range across any number of topics including air pollution, toxics, and impact on wildlife.
- **Socioeconomic analysis.** The task of assessing the impact of a plan or project on a neighborhood's social structure, on a

Since the nature of California's growth patterns is changing, in the future more attention will be focused on city neighborhoods and mature older suburbs, as well as newly developing areas on the metropolitan fringe.

Five Elements of Planning

community's fiscal health, on a region's economic basis, and similar socioeconomic considerations.

- **Political approval.** The task of winning the support of the public and elected representatives for a plan, a planning process, or a specific development project—everything from approval of a general plan to the issuance of permits for a particular project.

All five of these activities will be discussed in this book. However, the basic focus is on laws and regulations and, especially, on politics. Planning decisions are made in a legal and regulatory framework that is determined by political considerations, and very often those decisions come about directly as the result of political pressure.

Planning decisions are made in a legal and regulatory framework that is determined by political considerations, and very often those decisions come about directly as the result of political pressure.

Planning as Politics

In most textbooks, planning is described as a sober and objective process—the process used to arrange buildings, roads, and other built structures on the ground so that society can function efficiently and effectively. This description makes planning seem highly technical, and there is no question that technical skill (cartography, data analysis, legalistic interpretation, and so on) plays an important role.

But planning is a public decision-making process, and this means that in the end, planning is politics. All the technical skill in the world does not alter the fact that every planning decision rests with a group of five or seven (or in some cases more) elected officials—politicians, if you will—who must work within a highly constrained political environment. Ultimately, planning is getting three votes out of five, or four out of seven. This fact, more than any other, defines the character of planning in California.

Ultimately, planning is getting three votes out of five, or four out of seven. This fact, more than any other, defines the character of planning in California.

Because planning is politics, it is inevitably subject to political lobbying by interest groups. On a state or national level, such activity is often derided as surrendering the public good to the "special interests." But in local planning, no less than in Sacramento or Washington, interest group lobbying is simply an expression of the age old American political tradition of pluralism. Different groups of people with different points of view come together in a political context to hash out a consensus. Pluralism in local planning is necessary because the different players approach planning from such vastly different perspectives.

Pluralism in local planning is necessary because the different players approach planning from such vastly different perspectives.

The legal rationale for planning in California is straightforward and idealistic, and it carries a touch of the state's deeply rooted environmentalist ethic. Land, according to California's planning, zoning, and development laws, is "an exhaustible resource." The purpose of planning is "to insure its preservation and use in ways which are economically and socially desirable in an attempt to improve the quality of life in California." In this way, planning is supposed to serve the public interest.

But land is not only a resource requiring preservation. Under the American system of values, economics, and government—and, especially, in a fast-growing economy like California's—land is also a commodity to be owned, traded, and exploited for profit. Private property rights are respected by the courts and jealously guarded by civil libertarians. Private landowners' decisions about where to invest and what to build are dictated primarily by the demands of the private real estate market, not by the principles of good city planning.

Environmentalists, preservationists, and planners may want to preserve and protect scenic wonders, fragile ecosystems, and rare buildings. But developers want land uses arranged to maximize the marketability of their projects, and investors want to protect their investment by preserving the convenience, attractiveness, and future sales potential of the properties they own. (This last category includes California's 10 million or so homeowners, whose financial well-being, thanks to home prices that are double the national average, rests more than ever before in the value of their houses.)

This difference in attitude between the public goals of planning and the private goals of real estate investors is important, because most plans, however inspired, are not self-executing. They are translated into reality only when private developers try to build something. Planners may shape the broad contours of growth and development according to public concerns. But the specific patterns that go into the ground are created, ultimately, by private investors seeking to maximize financial gain.[1]

These two distinct world views—land as resource and land as commodity—come into conflict continuously in the planning process. In addition, these two views often run up against a third idea: land as the context for a human community.

Even as environmentalists want to preserve land and developers want to exploit it, those who live in an existing community want to make sure that, whatever is done, the future use of land enhances

---

1. Occasionally, public entities such as redevelopment agencies and port districts are able to initiate projects themselves, but they too must rely on the response of private investors for success.

their quality of life rather than detracts from it. As California has become more crowded and development battles have become more contentious, homeowner activists have more and more become staunch defenders of the status quo—at least in their neighborhoods and in their backyards. That's one of the reasons the slow-growth movement still holds a powerful allure for many Californians.

How Planning in California Really Works

Even given the narrow definition of planning presented above, when we speak of "planning," we are really speaking of two different processes: plan "making" and plan "implementation."

Plan "making" is the process of devising plans for communities—general plans, specific plans, district plans, and other policy documents designed to guide the future development of a community. Plan "implementation" is the process of carrying out those plans on a project-by-project basis through zoning decisions, permit approvals (or denials), and other individual actions on the part of local governments.

Plan "making" is the process of devising plans for communities—general plans, specific plans, district plans, and other policy documents designed to guide the future development of a community.

Because it is a broad-ranging policy process, plan making tends to be the classic pluralistic process. Many different interest groups jockey to influence the types of policies that will be adopted. (This process will be discussed in more detail in chapter 6, General Plans.) By contrast, plan implementation usually operates as a classic regulatory system—as a government mechanism designed to restrain private businesses in order to achieve a public good that the private market apparently can't provide. While plan making is proactive, plan implementation is usually reactive, as the regulators await private development proposals and then respond to them.

Plan implementation usually operates as a classic regulatory system—as a government mechanism designed to restrain private businesses in order to achieve a public good that the private market apparently can't provide.

These two processes sometimes become intertwined more in planning than in other areas of public policy. As will be discussed in later chapters, implementation tools such as zoning variances are sometimes used to create a de facto policy change without going through the plan-making process. Perhaps most important, the plan implementation process is subject to more direct political pressure than most regulatory mechanisms. Decisions are made by the same local politicians who set the policies, and they are often subject to the same kind of lobbying from the same interest groups during regulatory decisions as during policy discussions.

Throughout California, the planning scenario unfolds in similar fashion from city to city and county to county. Deep pocket developers bankroll local political campaigns and hire armies of consultants in hopes of getting their projects approved. Powerful citizen groups raise the banner of environmental protection, historic preservation, or quality of life in order to stop the developers or slow them down. Financially strapped city governments seek to extract from new development the funds they can no longer obtain from property taxes. On the community level, planning is a lever used by virtually every interest group on the local scene to get what it wants.

Indeed, the power of all interest groups—or at least their direct involvement in the planning process—seems to have grown in recent years. Citizen groups have gained tremendous leverage over the land use process, and, if well organized, they can snag virtually any project they dislike in California's vast legal underbrush.

Most state planning laws, buttressed by expansive court rulings, now require considerable public participation.

This power arises from the legal structure of planning in California, which is unusually open to the public. Most state planning laws, buttressed by expansive court rulings, now require considerable public participation. Other laws, such as the California Environmental Quality Act, require the release of vast amounts of information about proposed development projects, and establish intricate procedures that must be followed, so that local officials cannot shut the public out.

Citizen groups have also made effective use of California's longstanding tradition of "citizen enforcement" of laws in the planning field. Few state planning laws are enforced by the state government itself—that is to say, state bureaucrats do not stand over the shoulder of local planners and developers, threatening to punish them if laws are not followed. In most cases, the only way to hold developers and local governments accountable is by suing them.

In most cases, the only way to hold developers and local governments accountable is by suing them.

Despite the expansive involvement of citizen groups, the pendulum in recent years has actually swung toward the landowners. In a series of recent cases (that will be discussed in detail in chapter 13), the United States Supreme Court has reined in the power of government agencies to regulate the activities of private landowners. From the 1960s through the mid-'80s, the California courts gave government agencies a free hand in restricting construction and regulating land. Now the hand is no longer quite so free. Cities, counties, and state agencies can be held accountable by property owners who feel wronged by regulation. These cases have not fomented a revolution, but they have led to a subtle change in the balance of power between developers and local governments.

The overtly political nature of planning is a good thing, in many ways, because it serves to sort out the public interest and hold the planning process accountable. It is important to watch the interest groups closely, however. Planning, by its very nature, is a public policy system susceptible to manipulation by small groups of people—and especially small groups of property owners—with a narrow agenda.

It is ironic, for example, that the Supreme Court's recent property rights decisions are meant to protect property owners from overly restrictive land use regulations. As originally conceived and used early in the 20th century, land use regulations were actually meant to "protect" private property owners—or, at least, certain groups of private property owners.

The first important zoning ordinance in this country, the New York City ordinance of 1916, was designed (among other purposes) to halt the march of tenements up Fifth Avenue toward the mansions of the bourgeoisie. Thus, 90 years ago, well-to-do New Yorkers learned one of the basic facts of land use regulations: that even though they may be grounded in lofty statements about the public welfare, land use regulations are most powerful as a tool of manipulation by narrow interest groups. This fact remains at the root of many planning controversies today. Unfortunately, the manipulation of the land use system by a variety of interest groups (ranging from developers to environmentalists) often prevents planning from serving as a tool to help shape a vision for a community's future.

The manipulation of the land use system by a variety of interest groups (ranging from developers to environmentalists) often prevents planning from serving as a tool to help shape a vision for a community's future.

And because they are highly susceptible to political pressure, land use regulations can be exploited by anyone able to gain leverage over a city council or county board of supervisors—not just homeowners or slow-growthers, but also big-time developers who need a zone change or some other governmental approval in order to build a project. The history of zoning in America is filled with colorful examples of municipal corruption. During the first half of this century, it was not uncommon for elected and appointed officials in the "machine politics" cities of the Northeast and Midwest to "sell" zone changes for personal gain.

During the first half of this century, it was not uncommon for elected and appointed officials in the "machine politics" cities of the Northeast and Midwest to "sell" zone changes for personal gain.

California has been surprisingly clean of blatant corruption over the years. But large landowners still manage to influence the process in subtle ways. For example, developers bankroll many local political campaigns in California. The reason is simple: No other group of potential contributors has so much to gain from a local government's decisions. A local council member's vote one way or another can literally turn a pauper into a millionaire if he owns the right piece of property (or vice versa if he owns the wrong piece).

In larger cities—and in counties, which often have large areas of unpopulated territory—it is much harder to assemble a corps of campaign volunteers capable of counteracting developers' money.

In return for campaign contributions, these developers expect, at the very least, a sympathetic ear from local council members or supervisors. In small cities, the financial power of developers is often overcome by sheer grassroots power—precinct walking and telephone campaigning by dedicated volunteers. In larger cities—and in counties, which often have large areas of unpopulated territory—it is much harder to assemble a corps of campaign volunteers capable of counteracting developers' money.

California's state requirements for local planning are largely procedural, and these requirements are so numerous and so detailed that virtually any plan or development project can be held up in court.

Landowners large and small are also able to use legal pressure, just as environmentalists and homeowner groups do. (Remember that homeowners, as in the Fifth Avenue example, should often be viewed as simply another class of property owners.) California's state requirements for local planning are largely procedural, and these requirements are so numerous, and so detailed, that virtually any plan or development project can be held up in court, at least for a while.

Such legal challenges often try to stand planning or environmental laws on their head just for the benefit of an angry property owner. For example, when the city of San Francisco wanted to condemn a mortuary in crowded Chinatown, in order to tear it down and create a park, the mortuary sued—under the California Environmental Quality Act! Ignoring the benefits of creating a park in a crowded section of the city, the mortuary's lawyers claimed that the mortuary served as an important piece of the cultural environment because it was the only establishment in Chinatown that still performed traditional Chinese funerals. The court of appeal eventually slapped this argument down as a sham.

So planning is politics—the classic politics of interest groups with a narrow agenda seeking to acquire enough clout to impose

Planning works best in California when a broad variety of interest groups are at work, which are well organized and able to balance each other off. It works poorly when the local political scene is dominated by one interest group or another.

that agenda on a broader public. Planning works best in California when a broad variety of interest groups is at work, when those groups are well organized, and when they balance each other out. It works poorly when the local political scene is dominated by one interest group or another—environmentalists, homeowners, the chamber of commerce—that is able to ram its agenda through.

Current Trends in California Planning

While the planning process in California is shaped largely by the political forces described above, the planning environment is being shaped today by a series of socioeconomic trends that are driving growth and change in the state. Today, three underlying trends are helping to create the environment within which planning operates:

- Population growth and demographic change
- Dramatic redistribution of the population within the state and within metropolitan areas
- A dwindling land supply in most metropolitan areas

Population Growth and Demographic Change

As the discussion at the beginning of this chapter indicated, the future of California is being shaped not only by continuing population growth, but also by the demographic forces underlying that growth. The historic trend of population growth fueled by domestic in-migration has dwindled away, though in good economic times it still plays a role. In its place is a new trend, in which virtually all population growth comes from foreign immigration (mostly from Asia and Latin America) and natural increase.

It is hard to predict just what role this changing demographic pattern will play in California planning in the future. To a large extent, the impact will depend on the extent to which immigrant groups embrace America's pre-existing community values—and the extent to which they can afford to achieve traditional American goals even if they want to embrace them.

For example, crowded immigrant neighborhoods in California have a completely different character than even working-class suburbs. Community life is often very public in nature, revolving around churches, parks, and other community institutions that attract crowds. But as immigrant groups climb the economic ladder, will this aspect of their culture remain? Will immigrant families still congregate in public parks in large numbers even as they can afford larger homes in more privacy-oriented suburban neighborhoods? Or will they shed this public part of their life to become more "American"?

It is impossible to make a definitive statement at this point, but the answer to questions like this one will play a very important role in shaping the future of California planning.

Dramatic Shift in the Distribution of California's Population

At the same time that the nature of California's population is shifting, so is its distribution. Driven by many of the same forces, population

The future of California is being shaped not only by continuing population growth, but also by the demographic forces underlying that growth.

growth is moving in two different directions—inward to central cities and older suburbs, and outward to the metropolitan fringe and, very often, beyond the fringe to small towns and truly rural areas.

In many parts of the country where the middle class has fled to the suburbs, central-city neighborhoods have been more or less abandoned, leading planners to call for reinvestment and renewal. In California's metropolises, something different is going on. Middle-class residents of all races still seek to escape to bucolic suburbs if they can, but their departure is not causing older neighborhoods to empty out. Instead, they are becoming more crowded.

For example: In the 1970s, the working-class industrial suburbs around the Bell and Huntington Park areas of Los Angeles County fell victim to white flight. They have since become modest but burgeoning suburbs with a high population of Latinos, both native-born and immigrant. The result? Since 1975, the population in these cities has almost doubled, even though the cities themselves have not increased in geographic size. This kind of demographic pressure in older neighborhoods makes it hard for planners to argue that the familiar strategy of luring people back to the city is credible. The people are already there.

At the same time, however, the demographic changes are causing middle-class people, retirees, and others to flee, just as they have been doing for decades. For the past two decades, Southern California's middle-class has headed for the so-called "Inland Empire" of San Bernardino and Riverside Counties. More recently, Bay Area retirees and other equity refugees from metropolitan California have been moving to attractive rural areas, such as the Sierra Nevada foothills and the Central and North Coasts. All these areas are among the most environmentally sensitive in California, creating a host of new problems.

Dwindling Land Supply

Much of the concern about growth in California these days is focused on the rapidly changing landscapes in the inland areas, where farms and natural areas are visibly giving way to conventional suburban development. But most of the actual population growth is occurring in the mature urban areas closer to the coast—San Diego, Orange County, Los Angeles, and the Bay Area. And in all of these areas, available land supplies are dwindling fast. In a study for the Department of Housing and Urban Development, UC Berkeley Professor John Landis concluded that Orange and Santa Clara

In California's metropolises, middle-class residents of all races still seek to escape to bucolic suburbs if they can, but their departure is not causing older neighborhoods to empty out. Instead, they are becoming more crowded.

California Land Distribution

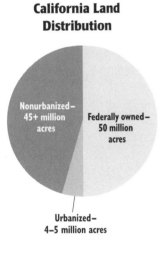

Nonurbanized—45+ million acres

Federally owned—50 million acres

Urbanized—4–5 million acres

Much of the concern about growth in California these days is focused on the rapidly changing landscapes in the inland areas, where farms and natural areas are visibly giving way to conventional suburban development.

Counties do not have enough land to accommodate expected future growth by 2010. Los Angeles, San Diego, and some other Bay Area counties are not far behind.

This dwindling land supply—combined with the other two trends described above—is the main reason that California growth issues are shifting in nature. In most areas where the population is growing, there is simply not enough land to accommodate the additional growth with traditional suburban development. Thus, both local governments and developers are gradually shifting toward "infill" development—high density housing and commercial projects, often in locations that were previously used for some other, lower intensity activity. Drive-in movies theaters have given way to shopping centers; older malls have been replaced by townhome projects. As time goes on, the dwindling land supply will become an ever larger issue, forcing California to squarely address the "second generation" of urban growth that is now upon us.

As time goes on, the dwindling land supply will become an ever larger issue, forcing California to squarely address the "second generation" of urban growth that is now upon us.

Ongoing Issues in California Planning

The political pressures on the planning process, combined with the socioeconomic trends described above, have combined to create six overriding issues that pervade all planning efforts in California. We will lay out these issues now, and return to them again and again throughout this book, because they underlie many of the difficulties California planning faces today. These issues are:

- The political nature of the planning process
- The ongoing state-local fiscal crisis
- Competition and lack of cooperation among local governments
- High housing prices
- The issue of sprawl versus compact urban form
- Property rights

The Political Nature of the Planning Process

Planning has always been political, and sophisticated interest groups on all sides have long used the planning process as a political tool. Still, one of the overriding issues in California planning today is that it has become more overtly political than ever before. Furthermore, three specific characteristics make it difficult to manage.

Planning has always been political, and sophisticated interest groups on all sides have long used the planning process as a political tool.

Heightened Political Awareness. The first characteristic is simply the heightened political awareness and organization on all sides. Beginning in the 1970s, developers and citizen groups transformed themselves into much more overtly political players. This transformation did not put an end to growth and development as a controversial issue, however. Rather, in community after community, it simply heightened the battle between developers and slow-growthers.

The more that the development community tried to exert its influence over local politics the better organized and more astute slow-growthers became. The more powerful the slow-growthers became, the more money developers shoveled into supporting pro-growth candidates and opposing local growth-control initiatives. Both sides honed their political skills, but in most communities they were not able to overcome the pro-growth/slow-growth confrontation.

Single-Issue Politics. The rise of citizen groups—along with increased use of the ballot and the lawsuit—has given planning in California the same polarizing, single-issue orientation that we see in Washington around abortion and gun control. The planning process is often characterized by political players (homeowners, developers, environmentalists) focused on a single objective and unwilling to compromise to achieve a broader vision of the public interest.

Frequently, for example, procedural attacks are used when a political battle over a project's merits has been lost. And the procedural attack need not be a bald perversion of the law, as in the case of the Chinese mortuary, in order for it to work against the defined public interest. Often, a group of environmentalists or homeowners will make some sort of technical or procedural challenge—the adequacy of an environmental impact report, for example, or consistency with the local general plan—simply because that is the only avenue left open to them. Their goal is not really to produce a better EIR, or a project more consistent with the general plan, but to kill the project altogether by making life miserable for the developer. The same dynamics are also at work when citizen groups place a development project or a land use plan on the ballot.

Easy access to the ballot or the courtroom encourages single-issue politics because it allows interest groups to reject the outcome of the political process. If you lose before the city council or board of supervisors, you can always sue or go to the ballot—and both a vote and a lawsuit are likely to be stark win-lose situations rather than arenas requiring compromise. You can stand true to your principles and gain an outright victory, or else fall on your sword in defeat. At the very least, the need to balance competing interests—a need basic to the concept of planning for a community's future—has been eliminated.

The planning process is often characterized by political players (homeowners, developers, environmentalists) focused on a single objective and unwilling to compromise to achieve a broader vision of the public interest.

EIR = Environmental impact report

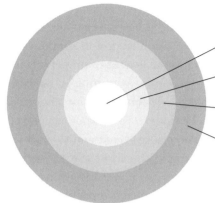

Politics of Proximity

Land owner—most interested in proposed project

Adjacent neighbors—strongest concerns, likely opposition to project

Surrounding neighborhood—concerned about mitigation of effects

Surrounding town or towns—little or no concern; may only be interested in project benefits

The Politics of Proximity. Because land use issues tend to be highly localized, the average citizen's interest in any particular land use issue usually depends on one's proximity to the piece of land in question.

Take, for example, a proposal to expand an old shopping center into a large regional mall. The person with the most intense interest in this proposal is the person who actually owns the property. Typically, the people who live adjacent to the shopping center will be the most active participants in the political process—most likely in opposition to the entire thing. People who live in the neighborhood—say, a couple of blocks away—will likely have specific concerns that might be mitigated, such as increased traffic. But people who live on the other side of town are probably just counting the days until the new Macy's opens. Their daily life is virtually unaffected.

Because planning is a political process susceptible to manipulation by small groups, it is likely that planning decisions about the mall will be made based on the concerns of those few residents and property owners who are most intensely involved in the process—the owner of the mall site and the immediate neighbors. Thus, the actual public interest in the mall project is hard to discern.

Because planning is a political process susceptible to manipulation by small groups, it is likely that planning decisions about the mall will be made based on the concerns of those few residents and property owners who are most intensely involved in the process.

Ongoing State-Local Fiscal Crisis

Since the passage of Proposition 13 close to 30 years ago, local governments have been experiencing an ongoing crisis in their funding and operations. As has been widely documented—and will be discussed in detail later in this book—the funding problems have a significant impact on the land use planning arena, as local governments jockey to attract land uses that will generate a net tax revenue surplus.

Since the passage of Proposition 13 close to 30 years ago, local governments have been experiencing an ongoing crisis in their funding and operations.

But underlying this apparent fiscal crisis is actually a much more complicated set of dynamics about local government organization and finance, which affect land use planning in subtle ways.

Though Proposition 13 constrains the levying of property taxes, government agencies do not lack for funds. According to taxpayer groups, California's state and local agencies take in a vast amount of money—about $130 billion a year, or close to $3,800 per capita. Part of the difficulty lies in how that money is collected and distributed among government agencies. For example, cities and school districts, while not as flush as they once were, are generally doing well. Counties, on the other hand, have serious financial problems. Many special agencies, including redevelopment agencies, special districts, and assessment districts, have independent sources of revenue that shield them, at least partly, from big picture financial problems.

The good old, post-war years when the state and federal governments paid most of the cost are over. Local governments are largely on their own for infrastructure projects.

Because of high real estate and labor costs, as well as stringent environmental regulations, nearly all infrastructure projects are very expensive. And the good old, post-war years when the state and federal governments paid most of the cost are over. Local governments are largely on their own for infrastructure projects. Even regional projects such as freeways are funded about half locally now. This is yet another reason that many cities and counties favor revenue generating retail developments over housing projects that produce only small amounts of property tax.

These problems will be discussed in greater detail in chapter 5, The Structure of Planning Decisionmaking. Suffice it to say, however, that a panoply of vested interests and turf battles makes it more difficult for local governments to make good planning decisions merely for the sake of doing the right thing. Virtually every planning decision carries with it the baggage of financial considerations and has an impact on other, often hostile local agencies, such as neighboring cities and counties, school districts, and special districts.

Competition and Lack of Cooperation

The ongoing fiscal crisis has also led to a competitive environment in which local governments use land use planning to fight for a financial advantage.

The ongoing fiscal crisis has also led to a competitive environment in which local governments use land use planning to fight for a financial advantage, and the fiscal elements of planning have made it much more difficult to discern the public interest in any given planning proposal.

As the Proposition 13 mentality has become more embedded in the California system, local governments have found themselves without the means to build new roads, sewers, schools, and the other essential building blocks of their communities. So they turned to the only source of funds over which they had any leverage—developers.

The" fiscalization of planning" took two forms. First, cities and counties began to encourage some types of development and discourage others based on financial considerations. In particular, big sources of sales tax revenue, such as auto dealerships, hotels, and shopping malls, became prize acquisitions, because Proposition 13 did not restrict the sales tax rates. Second, local officials, seeing the typical developer as a goose that lays golden eggs in their town, began leaning on developers to set aside a few eggs for public purposes, in order to make up for lost capital funds. Typically, developers now must build the infrastructure to serve their projects and set aside land for schools, parks, and libraries. In a growing number of jurisdictions, they also pay substantial development fees to assist in the construction of freeway interchanges, transit lines, low-income housing, and even childcare centers.

In a growing number of jurisdictions, developers pay substantial development fees to assist in the construction of freeway interchanges, transit lines, low-income housing, and even childcare centers.

The fiscalization trend fed into the politicization trend in several important ways. Perhaps most important was the fact that a city or county government's interests in the planning process gradually became more fiscally oriented.

Fiscalization, in turn, has led to an every-city-for-itself attitude that is damaging planning and quality of life at a regional level. In manipulating the land use system to their own financial advantage—using redevelopment and zoning to bring certain developments in and keep others out—cities and counties acting independently have created vast regional imbalances throughout California.

High Housing Prices

Up until the mid-1970s, California was an inexpensive place to live. Since then, the state's growth landscape has been shaped to a significant degree by high home prices—especially since the most recent run-up in housing prices began in 1999. The first round of home price increases in the '70s led to Proposition 13. The second in the '80s ushered in the era of widespread ballot box zoning. The most recent rise has led to average home prices approaching a half-million dollars—and the changed economics of housing has changed everything else.

Since the mid-1970s, the state's growth landscape has been shaped to a significant degree by high home prices—especially since the most recent run-up in housing prices began in 1999.

Although land use planning per se was not much of a factor in the most recent run-up, the cost of housing began to dominate planning discussions. Housing near job markets of the Bay Area and Southern California quickly got out of reach for working families. The new mantra was "drive until you qualify." Workers were forced to drive farther and farther away from the office until they reached a housing development they could afford.

This phenomenon made housing a more acceptable political issue than it was before. And it led to new political acceptance and financial feasibility of denser housing in infill locations.

Sprawl vs. Compact Urban Form

Most new development in California over the last half century has occurred on newly urbanized land outside central cities, and even when it has included high-density apartment housing or dense office centers, it has still been oriented around automobile travel.

Most new development in California over the last half century has been what might be called conventional suburban development. It has occurred on newly urbanized land outside central cities, and even when it has included high-density apartment housing or dense office centers, it has still been oriented around automobile travel. Much of California's planning practice is based on these assumptions, and many of the state's planning and development conflicts have been shaped by the idea that the development being proposed is conventionally suburban in nature.

In the last decade, the New Urbanism movement has begun to challenge the notions of conventional suburbia in California and throughout the country. The result has been a vigorous debate, for the first time in decades, over the form that new urban and suburban development should take. While not anti-growth or slow-growth, New Urbanists challenge the auto-oriented suburban model of development that has dominated California's landscape. They argue for a shift to more pedestrian and transit-oriented communities, with a greater mixture of land uses at the neighborhood level and stronger transit connections. This form of development is often described by advocates as "compact," to distinguish it from conventional suburban development patterns they view as more sprawling.

Over the past few years, land developers and builders have tussled with planners and environmentalists over the question of which pattern of development is better for the state.

Partly because of publicity generated by the New Urbanism, the debate about compact versus sprawling development patterns is also taking place in a broader context in California. Over the past few years, land developers and builders have tussled with planners and environmentalists over the question of which pattern of development is better for the state. As the land supply has dwindled, urban developments have become more compact because of economic necessity—but the philosophical debate over what form of development is better continues to rage.

Property Rights

The final overarching issue in California planning today is the issue of property rights. Much of the state's planning system was established in the 1960s and '70s, when the legal right of government agencies to regulate the use of land was at its most expansive. Since then, however, property owners and their allies—many of them ideologically driven lawyers and advocates—have made significant strides in reasserting the rights of landowners in planning and land regulation.

In particular, a series of rulings by the U.S. Supreme Court has forced government agencies, especially in California, to moderate their once aggressive regulatory agenda. For example, property owners now have a much stronger legal right to sue, and demand compensation, for excessive regulations than they did two decades ago. And government agencies must be much more careful about the types of exactions and conditions they impose on property owners today.

A series of rulings by the U.S. Supreme Court has forced government agencies, especially in California, to moderate their once aggressive regulatory agenda.

These changes mean that the planning process, in addition to balancing everything else on the local land use agenda, must also accommodate the rights of property owners. Agencies must be careful not to snuff out a property owner's rights completely, and usually they must monitor and document the relationship between a proposed development project and the conditions and exactions they impose. This is a far cry from the late 1970s and early '80s, when local governments were rarely forced to consider the impact of land use regulations on property owners. And it is likely that property rights will continue to be an important issue in planning, as property rights advocates continue to promote their agenda in both the courts and the legislative arena.

Agencies must be careful not to snuff out a property owner's rights completely, and usually they must monitor and document the relationship between a proposed development project and the conditions and exactions they impose.

Conclusion

This, then, is the world of planning in California today. It is a world far more open and inclusive than it was 30 or 40 years ago. In a way, it is a wonderfully messy, democratic process, with interest groups forming and creating coalitions, citizens assuming political power, and the future of each community being debated far more publicly and thoroughly than ever before.

Yet at the same time, it is a world disturbingly open to manipulation by special interests. It is a world where developers use heavy duty political firepower to try to get their projects approved. It is a world where cities and counties use their land use powers to maximize their own financial gain. It is a world where home-owners use both political and legal tactics to protect their investments. It is a world where civic organizations use their leverage over new development to finance their pet projects. It is a world, in other words, where so many narrow claims are made to the public interest that the term "public interest" has lost much of its meaning.

This is not to say that planning does not "work" in California today. There are planners out there with vision, and developers who want to build good projects, and politicians and citizens who want to make their communities better. These people often work together well, and no doubt the public interest sometimes emerges from their joint effort, as it often does in the legislative forum. In particular, many communities and their planners have begun to squarely confront the "post-suburban" issues that are emerging out of demographic change and dwindling land supply.

It is important to understand from the outset that the system works to the advantage of the manipulators, and as a result the ideal is rarely achieved.

Nevertheless, for anyone who hopes to operate in the world of planning in California, it is important to understand from the outset that the system works to the advantage of the manipulators, and as a result the ideal is rarely achieved. In the chapters ahead, we will discuss in great detail the processes and laws that must be observed in California planning, and how they are supposed to be used to create better communities. But we also hope to show how those processes and laws are used—for better or worse—by the people who play the game.

Chapter 2

The Californias

Many years ago, the state of California embarked on a tourist marketing campaign called *The Californias*. The goal was to persuade tourists—from both inside the state and elsewhere—that California was not just one place but many. If you didn't want to spend a week at Disneyland and Universal Studios, you could always go fishing along the Sacramento River, some 700 miles to the north. If you didn't like the beach, you always had the mountains. The state even hired sports commentator Howard Cosell, a quintessential New Yorker, for *The Californias'* ad campaign. The idea was that no matter where you were from or what you liked, there was a California waiting there for you somewhere.

Whether or not it was successful, *The Californias* campaign did have one ingredient you don't always find in a typical marketing campaign—It was true. California is not one state but many: mountains, deserts, beaches, cities, rivers, farms, forests, and so on. And no matter which California you might like to visit as a tourist, you need to understand all of them—and, especially, the relationships among them—to understand how planning in the state truly works.

No matter which California you might like to visit as a tourist, you need to understand all of them—and, especially, the relationships among them—to understand how planning in the state truly works.

Although California is the most populous state in the Union, it is so geographically large that, on average, it is not densely populated. The state's density is about 2200 people per square mile—more than most other Western states, but well below other urban states such as New Jersey (the national leader), New York, Massachusetts, and even Florida.

This statistical average, however, hides an important reality that plays a key role in shaping the way planning in California works: The state is unevenly populated. The vast majority of Californians are crowded into a few large metropolitan areas, which take up relatively little space. And the vast majority of California's geographical area contains very few people—sometimes, none at all.

California is the most urbanized state in the nation. According to the 1990 Census, more than 80 percent of Californians live in metropolitan areas of one million people or more.

Despite the low population density, California is the most urbanized state in the nation. More than 80 percent of all Californians live in metropolitan areas of one million people or more. (By contrast, the national figure is about 50 percent, and even in New York the figure is only about 75 percent.) Most of these metropolitan dwellers live in four well-established metropolitan areas: Greater Los Angeles, San Diego, the San Francisco Bay Area, and Sacramento. Yet even this description does not accurately convey the geography of urbanized California.

In fact, virtually all of California's metropolitan dwellers live in one of the state's two great metropolitan triangles—one in the north and one in the south. These two triangles each encompass hundreds of cities and stretch beyond the traditional boundaries of a single metropolitan area. [1]

The northern triangle, focused around Sacramento and the Bay Area, stretches from Sonoma County by the ocean inward about 100 miles to Sacramento, then southeast another 100-plus miles to Monterey County. This area encompasses virtually all of Northern California's large cities, including San Francisco, Oakland, San Jose, Sacramento, and Stockton.

The southern triangle—even larger—stretches from Ventura on the coast inland some 130 miles to San Bernardino and Riverside, and then southward another 100-plus miles to San Diego. This triangle encompasses most of the rest of the state's population, including Los Angeles, Orange County, San Diego, Riverside, and San Bernardino.

The two metropolitan triangles contain some 30 million people, or about 85 percent of the state's population. But these areas are not cohesive regions; nor are they consistently urban in character.

These two triangles contain about some 30 million people, or about 85 percent of the state's population. Of course, these areas are not cohesive regions; few people in Monterey believe they have much in common with people in Sacramento.

1. The definition of these metropolitan triangles is not commonly used by the Census Bureau. Most people who live inside these two triangles would consider themselves citizens of some smaller unit, such as San Diego or Los Angeles or the Bay Area. Nor do their definitions imply that everything inside their boundaries is "urbanized." Indeed, large areas inside these triangles are in agriculture or natural use. Nevertheless, the identification of these two triangles best describes the way the state's urban population is distributed.

Nor are they consistently urban in character. In fact, these areas take in wide swaths of farmland and natural areas. And they are characterized most frequently by small to medium-sized suburban communities. California has some 63 cities with a population of 100,000 or more, but only 10 with a population of 300,000 or more. The combined population of these 10 cities, all located (except one) within the two metropolitan triangles is about 9.4 million. Less than one person in three inside the metropolitan triangles lives in one of California's 10 large cities.

These areas are not even similar in terms of partisan politics. Some are very liberal, others very conservative, and many more are somewhere in between.

What is important, however, is that almost all of the people who live inside these two triangles are metropolitan dwellers. They live in cities or suburbs. They commute almost every day to an office or a factory or some other workplace (usually no more than a half hour from home). They travel short distances, usually by car, to gain access to a wide variety of activities: retail shopping, medical care, government services, recreation.

Politically, they may prefer big government or small government, but they have high expectations about what their community living environment will be. They expect that it will be rich with opportunities (especially jobs and shopping), yet manageable in terms of day-to-day living. They expect to be able to afford a comfortable house in a neighborhood they like, yet they're committed to preservation of open space nearby. Perhaps most important, in a large metropolis where so many things seem beyond their control—crime, job security, traffic jams—they expect a high degree of control in shaping the future of their own communities.

Not surprisingly, these are the values reflected in California's system of local planning: a high degree of local control, a focus on the real estate development process, a bias in favor of environmental protection, and a heavy concern with traffic issues. The reason that these are the values embedded in California's planning system is simply that these are the values held by the state's most politically powerful voters during the last 30 years—the suburban middle class.

The underlying assumption for much of California's planning system is that the venue for all this planning is the still emerging small suburban city that is part of a larger metropolis—the places where stereotypical suburban families live. In this respect, it is only appropriate that the planning system reflects these values. The

California has some 63 cities with a population of 100,000 or more, but only 10 with a population of 300,000 or more. The combined population of these 10 cities is about 9.4 million.

The values embedded in California's planning system are the values held by the state's most politically powerful voters during the last 30 years—the suburban middle class.

San Francisco

Sacramento

San Jose

Riverside

Los Angeles

San Diego

40   0   40   80 Miles

50   0   50   100 Kilometers

California's Metropolitan Triangles

planning laws are created by the legislature and the governor, which in turn must respond to the electorate.

Yet at the same time, the stereotypical suburban mentality is not always appropriate everywhere in California. The metropolitan triangles are so dominant that they contain more than 80 percent of the population, even though they make up only about 20 percent of the state's land. Outside the metropolitan triangles, life is very different. In the rural mountain, desert, and coastal areas, population is small, economic growth is an iffy proposition at best, and the role of the federal government is enormous. In the state's remaining agricultural valleys, including portions of the Central Valley, communities retain the scale and feel of small towns, much more in keeping with farm towns in the Midwest or the South than with

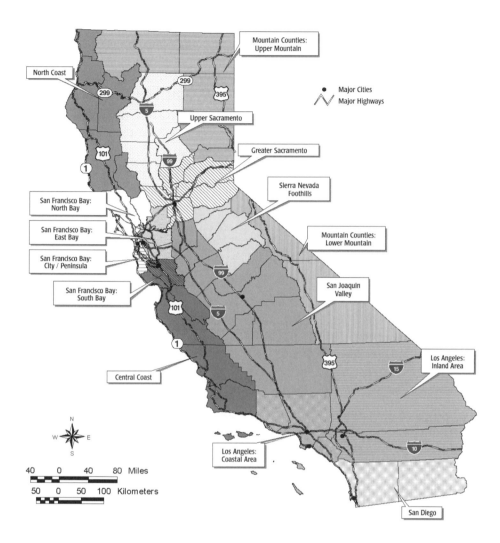

Major Cities
Major Highways

North Coast
Mountain Counties: Upper Mountain
Upper Sacramento
Greater Sacramento
Sierra Nevada Foothills
San Francisco Bay: North Bay
San Francisco Bay: East Bay
San Francisco Bay: City / Peninsula
San Francisco Bay: South Bay
Mountain Counties: Lower Mountain
San Joaquin Valley
Central Coast
Los Angeles: Inland Area
Los Angeles: Coastal Area
San Diego

40   0   40   80 Miles

50   0   50   100 Kilometers

California. Large parts of California have more in common with surrounding states like Oregon, Idaho, Nevada, and Arizona than with the metropolitan triangles.

Yet all these areas must play by the same rules. They must produce sophisticated general plans, run their development projects through the gauntlet of the California Environmental Quality Act, abide by the limitations and restrictions of Proposition 13, and follow dozens of other state laws and planning expectations designed to appeal to the voters of the metropolitan suburb. This point cannot be overemphasized, because as the metropolitan triangles fill up, and growth overflows into previously rural areas, suburban planning values will shape these new communities—whether or not they become metropolitan.

California's Population Regions

California's Regions

In recent years, it has become fashionable to say that California is no longer divided by north and south, but, rather, by east and west. The point of this observation was that, whatever historical animosity Northern and Southern California may have for one another, the most significant fault line in the state is now between the mature urban areas along the coast and the rapidly growing and more rural areas in the inland part of the state.

There is a good deal of truth to this observation, especially in discussing the relationship between the Bay Area and Los Angeles on the one hand and their emerging inland counterparts (Sacramento, Stockton-Modesto, Riverside-San Bernardino) on the other. But, as the earlier discussion indicates, the geographical reality of California is a good deal more subtle than any simplistic fault line discussion suggests. Here is a quick description of California's regions.

Metropolitan Los Angeles / Southern California

Broadly defined, the Southern California metropolis that revolves around Los Angeles is the second largest metropolitan area in the nation, comprising five counties and more than 18 million people. Furthermore, unlike most huge metropolises in the United States, such as Chicago and New York, it is still growing fast (36 percent, or some 5 million people, in the last 20 years).

The coastal inland fault line applies appropriately to metropolitan Los Angeles. The five county region breaks down logically between the three coastal counties and the two inland counties.

Coastal Area
Los Angeles, Orange, and Ventura Counties

The three coastal counties around Los Angeles represent perhaps the most heavily populated coastal plain anywhere in America. It is home to more than 12 million people, and while it has slowed somewhat, growth still runs close to the statewide average of approximately 2 percent per year. All told, the three counties contain nearly 40 percent of California's population on about 4 percent of the land.

Los Angeles is by far the most populous county in the United States, with more than 10 million people. Orange County has matured dramatically in recent years, with population growth slowing and business growth so ascendant that the county is now an economic powerhouse all by itself. Ventura has tracked Orange's growth on a smaller scale, but with economic growth tempered by strong slow-growth policies.

The continued urban expansion in the Los Angeles area has placed tremendous pressure on surrounding natural areas, including the Santa Monica Mountains National Recreation Area and Angeles National Forest. It is important to note that even though the population growth rate has slowed, the sheer numbers being added are still very large. Los Angeles County alone, for example, added almost 2 million people between 1990 and 2004, a figure higher than the total population of any other county in the state except Orange and San Diego.

Inland Area
San Bernardino and Riverside Counties

The Inland Empire has become synonymous in the public's imagination with rapid suburban growth. Since 1980, the population of these two counties has more than doubled, from 1.5 million to more than 3.6 million—making Riverside/San Bernardino the fastest growing large metropolitan area in the nation. All by itself, the Inland Empire has as big a population as Atlanta or Miami. By many definitions, however, it remains part of Greater Los Angeles. Both counties and the cities within them belong to the Southern California Association of Governments (SCAG), and strong commuting relationships exist between the bedroom communities in the Inland Empire and job centers in Los Angeles and Orange Counties.

Despite rapid urbanization, the Inland Empire remains an area of remarkable environmental diversity. At 20,000 square miles, San Bernardino County is by far the largest county in the state, bigger than Vermont and New Hampshire combined. At 7,000 square miles, Riverside County is about the size of Massachusetts. Vast stretches of both counties remain more or less unpopulated deserts, filled with a rich mixture of plant and animal species. In Riverside especially, endangered species issues have dominated the planning agenda for the last decade, and the federal government owns enormous chunks of both counties.

Both also have charming old towns such as Redlands and Riverside, as well as sprawling new suburbs. The population regions are concentrated in the western parts of these counties along freeway corridors—the areas with easiest access to Los Angeles and Orange Counties. Even so, they are sprawling by California standards. According to one national study in 2002, Riverside County was, by

California's Regions

Metropolitan Los Angeles / Southern California
Coastal Area: Los Angeles, Orange, and Ventura Counties
Inland Area: San Bernardino and Riverside Counties

San Diego "Empire"
San Diego and Imperial Counties

Central Coast
Santa Barbara, San Luis Obispo, Monterey, Santa Cruz, and San Benito Counties

San Francisco Bay Area
Alameda, Contra Costa, Marin, Napa, San Francisco, San Mateo, Santa Clara, Solano, and Sonoma Counties

North Coast
Del Norte, Humboldt, Lake, Mendocino, and Trinity Counties

San Joaquin Valley
Fresno, Kern, Kings, Madera, Merced, Tulare, San Joaquin, and Stanislaus Counties

Greater Sacramento
Sacramento, Yolo, Sutter, Yuba, Placer, El Dorado, and Nevada Counties

Upper Sacramento Valley
Butte, Colusa, Glenn, Tehama, and Shasta Counties

Sierra Nevada Foothills
Amador, Calaveras, Mariposa, Tuolomne, plus El Dorado, Placer, and Nevada Counties

Mountain Counties
Upper: Lassen, Modoc, Plumas, Sierra, and Siskiyou Counties
Lower: Alpine, Inyo, and Mono Counties

SCAG = Southern California Association of Governments

far, the most sprawling metropolitan area in the nation, and far different in character from every other metro area in California.

The San Diego Empire
San Diego and Imperial Counties

Between the Los Angeles metropolis and the Mexican border lies San Diego County, which is usually thought of as a separate metropolis, and Imperial, a sparsely populated agricultural area that was carved out of San Diego County in 1907, making it the newest county in California.

With more than 3 million people, San Diego is the second-largest county in the state, and it is dominated by the city of San Diego, the second largest city in the state.

With more than 3 million people, San Diego is the second largest county in the state, and it is dominated by the city of San Diego, whose population of some 1.2 million makes it the second largest city in the state after Los Angeles. (The county has 17 other cities, and only three with a population in excess of 100,000.)

Growth and planning issues have been predominant in San Diego at least back to the 1970s, when Pete Wilson was a growth management innovator as San Diego's mayor. More recently, land planning in the San Diego area has been dominated by endangered species issues, as both city and county have participated in a state led effort to create multiple species conservation plans.

SANDAG = San Diego Association of Governments

Imperial County is not usually viewed as a part of the San Diego region and, in fact, the county and its cities belong to the Southern California Association of Governments, rather than the San Diego Association of Governments (SANDAG). But the two counties are adjacent and may soon be linked by a pipeline to ship Colorado River water from Imperial Valley farms to the coastal cities in San Diego County.

Irrigation with Colorado River water has transformed Imperial from a hot, dry desert area to a fertile agricultural valley. The county has only 160,000 residents (two-thirds of them Latino), but produces approximately $1 billion per year in crops.

Central Coast Santa Barbara, San Luis Obispo, Monterey, Santa Cruz, and San Benito Counties

The Central Coast, stretching from below Santa Barbara to beyond Santa Cruz, consists of some 300 miles of coastal area and nearby inland valleys between metropolitan Los Angeles and the San Francisco Bay Area.

The Central Coast, stretching from below Santa Barbara to beyond Santa Cruz, consists of some 300 miles of coastal area and nearby inland valleys between metropolitan Los Angeles and the San Francisco Bay Area. These four coastal counties (plus tiny San Benito just inland from the Monterey Peninsula) contain some of the state's most beautiful landscapes, most productive agricultural land (it is increasingly a wine-growing region), and strictest land use planning regulations. Among other things, this region generates a disproportionate amount of high profile litigation over land use and environmental planning issues.

The Central Coast is sparsely populated compared with the giant metropolises to the north and south, and it is not growing as fast as the rest of California, but it is growing fast because of its proximity to these areas. Some 1.43 million people live on the Central Coast, an increase of 15 percent since 1990.

The Central Coast is sparsely populated compared to the giant metropolises to the north and south, and it is not growing as fast as the rest of California.

Though not included in the traditional definition of the adjacent metropolises, the northern (Monterey and Santa Cruz) and southern (Santa Barbara) portions of the area are clearly part of the emerging metropolitan triangles where the majority of the state's population live. Santa Barbara contains some 400,000 people, while Santa Cruz and Monterey together contain almost 760,000. However, the fastest growing county in this area is San Luis Obispo, located halfway between San Francisco and Los Angeles. Though its growth rate has dropped in recent years, its population is driven largely by retirees and other "equity refugees," rather than high fertility rates.

San Francisco Bay Area
Alameda, Contra Costa, Marin, Napa, San Francisco, San Mateo, Santa Clara, Solano, and Sonoma Counties

With a population of more than 7.6 million, the San Francisco Bay Area is the second largest metropolis in California and the fourth largest in the nation, exceeded in population only by New York, Los Angeles, and Chicago. The region is generally defined as encompassing the nine counties that touch the Bay. The Bay Area is regarded as one of the most desirable metropolitan areas in the nation, although it did suffer an economic decline following the recent dot-com bust.

With a population of more than 7.6 million, the San Francisco Bay Area is the second-largest metropolis in California and the fourth-largest in the nation.

The Bay Area is a hotbed of environmental activism and slow-growth sentiment that is measurably more liberal than any other part of the state. Home prices are consistently the highest in the nation. Regulatory restraints on land development are probably tighter in the Bay Area than anywhere else in California. The region has a large infrastructure of organizations dedicated to preserving open space, and several counties have approved taxes to buy open land. In recent years, environmentalists have focused on creating "urban growth boundaries" in the Bay Area counties, clearly delineating where urban development will be accommodated and where it will not be permitted.

Between 1990 and 2004, population in the Bay Area grew by 14 percent, while population in the rest of California grew 18 percent.

Although the Bay Area added more than one million residents between 1990 and 2004, it is actually growing at a noticeably slower rate than the rest of the state. During that 14-year period, population in the Bay Area grew by 14 percent, while population in the rest of the state grew 18 percent. And the population growth in the Bay Area is not evenly distributed. Instead, it has been concentrated on the fringes—in particular, Solano and Sonoma Counties and eastern Contra Costa and Alameda Counties.

The region can be easily divided into four subregions—the North Bay (Marin, Sonoma, and Napa Counties), the East Bay (Contra Costa, Alameda, and Solano Counties), the City/Peninsula area (San Francisco and San Mateo Counties), and the South Bay (Santa Clara County). Unlike Los Angeles and other major metropolitan areas, the Bay Area has no single dominant city. Rather, there are three major cities, each in a different part of the region (San Francisco, Oakland, and San Jose) and 12 other cities with a population of 100,000 or more located all around the Bay.

The older areas of San Mateo County, San Francisco, Marin County, and Santa Clara County are adding population very slowly.

The older areas of San Mateo County, San Francisco, Marin County, and Santa Clara County are adding population very slowly. These areas have lost some of their economic luster since the dot-com bust, but home prices have continued to rise.

North Coast Del Norte, Humboldt, Lake, Mendocino, and Trinity Counties

The three North Coast counties (plus inland Lake and Trinity Counties) are generally better known for trees and owls than for people—though, increasingly, the area is best known for the conflicts among all three.

Though relatively unpopulated, the Redwood Empire has a strong relationship to the San Francisco Bay Area, the source of many tourists, visitors, business connections, and second home buyers.

Though relatively unpopulated (a little over 300,000 total in 2004), the Redwood Empire has a strong relationship to the San Francisco Bay Area, the source of many tourists, visitors, business connections, and second home buyers. The area covers 300-plus miles from the Bay Area to the Oregon border, and its political and natural environments are varied. Lake County is a funhouse mirror image to its southern neighbor Napa; whereas Napa is a hideout for the rural chic, Lake County—revolving around the natural lake of Clear Lake—is a working-class vacation paradise, where the buying and selling of small and substandard lots is a major industry.

The coastal counties vary as well, but their planning issues focus in large part on the ferocious debate over the harvesting of trees on public and private land. Though some coastal areas are big tourist attractions—the Mendocino Coast is a favorite destination for upper class Bay Area residents, the North Coast's planning debates in recent years have been largely defined by the twin poles of the forest industry and local environmentalists.

With its old-growth forests and ample raw material, the North Coast has always been the logging capital of California. Most of the coastal cities in the area have some tie to the timber industry. At least one, Scotia, is a classic company town, built more or less in its entirety by Pacific Lumber Company. In recent decades, the North Coast has also become a center for environmental activism. With the listing of the spotted owl, endangered species issues became the dominant planning (and political) issue in the region, with forest interests and environmentalists engaged in pitched battle over how much logging to allow on federally owned forest land that serves as habitat for the spotted owl.

With its old-growth forests and ample raw material, the North Coast has always been the logging capital of California.

Recent activity has centered around Pacific Lumber's rapid harvesting of privately owned redwood forests in Humboldt County. But in general the region remains stymied by the long-term question of how to manage forest resources and whether (and how) to build future economic development around other industries.

The San Joaquin Valley
Fresno, Kern, Kings, Madera, Merced, Tulare,
San Joaquin, and Stanislaus Counties

There is little question among the experts that the San Joaquin Valley will be California's greatest planning problem over the next 20 years.

The San Joaquin Valley includes the eight southernmost counties of the Great Central Valley—the counties whose land drains into the San Joaquin River and, ultimately, into the Sacramento Delta from the south. (The Central Valley also includes counties in the Sacramento Valley to the north.) The eight counties in the San Joaquin Valley traditionally form one of the most powerful agricultural economies anywhere in the world. In 2003, San Joaquin Valley counties occupied six of the top seven spots on the list of farm counties, and all eight ranked among the top 14. Together they produced about $16.5 billion in agricultural products in 2003, or about 60 percent of the statewide total.

The eight counties in the San Joaquin Valley traditionally form one of the most powerful agricultural economies anywhere in the world.

Yet these eight counties are now subject to intense urbanization pressure. Their population almost doubled between 1980 and 2004 and their growth is expected to continue unabated in the years ahead. Even the San Joaquin Valley's large cities, such as

Fresno, Bakersfield, and Modesto, have been among the fastest growing in the state. The Public Policy Institute of California recently found that the San Joaquin Valley's population is growing faster than Mexico's. Furthermore, their growth rates have been exceeded only by the rate of their physical expansion. With a seemingly endless flat plain at hand, and little economic or political pressure to conserve land, urban development in the San Joaquin Valley has sprawled across important farmland. The PPIC recently concluded that the population will double again by 2040, but the amount of urbanized land will triple at least. Simply put, it is by far the largest expanse of flat farmland available for urban growth anywhere in the West. Nowhere else is even close. And there are few barriers to developing virtually all of it in the long run.

Although urban development in the San Joaquin Valley is partly driven by low land and housing costs, the specific growth dynamics vary from county to county. San Joaquin, Stanislaus, and Merced Counties have grown rapidly, largely because of spin-off development from the Bay Area, where homebuilders and businesses must deal with high land and housing prices. Fresno, Madera, and Tulare Counties—the heart of the San Joaquin Valley—have also grown rapidly, but their growth has been driven more by internal economic expansion; this area remains the largest agricultural economy in the state. Kern County (Bakersfield) has seen an expanding agricultural and oil economy and some spin-off from Los Angeles to the south.

Greater Sacramento
Sacramento, Yolo, Sutter, Yuba, Placer, El Dorado, and Nevada Counties

Greater Sacramento is the state's fourth-largest metropolitan region, with a population approaching two million. Once centered around the State Capitol in downtown Sacramento, the metropolitan region now sprawls across all of the lower Sacramento Valley and then eastward into the foothills of the Sierra Nevada Mountains.

Metropolitan Sacramento has changed character considerably in recent years. At least until the 1970s, it maintained many characteristics of a sleepy Central Valley town despite the presence of the State Capitol. But as the coastal areas have filled up and become more expensive, Sacramento is an attractive alternative for many businesses and many residents. In the mid-1980s, the population of Sacramento County hit the one million mark, meaning the area suddenly popped up in business location searches. Sacramento's

PPIC = Public Policy Institute of California

Fresno, Madera, and Tulare Counties—the heart of the San Joaquin Valley—have also grown rapidly; this area remains the largest agricultural economy in the state.

Greater Sacramento is the state's fourth-largest metropolitan region, with a population approaching two million.

relatively low land and housing prices, and its position at the cross-roads of major north-south and east-west freeway corridors, also made it an attractive alternative to the Bay Area. With its nearby foothills, metro Sacramento is virtually the only inland location in the state where high-tech companies have been willing to relocate major operations.

The city of Sacramento, with about 450,000 residents, comprises a fairly small part of this area. Most people who live in metropolitan Sacramento live in unincorporated suburbs in Sacramento County, in the newly incorporated cities of Citrus Heights, Elk Grove, and Rancho Cordova, and in rapidly growing western Placer County. The surrounding farm counties (Yolo, Sutter, and Yuba) are relatively unpopulated. Major development plans have been proposed from time to time (Sutter and Yuba are located close to downtown Sacramento and the Sacramento International Airport), but only during the last few years have large projects started to develop.

Most people who live in metropolitan Sacramento live in unincorporated suburbs in Sacramento County.

The real growth has come to the east and northeast of Sacramento, along the Interstate 80 and Highway 50 corridors leading into Placer and El Dorado Counties. Since 1980 the population of these two counties has more than doubled—a level of growth that is among the highest in the country. (Nevada County, another foothill county to the north that is somewhat outside of Sacramento's commuting shed, experienced nearly the same rate of growth.)

Since 1980 the population of Placer and El Dorado Counties has more than doubled.

Upper Sacramento Valley
Butte, Colusa, Glenn, Tehama, and Shasta Counties

The Upper Sacramento Valley includes five agricultural counties that are adding population rapidly but are located outside the influence of any large metropolitan area. Unlike the San Joaquin Valley counties, the Upper Sacramento Valley counties (and the adjacent farm counties near Sacramento) do not produce enormous agricultural profits. Of these five counties, only Colusa, with some $300 million in agricultural production per year, ranks in the top 20 statewide. Nevertheless, agriculture—both farming and ranching—is the leading industry throughout the region.

Unlike the San Joaquin Valley counties, the Upper Sacramento Valley counties do not produce enormous agricultural profits. Nevertheless, agriculture—both farming and ranching—is the leading industry throughout the region.

On their own scale, however, the five counties are beginning to grapple with the same issues of urban development seen in other parts of the Central Valley. The area's two largest cities, Redding and Chico, have both doubled in population since 1980. Environmental issues—including endangered species, wetlands, and riparian areas—have become increasingly important.

Sierra Nevada Foothills
Amador, Calaveras, Mariposa, Tuolomne, plus El Dorado, Placer, and Nevada Counties

The seven foothill counties (three near Sacramento, four farther south) have traditionally been the center of the Mother Lode, the colorful gold mining towns along Highway 49. Until recently, a fair argument could be made that their best years were behind them—back in the 19th century, when gold mining was the predominant activity.

Five of the seven the foothill counties ranked in the top 10 in percentage of population growth between 1980 and 1995.

In recent years, however, the foothill counties have become a new center of urban and suburban growth. Their population too has doubled since 1980. Between 1980 and 1995, the population of the foothill region grew by 74 percent, outstripping every other part of the state except the Inland Empire. Five of the seven counties ranked in the top 10 in percentage of population growth during that period, and all seven ranked within the top 21.

The dynamics driving growth in the upper and lower foothill counties are somewhat different. As stated above, the upper foothill counties (Nevada, Placer, and El Dorado) are growing in large part because of their proximity to Sacramento. About two-thirds of the population of these seven counties lives in only two counties: Placer County, which lies along Interstate 80 northeast of Sacramento, and El Dorado County, which lies along Highway 50 east of Sacramento. Both counties have had bruising general plan debates in recent years, as property rights advocates and landowners have gone toe-to-toe with environmentalists and emerging slow-growth groups.

About two-thirds of the population of the foothill counties lives in Placer County and El Dorado County.

The four lower foothill counties are also growing fast, but they are not located near a major metropolitan area. In large part, their growth is being driven by retirees and other Bay Area dropouts who are drawn by inexpensive housing and the natural environment. The demand for large lot subdivisions in these counties is a major planning challenge. This issue is compounded by the need for good fire hazard management. As more large lot subdivisions are built in rural and forested areas, firefighters must concentrate more on protecting residential structures, often at the expense of managing wildfires in a more environmentally sensitive manner.

Mountain Counties
Upper: Lassen, Modoc, Plumas, Sierra, and Siskiyou Counties
Lower: Alpine, Inyo, and Mono Counties

Stretching from Death Valley to the Oregon border along the eastern part of the state, the eight mountain counties represent, in many ways, the forgotten California. Together they comprise more than 30,000 square miles—some 20 percent of California's total land area, an area approximately the size of Maine. But their total population is only about 150,000, and almost all of these counties are growing more slowly than the statewide average. While Siskiyou County, which includes Mount Shasta, has 10 incorporated cities, the other seven counties have only six incorporated cities among them—and in recent years one of those (Portola in Plumas County) has been the subject of dissolution attempts.

The Upper Mountain Counties (Lassen, Modoc, Plumas, Sierra, and Siskiyou) form a ring to the east and north of the Sacramento Valley. Two of these counties, Modoc and Lassen, are extremely remote, lying on the other side of California mountain ranges. The Lower Mountain Counties (Alpine, Inyo, and Mono) take in large portions of the Sierra Nevada mountain range on the east side of the Central Valley. Alpine is the least populous county in the state, with only about 1,300 people. Mono and Inyo are geographically large counties that have suffered the historical fate of being, in certain ways, colonies of Los Angeles. The famous L.A. aqueduct diverts water from the Owens Valley and sends it southward down the mountains and through the desert to Los Angeles.

Alpine is the least populous county in the state, with only about 1,300 people.

These counties remain economically dependent on extractive industries and, in a few cases, on tourism. Because the federal government owns most of the land, they have been California's hotbeds of home rule sentiment. Many have adopted the view, at least rhetorically, that the federal government's ownership of land in their counties should not be recognized. Even those with a more moderate stance are clearly frustrated by the federal government's dominance. With counties already squeezed financially, vast federal ownership has left these counties with little land available for commercial or residential development that could increase local government revenue.

Chapter 3

The Emergence of Urban Planning and Land Use Regulation in California

In 1867, just two years after the end of the Civil War, a certain Mr. Shrader petitioned the California Supreme Court to overturn his conviction in San Francisco Police Court on a charge of operating a slaughterhouse. The year before, the city's Board of Supervisors had banned slaughterhouses in a particular district of San Francisco. They passed the ordinance under broad power the city had received in a state law passed in 1863, which authorized San Francisco "to make all regulations which may be necessary or expedient for the preservation of the public health and the prevention of contagious diseases."

A state law passed in 1863 authorized San Francisco to make all regulations necessary or expedient for the preservation of the public health and the prevention of contagious diseases.

Mr. Shrader continued to operate his slaughterhouse in violation of this law, and as a result the authorities threw him in jail. In front of the Supreme Court, Mr. Shrader argued that his property rights had been violated. He said that he had been stripped of his inalienable right, guaranteed under the California Constitution, to use his property as he wished. Further, he argued, his property had been "taken" via regulation without just compensation.

But Mr. Shrader got no further in the California court system than most of his modern counterparts. Writing for a unanimous bench, Justice Oscar Shafter went out of his way to put the slaughterhouse operator in his place. "The result of which the prisoner complains is personal imprisonment for a misdemeanor," Justice Shafter said, "and not a condemnation of his property to the public use without compensation."

In upholding San Francisco's conviction of Mr. Shrader, Justice Shafter made it clear that property ownership "does not deprive the Legislature of the power... of regulating the conduct and relations of the members of society in respect to property rights." He concluded his ruling by stating that if governments did not have the power to protect public health, safety, and morals, "there would be few social or common rights which individual caprice or rapacity would be bound to respect."

Property rights lawyers today would no doubt characterize Mr. Shrader as the first victim of California's now-famous oppressive approach to land use regulation. But in fact he was a minor player in the lengthy history of California land use planning as it evolved from the ancient legal doctrine of nuisances into the highly sophisticated modern system of land use planning that is used today.

The emergence of California's common land use planning tools is the result of a century of struggle—between the private real estate market and government regulation, between architecture and law, between rich and poor, and even, in a sense, between the idealistic promise of the future and the tangible benefits of the present.

Though some rudimentary tools date back to 19th century San Francisco, most land use regulations were first forged outside California.

Though some rudimentary tools date back to 19th century San Francisco, most land use regulations were first forged outside California—largely in the crucible of New York City in the late nineteenth and early twentieth centuries when that city was afflicted by a rampant growth not unlike our own in California today. These tools were later pieced together in California, appropriated by environmental do-gooders, suburban snobs, and even the real estate development industry itself to further their own ends.

Since planners and planning processes are often called upon to balance competing interests in their communities, it is perhaps appropriate that the idea of planning itself rests on the assumption of balance as well. Throughout the 20th century, this balance shifted back and forth among various points of view. The balance of power between the private property owner and the land use regulator often changes, depending on prevailing political and legal winds. The leeway that states allow local governments in regulating land varies. And planning, a process that deliberately grants centralized regulatory power to government agencies, sometimes comes into conflict with the goals of a democratic society. In many ways, these three conflicts shape the regulatory tools used in planning.

Throughout the 20th century, the balance of power between the private property owner and the land use regulator often changes, depending on prevailing political and legal winds.

The battle between land use regulators and private property owners has been going on before the U.S. Supreme Court for more than 70 years now, from *Euclid v. Ambler* in 1926, which first upheld the constitutionality of zoning, to *Tahoe-Sierra Preservation Council v. Tahoe Regional Planning Agency,* 535 U.S. 302 (2002), which up-held the ability of local government to impose building moratoria. Regulators and property owners are always engaged in legal skir-mishes on the frontier of land use planning, moving the boundary of acceptable regulation back and forth.

During two periods in recent American history, states have reached out and grabbed considerable power from local gov-ernments over the regulation of land. The first period was in the early '70s, when environmental consciousness was at its zenith; it was during this period, for example, that the California Coastal Commission was established. The second period was in the late '80s, when concerns about traffic congestion and suburban sprawl led to state-level growth-management movements in states such as Florida and New Jersey.

During the early '70s and the late '80s, states have reached out and grabbed considerable power from local gov-ernments over the regulation of land.

Part of the reason California resisted this recent movement—indeed, part of the reason that land use regulation has remained largely in the hands of local governments everywhere—is the citi-zenry's understandable skepticism about centralized control of land. But some of the original impulses for land use planning can fairly be described as elitist, and much of the recent history of the field has been a struggle to democratize a field not easily adapted to democratic processes.

Planning commissions and planning processes were originally designed, at least in part, to counterbalance the teeming and often corrupt political atmosphere in large cities in the early part of the 20th century. Planning was too important to leave to the politicians, or so believed the old-line business leaders and power brokers who didn't trust the political machines that thrived in immigrant neigh-borhoods. Therefore, planning would be removed from politics and placed in the hands of nonpartisan citizens (planning commission-ers) and impartial experts (the professional planners themselves).

Planning commissions and planning processes were originally designed, at least in part, to counterbalance the teeming and often corrupt political atmosphere in large cities in the early part of the 20th century.

In California, this idea was reinforced by the Progressives, who led an influential movement a century ago that promoted the idea of professionalism, not politics, in government. Planners and civic leaders often constituted an oligarchy that governed the devel-opment and redevelopment of their communities without much involvement from the citizenry. Many of our most handsome com-munities (Santa Barbara, Pasadena, and Carmel) were created by these oligarchies, which were able to impose strict aesthetic stan-dards without much regard for the democratic process. In time, how-ever, the unrest of environmentalists, homeowners, preservationists, and others forced democratization. The goal of planning is neat and orderly development; democracy, on the other hand, requires a certain degree of messiness. And these conflicting requirements still do not rest comfortably next to each other in most planning processes.

Planning's Twin Traditions

Planning has emerged from two distinct traditions: architecture and landscape architecture and the tradition of law.

In California and elsewhere in the United States, planning has actually emerged from two somewhat related, but distinct traditions. The first evolved from architecture and landscape architecture—the physical organization of land uses and the creation of their architecturally styled connections into a coherent environment that is today often called urban design. The second is strongly grounded in the tradition of law— the legal rationale for imposing public limitations on private land.

The idea of the general plan is that the future physical form of a community should be envisioned and laid out in a forward looking and wide-ranging document, often accompanied by maps and other graphic representations of the community's physical form.

The legacy of the first tradition is the comprehensive plan, or what we in California call the general plan—the idea that the future physical form of a community should be envisioned and laid out in a forward-looking and wide-ranging document, often accompanied by maps and other graphic representations of the community's physical form. The legacy of the second tradition is our system of land use regulations—the extremely detailed and legalistic set of rules about land and activities on the land that often goes by the name of zoning.

California has played an instrumental role in the evolution of both traditions—and, in recent decades, in attempting to integrate them into a cohesive whole. Indeed, the concept of consistency between the general plan and the zoning ordinance—which is perhaps one of the most deeply embedded ideas in modern California planning practice—represents a serious attempt to reconcile these two traditions.

Of course, the traditions of "the plan" and the law" are not quite as separate as the following discussion will sometimes make them seem. Theoretically, as the consistency requirement suggests, they fit together nicely: The plan provides visionary guidance, while the law provides the power to implement that vision. But over the last century, the plan and the law have had an uneasy relationship.

Throughout most of human history, city plans did not need a complicated legal substructure, because they were drawn up with the approval of monarchs and other rulers who did not need to consider the legal rights of their subjects. To this day, planning remains populated by many would-be monarchs who dream of great plans and wish for absolute power.

It was the phenomenon of the crowded industrial city in a democratic society that created the need for a legal process as part of planning. Ironically, for most of the 20 century, the legal aspects of planning developed a life independent of—and, indeed, sometimes more important than—the plans themselves.

But there is no question that both these traditions evolved out of the hurly-burly of the industrial city of the late 19th century—out of the reality of congestion and geographical confinement in cities such as San Francisco and Chicago and especially New York, a reality that stood in sharp contrast to the wide-open-spaces tradition of American development. And there can be no question that the modern California landscape—low-rise, suburban, auto-oriented, seemingly the antithesis of the industrial city—strongly bears the imprint of both.

The History of Planning as Urban Design

All that is good about American city planning, the great urbanist Lewis Mumford once wrote, began with the design of Central Park. By this statement Mumford meant simply that most design traditions of American urban development are derived from the pastoral and romantic vision of landscape architecture Frederick Law Olmstead and Calvin Vaux created in the 1850s at Central Park. And he was right.

Most design traditions of American urban development are derived from the pastoral and romantic vision of landscape architecture Frederick Law Olmstead and Calvin Vaux created in the 1850s at Central Park.

Prior to Central Park, American city planning, such as it was, consisted mostly of subdividing and speculating. Whether it was the creation of the grid system in Manhattan in 1811 or the invention of Midwestern town plats from whole cloth, pre-Central Park planning had been focused on creating a system of roads and lot configurations that would maximize the speculative value of urban real estate. After Central Park, American city planning was planted on a foundation of specific ideas about how urban places should be designed.

California today is covered with the remnants of these ideas. They can be seen in San Francisco's Golden Gate Park, in stately older neighborhoods such as Land Park in Sacramento, in the formal design of older portions of San Diego, and in William Pereira's circular design for the University of California, Irvine. Central Park is present on every curvilinear suburban collector street and in every quiet suburban cul-de-sac, which stands as testimony to Olmstead and Vaux's belief that it is possible to create a respite in the midst of a bustling metropolis.

California today is covered with the remnants of post-Central Park planning ideas.

The desire to create such places—to use the process of urban development to construct artificially pastoral settings for human consumption—has been with us for more than two centuries. Since the onset of the Industrial Revolution, we have been driven by a desire to move outward and replicate the rural or small-town life we believe we have left behind. Since the invention of the streetcar in the 1870s, many of us have been able to pursue this goal.

In opening up to suburban development land that was previously too remote to be usable, the streetcar also caused the invention of our modern idea of a suburb—a mostly residential place, far from the grubby world where work was done and profits were made, where all who could afford it could experience community life on a more human scale. The streetcar also transported many of the Central Park design ideas to the suburbs and led to intertwined movements in architecture, landscape architecture, urban design, and city planning that have shaped current planning in California in a profound way.

Even before the suburb gained a dominant place in American city planning, architects and designers had begun to grapple with how to transform a sooty, crowded, and ugly city into one that was clean, beautiful, and manageable.

Even before the suburb gained a dominant place in American city planning, architects and designers had begun to grapple with how to transform a sooty, crowded, and ugly city into one that was clean, beautiful, and manageable. After Central Park, the next seminal event was the Columbian Exposition in Chicago in 1893—a world's fair for which leading architects had created a temporary White City of plaster. The White City so captured the American imagination that its neoclassical architecture was soon mandatory for most civic buildings, and its formalistic pattern, along with the Central Park notion of a landscaped park, served as the design foundation for the City Beautiful movement.

Similar characteristics are evident in the handsome streetcar suburbs built between approximately 1890 and 1920. Though not as self-consciously monumental as the City Beautiful designers, the designers of these suburbs emphasized formal streetscapes oriented around local transit stops. Other urban designers during the go-go years of the 1920s adopted a similar approach, emphasizing public spaces, civic buildings, and orderly neighborhoods.

All these efforts revolved around a particular set of design principles in order to shape the new urban forms emerging at the time on a more human, village-like scale.

All these efforts revolved around a particular set of design principles in order to shape the new urban forms emerging at the time (suburbs, resort towns, factory towns) on a more human, village-like scale. The work of John Nolen, one of the leading urban designers of the early 20th century, is a model of this type of planning. In factory towns, boom towns, and city plans—such as his 1909 plan for San Diego—Nolen's style is characterized by, in the words of planning historian Mel Scott, "some rather formal, almost baroque, street arrangements with naturalistic parks and open spaces," as well as a strong emphasis on public buildings and public spaces.

At the same time, another movement was seeking to restore village life to urban living and to create a "sense of place." But the Garden City movement was less formal and more oriented toward natural green areas rather than streets carrying automobiles as the spine of a community. The Garden City movement began with English designer Ebenezer Howard's ideal for creating self-contained new towns surrounded by greenbelts. (The garden suburb ideas of English designer Raymond Unwin also played an important role.) In America, a group of designers, organized as the Regional Planning Association of America, sought to restore village life by taking a different and less urban approach to creating communities.

Led by such figures as Clarence Stein, the Garden City designers sought to create new towns on the metropolitan fringe that maintained a village atmosphere, yet accommodated the automobile and incorporated farmland and natural areas into their design. Whereas Nolen and others oriented their designs around urban streets (a principle many New Urbanists would later adopt), Stein and his associates sought to separate automobile and pedestrian traffic with overpasses and greenways. The Garden City designers also adopted the concept of the "neighborhood unit"—a large meandering block permitting no through traffic, and oriented around green space and school sites. The Garden City approach—more suburban, at least on the surface—is still on display in California at Baldwin Hills Village, a residential project designed by Stein and built in 1941.

The Garden City designers sought to create new towns on the metropolitan fringe that maintained a village atmosphere, yet accommodated the automobile and incorporated farmland and natural areas into their design.

In their purest form, all these approaches fell by the wayside in the rush toward postwar American suburbanization. In bastardized form, however, the Garden City approach came to dominate suburban planning during this period and profoundly shaped the urban landscape of California that even today revolves largely around postwar suburbs.

It's true that many postwar land developers, including those who worked in southern L.A. County, northern Orange County, the San Fernando Valley, and San Francisco's Peninsula, were drawn to the miraculous profitability of the old-fashioned grid, which maximized the number of building lots in 1950 just as it had in 1811. This arrangement suited the new techniques of mass-production homebuilding perfectly. Yet once the pent-up demand for new housing had been sated after the war, California's prominent land developers acquired a more discriminating taste. Especially around Los Angeles, major landowners embarked on design and construction of master-planned projects that sought to avoid the piecemeal

Once the pent-up demand for new housing had been sated after the war, California's prominent land developers acquired a more discriminating taste.

approach of the 1940s and '50s suburb and to create, instead, entire suburban communities.

Southern California was a logical centerpoint for the master-planned movement because of intense growth pressure and because California's peculiar political history had permitted huge pieces of land, such as the 140,000-acre Irvine Ranch and the 44,000-acre Newhall Ranch, to remain intact. Indeed, the work architect William Pereira did for The Irvine Company is the best example of early master planning in California. Unlike other developers, who simply built houses and a shopping center, The Irvine Company, at Pereira's direction, created the footprint for an entire community from scratch, with houses, apartments, a university, office complexes, and so forth.

Pereira and his counterparts elsewhere in California were seeking not to combat suburban sprawl but, rather, to improve it by adapting the principles of the Garden City movement. Though much more auto-oriented and less small-townish than originally envisioned, the city of Irvine became the standard by which most suburban development in California was measured.

Though derided by Mumford and other Garden City leaders, Irvine and its knock-offs were auto-dominated derivations of their idea, complete with the idea of a superblock and a setting close to nature.

Though derided by Mumford and other Garden City leaders, Irvine and its knockoffs, based on the neighborhood-unit model, actually were auto-dominated derivations of their idea, complete with the idea of a "superblock" (which insulated the neighborhood from through traffic) and a setting close to nature. The Garden City model was much easier to mutate for suburban needs than the more urban (and urbane) formal towns and villages Nolen and others designed. And even today most private master-planned communities in California follow an altered Garden City model, with greenways, walking paths, and houses or apartments positioned along golf courses.

The History of Planning as Land Use Regulation

For nearly 100 years, however, land use planning in America has been driven at least as much by lawyers as by architects and landscape architects. Zoning emerged for the same reasons as the city planning movements described above: to provide an alternative to the congested and unsanitary urban conditions in turn-of-the-century industrial cities. But far more than the city planning movements, zoning was reactive—an attempt by progressive reformers to rein in the excesses of the private market through government regulation.

Zoning emerged in response to congested, unsanitary urban conditions in turn-of-the-century industrial cities.

Zoning soon gained a life of its own, separate and apart from the visionary physical solutions of city planners. This came about partly because it emerged from a different, more legalistic tradition. But it also came about because the idea of zoning was susceptible to appropriation by small groups of private property owners trying to protect their own interests.

As this chapter's opening story suggests, the use of governmental authority to restrict the activities of private property owners dates back well into the 19th century, when urban crowding first set noxious industrial businesses cheek-by-jowl with residential neighborhoods. The legal tradition that formed the basis for this action was "nuisance law," and the concept that allowed nuisance law to expand into a broad-ranging system of land use regulation was the police power.

Governments may regulate the use of land because governments hold police power—the power that permits them to restrict private activities in order to protect the public health, safety, welfare, and (under the California Constitution) public morals. Under common law, the informal legal traditions stretching back to England, governments have always had the power to curtail activity that constitutes a nuisance.

Governments may regulate the use of land because governments hold police power—the power that permits them to restrict private activities in order to protect the public health, safety, welfare, and public morals.

As the case of Mr. Shrader shows, in the mid- and late 19th century, both state legislatures and the courts gradually permitted local governments more power in restricting the use of land. Most of these early ordinances sought to restrict particularly noxious industrial uses (slaughterhouses, glue factories, brickmaking operations) from close proximity to residential neighborhoods. Racism played a role too, especially in California, where many early ordinances (in San Francisco, Modesto, Los Angeles, and elsewhere) prohibited commercial laundries in residential neighborhoods—a direct attack on the livelihood of many Chinese immigrants.

Zoning was especially popular among political reformers from the Progressive movement, who saw rational land use controls, along with publicly owned utilities and similar issues, as a necessary public restraint on private business. Los Angeles's Progressive-dominated government imposed one of the nation's first wide-ranging zoning ordinances in 1909—an ordinance that sought to restrict industrial uses to only four districts in the city. The United States Supreme Court upheld this ordinance against intense attack in 1915. A brickmaker whose operation predated the zoning ordinance—indeed, predated his property's annexation to the city—had unsuccessfully challenged his prosecution under the ordinance. "There must be progress," the Supreme Court said, "and if in its march private interests are in the way, they must yield to the good of the community." *Hadacheck v. Sebastian*, 239 U.S. 394 (1915).

Los Angeles's Progressive-dominated government imposed one of the nation's first wide-ranging zoning ordinances in 1909—an ordinance that sought to restrict industrial uses to only four districts in the city.

The Los Angeles ordinance, though it covered much of the city, was not comprehensive. And while many of the underlying ideas of zoning were contained in the Los Angeles ordinance, they were brought to fruition in New York. If all American city planning derives from Central Park, then all American zoning derives from Fifth Avenue, the adjacent street that has always catered to the carriage trade. Even from a California perspective, New York's dominant influence on the early development of planning tools is undeniable.

New York's comprehensive zoning ordinance—the first in the country—resulted from a series of problems caused by the city's remarkable growth at the turn of the century. In 1900, New York was the center of the nation in almost every way—it was the nation's financial capital, center of the bustling garment industry, the favored headquarters location for emerging national chains such as Woolworth's, and gateway for a huge wave of immigrants from Europe. The result was a huge disparity between rich and poor, and a dramatic set of urban conditions.

Crowded and unsanitary conditions, first documented by journalist Jacob Riis in *How the Other Half Lives,* evoked a public outcry to improve tenement housing. The use of steel construction (and the opening of the city's subway) permitted the construction of skyscrapers, clogging the city streets with workers. Perhaps most important, the growing city created massive land speculation along Fifth Avenue, driving the well-to-do farther and farther north.

All of these changes spawned opposing constituencies: poverty advocates who wanted better tenements, other reformers who wanted to restrict building height, and the well-to-do who wanted to freeze the neighborhood in place. The alliance of all these groups led to the passage of the 1916 ordinance. But as author Seymour Toll retells the story in his book *Zoned American,* zoning, unlike planning, was not visionary or forward-looking. Instead, "zoning's first objective was to solidify a very particular status quo." The ordinance's organizing principle "was a concept of hierarchy, a kind of fixed, developmental pecking order for every square inch of city land and every cubic foot of city building."

During the 1910s and '20s, zoning took hold as an idea not just in New York but in most major American cities. The boom began after the National Conference on City Planning in 1913, which published several model ordinances for states and localities to follow. In the 1920s, under the leadership of Commerce Secretary Herbert Hoover, the federal government proposed two pieces of model legislation that proved to be of great importance: the Standard State Zoning Enabling Act (SZEA) in 1922 and the Standard City Planning Enabling Act (SPEA) in 1928. These were not laws but merely publications laying out model ordinances and laws that states and localities might implement or adapt. But especially because of the involvement of the then-esteemed Hoover, the model laws stamped the federal government's symbolic imprint on the idea of creating comprehensive plans and zoning ordinances.

SPEA = Standard City Planning Enabling Act

SZEA = Standard State Zoning Enabling Act

SZEA sanctioned the idea of local governments dividing territory into zones, with uniform regulations in each zone—a key characteristic of what later became known as Euclidean zoning. SPEA created a model ordinance dealing with what today's Californians would call the general plan process—powers of a planning commission, content of the plan, and so on—as well as a municipality's subdivision powers.

These two models created a tidal wave of activity in state legislatures and local governments throughout the country. Using SZEA as the framework, state legislatures passed their own enabling legislation, formally confirming that local governments' police powers extended to zoning. In response to SPEA, many states also passed planning laws, encouraging or requiring local governments to draw up comprehensive plans. According to one estimate, the number of American cities with zoning ordinances grew from eight in 1916 to more than 800 in 1930.

Ira Michael Heyman, UC Berkeley law professor, has written that early zoning ordinances were built on five crucial assumptions:

- Segregation of uses would improve the quality of the urban environment
- The zoning map would provide a vehicle "to formulate an intelligent all-at-once decision to which the market would conform"
- Once the zoning was in place, local governments would rarely change the rules
- Nonconforming uses would go away
- Municipal governmental power would be sufficient to accomplish these goals

"Most of these," Heyman concluded, "have proven to be wrong."

Furthermore, in failing to achieve these original goals, zoning succeeded in being used by single-family homeowners (then a small minority of the overall population) and residents of affluent suburbs to exclude others from their neighborhoods.

Cumulative Zoning

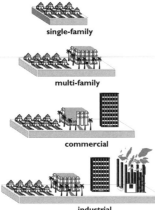

single-family

multi-family

commercial

industrial

The constitutional arguments against zoning generally fell into three categories: due process, equal protection, and just compensation.

From the beginning, most of these zoning ordinances shared a common goal: the preservation, above all else, of the single-family neighborhood. All early zoning ordinances called for a separation of land uses, but the system, called cumulative zoning, was really a pyramid, with industrial property at the bottom and single-family homes at the top. Any land use zone could accommodate uses above it on the pyramid, but not those below. Thus, anything could be built in industrial zones: commercial development, apartments, even single-family houses. In commercial zones, located just above industrial on the pyramid, anything could be built except industrial buildings. At the top of the pyramid stood the single-family zones, which permitted no construction of any kind except for single-family homes.

The hallowed status of the single-family neighborhood as a social institution that is somehow inviolate—even as all other land uses are subject to change and encroachment—remains with us today, not only in the wording of zoning ordinances but also in the psychology of the homeowners, developers, planners, and politicians who work with zoning every day.

Euclid v. Ambler and the Constitutionality of Zoning

The quick passage of so many zoning ordinances and state enabling laws forced a constitutional crisis. Though the *Hadacheck* ruling in 1915 seemed to favor government restrictions on the use of land, the Supreme Court had never definitively ruled that zoning ordinances were constitutional.

The decade of the 1920s was perhaps the zenith of private enterprise in the United States, and property owners often regarded these new regulations as an unconstitutional infringement of their rights. There were several different constitutional arguments (and they have gone in and out of fashion ever since), but, in general, they fell into three categories: due process, equal protection, and just compensation.

"Due process," in particular, was a sticky legal point, because in the latter half of the 19th century, as government regulation grew, the courts had created a concept called substantive due process. A government might violate one's constitutional rights to "procedural" due process by not according an individual a fair hearing in some way. But it might also be unconstitutional in the sense that the regulation does not advance a legitimate governmental purpose. In the '20s, many landowners argued that zoning was not a legitimate use of the police power, and therefore their property had been taken through a violation of substantive due process.

The "equal protection" argument was easier to understand but no less important. By dividing land into different use categories, the argument went, a zoning ordinance favored some landowners over others, therefore denying equal protection under the law.

The "just compensation" argument arose from the Fifth Amendment to the Constitution, prohibiting the government from taking a citizen's property without paying the citizen just compensation; it would not emerge as the leading issue in constitutional land use law until the 1970s. In the 1920s, the arguments were associated instead with the Fourteenth Amendment's guarantees of due process and equal protection.

The legal issues finally came to a head in 1926, when the constitutionality of zoning power was debated by a conservative United States Supreme Court that could not, in advance, have been expected to uphold it. As Seymour Toll explained in his fine account of the case in his book *Zoned American, Euclid v. Ambler* was a test case brought by the real estate industry, selected because it provided a strong and clear-cut attack on zoning. *Euclid v. Ambler Realty Co.,* 272 U.S. 365.

The legal issues finally came to a head in 1926, when the constitutionality of zoning power was debated by a conservative U.S. Supreme Court that could not have been expected to uphold it.

Euclid was a pleasant streetcar suburb of Cleveland that had enacted a zoning ordinance in 1922 to forestall the encroachment of industry and apartment buildings. Ambler Realty owned 68 acres of land in Euclid. Most of Ambler's property was zoned for broad commercial and industrial use, but some of it was restricted to one- and two-family houses.

Ambler claimed that the zoning ordinance took its property without due process of law and denied the company equal protection under the law. Ambler's prospects looked good. There was little doubt that the zoning ordinance had reduced the value of Ambler's property, and the Supreme Court in the 1920s, under the leadership of former President William Howard Taft, was perhaps the most reactionary of the century.

Yet the court upheld the Euclid ordinance on a 6 to 3 vote. In part, this decision arose from a recognition of "the complex conditions of our day," as compared with the "comparatively simple" urban life that had existed only a few decades before. Crowded cities, the justices seemed to suggest, provided a legitimate rationale for more regulation.

At the same time, there can be no question that the elitist nature of zoning in suburban communities also appealed to these conservative justices. The decision is littered with remarks that seem to reveal a certain prejudice against the lower classes and a sympathetic attitude toward keeping them out of the suburbs. In the course of their opinion, the justices attribute nerve disorders, street accidents, and assorted other social maladies to apartment life, and call the apartment house "a mere parasite, constructed in order to take advantage of the open spaces and attractive surroundings created by the residential character of the district"—as if only single-family neighborhoods, and not apartment blocks, could be deemed residential.

Euclid v. Ambler upheld the constitutionality of zoning. But just as important, it helped to legitimize zoning's hidden and somewhat elitist agenda. The U.S. Supreme Court reaffirmed the belief that the single-family home provided a particularly healthful way of life, and that single-family neighborhoods (and their property values) were singularly entitled to legal protection. After a clarifying ruling two years later, the Supreme Court departed from the land use scene for almost 50 years, returning to deal with the issue of takings only in the 1970s and '80s. In the meantime, affluent suburbanites used zoning aggressively to reinforce the social values the Supreme Court had laid out in *Euclid*.

With *Euclid* in hand, planners and land use lawyers set out to apply the legal principles of the case to zoning ordinances throughout the country. The two most important principles were the division of all of the municipality's land into use districts and the more or less equal treatment of property owners within each district. Both of these principles were meant to ensure that police powers advanced a legitimate governmental purpose—protecting substantive due process rights—and to provide landowners with equal protection under the law. Together they formed the basis of what became known, both for its connection with the Supreme Court case and its geometric appeal, as Euclidean zoning.

Life After *Euclid*

Euclid may have made zoning constitutional, but it did not wed zoning irrevocably to a rational planning process. SZEA and many state enabling acts called for zoning ordinances to be prepared "in accordance with a comprehensive plan." By and large, however, they were not. Urban designers and civic visionaries went about the business of preparing "end-state" comprehensive plans, which showed how a city was supposed to look at some endpoint 20 or 30 years down the road. Meanwhile, in the day-to-day business of city-building, lawyers worried about zoning and ignored plans.

Euclid v. Ambler *upheld the constitutionality of zoning. But just as important, it helped to legitimize zoning's hidden and somewhat elitist agenda.*

Two important principles of Euclid *were the division of all of the municipality's land into use districts and the more or less equal treatment of property owners within each district.*

Euclid *may have made zoning constitutional, but it did not wed zoning irrevocably to a rational planning process.*

"If a plan was thought of, more often than not it consisted of a map of blobs vaguely suggesting how the community should look in twenty-five years," wrote the eminent planning lawyer Richard Babcock in his chapter on zoning in *The Practice of Local Government Planning.* "Once drawn, such a 'plan' was tacked on a wall and was forgotten while the local plan commission and city council went about the business of acting upon innumerable requests for changes in the zoning map."

Instead of being used to further its stated goal, the implementation of local comprehensive plans, the power of zoning was, characteristically, usurped for whatever purpose the local economic and political elite had in mind. In Los Angeles during the 1920s and '30s, when frenetic subdivision of land lowered property values, the Board of Realtors used zoning aggressively to encourage "quality" development as a means of propping up values. Big-city political bosses quickly recognized zoning's value in rewarding or penalizing developers, depending on their political loyalties. In the suburbs, the emergence of the special permit, sometimes called the conditional use permit, allowed local governments to deny a landowner permission to build even if the project otherwise met all legal requirements. This additional discretionary power was used frequently against supposedly undesirable land uses—however they might be defined by a particular local government.

Instead of being used to further its stated goal, the power of zoning was usurped for whatever purpose the local economic and political elite had in mind.

In California, planning and zoning laws moved along faster than in the rest of the country, partly in response to rapid growth. California had entered the land use field some 20 years earlier in 1907, when the legislature passed the first Subdivision Map Act. But like other states, California did not pass the first laws dealing with planning and zoning until the 1920s. In 1927, just prior to the issuance of SPEA, the state legislature passed the first law authorizing cities and counties to prepare "master plans." (This law was among the first in the country dealing with comprehensive plans.) Two years later, shortly after the issuance of SPEA, the general plan law was amended to reflect its provisions. Most significantly, any city or county that had established a planning commission, as SPEA had called for, was now required to prepare a general plan. In 1937, the state amended the law again to require all cities and counties to prepare general plans. This step was remarkably ahead of its time; even today, local planning and zoning is not required in all states.

California entered the land use field in 1907, when the state legislature passed the first Subdivision Map Act. In 1927, the legislature passed the first law authorizing cities and counties to prepare master plans.

When the postwar prosperity led to the construction of massive housing tracts in the suburbs, however, one early tenet of zoning fell by the wayside: cumulative zoning. In its place, planners created "exclusive" zoning, a system that permitted one—and only one—use in each zoning district. Thus, just as only single-family homes could be built in single-family zones, now only industrial buildings could be built in industrial zones, or apartment buildings in apartment zones. Such separation was facilitated, of course, by the automobile, which permitted easy mobility from one zone to another (at least in those days!).

In the same way that an earlier generation of zoning laws had reinforced the idea that single-family living was a superior way of life, exclusive zoning cemented in the public consciousness the notion that any mixing of land uses was unhealthy. In the postwar era, suburban jurisdictions throughout the country were able to use their zoning powers—along with these two widely accepted principles of planning philosophy—to create "exclusionary" zoning policies. Large lot requirements, setback standards, and a general reluctance to zone land for anything other than single-family residential use ensured that teeming cities would not spill over into affluent, pastoral suburbs.

During the postwar construction boom, however, California's system of planning and zoning was hard-pressed to keep any semblance of control over growth. This growth was driven in large part by a booming economy, rapid population increases, and pent-up demand for housing from the Depression and World War II. But it was also driven by several other important factors, including the construction of the statewide freeway system (which began in earnest in about 1950) and the emergence of mass-produced housing.

"Production housing," as it is known, was not invented in California—that distinction belongs to the Levittowns of the northeast—but it was perfected here. The classic production-home California suburb—still a sterling example today—was Lakewood, a lower middle-class community in southern Los Angeles County. Lakewood's houses were built on a huge grid system surrounding a shopping mall in three years, between 1950 and 1953. A year later, pioneering a California system of running municipalities on the cheap by contracting for services from county government, Lakewood became a city.

Lakewood's incorporation in 1954 revealed one of the state's biggest problems in planning for postwar growth: the fragmentation of its growing communities into small suburban municipalities, and the increasing competition among local governments (large and small) for new development. During the growth boom of the 1950s and '60s, many landowners engaged in leapfrog development—jumping far ahead of existing municipal boundaries and urban services to

Exclusive Zoning

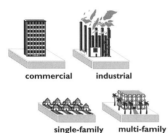

commercial   industrial

single-family   multi-family

The classic production-home California suburb—still a sterling example today—was Lakewood, a lower middle-class community in southern Los Angeles County.

During the growth boom of the 1950s and '60s, many landowners jumped far ahead of existing municipal boundaries and urban services to build subdivisions without central water and sewer systems.

build subdivisions without central water and sewer systems. By and large local governments accommodated these developers. Cities happily annexed distant property. Counties permitted growth wherever landowners wanted to put it. And, in many cases, the two competed to obtain municipal control of this same land.

Within a few years, a backlash began to occur. Citizen activists in San Francisco opposed freeway construction in their city in the late 1950s. In 1961, the California Tomorrow organization issued the first of many dire predictions that California's growth was becoming unmanageable. In a pamphlet called *California Going, Going...*, the organization decried the creation of "slurbs" and asked, "How polluted can a bright land become, and still be bright?"

Within a few years, the state was rife with planning reform. Throughout the 1950s and '60s, the state's local planning laws were repeatedly moved around in state codes and amended until they began to take their current shape. Today all of California's cities and counties must establish a planning agency and prepare and adopt a general plan. These requirements were first centrally organized in the state's government code in 1953 (sections 65000 *et seq.,* where they remain today as the "Planning and Zoning Law").

Two years later the state imposed its first specific requirements on general plans: all plans had to contain at least two "elements," one dealing with land use and the other dealing with circulation. Thus, a general plan prepared in the late '50s would bear at least a passing resemblance to a general plan of today.

The '60s and '70s:
More Requirements, Environmental
Protection, and Citizen Empowerment

In the 1960s and early '70s, most of the current elements of the general plan were added: open space, conservation, housing, etc. State law did not require consistency between general plans and zoning until 1971—more than 40 years after the passage of the first general plan law. (Although the courts now take this legal requirement seriously, many cities and counties were slow to comply. Los Angeles did not undertake a reconciliation between planning and zoning until forced by court order to do so in the late 1980s.)

State law did not require consistency between general plans and zoning until 1971—more than 40 years after the passage of the first general plan law.

In a state filled with small municipalities, however, tweaking the requirements for local planning was not enough. Most of the planning reform activity undertaken in the 1950s and '60s dealt with the regional and statewide consequences of growth. In 1955, the state

LAFCO = Local agency
formation commission

passed the Agricultural Exclusion Act, which prohibited cities from annexing agricultural land without a property owner's consent and also sought to reduce leapfrog development. In 1963, the state created a local agency formation commission (LAFCO) in each county in an attempt to bring rationality to municipal boundaries. In 1965, the state passed the Williamson Act, a tax break for farmers who agree to keep their property in agriculture for 10 years or more. Also in 1965, the state took the bold step of creating the Bay Conservation and Development Commission—the first time land use authority had ever been taken away from local governments and given to a state agency.

Taken together, all these changes did not alter the state's basic trajectory. But they set the stage for even more profound changes in the late 1960s and early '70s—changes that challenged virtually all of the longstanding tenets of law and practice in land use planning.

The Democratization of Planning

The tumultuous social changes of the '60s and '70s created a new set of public policy priorities that, while they did not always affect land use planning directly, had a major impact on the field indirectly.

The tumultuous social changes of the '60s and '70s created a new set of public policy priorities that, while they did not always affect land use planning directly, had a major impact on the field indirectly. These new priorities were characterized by a greater sensitivity to environmental damage and a much more open and inclusive decision-making process. As a result, such traditional staples of planning as uniform zoning requirements, the end-state plan, and broad use of the police power were first altered and then dramatically changed.

In general, these changes can be traced back to four somewhat related trends: stricter environmental laws, greater citizen power, the fiscal problems of local government, and the rise of the modern property rights movement.

The Greening of America:
Environmental Laws

"There is a new mood in America," the Rockefeller Brothers Fund Task Force on Land Use and Urban Growth reported in 1973. "Increasingly, citizens are asking what urban growth will add to the quality of their lives. They are questioning the way piecemeal urbanization is changing their communities and are rebelling against the traditional processes of government.... They are measuring new development proposals by the extent to which environmental criteria are satisfied—by what new housing or business will generate in terms of additional traffic, pollution of air and water, erosion, and scenic disturbance."

This new mood helped force passage of two landmark environmental laws: the National Environmental Policy Act, or NEPA, passed in 1969, and the California Environmental Quality Act, or CEQA, passed in 1970. Both (but especially CEQA) had a profound effect on planning by establishing systems of environmental review for development projects in California.

In a sense, these new laws represented an approach that was different from traditional planning principles. Unlike zoning, these laws did not constitute a set of development limitations intended to ensure that all pieces of property dedicated to similar uses were treated the same. Quite the opposite: They established procedures, such as preparation of environmental impact reports, also known as EIRs (or environmental impact statements, or EIS's, in federal jargon), designed to assure that each piece of land's differences were taken into account. The same project built on different pieces of land might affect the environment and the surrounding communities in entirely different ways, and therefore might be subject to completely different regulations. Thus, a procedure that stood somewhat in conflict with traditional land use planning was simply grafted onto that system.

The environmental laws also opened up the planning process to more citizen empowerment.

Citizen Power

Up until the 1960s, public participation in the planning process rarely consisted of much more than perfunctory public hearings before the local planning commission. The real decisions about planning in a community were still made largely behind closed doors, by elected officials, developers, public works officials, and planners. The '60s and '70s, however, saw the rise of "citizen power"—a term that can be applied loosely to encompass the empowerment of slum dwellers, consumer activism, neighborhood organizing, and the birth of both the environmental movement and the historic preservation movement.

In part these organizations obtained power over the land use planning process simply by grabbing it—through direct action such as street demonstrations, political organization, and use of the media. When politicians and courts didn't respond, citizens were able to take large-scale political action that sent a ringing message to the authorities. Perhaps the most dramatic example in California was the passage of Proposition 20, the 1972 coastal initiative, which took land use planning power along the coast from local governments and gave it, instead, to a new state coastal commission.

CEQA = California Environmental Quality Act

EIR = Environmental impact report

EIS = Environmental impact statement

NEPA = National Environmental Policy Act

The 1960s and '70s saw the rise of citizen power—a term applied loosely to encompass the empowerment of slum dwellers, consumer activism, neighborhood organizing, and the birth of both the environmental movement and the historic preservation movement.

Perhaps the most dramatic example of political action was the passage of Proposition 20, the 1972 coastal initiative, which took land use planning power along the coast from local governments and gave it instead to a new state coastal commission.

In time, however, both politicians and the courts responded to these demands for power by creating a more wide-open process. And this process contained many levers a citizen group could use to advantage. CEQA, for example, was designed mostly to empower ordinary citizens; its chief function remains to bring lots of information about a project's environmental impact into public view. Under CEQA, public access to the information is as important as the information itself, meaning that citizen groups have many legal steps at their disposal to flush the information out if they can't get it any other way.

In this environment of citizen activism, even the long-ignored general plan took on new importance. California courts in the '60s began taking seriously the language contained in state law about the general plan's significance. In 1965, an appellate court called the plan "a constitution for all future development in the city." Six years later, the legislature required, at last, that zoning ordinances be consistent with their accompanying general plans. These changes made the general plan a significant lever for citizen groups seeking to hold local governments and developers accountable.

Thus, by the mid '70s, citizen activists had forced onto the land use agenda the social and environmental costs of development that zoning had never addressed. Just as important, the rise of citizen power encouraged a flexibility that land use planning had never before seen. No longer were certainty and consistency the system's goals; instead, the goals were to minimize social and environmental costs and to mollify the citizen groups that could stop a project. For the first time since the inception of zoning, landowners did not always know in advance what they would be able to build. In this environment, the end-state plan seemed less relevant than ever.

The '70s and '80s: Fiscal Problems and Property Rights

Fiscal Problems

The rapid urban growth of the 1960s and early '70s brought about a voracious need for new public facilities like roads, sewers, police stations, schools, and libraries. In time, an elaborate financing system sprung up to provide these facilities—a combination of federal grants (for water and sewer systems), state grants (for roads and schools), and local bond issues (for the rest of the facilities).

In the '70s, however, this system came crashing down. Federal and state budget cuts virtually eliminated local grants. The passage of Proposition 13 in 1978 cut local property taxes by two-thirds, and

In 1965, an appellate court called the general plan "a constitution for all future development in the city." Six years later, the legislature required that zoning ordinances be consistent with their accompanying general plans.

In time, an elaborate financing system sprung up to provide for new public facilities—a combination of federal grants (for water and sewer systems), state grants (for roads and schools), and local bond issues (for the rest of the facilities).

made it virtually impossible for local governments to raise those taxes again in order to pay debt service. Especially under Proposition 13, citizens began to question the long-held assumption that "growth pays for itself" through increased tax revenues.

These financial problems have probably helped to shape California's development patterns during the last three decades almost as much as the land use planning system itself. Strapped for capital funds, most cities and counties demanded that developers provide the money needed for public infrastructure—a trend that has altered the scale and price of new buildings of all sorts. Also, financially strapped communities, which might once have purchased land for open space or parks, are now more inclined to place severe use restrictions on that land in order to preserve it, or to demand dedications of park lands in return for development permits. The recent passage of Proposition 218 in 1996, making it more difficult to create assessment districts, has added to this trend.

Just as important, California's communities entered into a brutal economic competition for new development, which was virtually the only way to obtain new tax revenue. Many communities engaged in "fiscal zoning"—encouraging construction of tax-rich projects (shopping malls, auto dealerships, hotels), while discouraging construction of tax-poor projects (principally housing and especially lower-cost housing). Many more have used redevelopment aggressively to subsidize tax-rich projects. The result is an imbalance of land uses in many communities because of financial considerations.

Many communities engaged in fiscal zoning—encouraging construction of tax-rich projects, while discouraging construction of tax-poor projects.

Property Rights

Toward the end of the 1970s, the dramatic changes of the previous 15 years spawned another trend: the "property rights" movement. Especially in California, landowners and developers felt ravaged by uncertainty, by fiscal demands, and by the opposition of citizen groups. So, for the first time since the 1920s, they launched a broad-based counterattack, claiming that modern land use regulation had gone so far that it had actually become confiscatory and, therefore, unconstitutional.

Especially in California, landowners and developers felt ravaged by uncertainty, by fiscal demands, and by the opposition of citizen groups.

At first the property rights movement fared poorly. In the '70s, developers lost a series of cases on the issue of "vested rights," and the result was that developers had a harder time vesting their right to build in California than in any other state. In 1979, the California Supreme Court ruled against developers in *Agins v. City of Tiburon*, 24 Cal. 3d 266, by stating that a landowner who claimed his property had been "taken"

In the '70s, developers lost a series of cases on the issue of "vested rights," and the result was that developers had a harder time vesting their right to build in California than in any other state.

by regulation was entitled only to an invalidation of the ordinance, not to just compensation. (As a result, for years most California landowners could not even get a court hearing in a regulatory taking case.)

As the political winds shifted to the right, however, the property rights movement began to score some victories. In 1981, the legislature passed the "development agreement" statute, which permits developers to enter into long-term contracts with local government that secure a developer's vested rights. And since 1987, the U.S. Supreme Court has issued a series of rulings—most of them from California—that have begun to swing the balance of power in land use regulation back toward property owners.

Since 1987, the U.S. Supreme Court has issued a series of rulings that have begun to swing the balance of power in land use regulation back toward property owners.

A System Filled With Friction

In recent years, another generation of change has been layered onto the planning system—including such diverse considerations as federal environmental policies on endangered species protection, the need for more infill housing, and the challenges posed by big-box retail.

California's system of planning today is the result of more than a century of incremental change in response to changing trends—from Mr. Shrader's illegal San Francisco slaughterhouse of the 1860s to attempts by some cities to ban Wal-Mart more than 140 years later. Over those years, other changes have included the L.A. Board of Realtors' use of zoning in the 1920s, the suburban boom of the '50s, the environmental movement of the '70s, and the tax revolt of the '80s.

As the new century begins, it is clearer than ever that planning in California is a system characterized by friction everywhere.

As the new century begins, it is clearer than ever that planning in California is a system characterized by friction everywhere. There is friction between traditional zoning, in which like landowners are treated alike, and environmental review, in which each piece of land is dealt with differently. There is friction between the power of citizen groups, which breeds uncertainty, and the renewed property rights of landowners. There is friction between those same property rights and the fiscal demands cities and counties place on developers. And there is friction between the uncertain and somewhat flexible nature of current land use planning, created by all of the above conditions, and the traditional concept of the end-state general plan.

In short, over the past century, generation after generation of planning tools and techniques have been added to the pile, with little thought given to how they all work together. In the next several chapters, we will discuss these tools and techniques individually. But it is important to remember that many of California's planning problems are inherent in the conflicts among these competing planning tools.

Part Two

The Local Planning Process

Chapter 4

The Structure of
Planning Decisionmaking
Part 1—Local Governments

Whether you want to put up a building or stop somebody else from doing so, your first stop will probably be city hall or the county administration building. That's because local governments are on the front lines of land use planning. Zoning ordinances and general plans are drawn up at the local level. Building permits and other development approvals are issued at the local level. Environmental review is usually conducted under the guidance of local planning departments. Virtually everybody engaged in planning and property development winds up standing in front of a local planning commission or city council sooner or later.

But planning does not begin and end at city hall. In fact, the structure of planning decisionmaking encompasses a wide range of people, places, and institutions, stretching all the way from the typical neighborhood group to the Capitol in Washington, D.C.

Virtually all the players in the vast array of our political/governmental system have a role in determining how planning works at the local level in California. The local planning commission or city council may have power over the zone change or the building permit, but the nature of that power is shaped by other forces, usually involving higher levels of government. Judges, the state legislature, various governmental agencies, even Congress and the U.S. Supreme Court all play a role in determining how the local planning commission or city council is permitted to regulate the use of land.

Judges, the state legislature, governmental agencies, Congress, and the U.S. Supreme Court all play a role in determining how the local planning commission or city council is permitted to regulate the use of land.

Private companies and the private marketplace also play an important role in determining what the final product of the planning process will be. Developers will not propose building something

The Permit Process

Developer brings application to the Planning Department which examines project and conducts environmental review.

Developer then presents project to the Planning Commission.

Citizens comment.... Under the Permit Streamlining Act, the Planning Commission must act within one year of original application. Decision may be appealed to City Council or Board of Supervisors.

unless they believe there is a market to buy it (home purchasers, commercial tenants, etc.), and usually they won't be able to borrow the money to build it unless there is a financial institution willing to invest. These considerations play a major role in shaping general plans, for example. Most planning ideas won't survive the intense public scrutiny of the planning process unless organized real estate interests believe the ideas have some relationship to the realities of the private real estate market.

Nevertheless, local governments usually constitute the main event in land use planning in California. It is impossible to understand how planning works without first understanding how local governments are structured. (Other players will be covered in the next chapter.)

Local Governments: Cities, Counties, and Everybody Else

Government isn't always a popular institution these days, but people tend to like government when it's close to them. Maybe that's why California has so many local governments—more than 7,000 different entities in all. Most of these (between 3,000 and 5,000, depending on the criteria used) are special districts, established to perform specific functions. About 1,000 are school districts, a figure significantly reduced from 3,000 because of consolidations in the 1960s. California has 478 cities, a large number by any standard. And the state has 58 counties—a relatively small number. Many of California's counties, especially those in Southern California, are among the largest in the nation geographically.

All of these local agencies play a role in the planning process, but cities and counties are by far the most important. Because they are California's only "general purpose" local governments, they are the only local agencies holding regulatory power. With a couple of exceptions at the state level, such as the Coastal Commission, virtually all land use permits in California are issued by the cities and the counties.

(Unlike many other states, California does not have legally established towns or townships.)

Cities and counties can create and administer land use regulations because the state constitution specifically gives them that power. Like all governmental power in this country, the power to regulate the use of land stems ultimately from the U.S. Constitution. The Tenth Amendment to the Constitution, the so-called "reserved powers doctrine," states that any powers not specifically granted to the federal government in the Constitution are reserved by the states. Chief among these is the "police power." No legal term is more important to planning.

The Tenth Amendment to the Constitution states that any powers not specifically granted to the federal government in the Constitution are reserved by the states.

The police power is the power of a governmental entity to restrict private activity in order to achieve a broad public benefit. In California, police power is used to protect the health, safety, morals, and welfare of the public. Throughout legal history, the police power has been used as the basis for a broad range of governmental activities from the court system to general relief. For more than a century, it has also been the legal vehicle used to justify governmental regulation over the use of land.

But police power does not rest inherently at city hall. Local governments in California exercise police power over land uses only because the state government delegates that power to the counties and cities. Article XI, section 7, of the California Constitution states: "A county or city may make and enforce within its limits all local, police, sanitary, and other ordinances and regulations not in conflict with general laws."

A county or city may make and enforce within its limits all local, police, sanitary, and other ordinances and regulations not in conflict with general laws.
— Article XI, section 7, California Constitution

The courts have interpreted this clause liberally, and the term most often used to describe the police power in dealing with land use is "elastic." For this reason, land use regulation has expanded in scope a great deal over the past few decades. Nevertheless, the local exercise of police power is far from absolute. Local actions must be "reasonably related" to the public values of health, safety, morals, and welfare. They must not contradict constitutional principles, especially the concepts of due process, equal protection, and the unlawful taking of property without compensation. And they are subordinate to state laws.

So even though local governments think they have a lot of land use power, they are really at the mercy of the state and federal governments, which shape their land use power through both legislation and litigation. This means that legislators, judges, bureaucrats, and others become players in the land use game just as much as planning commissioners or city council members. But again, only cities and

The Legal Structure
of California Planning

PLANNING PROCEDURES in California derive from a broad array of state laws. The ones most directly applicable to conventional land use planning appear in the Government Code, which is the section of the state's laws dealing with governmental actions. Many others are scattered throughout other sections of state law, including the Public Resources Code and the Health and Safety Code. Together they form the basis for California's planning system. The most important pieces of this legal structure include the following:

Planning, Zoning, and Development Laws
Govt. Code § 65000 *et seq.*

This set of laws lays out the legal basis for the state's interest in planning and establishes the requirement that all local governments create "planning agencies."

General Plan Law
Govt. Code § 65300 *et seq.*

These code sections require that all local governments prepare a "general plan" for the future development of the city or county, and lay out all the state's requirements governing what a general plan should contain. The general plan is the same as the document that most planners outside California refer to as the "comprehensive plan" or the "master plan"—that is, a comprehensive document that establishes the land use policies and also details the likely future development patterns of the city or county.

Subdivision Map Act
Govt. Code § 66410 *et seq.*

This law governs all subdivision of land. It requires that local governments establish regulations to guide subdivisions, and grants powers to local governments to ensure that the subdivision occurs in an orderly and responsible manner.

counties issue the actual land use permits that lie at the heart of most local planning processes.

Cities and Counties

Cities and counties divvy up the power to regulate land use in a very simple way: Cities have jurisdiction over land inside their borders, and counties control what's left—the so-called "unincorporated" territory. Thus, cities have a certain strategic territorial advantage. Any time a city incorporates or annexes more land, it wrests land use power (as well as tax revenue) away from the county.

Although cities and counties have identical authority over land use in their jurisdiction, they exercise that authority somewhat differently. The reason for this is simply that cities and counties are fundamentally different governmental beasts.

Counties are creatures of the state government whose basic mission is to implement state policy on a regional basis. They are subdivisions of the state; every square inch of California falls within one of its 58 counties.

Counties focus most of their attention—and their money—on health, welfare, and criminal justice, services they must deliver on a regional basis to all residents whether they live inside cities or not. In legal terms, at least, counties are in the land use planning business by default, because they have responsibility for land outside cities.

Because they control so much agricultural and other nonurban land, county-level land use planning often has a rural or resources focus. But counties are often in the "urban" land use planning business as well, because new developments often locate in unincorporated areas. Many of these communities eventually incorporate or annex to cities, but others do not. Thus, virtually all counties are responsible for some communities that are essentially urban or suburban in character, while some counties serve as the "municipal government" for hundreds of thousands of people who live in unincorporated areas.

Unlike counties, California's cities are not creatures of the state. Rather, they are created by local citizens to serve their own purposes, especially to provide urban services (such as water and sewer service and a police force). Most counties are geographically large, while cities range from one square mile (Lawndale) to more than 400 (Los Angeles). Cities range in population from only a few hundred to about 4 million in Los Angeles. Counties vary widely in population as well. Most of California's residents live in the eight large urban counties with a population of one million or more. Yet 22 rural counties have populations of less than 100,000 residents, including Sierra (3,500) and Alpine (1,200).

Not all cities are created equal in California. Larger cities—as well as many smaller, older ones—are "charter cities," meaning they have more discretion within their city charters to establish land use processes (subject to a vote of the city's residents). Most smaller cities are "general law cities," meaning they do not have a city charter and must adhere to state law. Thus, charter cities are more clearly separate entities from the state government, while general law cities are more dependent.

Local Planning Powers

Under state law, every county and every city has a legislative body and a planning agency. A county's legislative body is called the board of supervisors, while a city's is called the city council. Almost all boards of supervisors, as well as most city councils, have five members. But there are some exceptions. The Board of Supervisors of the combined city and county of San Francisco (the only combined city and county in the state) has 11 members, while the Los Angeles City Council has 15. Most other large cities have

California Environmental Quality Act
Pub. Res. Code § 21000 *et seq.*

This law requires local governments to conduct some form of environmental review on virtually all public and private development projects. CEQA's requirements, which are mostly procedural, sometimes cause local governments to prepare environmental impact reports on specific development projects, detailing the likely environmental damage the projects would cause.

Coastal Act
Pub. Res. Code § 30000 *et seq.*

This law, originally passed as a ballot initiative in 1972, establishes special planning requirements for coastal areas and creates a powerful state agency, the Coastal Commission, to oversee coastal planning.

Community Redevelopment Law
Health & Safety Code § 33000 *et seq.*

This law gives cities and counties great power to redevelop blighted areas. It is perhaps the most powerful single tool local governments possess, other than the basic laws permitting them to engage in planning at all.

Cortese-Knox-Hertzberg
Local Government Reorganization Act
Govt. Code § 56000 *et seq.*

This law is not strictly speaking a planning law. However, its provisions play an important role in local planning because it governs procedures by which local government boundaries may be changed. Under the Cortese-Knox-Hertzberg Act, all annexations, incorporations, and other boundary changes must be processed through a special countywide agency called the local agency formation commission (LAFCO).

Many other laws come into play at one time or another, and these will be dealt with in the chapters to come. However, these seven sets of laws form the core of California's planning system. ■

Types of Local Government Decisions

CEQA = California Environmental Quality Act

Legislative acts are general policy decisions, such as general plan revisions and zoning ordinances.

seven-member city councils. But the board of supervisors in Los Angeles County, the largest local government in the country (with 10 million residents), has only five members, meaning a Los Angeles County supervisor has more constituents than any lawmaker except a U.S. senator.

Most local governments have separate planning commissions. In about 30 small cities and one or two counties, the governing body itself serves as the planning commission. Most planning commissions consist of five or seven members appointed by the legislative body (though in Los Angeles and San Francisco the commissioners are appointed by the mayor as a check against the legislative body's power). Most local governments have a slew of other boards and commissions, but the planning commission is one of the few local bodies, other than the city council or board of supervisors, with the power to make legally binding decisions. (Most, if not all, such decisions can be appealed to the local legislative body.)

Not all decisions made by local government hold the same legal status. That's because local governments play more than one role. On the local level, the city or county can act, in a way, as legislature, court, and bureaucracy, so local decisions are divided into three categories: legislative, quasi-judicial, and ministerial. These categories are extremely important, because they define the duties of the legislative body and the planning commission; they determine which decisions are subject to initiative and referendum, and to CEQA; and they often determine the type of review a local decision will receive in court.

Legislative acts are general policy decisions, such as general plan revisions and zoning ordinances. These acts, which usually take the form of local ordinances, are no different than laws passed by the legislature or by Congress. They are policy statements establishing the rules by which everyone must play. For this reason, legislative acts are binding only when they are approved by the city council or board of supervisors. A planning commission may recommend a general plan amendment or zoning ordinance, but only the legislative body can approve and adopt it. Under California law (liberally construed by the courts), any legislative act is subject to initiative and referendum. Virtually any general plan amendment or rezoning can be placed on the ballot by the voters.

Legislative Acts (discretionary)	vs.	Quasi-Judicial Acts (discretionary)	vs.	Ministerial Acts (not discretionary)
Creating policy • General plan revisions • Zoning ordinances

Approved / Adopted by city council

Subject to initiative and referendum | | Applying discretionary policy to individual projects • Conditional use permit • Zoning variance

Approved / Declined by planning commission (appeals decided by city council)

Not subject to initiative and referendum | | Applying nondiscretionary policy to individual projects • Building permit (on an approved project) • Other permit (where all necessary conditions are met)

Approved by staff

Not subject to initiative and referendum |

Quasi-judicial acts are decisions that apply legislative policy to individual development projects, much as a court might apply legal precedents to a particular case. Like legislative acts, quasi-judicial acts involve some discretion on the part of the local government, meaning that an application for a conditional use permit (CUP) or a zoning variance could be turned down based on the judgment of local officials. However, because quasi-judicial actions merely interpret rather than set policies, the planning commission's ruling is legally binding, though these decisions can be appealed to the city council or board of supervisors. For this same reason, quasi-judicial decisions cannot be placed on the ballot through the initiative and referendum process. (However, local citizens might force a reconsideration of the matter by the local council or board if they file a lawsuit with merit.)

CUP = Conditional use permit

Ministerial acts are actions in which the local government has no discretion. Usually a ministerial act involves the mandatory issuance of a permit if certain conditions are met. For example, if a development project has already been approved by a planning commission or city council, then most likely the issuance of the building permit is a ministerial act, meaning the permit must be issued if the conditions of the development approval are met. Because they involve no discretion, ministerial decisions are delegated to the staff level. Significantly, ministerial acts are not subject to initiative and referendum. And, unlike legislative and quasi-judicial acts, they are also exempt from environmental review under CEQA.

Ministerial acts are actions in which the local government has no discretion.

Local Planning Staffs

Although they merely recommend actions to planning commissions, city councils, and boards of supervisors, local planning staffs wield tremendous influence over planning in California.

The planning department is typically headed by a planning director, who is in charge of all cases that come before the commission.

EPA = Environmental Protection Agency

LAFCO = Local agency formation commission

Putting the Pieces Together in Local Planning

PLANNING IS A BALANCING ACT. The creation of a general plan or any other planning document requires the ability to understand a wide range of issues and goals—many in conflict with one another—and synthesize them into a cohesive and consistent package. For this reason, local planners are often best described as "generalists"— professionals who may have expertise in a particular field such as land use, but who recognize that their most important job is fitting all the pieces of a community together.

This is not an easy job, because most of the laws and most of the other government agencies involved in the planning process focus on specific topics with little regard for how to meld them. State and federal laws cover such discrete topics as air quality, housing, transportation, wildlife, parks, and water. As a result, state and federal agencies are arranged under this same hierarchy. Each agency concerns itself with just one narrow area of what to a planner appears to be an overall, integrated portrait of that community.

Even in local government, other departments and agencies are similarly segmented, focusing on such topics as public works, parks, traffic, or fire protection, with little concern for how the pieces fit together. Planners themselves are often asked to confine themselves to such pigeonholes. This is especially true if they work in the "current planning" section, which focuses on reviewing development applications and administering land use regulations.

Yet it is the special job of planners—especially when they work on "advance planning," or the creation of long-range documents such as general plans—to find a way to meld all these different policy issues. Often they must do so under the shadow of conflicting laws and policies from the state or federal governments—requiring them, for example, to provide a wide range of housing opportunities while at the same time calling for protection of wildlife and open space.

To provide an idea of the range of issues local governments face, here are some of the topics contained in a typical ➡

In many cities, the planning department is part of a larger community development department, which encompasses related city activities such as housing, transportation, and building code enforcement. A city or county community development director will often interact with both planning commission and city council, especially on matters of policy, such as general plan amendments and zoning ordinances. A city manager or county administrative officer, though responsible for all day-to-day operations of the jurisdiction's departments, may also become involved in land use issues when they are significant. Thus, these staff members hold primary responsibility for research and recommendations on virtually all actions of local government.

Staff members at the local level exert considerable influence for one particularly important reason. While state legislators, members of Congress, and judges work essentially full-time at their jobs, most members of city councils and planning commissions serve only part-time, often with no pay. (Large cities such as Los Angeles and San Diego have full-time council members, and most county supervisors receive a full-time salary as well, though in rural counties the salary is often quite low.)

Of course, officials at higher levels of government must rely on their staff members as well, especially because they have such a broad range of responsibilities. But because most local council members and planning commissioners have full-time jobs outside city government, they rarely have the opportunity to investigate an issue or a case independently. They have no choice but to rely on the information they receive from their staff. A planning commissioner may drive by and look at a parcel of land before a meeting, but it is the staff planner who will research the property's history and the codes that govern its use, and examine a proposal in detail for its merits.

Not all city council members or planning commissioners follow staff recommendations; in fact, some are hostile to the staff's ideas because they want to appear independent (or sometimes for ideological reasons). And, of course, local officials are not entirely dependent on the staff, because public hearings give them a chance to hear the views of the proponents and citizens directly. The truth is, however, that staff members control most of the information that goes to a local city council or planning commission, and they always have the last word in a debate at a public hearing.

Also, in many communities staff members can assume some of the planning commission's functions by conducting public hearings and approving conditional use permits, or their equivalents, by sitting as "zoning administrators." The government code allows such quasi-judicial authority to be delegated to the staff by local ordinance.

Staff members do not always wield great power. In many cities they are mere functionaries who carry out the demands of elected officials, whether those officials have a slow-growth bent or close ties to developers. But because of their training and experience, top staff members are often regarded by their employers as experts in the field whose views must be given great weight. Their influence is far greater than their job descriptions might suggest.

Drawing Boundaries

Because local governments are responsible for land use planning and permitting, the general plan, along with a list of some of the state and federal agencies that regulate or execute policy in these areas:

- **Land Use Planning**
  - Local control
- **Housing**
  - California Department of Housing and Community Development
  - U.S. Department of Housing and Urban Development
- **Transportation**
  - Regional Transportation Planning Agencies
  - Caltrans
  - U.S. Department of Transportation, including both Federal Highway Administration and the Federal Transit Administration
- **Natural Resource Protection**
  - California Department of Fish and Game
  - Regional Water Quality Control Boards
  - U.S. Fish and Wildlife Service
  - U.S. Environmental Protection Agency
  - Army Corps of Engineers
- **Parks and Recreation**
  - California Department of Parks and Recreation
- **Sewers and Other Public Infrastructure**
  - Federal and State Environmental Protection Agencies
- **Schools Capacity**
  - California Department of Education
  - Local School Boards
- **Air Quality**
  - Regional Air Quality Management Districts and Air Pollution Control Districts
  - California Air Resources Board
  - U.S. Environmental Protection Agency

It is the unenviable task of local planning not only to balance these various topic areas off one against the other—the basic task of local planning—but also to fulfill the often conflicting agendas of these single-purpose agencies (or at least keep the agencies' top bureaucrats happy enough to leave the local officials alone). How these bureaucrats and other nonlocal players approach planning issues will be discussed in the next chapter. ▪

Managing the Contours of Local Empires: Incorporations and Spheres of Influence

PROBABLY THE TWO MOST controversial—and, from a land use planning point of view, significant—actions that LAFCOs can take are incorporations and the designation of "spheres of influence."

Communities usually seek to incorporate as cities for one of two reasons. The first is a desire to control local tax dollars, a feeling that often arises when a community is located far from the county seat. The second is a desire to control a community's growth. Because they must rely on new development to increase tax revenue, counties often encourage growth in unincorporated areas, which can lead to a backlash by local residents. In this context, incorporation becomes a slow-growth measure, whose purpose is to draw a line around the area and then elect a local city council that will change the planning policies.

LAFCOs must conduct a fiscal review on any proposed new city. Unless a new city is going to show a healthy budget surplus, the LAFCO is not supposed to approve it. But this fiscal review is not as simple or nonpolitical as it might seem.

In several instances, incorporation proponents have engaged in bitter disputes with LAFCO fiscal consultants over the likely cost of city services. High-end assumptions can sink a cityhood movement; low-end assumptions can help it. Also, a city's likely policies after incorporation can enter into the equation. For example, suppose a new city is proposed by citizens who have made it clear that they will pursue slow-growth policies if incorporation succeeds. Obviously, the slow-growth policies will affect the proposed city's fiscal health. A change in development plans might harm the city financially by slowing down new construction. This financial information may be used to support or oppose incorporation, depending on the political motivations of the city and county officials who sit on the LAFCO.

Pessimistic fiscal projections have killed more than one proposed city. But optimistic projections can lead to equally sad ➡

fate of any particular parcel of land or neighborhood depends on the jurisdiction within which it is located. For this reason, the question of drawing local government boundaries is an extremely important issue in determining land use patterns throughout the state.

Boundary wars are common in most states, as aggressive cities and towns try to out-muscle one another for choice territory. In California, the process is at least nominally more rational. With the exception of redevelopment boundaries, all local government boundaries in California are drawn not by the local governments themselves, but by a special agency in each county called the local agency formation commission, or LAFCO.

Communities have always used boundaries as weapons—to keep out poor people or noxious industries, to maximize tax revenue, and to gain control over newly emerging areas. The passage of Proposition 13 and the legislature's shift of property tax revenue to school districts have caused this local warfare to increase. By virtually prohibiting property tax increases, Proposition 13 turned local government finance into a game of winner-take-all. The property tax shifts that were implemented to balance the state budget starting in the early 1990s made sales tax even more attractive. Thus, cities constantly battle counties and each other to control territory that holds the potential for a valuable sales tax base, because gaining control of land for retail development is one of the few ways for a city or county to increase tax revenue. The battleground where these fights take place is the LAFCO.

The legislature approved the first LAFCO law in 1963, following a report by Governor Pat Brown's Commission on Metropolitan Problems. The newly created LAFCOs were intended to stop the competition for desirable raw land among cities, which was leading to leapfrog development and suburban sprawl in rapidly urbanizing metropolises such as San Jose. LAFCOs were specifically charged with creating orderly local boundaries in order to minimize sprawl. For example, a LAFCO may not approve a city's annexation of land that is not contiguous to existing city boundaries.

Theoretically, a LAFCO is a state entity separate from all local government jurisdiction. LAFCOs exist because boundary decisions, unlike local land use planning, are considered matters of state concern. (Thus, boundary decisions are not subject to local initiative and referendum.)

However, the LAFCO process can often become very political because a majority of the LAFCO board members are elected local officials. Some LAFCOs have been accused of being controlled by city or county officials who want to accommodate developers that are big campaign contributors. In some instances, this accommodation may lead to the annexation of a key piece of property to a city able to provide water and sewer service to that property. At other times, a developer's influence may mean LAFCO votes to exclude a particular piece of property from a city or its sphere of influence, especially if the city is unfriendly to growth. So even though LAFCOs have no land use power, their decisions affect

results. For example, the only city in recent California history to incorporate with a questionable financial future was East Palo Alto. The area is a minority ghetto in San Mateo County, just across the county line from the affluent city of Palo Alto; it is afflicted with crime and poverty, and has little tax base. Nevertheless, East Palo Alto was permitted to incorporate in 1983 as an affirmation of social justice. The city has struggled to provide services ever since.

Once the LAFCO has approved an incorporation, the issue usually proceeds to a vote. State law includes protest procedures that may avert an election,* but in fact a vote is almost always held. And if cityhood makes it to the ballot, it almost always wins. Shortly after the passage of Proposition 13 in 1978, many cityhood advocates realized that incorporation is *free* because property taxes cannot be increased. The county is forced to surrender much of its tax base inside the city limits to the new city government, while the new city obtains a revenue stream without raising taxes. Between 1978 and 1992, new cities were formed at a rapid rate.

A new state law passed in 1992, however, requires that counties be held financially harmless in city incorporations. Thus, an incorporation must meet two seemingly conflicting tests: It must provide a positive cash flow for the new city without harming the county's financial well-being. Needless to say, few new cities have been incorporated since the new law was passed. Citrus Heights became the first new city in Sacramento County to incorporate in 50 years, while Orange County worked with a large number of communities to facilitate cityhood while still meeting the revenue neutrality requirement.

A LAFCO can also establish a city's sphere of influence, which will usually extend beyond the current boundaries into undeveloped areas. By creating a sphere of influence, a LAFCO defines the probable ultimate boundaries of a city. Because the

---

* Under state law, after approving an incorporation LAFCO must conduct a protest hearing and hold the comment period open for 30 days. If opposition is expressed by 25 to 50 percent of the people who live in the area or by the owners of 25 to 50 percent of the property, then a vote must be held. (If more than 50 percent of either group complains, then the incorporation cannot occur.)

➡

sphere indicates what property the LAFCO will permit the city to annex, a city can draw up a general plan that includes the sphere area.

As with incorporation, the creation of a sphere of influence might seem to be a technical, nonpolitical decision that simply acknowledges likely future development patterns. In fact, sphere decisions are highly political. Some landowners and developers will lobby the LAFCO to be included in a city's sphere; others will lobby to be left out. And because developers are major contributors to both city and county election campaigns, the city and county officials who sit on the LAFCO will often try to accommodate the developers.

The most celebrated sphere battles have occurred in Los Angeles County, where the LAFCO has tried to limit the spheres of new cities because developers prefer to deal with the county planning department. When the city of Agoura Hills incorporated in 1982, for example, the Los Angeles County LAFCO created a sphere of influence co-terminus with the city's boundaries. Fearing rampant development in nearby unincorporated areas, Agoura Hills sued, claiming that a city's sphere must be larger than its boundaries. But the court of appeal rejected the argument, saying the LAFCO had acted properly.

The city of Santa Clarita suffered a similar fate when it incorporated five years later. Consisting of unincorporated areas such as Valencia, Newhall, and Saugus, the city had incorporated partly to stop what it regarded as irresponsible development under Los Angeles County policies. Therefore, Santa Clarita asked the L.A. County LAFCO for a sphere of influence of 90 square miles (compared with the city boundaries of 40 square miles). Under pressure from homebuilders in the area, however, the LAFCO denied the request and, as with Agoura Hills, established a sphere that was co-terminus with city boundaries. Undaunted, Santa Clarita returned to the LAFCO two years later with a request for a sphere covering 200 square miles! This request, at least, motivated the LAFCO staff to recommend the 90-square-mile sphere Santa Clarita had wanted originally, but again the LAFCO commissioners turned down the request. ▪

development patterns because LAFCOs determine which local jurisdiction will have responsibility for planning new areas.

For decades, counties closely controlled LAFCO policies and day-to-day activities because counties, by law, were required to provide LAFCO offices and to fund agency expenses. Many counties went a step further and had the county administrator or planning director also serve as the LAFCO executive officer. Given the contentious relationship among cities, counties, and special districts over boundary issues, the county's close relationship with the LAFCO created credibility issues.

Despite their importance, LAFCOs remain one of the most obscure local government agencies. Thus, the attention given to LAFCOs by state lawmakers and policy wonks several years ago came as something of a surprise. In 1997, San Fernando Valley Assemblyman Robert Hertzberg authored a bill that created the Commission on Local Governance for the 21st century. The 15-member commission was charged with reviewing and making recommendations regarding LAFCO law (known as the Cortese-Knox Act).

Led by former San Diego Mayor Susan Golding and future Bush administration official Ruben Barrales, the 21st century commission conducted two dozen public hearings all over the state and consulted with a variety of academics, local officials, civic activists, developers, and others. In 2000, the commission released a wide-ranging and well-received report concluding that the state and local governments were poorly prepared to handle the intense demands of California's rapid growth. By the time the commission issued its report, Hertz-berg had become the Speaker of the Assembly. In his new role as one of the state's most important politicians, Hertzberg pushed through the legislature a bill containing many of the commission's recommended overhauls of the LAFCO law, which became known as the Cortese-Knox-Hertzberg Act. (The commission's broader recommendations for things such as a new state-local fiscal relation-ship were largely unheeded.)

The revised law made LAFCOs more independent and gave them an even larger role in local planning. To force a more inde-pendent approach, the Hertzberg amendments require all cities and special districts to help fund LAFCOs, ending the agencies' finan-cial dependence on counties. The bill also requires a LAFCO board to appoint an executive officer and lawyer, and not simply accept whatever staff members the county assigns. The Hertzberg changes also extended lobbying and campaign disclosure requirements to LAFCOs for the first time, so that everyone may see who is trying to influence the agencies' often obscure decisions.

The Cortese-Knox-Hertzberg Act made LAFCOs more independent and gave them an even larger role in local planning.

As for planning policies, the updated law required OPR to produce statewide guidelines for incorporation. More significantly, the bill requires every LAFCO to review how municipal services are provided throughout the county by 2007, and then to adopt spheres of influence for every local government agency based on those re-views. A LAFCO is supposed to update the spheres of influence every five years. Furthermore, the Hertzberg amendments require individual LAFCOs to adopt and abide by written policies for the first time. Also for the first time, the amendment stated that the law's intent is to preserve open space and agricultural lands.

The Hertzberg revisions expanded LAFCO board membership to ensure special district representation, although some LAFCOs already had special district appointees. With a few exceptions, LAFCO boards must now be composed of two county supervisors, two rep-resentatives of the county's cities, two representatives of special districts within the county, and one member of the public.

The Hertzberg revisions expanded LAFCO board membership to ensure special district representation, al-though some LAFCOs already had special district appointees.

LAFCO policies vary from county to county. In Ventura and Santa Clara Counties, the LAFCO has a strong tradition of directing growth inside city boundaries, and as a result only 5 to 10 percent of the population lives in unincorporated areas. Sacramento County, on the other hand, grew from 200,000 to one million residents in the half century between 1946 and 1996 without forming a single new city. Even with the incorporation of the cities of Citrus Heights,

Elk Grove, and Rancho Cordova since 1996, about 40 percent of Sacramento County residents live outside city boundaries.

LAFCOs deal with a broad range of boundary actions, including incorporations, annexations, dissolution (the opposite of incorporation), detachment (the opposite of annexation), and the creation of spheres of influence for cities. LAFCOs also adjust the boundaries of special districts. Dissolutions are rare, but detachments are quite common, as cities are constantly making small adjustments to their boundaries.

Passage of the Herzberg revisions forced LAFCOs to produce numerous policy documents, a mandate that has received a mixed reception from LAFCOs.

During the boom years of the 1980s, LAFCOs spent much of their time dealing with proposed incorporations and annexations. Though annexation activity remained heavy, incorporations dropped off after a 1992 law required that the formation of new cities not come at the financial expense of counties. (*See* Managing the Contours of Local Empires, page 74.) During the 1990s, LAFCOs focused heavily on the need for the state's thousands of special districts, which do not directly affect land use, but whose service areas and organizational structure often reflect—and foreshadow—the geographical boundaries of urban development. Most special districts, however, proved effective at protecting their turf. Passage of the Herzberg revisions forced LAFCOs to produce numerous policy documents, a mandate that has received a mixed reception from LAFCOs.

Chapter 5

The Structure of Planning Decisionmaking
Part 2—Other Players in the Planning Process

Cities and counties may make the actual planning decisions, but they are far from the only players in the planning arena. Although they hold the actual land use permitting authority, cities and counties are only two of dozens of players in the planning process. In fact, they are constantly squeezed, pressured, dictated to, and lobbied from above and below. Contrary to popular belief, cities and counties are not free to do as they wish; they must follow the rules set by others and adhere to the pressures of both politics and the private marketplace.

In general, besides local governments, the planning world's other players fall into four other categories:

- **Rulemakers,** such as the California legislature, Congress, and the court system, all of which set and often apply the rules by which local governments play the planning game
- **Other government agencies,** mostly on the state and federal level, which have some influence over the local planning process
- **The private real estate industry,** including developers, lenders, and the buyers of improved real estate, who influence the planning process through their private business decisions
- **Citizen groups,** including homeowner associations, environmentalists, historic preservation advocates, and others, who become politically involved in the planning process in order to further their group's agenda, rather than for private business reasons

The Rulemakers

Local governments that operate the planning process do not have much autonomy, at least in organizing the way the planning process

Other Players in the Planning Process

- **Rulemakers**
  - Legislature
  - Congress
  - Court system

- **Federal and State Agencies**

- **Real Estate Industry**
  - Developers
  - Lenders
  - Buyers

- **Citizen Groups**

is set up. In fact, these local governments are very much at the mercy of the rulemakers—the U.S Congress, the California legislature, and the state and federal court systems—which shape their land use power through both legislation and litigation.

Congress

Congress is important because of the ubiquitous nature of the federal government, but its role in planning is indirect. The concept of a "national land use policy" was kicked around on Capitol Hill in the 1970s, but Congress has never interfered directly in the land use area, preferring to leave those matters up to the states. Nevertheless, Congress has passed a vast array of laws, mostly environmental in nature, that affect the land use process at the local level.

Laws designed to protect endangered species and wetlands, for example, give federal agencies the power to block development, even if local officials disagree. Federal air and water quality laws often affect the size, location, and nature of industrial plants by requiring a reduction in pollutants. Also, federal projects are not subject to local land use controls, though, in practice, some federal/local negotiation usually takes place. Congress often appropriates funds to buy land for conservation purposes (for example, in creating the Santa Monica Mountains National Recreation Area in Los Angeles and the Golden Gate National Recreation Area near San Francisco). During the 1980s and '90s, Congress also had a dramatic effect on local land use patterns around the state by closing dozens of military bases, thus creating a whole new set of planning processes for base reuse. More recently, Congress has been overshadowed by presidential administrations' use of agencies such as the U.S. Fish & Wildlife Service and the U.S. Forest Service to shape the application of environmental regulations.

The California Legislature

During the past century, the legislature has created the entire framework for local planning in California.

The California legislature plays a far more direct part in establishing the roles of local planning. During the past century, the legislature has created the entire framework for local planning in California. The legislature passed the precursor to the Subdivision Map Act in 1893 and the first general plan law in 1927. Specific elements were first required in a general plan during the 1950s, and the requirement that a zoning ordinance and general plan must be consistent with one another passed the legislature in 1971. The legislature has also passed a host of other laws affecting land use, including the Community Redevelopment Law, which dates from the early 1950s, and the California Environmental Quality Act, which dates from 1970.

Furthermore, these laws do not simply go on the books and stay there. The legislature tinkers with every one of them every year. The exact process by which the California Assembly and Senate pass a bill is complicated and does not merit much discussion here. (The process is virtually the same as the one in Congress—committee hearings, votes in both Houses, conference committee, and review by the executive, who has veto power.) But thousands of bills are introduced each year and hundreds pass, most of them amending laws already on the books. Sometimes these amendments create marginal, almost imperceptible changes, but over a period of time they can significantly change the thrust of a law.

Many laws are passed simply because the legislature has reached a consensus that they serve the public interest. But such purity of motive is not always the rule. The legislative arena is highly susceptible to politics and other external forces. Typically, bills are proposed—or even written—by lobbying organizations with something to gain. Many of the bills cracking down on redevelopment, for example, have been proposed by California's counties, which lose considerable tax revenue when redevelopment projects are created. And occasionally, a developer will ask a friendly legislator to carry a so-called "juice" bill—a bill that looks general on its face, but actually carries a specific provision designed to help the developer push his project through back home.

Once a bill is introduced, many different interest groups lobby the legislators (and the governor), encouraging them to pass, defeat, or amend the bill to make it more favorable to their interests. On land use bills, influential lobbyists typically include the League of California Cities, the California State Association of Counties, the California Building Industry Association, affordable housing advocates from California Rural Legal Assistance, perhaps the California Association of Realtors or the California Business Properties Association, and sometimes environmental groups such as the Sierra Club. The opposition of any one of these groups can be enough to kill a bill. Sometimes they neutralize each other's impact, meaning that a successful bill is likely to be a cautious one. This has become even more true since the introduction of term limits and the departure of powerful and experienced legislators. Rather than

Many of the bills cracking down on redevelopment have been proposed by California's counties, which lose considerable tax revenue when redevelopment projects are created.

Once a bill is introduced, many different interest groups lobby the legislators and the governor, encouraging them to pass, defeat, or amend the bill to make it more favorable to their interests.

solving large-scale problems, today's California legislature is much more likely to pass small bills dealing with small problems.

The legislature is not the only statewide forum for resolving public policy issues in California. Any issue may also appear on the statewide ballot as an initiative or a referendum if enough signatures are gathered. As we shall see, initiatives and referenda have played a much more direct role in planning on the local level; but statewide ballot measures can be just as influential as the legislature in shaping the local planning environment. Perhaps the leading example in this area is Proposition 20, the 1972 initiative that established the Coastal Commission and gave it direct jurisdiction over development permits and planning in all coastal areas of California. An initiative with an indirect but perhaps more pervasive impact on local planning is Proposition 13, the 1978 measure that cut property taxes dramatically. By weakening local governments' general property tax base, Proposition 13 ushered in an era of intense competition among cities and counties for sales tax-producing development, a competition often reflected in local land use plans and development strategies that favor retail stores at the expense of almost everything else.

By weakening local governments' general tax base, Proposition 13 ushered in an era of intense competition among cities and counties for tax-producing development.

Starting in 1996, state voters—with the support of many state and local elected leaders—began approving bonds in unprecedented amounts to fund a variety of state and local public works projects and for natural resource protection. In several instances, money from these bonds has allowed the state to purchase land where controversial development projects were planned, including the 2,800-acre Ahmanson Ranch in eastern Ventura County where a housing subdivision was planned, an old industrial site in park-deficient downtown Los Angeles known as the "Cornfield," and part of the Playa Vista mixed-use project site near Playa del Rey.

Proposition 204 in 1996 provided $995 million for various water projects, such as restoration of the Bay-Delta ecosystem. Propositions 12 and 13 in 2000 jointly provided $4 billion for water and sewer projects, open space and habitat acquisition, neighborhood park development, and coastal protection. Two years later, Propositions 40 and 50 provided even more money. Together they offered $6 billion for land purchases and park development. Propositions 40 and 50 also provided money for a wide variety of projects intended to clean up waterways and the air, such as watershed purchases and stream projects intended to preserve the clarity of Lake Tahoe. With the state budget shortfalls of recent years, however, more than a little of the bond money has paid for ongoing state expenses rather than capital projects.

The Courts

Litigation is rife in land use disputes, especially in California. Indeed, many participants in the process simply accept litigation as a part of planning, while many critics complain that the courts wind up reviewing cases that seek to use legal arguments to resolve what are, in essence, political conflicts. It is not surprising why so much litigation occurs. Because it deals with the issue of regulating private property, planning often raises constitutional issues. And because planning law is based on the concept of "citizen enforcement," local governments are held accountable to the law only through litigation.

Land use cases usually fall into one of two categories. First is the "constitutional case," in which the plaintiff argues that the local planning process has violated his or her constitutional rights. Often developers will believe, for example, that because their project was turned down, they were not accorded equal protection under the law, because, under the same circumstances, another developer's project might have been approved. Or landowners might feel that if their property is downzoned, some of its value has been taken from them by the government without just compensation.

In a constitutional case the plaintiff argues that the local planning process has violated his or her constitutional rights. In a statutory case the plaintiff argues that some state or federal law has been violated.

The second category is the "statutory case," in which the plaintiff argues that a state or federal law (sometimes called a statute) has been violated. For example, a homeowner group might argue that the local general plan is not consistent with the local zoning ordinance, or that an environmental impact report should have been prepared on a project, as required by state law.

Statutory cases are fertile ground for disgruntled homeowners or developers because California planning statutes are so procedural in nature. A minor glitch can create an inconsistency between a general plan and a zoning ordinance; similarly, environmental review under the California Environmental Quality Act contains so many procedural requirements that it's hard to imagine any EIR that isn't legally vulnerable in some way. Statutory cases can be productive because of the citizen enforcement concept. The government can use this same enforcement process, and does so on occasion. For example, the state attorney general can sue local governments over housing element compliance just as a private citizen could.

Statutory cases are fertile ground for disgruntled homeowners or developers because California planning statutes are so procedural in nature.

EIR = Environmental impact report
HCD = California Department of Housing and Community Development

Because most laws affecting local planning are state laws, many statutory cases wind up being heard in state courts. However,

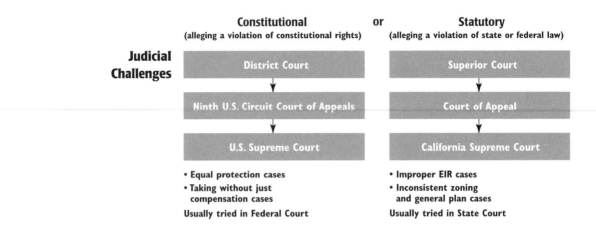

Judicial Challenges

Constitutional
(alleging a violation of constitutional rights)

or

Statutory
(alleging violation of state or federal law)

District Court → Ninth U.S. Circuit Court of Appeals → U.S. Supreme Court

Superior Court → Court of Appeal → California Supreme Court

- Equal protection cases
- Taking without just compensation cases

Usually tried in Federal Court

- Improper EIR cases
- Inconsistent zoning and general plan cases

Usually tried in State Court

because protections for wetlands and endangered species often result from federal laws and administrative regulations, suits involving those issues often are filed in federal court.

Because most of the constitutional questions in land use involve the U.S. Constitution, many constitutional cases wind up in federal courts. This division, though, is not always stark. State courts often hear "takings" or due process cases. (In fact, the federal judiciary encourages this, in order to clear out its logjam of cases.) And landowners can occasionally sue under federal statutes, such as the Civil Rights Act [42 U.S.C. 1983], which permits them to claim that their civil rights were violated by a local government that refused to let them build their project. Because some state and federal laws are similar, many land use lawyers are able to go "forum shopping" by filing a case in either state or federal court, depending on where they think they'll find the more sympathetic hearing.

Both court systems are set up in a similar, three-tier fashion. Cases begin before local, trial-level judges (superior court judges in the state system and district court judges in the federal system). Cases can then be appealed to an "intermediate" court (the six courts of appeal on the state side and the United States Court of Appeals for the Ninth Circuit in San Francisco on the federal side). Important matters of legal dispute may then be appealed to either the California Supreme Court for state issues or the U.S. Supreme Court for federal issues, although neither high court is obligated to consider the appeal. (A matter from the California Supreme Court can be appealed to the U.S. Supreme Court if a federal constitutional issue is involved). Cases usually have no value as a precedent until an appellate court has issued a published ruling, and the vast majority of appellate court decisions are not published.

Because some state and federal laws are similar, many land use lawyers are able to go forum shopping by filing a case in either state or federal court, depending on where they think they'll find the more sympathetic hearing.

To a surprising degree, the success or failure of any particular case depends not only on the legal arguments, but also on which judges hear the case. Lawyers generally know the orientation of each judge, but it is difficult to generalize. Trial-level judges, especially at the state level, often side with the landowners who come before them feeling wronged. On the other hand, appellate judges, who frequently are more detached from the human emotions involved in a legal case, are often deferential to the actions of local governments.

Trial-level judges often side with the landowners who come before them feeling wronged. Appellate judges are often deferential to the actions of local governments.

These trends are not necessarily related to the political leaning of a particular judge. Liberal judges may be deferential to local governments because their philosophy gives them a preference for strong governmental intervention in land use matters. On the other hand, the deference of conservative judges may come from a reluctance to appear to be judicial activists in overturning local government actions. In recent years, many trial courts have been deferential to government agencies simply because, under Governors George Deukmejian and Pete Wilson, so many judges were plucked from the ranks of local prosecutors. Although he tapped a number of public defenders and trial lawyers for judgeships, Governor Gray Davis continued to name prosecutors to the bench. Although many of these judges have a "law and order" bent, they can be surprisingly liberal when it comes to environmental protection. Slow-growth advocates and environmentalists have continued to rack up important victories in court no matter who is wearing the black robe.

State and Federal Agencies

Congress, the legislature, and the courts may set the rules, but state and federal agencies play a much more important day-to-day role in California's planning process. This role includes dealing with many important and often conflicting issues that help shape local land use planning. Among other things, state and federal agencies:

- **Regulate the activities of both private landowners and local governments** under environmental laws such as the Clean Water Act and the Endangered Species Act

- **Manage vast amounts of land,** especially in California's mountain and desert areas—some California counties consist almost entirely of federally owned land

- **Construct roads, water systems, and other critical pieces of infrastructure** that often guide the direction of growth

- **Provide funding to local governments** in some areas associated with planning, such as affordable housing programs

Caltrans = California Department of Transportation

CDF = California Department of Forestry and Fire Protection

CEQA = California Environmental Quality Act

DOT = U.S. Department of Transportation

DWR = California Department of Water Resources

GSA = General Services Administration

HUD = U.S. Department of Housing and Urban Development

OPR = Governor's Office of Planning and Research

Policy Approaches in California Planning

THE STATE LEGISLATURE AND THE COURTS play an important role in creating and carrying out the policy approaches used in California planning. In general, the California policy approach establishes a decentralized system with four different aspects:

• The state establishes the procedural structure

• Local governments are required to address specific issues but are given considerable leeway in determining policy direction

• Planning laws are generally enforced via citizen enforcement

• Little formal coordination is required, although certain laws and funding programs encourage cooperation among local, regional, state, and federal agencies

State Establishes Procedural Structure

Most of California's planning-related laws are not prescriptive or substantive in nature. That is, they do not seek to dictate specific policies to local governments. Rather, they lay out a detailed set of procedural requirements that local governments must follow in adopting and implementing their plans.

This is true for policy-level planning documents, for actions under the California Environmental Quality Act, and for implementation of land use regulations under such laws as the Subdivision Map Act.

California law requires local governments to cover certain policy areas in drawing up their general plans; to follow extensive process and format requirements (which are laid out in the state's General Plan Guidelines); and to assure that the resulting planning documents are consistent internally and with one another. CEQA is so procedural in nature that it does not prohibit decision makers from approving any project, no matter the impacts on the environment. CEQA simply requires decision makers to identify those impacts.

The Subdivision Map Act is also a smorgasbord of procedural requirements whose general goal is to permit local governments to influence the configuration of subdivided lands by affecting the "design" and "improvements" associated with those subdivisions. But as with the other laws, the Map Act does not dictate many policy outcomes. The law does not say what those designs and improvements should be.

➡

Traditionally, state and federal agencies are somewhat remote from the day-to-day nitty-gritty of local planning issues. This distance is the result of several factors.

First, compared with local governments and local planners, state and federal agencies are much more bureaucratic and much less overtly political. Ultimately under the bureaucratic control of an elected politician (the governor and the president), these agencies are large and far-flung organizations in which the bureaucratic chain of command is perceived to be far more important than responding to a local situation.

Second, their size and scope cause these organizations to operate in a way that often seems unresponsive. Field offices of Caltrans or the U.S. Fish and Wildlife Service cover large geographical areas, so that even their field staff cannot always be on the scene or attend important meetings. These agencies frequently try to participate by commenting on environmental impact reports, but their heavy workload and bureaucratic routing requirements often cause their comments to be late, adding to the perception of unresponsiveness.

Finally, because they are not usually dependent on local land use regulatory authority to achieve their objectives, state and federal agencies often do not see the need to cooperate with local government. Many agencies have their own regulatory authority—such as endangered species laws and clean air and clean water laws—which they believe places them in a strong power position *vis-à-vis* local government. Landowning and infrastructure agencies do not have to comply with local land use authority and therefore are unaccustomed to dealing with local concerns.

It is important to note that state and federal agencies have traditionally been so insular and bureaucratic that they've had as much trouble cooperating with each other as they have with local government. For example, the U.S. Fish and Wildlife Service administers the Endangered Species Act, while the California Department of Fish and Game administers the California Endangered Species Act. For many years, these two agencies operated completely separate permitting systems and communicated with each other rarely.

During the 1990s, their approach began to change. Many state and federal agencies started to cooperate with local governments and with each other. In part, this resulted from a concerted partnership effort on the part of state and federal agencies dealing with the protection of natural resources. Beginning in

This procedural approach stands in contrast to the approach to planning in several other important states. In Oregon, Florida, and New Jersey, for example, the state government plays a more direct role in policy making on land use matters, establishing specific policy goals local governments must pursue in land use planning. Maryland uses a different approach—providing financial rewards in the form of state funding for infrastructure and land conservation projects that conform to the state's own policy goals. Admittedly, these states are in the minority (there are perhaps a dozen nationwide), but they have been on the cutting edge of land use regulation since the 1970s, and process driven California has not followed their lead.

Local Governments Are Required to Address Specific Issues, But Are Given Leeway in Determining Policy Direction

State law does not dictate particular land use planning policies, but does require a local government to consider a wide range of policy issues when drawing up and implementing its plans.

Perhaps the best example of this approach is contained in the state's general plan law. The general plan law requires that local governments include at least seven different topic areas (called "elements"): land use, circulation (transportation), housing, open space, conservation, safety, and noise. The state's General Plan Guidelines establish a set of norms local governments typically must follow when analyzing these topic areas, including the expectation that technical analyses will be used where appropriate to document a community's problems and substantiate the policy decisions contained in the general plan. The 2003 update of the General Plan Guidelines also emphasized the necessity for public participation in general plan updates, and the need to consider environmental justice when planning for public facilities and services, industrial areas, schools and homes. But, with a few exceptions, local governments can choose their own policy direction: they can set their own goals and decide how much weight to accord such potentially competing issues as transportation, housing, and parks and open space.

Even when they have theoretically unlimited freedom to choose their own policy direction, local governments are still sometimes constrained by state and federal laws and regulations. A city might, for example, choose to devote an undeveloped area of land to affordable housing, only to have the U.S. Fish and Wildlife Service block construction if an endangered species is located on the property. In general, such direct

➡

action by state and federal regulators is rare, and usually occurs outside a typical local planning process.

Planning Laws Are Generally Enforced Via Citizen Enforcement

In most areas of public policy, if the state government asserts control over the field, the state issues regulations, which are then enforced by a state administrative agency located in Sacramento. If you don't follow state welfare policy, for example, some bureaucrat in Sacramento will crack the whip on you.

Because planning laws are mostly procedural, however, few state administrative agencies enforce them on local governments. The Department of Housing and Community Development enforces the housing element law, but its power to punish local governments is weak. The Resources Agency and the Office of Planning and Research prepare the General Plan and CEQA Guidelines, but the General Plan Guidelines are voluntary, and neither the Resources Agency nor OPR has the legal power to enforce the CEQA Guidelines. In other areas of planning law, no administrative mechanism exists in state law at all.

This situation is a deliberate political decision on the part of California's voters, its politicians, and its lobbyists. Local governments do not want strong state oversight of their planning obligations, and neither voters nor politicians are interested in expanding the state bureaucracy to make sure planning laws and CEQA are carried out in a lawful manner.

Because there is no administrative agency to enforce them, the planning laws and CEQA are supposed to be enforced by direct citizen action—or "citizen enforcement" in Sacramento parlance. Citizen enforcement simply means that citizens and citizen groups are supposed to be the watchdogs of the planning process, holding local governments accountable. When they believe local governments are not following planning laws or CEQA, citizens are supposed to file lawsuits in order to compel local agencies to follow the law. In other words, if the land use planning arena often seems rife with lawsuits, it's supposed to be that way. And if citizens are not paying attention, a city council or board of supervisors can often get away with creative interpretations of planning laws and CEQA.

Since Bill Lockyer became attorney general in 1999, the state has played a slightly larger role in enforcement of planning laws and CEQA. For example, Lockyer sued Tulare County because the county was allowing

➡

1991, both regulatory and land-owning agencies signed a series of mutual agreements promising cooperation on biodiversity and related issues.

Greater cooperation with local governments has emerged from a growing awareness that state and federal programs are often unpopular and local political buy-in is necessary to make them successful. Perhaps the most prominent example of this trend is in the arena of endangered species protection. In the 1970s and early '80s, most endangered species problems were found, and could be solved, on public land. Beginning in the late 1980s, however, the problem had moved onto privately owned land, especially in California. Thus, protecting habitat could not be achieved without cooperation between private landowners and the local governments that regulate private land use.

Although bureaucracies always have a life of their own, the attitude of state and federal agencies toward local land use planning also derives from the political priorities of the governor and the president. The involvement of state and federal resource agencies in local land use planning during the 1990s was largely the result of initiatives by Governor Pete Wilson (and his Resources Secretary Douglas Wheeler) and President Bill Clinton (and his

Interior Secretary Bruce Babbitt). That involvement continued even under new administrations, as state and federal agencies work closely with local governments on large-scale plans to preserve habitat for plants and animals (*see* chapter 23).

Types of State and Federal Agencies

State and federal agencies are engaged in a wide variety of activities, but in general they can be divided into two types: "conservation agencies" and "development agencies." Conservation agencies include agencies that regulate the use of land indirectly through the enforcement of environmental laws, as well as land-owning agencies charged primarily with land conservation and resource management. Development agencies include agencies in the business of constructing infrastructure, installations, and buildings required by state and federal governments.

State Infrastructure and Development Agencies

- **California Department of Transportation.** Caltrans is charged with building and maintaining the state highway system. In recent years, the power of Caltrans to plan these facilities has been assumed by regional transportation planning agencies around the state.

dozens of large dairies to be developed with almost no review of the effects on air and water quality resulting from tens of thousands of cows concentrated on feed lots. Lockyer's action forced Tulare and other counties in the San Joaquin Valley to dramatically slow dairy development while the counties prepared program EIRs on the rapidly expanding dairy industry.

Little formal coordination is required, although certain laws and funding programs encourage cooperation among local, regional, state, and federal agencies.

One of the great weaknesses of California's approach to planning policy is that even neighboring jurisdictions are rarely required to work together or even take each other's plans into account. The issues of metropolitan growth which form the basis for most planning efforts are clearly regional in nature. Housing, commercial, and industrial development projects must, for example, appeal to a regional market that extends far beyond the political jurisdiction within which their land happens to be located.

Yet the state planning law does not address this reality. Planning is done on a municipal level. Each city produces its own plan and has no obligation to any other jurisdiction. Each county produces plans only for its unincorporated areas, without any regard for adjacent counties or for the cities located within that county. Each jurisdiction's planning effort is accountable only to its own voters, no matter how parochial the voters' concerns may be or how great the impact of plans or projects on adjoining jurisdictions.

This situation leads to a great temptation: to draw up plans or approve projects in which the benefits (often taxes) flow to your jurisdiction, while the harmful side effects (traffic, for example) waft across the city or county line to your neighbors. Many communities, for example, place shopping centers (high taxes but also high traffic) in "island" locations that are removed from their own neighborhoods, yet close to the boundaries with neighboring cities or counties.

In most cases, the only way one local government can gain any influence over its neighbor is to follow the citizen enforcement route and sue. Increasingly, CEQA lawsuits have been filed not by environmentalists seeking to minimize damage to the environment, but by neighboring jurisdictions seeking to lessen the impact of a development project in a neighboring community. Oftentimes these lawsuits are settled for "mitigation money"—funds for traffic improvements, for example—without ever going to trial. This is one of the many reasons why CEQA has been transformed in recent years from a tool to stop projects into a mitigation machine that spews forth mitigation measures.

State lawmakers have tried using both carrots and sticks to get local governments to work together, with limited success at best. For example, the Interregional Partnership provides modest financial incentives for cities and counties in a five-county region of the Bay Area and the Central Valley to coordinate the planning of housing and employment centers. The legislature wielded the stick when it outlawed the practice in which one city provides subsidies—such as free land or sales tax "rebates"—to get a large retail store or car dealership to relocate in a new city.

A Troubled and Confusing System

California's complex system of funding state and local government has only become more difficult to understand—and some say easier to manipulate—since the early 1990s. It's a system that rewards cities and counties for approving retail development and penalizes local governments for allowing new housing. And it's a system that virtually ensures cities and counties will not work together, even when they struggle with the same regional issues such as traffic congestion and air pollution.

More than a decade ago, the term "fiscalization of land use" became popular. The term reflects the tendency of cities and counties to make land use decisions based on the immediate fiscal impacts of a proposed development. Indeed, a comprehensive survey by the Public Policy Institute of California found that city managers favor retail development above all else, including employment centers such as offices and factories. Under the current system, a city is likely to look favorably upon—and might even provide subsidies for—a proposed shopping center or car dealership because those developments would provide sales tax revenue to the city. The same city might not be open to a proposed housing development because houses generate only property taxes. Because of the low property tax rates mandated by Proposition 13 and the complicated way that Proposition 13 has been implemented, most new houses do not produce enough property taxes to fund the city services that the house and its residents require. Even if the city were to approve the housing development, the city would likely impose heavy development impact fees or saddle future homeowners with assessment districts. Many cities would simply rather see the houses get built in the city next door.

- **The Department of Water Resources.** DWR owns, operates, and maintains the State Water Project, which brings water from Northern California and the Sierra Nevada Mountains to agricultural and urban users in the Central Valley and Southern California. DWR's facilities include the California Aqueduct and the massive San Luis Reservoir near Los Banos.

- **California Department of Housing and Community Development and California Housing Finance Agency.** These agencies do not construct affordable housing projects but do provide funding to local governments, nonprofits, and developers that do. In addition, HCD has oversight (but not regulatory power) concerning local housing elements.

- **California Department of Corrections.** The Department of Corrections oversees the state's prison-building program. During the 1980s and 1990s, the state government built dozens of prisons, many in rural communities that were happy to get the stable jobs that prisons provide. As the crime rate fell and the state budget tightened, prison construction slowed.

- **California Department of General Services.** The Department of General Services is responsible for all of the state's real estate and facility planning activities, including construction and leasing of necessary buildings. During the 1990s, the agency pursued real estate acquisitions, and office development and leases in downtown areas, including major office projects in the downtown areas of Sacramento, Oakland and Los Angeles. More recently, Governor Davis strengthened the state agency's commitment to core urban areas when he signed an executive order directing General Services to select locations near public transit, close to areas with affordable and available housing, and within walking distance of stores and commercial areas. The executive order also directed General Services to develop "mixed-use" buildings.

- **University of California and California State University.** These agencies are responsible for siting and maintaining the state's public universities. Few new campuses are built these days, although during the '90s Cal State built a campus in San Marcos and converted the defunct Fort Ord military base near Monterey to a campus. In 2002, CSU Channel Islands opened at a former state mental institution in Camarillo. Meanwhile, the University of California is building a campus in Merced, the first new UC campus since the 1960s. Because many campuses, especially UCs, are located in areas with high housing prices, the state has developed thousands of apartments and dormitory rooms both on and off campuses during recent years. The CSU Channel Islands project also includes 900 new houses for faculty and staff members.

State officials exacerbated the situation during the early 1990s when they began an annual shift of property tax revenue away from counties and cities and to school districts, thereby relieving some of the state's obligation for funding schools. Thus, the majority of property taxes go to local school districts, with cities and counties receiving only about 10 percent to 20 percent of property tax revenues.

In recent years, state officials have appointed a number of task forces and commissions to examine the situation. The Legislative Analyst's Office has addressed the subject. Numerous academics and interest groups have also weighed in. These efforts have reached similar conclusions: The fiscal relationship between the state and local governments is broken, and the method by which local governments are funded should be overhauled. Most of the people and committees that have looked at the issues have recommended giving cities and counties a larger cut of property tax revenues, and possibly divvying up sales tax revenue based on something other than where an item was purchased. The idea is to give cities and counties fiscal reasons to approve the land uses their communities truly need and to consider the regional implications of local decisions.

State lawmakers have conducted countless hearings on the subject and have introduced bills, but the legislature has not approved substantive changes. Recent administrations have shown little interest in overhauling the system. The only significant recent change is, in some ways, just another defensive move—the passage of Proposition 1A in 2004—which permitted the state to reallocate additional property tax funds from cities and counties to school districts for only two more years. Prop 1A was a win for local governments, but it only further cemented the current system in place.

This stalemate results from the zero-sum nature of the problem. The current system has a set of winners (such as cities with large auto malls) and losers (such as cities with extensive amounts of affordable housing). The winners defend the existing system, saying they have played by the rules that exist. Changing the system would create a different set of winners and losers. When reforms are proposed, the winners complain to the legislature and administration and the reforms die, in part because the public at large does not care. The system is too complicated for the average citizen to grasp. The result is policy paralysis, even though many people believe the policy is a failure. ∎

Governor's Office of Planning and Research

UNLIKE MANY STATES, California has no cabinet-level administrative department dealing with land use planning or community affairs. But the state does have one office in Sacramento that is supposed to deal with planning issues: the Office of Planning and Research (OPR), which is housed administratively in the governor's office (and located in the historic Fruit Exchange building across the street from the State Capitol in Sacramento).

OPR has several statutory duties, including the preparation of the CEQA Guidelines, that despite their name are binding on local governments, and the General Plan Guidelines, which really are mere guidelines. The office also provides assistance to local government on planning issues and administers certain other procedural requirements, such as the collection of all EIRs around the state.

State agencies often comment on local planning documents, especially the EIRs prepared for general plans. Certain other documents must be submitted to certain other agencies. Safety elements, for example, must go to the Division of Mines and Geology. Even though they may comment on local documents, state agencies usually do not have the ability to force local governments to act on the state's comments.

Ultimately, because it is housed in the governor's office, the Office of Planning and Research is hostage to the governor's political agenda. If the governor is interested in planning issues, OPR is used to advance that interest. If the governor has little interest in planning issues, OPR simply provides the minimal amount of bureaucratic support for planning required by law. ■

State Conservation Agencies

Note: Most of these agencies are part of the cabinet-level California Resources Agency.

- **Department of Fish and Game.** Fish and Game regulates private landowners through the California Endangered Species Act and also administers a large amount of land set aside for wildlife.

- **Department of Forestry and Fire Protection.** CDF, as this agency is commonly known, is responsible for fighting wildland fires all around the state. For this reason, the agency has become increasingly involved in recent years in subdivision planning in forested counties, especially in the Sierra foothills.

- **Department of Parks and Recreation.** Parks and Recreation owns and operates all of the California state parks. The department also participates in land use and land management activities that affect state park land.

- **Department of Conservation.** Conservation administers the Williamson Act, the Surface Mining and Reclamation Act, and other resource-oriented laws.

- **California Energy Commission.** The Energy Commission regulates the siting of power plants around the state. After blackouts and sky-high electricity prices hit the state in late 2000 and early 2001, some of the commission's processes for reviewing new power plants were shortened. A flurry of power plant development followed, often despite local opposition.

- **Regional Land Use Agencies.** Four state agencies are responsible for land use in specific geographical areas: the Bay Conservation and Development Commission (San Francisco Bay), the Coastal Commission (the Coast), the Tahoe Regional Planning Agency (Lake Tahoe area), and the Delta Protection Commission (Sacramento Delta). All but the Delta Protection

Commission have explicit land use regulatory authority that usurps the power of local governments.

Federal Development Agencies

- **Bureau of Reclamation.** Like the California Department of Water Resources, the Bureau of Reclamation is responsible for building and maintaining water systems, including a variety of dams around the state and the Central Valley Project, the large system of dams and canals that feeds water from Northern California and the Sierras to agricultural businesses in the Central Valley.

- **Department of Transportation.** Unlike Caltrans, the federal Department of Transportation is not engaged in actually constructing roads and transit facilities. However, as a major funding source for both highways and transit projects, DOT plays a key role in determining which facilities are built, where, and when.

- **Department of Housing and Urban Development.** Like the federal Department of Transportation, HUD does not actually construct community facilities but plays an important role in funding them. HUD continues to subsidize public housing authorities that own and operate publicly owned low-income housing projects around the country. But HUD has also traditionally operated many other programs that provide funding for affordable housing owned by nonprofits, commercial development projects in struggling downtowns, and other urban redevelopment efforts.

- **General Services Administration.** Like the state Department of General Services, GSA plays an important role in the health of downtowns and other local real estate markets because it is responsible for the

Regional Planning: The Endless Struggle

PLANNING PROBLEMS, obviously, do not begin and end at the city line. Almost all planning problems spill over city or county boundaries. Air pollution and traffic congestion are perhaps the classic examples. But housing and job markets are also regional in nature, so often they cannot be tackled on a city-by-city basis.

In short, planning problems are regional in nature, but planning solutions are typically tied to the parochial boundaries of local government jurisdictions. Finding politically acceptable ways to attack planning problems on a regional basis has always been one of the most vexing problems in the field, both in California and across the United States. While some states have had varying levels of success with regional models, California has found no useful and politically acceptable solution.

In rare instances, the state has proven willing to create regional land use regulatory agencies that usurp local land use authority in the hope of creating a consistent planning regimen across an entire region. The three regional agencies with this power are the San Francisco Bay Conservation and Development Commission, the Coastal Commission, and the Tahoe Regional Planning Agency, which was created as part of a bistate compact with Nevada. All of these agencies are the result of the environmental movement in the late '60s and early '70s, however.

Since then, the state has called out particular geographical regions for special planning attention, but it has been politically impossible to create other regional agencies with regulatory power. In the 1970s, for example, the federal, state, and local governments all signed off on a comprehensive plan for the Santa Monica Mountains near Los Angeles. But the state declined to create a Coastal Commission-style regulatory agency, choosing instead to create a land acquisition and management organization, the Santa Monica Mountains Conservancy. Regulatory authority in the Santa Monica Mountains remains in the hands of a fragmented group of local governments.

In 1993, the state created its first regional planning agency since the 1970s, the Delta Protection Commission. Unlike the Coastal Commission and other agencies, however, the Delta Commission is not really a regulatory body. It has drawn up a plan for the five-county region around the Sacramento Delta, but—in similar fashion to the Santa Monica Mountains—the plan must be implemented by the counties and their cities as part of their own planning and regulatory functions.

In somewhat similar fashion, large-scale endangered species problems have forced a kind of regional land use and conservation planning to occur in various parts of the state with the cooperation of federal, state, and local governments. These conservation plans have been created under the state's rubric of "natural communities conservation planning," or under the federal government's habitat conservation planning. The goal of both is setting aside whole ecosystems permanently while allowing development that could harm rare species to continue.

As on the state level, the agencies that build infrastructure on a regional level are among the most powerful entities in the planning and development process. Like Caltrans, the Metropolitan Water District of Southern California, or MWD, has played a crucial role in establishing the state's development patterns. Essentially a consortium of local governments, MWD operates the Colorado River Aqueduct and allocates water to cities and counties. Many other regional and local water agencies have also played an important role in establishing

leasing and real estate decisions of federal agencies.

- **Department of Defense.** Traditionally, the Pentagon has played a very important, but needless to say somewhat hidden, role in shaping California's growth patterns and maintaining the health of its communities. The rapid growth of military bases and defense industries during World War II essentially created the modern industrial economy of California overnight, and many communities became economically dependent on local bases. More recently, the Pentagon's role in land use has become more obvious, as Defense closed dozens of military bases around the state. More base closures are likely in the future. The resulting base reuse efforts have been among the most important large-scale planning efforts in the state, in part because the bases often are composed of big parcels of desirable real estate, such as El Toro in Orange County, Fort Ord near Monterey, and the Presidio in San Francisco. The Pentagon has played an important role in all of these base reuse efforts.

Federal Land and Conservation Agencies

- **Environmental Protection Agency.** EPA is one of the most wide-ranging regulatory agencies in the federal government, with responsibilities covering a broad range of environmental issues including toxics, air pollution, and water quality. EPA often plays an important indirect role in local planning by administering the Clean Air Act. That law's regulations have discouraged further heavy industrial development in some parts of California and also encouraged local governments to engage in carpooling programs and similar efforts to reduce the number of vehicle trips.

- **U.S. Fish and Wildlife Service.** The Fish and Wildlife Service's role in local planning is defined largely by the federal Endangered Species Act. Fish and Wildlife writes and administers Endangered Species Act regulations, including the designation of land as "critical habitat" for endangered species—which under the law can't be disturbed without Fish and Wildlife's permission. Thus, the agency serves, in effect, as the ultimate land use regulator in undeveloped areas where species are listed and critical habitat has been designated. The agency has not designated critical habitat for most species on the endangered list, however, because the agency has lacked money for the expensive planning process and because Fish and Wildlife contends species are protected with or without the designation. Environmental groups have filed—and won—numerous lawsuits seeking to force Fish and Wildlife to designate more critical habitats. At the same time, development interests have pushed the agency to consider the economic impact of such designations.

- **U.S. Army Corps of Engineers.** In most parts of the country, the Corps plays a major role as a federal development agency, building public works. In California and other parts of the West, its role as a builder is limited. But the Corps remains important because it administers permits to dredge and fill wetlands under Section 404 of the Clean Water Act. Thus, most landowners who have wetlands on their property (or waterways they wish to dam) must obtain a permit from the Corps to take any action.

- **Bureau of Land Management.** BLM owns and manages vast amounts of desert development patterns by deciding which areas would receive water and which would not. As with Caltrans, these agencies historically did not make an effort to link their actions with the planning actions of local governments, nor has there ever been anything that might be called a statewide comprehensive plan for such agencies to follow. Recent legislation has pushed water providers, cities and counties to coordinate to some extent so that decision makers will know whether adequate water exists to serve a particular development project or to carry out a general plan.

The nominal regional government in most parts of the state is the council of governments (COG)—the Southern California Association of Governments (SCAG) in Los Angeles, the Association of Bay Area Governments (ABAG) in northern California, the San Diego Association of Governments (SANDAG), and so on. These agencies were formed during the '60s, when state and federal officials thought powerful regional governments would serve a useful purpose. Their only real power, however, came from administering federal and state grants; when those grants waned, so did the power of the COGs.

And because they were usually run by a group of local officials, rather than officials with a regional constituency, the COGs rarely proved effective as regional governments. Because they draw up regional transportation plans and administer some transportation grants, COGs still have some power in this area. Generally, however, they serve mostly as information sources and think tanks for regional problems.

One significant exception is SANDAG, which does some true planning for San Diego County and its 18 cities. Though it has no regulatory authority, for years, SANDAG has reflected a fairly cohesive attitude among public officials in the county. State legislation approved during 2002 consolidated transit planning and project delivery in SANDAG's hands, greatly weakening two transit agencies that had become increasingly parochial. With its regional transportation plan and a comprehensive land use plan, SANDAG has gone further than any other COG in attempting to coordinate transportation projects with land development.

Some COGs also serve as metropolitan planning organizations, or MPOs, under federal transportation rules, and this designation carries considerable power. For example, SCAG is the MPO for the greater Los Angeles area. In the Bay Area, the designated MPO is the Metropolitan Transportation Commission (MTC), a sister organization to ABAG. As will be explained later in the book, the MPOs have considerable power in allocating federal and state funds for transportation projects.

Momentum for true regional planning or even regional government has built and waned several times during the last three decades. During the 1980s, Assembly Speaker Willie Brown carried the torch for regional government, possibly in lieu of county government. In the early '00s, there was a fresh surge of interest that culminated with a report by the Speaker Robert Hertzberg's Commission on Regionalism. The report identified a number of ills that result from the lack of coordinated, regional planning, such as traffic congestion, the loss of open space, the lack of affordable housing and competition among government agencies. The commission made extensive recommendations aimed at getting local and state officials to think regionally, but those recommendations have gone largely unheeded. In 2004, new Senate Pro Tem Don Perata—a former Alameda County supervisor—suggested the state should make more land use decisions. While many of the recommendations might sound reasonable, city councils and boards of supervisors are loathe to surrender any of their land use police power. And citizens, though they may complain about their council members and supervisors, have repeatedly indicated they favor "local control" over regional considerations. ■

and mountain land in California. Much of it is among the most environmentally sensitive land in the state. Though urban development is generally not permitted, the agency must balance off conservation and environmental protection goals against the desires of many other user groups, such as off-road vehicle enthusiasts, film companies, miners, and hunters. BLM has shown willingness to trade land it owns in or near urban areas to developers in exchange for privately held land further out of town.

- **U.S. Forest Service.** The Forest Service also owns large tracts of land and often finds itself in a position similar to BLM. Though charged with land conservation, the Forest Service is also required by law to accommodate the needs of many other users, especially loggers and recreationists such as skiers. The Forest Service's difficult role in balancing all these uses came starkly into public view during the controversy over the endangered spotted owl in Northern California, Oregon, and Washington. Owl protection required a reduction in logging on Forest Service land.

- **National Park Service.** The National Park Service owns smaller and more discrete pieces of prime environmentally sensitive land around the state, principally in the Sierra Nevada and the deserts of Southern California. Unlike BLM and the Forest Service, the Park Service is charged with recreation and conservation activities only. However, in recent years, the growing popularity of the parks—especially Yosemite National Park, the state's most popular—has created planning problems of its own. Yosemite has increasingly relied on crowd management plans and may someday have to restrict the number of visitors on any given day.

The Private Real Estate Industry

When examining any local planning situation, you'll always find someone who's popularly called "the developer." The developer is usually the front person or organization applying for approval of a particular project—or, in the case of a broader planning process, advocating the views of private developers generally.

In fact, the developer who applies for a land use permit or testifies at a planning meeting represents only the tip of the iceberg. He or she actually represents an entire sector of our private economy dealing with real estate development and real estate transactions. This sector includes not just developers, but also landowners, homebuilders, and real estate lenders and investors. In an indirect way, the developer also represents his or her customers, the "consumers" of improved real estate, including homebuyers and apartment tenants, and companies that lease retail stores, office space, and factories and other industrial buildings.

What binds all of these people and organizations together is that they are connected to the planning process by business interests. They are in the business of profitably trading land, constructing buildings, and leasing and selling those buildings. Even the consumers usually have a business interest in the outcome of the planning process. Business profitability is heavily influenced by the location, quality, quantity, and price of the buildings they buy and lease. Homeowners and renters also have an important financial stake in the process. Though they don't usually view the purchase or rental of a home as a business decision, their entire lifestyle, and their family budget, clearly depends on the kinds of buildings and neighborhoods produced by the planning process.

The principal difference between the private real estate industry and private citizen groups, which are discussed below, is that the real estate industry can afford to spend money on the planning process as a business investment. Indeed, the mere fact of planning approval can greatly increase the value of property. "Entitled" real estate—that is, property which comes with approved land use permits—is far more valuable than real estate without entitlements.

Simply put, developers are in business, and their actions, if successful, will lead to profit, while citizen groups, even if they are well-organized national institutions like the Sierra Club, must rely on memberships, donations, and grants for their funds. Thus, a developer trying to gain approval for a project can probably afford to hire lawyers, economists, site planners, and other consultants to bolster his case, while local homeowners must plot out their response in someone's living room, often without any professional help. Similarly, a local slow-growth group campaigning for a growth-control initiative must rely on volunteers to run a successful campaign, while developers who oppose the initiative can probably pay campaign workers.

But the range of businesses and individuals that influence the actions of the private real estate industry is far more broad and nuanced than most people think. Among other players, these businesses and individuals include the following:

- **Landowners**. These are the institutions and individuals who actually own property. Often they are passive participants in the planning process.

- **Land Developers**. These businesses and individuals specialize in planning real estate developments and obtaining land use approvals. They can be one-person operations or gigantic landowning companies like The Irvine Company. Many developers don't actually buy the land for which they are seeking approvals; instead, they go into partnership with passive landowners or buy options to purchase the property if approvals are obtained. Similarly, many developers don't actually build the projects they plan. Once approvals are obtained, they sell the entire project, or pieces of it, to companies that specialize in building.

- **Builders**. These are the companies and individuals who specialize in actually constructing the buildings. Larger builders will also act as developers and obtain their own project approvals. More typical is the approach of a merchant homebuilder, who will buy and construct one neighborhood in a larger development for which a land developer has already obtained approvals.

- **Investors and Lenders**. These are the institutions that provide the financial resources required to obtain land use approvals and construct buildings. Because they place their money at risk, investors and lenders tend to be cautious. They will only provide financial support for projects they believe will succeed in the marketplace. Thus, developers' actions are driven largely by the demands placed upon them by investors and lenders.

There are many different types of investors and lenders in real estate, but they are all important. These include commercial banks, which typically provide the short-term loans required for

Private Real Estate Industry

construction; pension funds, such as the California Public Employment Retirement System, which purchase and own buildings and development projects for long-term gain; institutional investors, such as life insurance companies and international banks, which have the same goal; and small investors, such as wealthy individuals, who often see real estate development as a way to make quick lucrative returns on their investment capital. Also important are the so-called "secondary mortgage markets," such as Fannie Mae (the federally chartered Federal National Mortgage Association), which buy mortgages from banks, package them together, and sell them to Wall Street investors. Especially in residential real estate, the secondary mortgage market demands standardized buildings and development projects. Thus, suburban residential patterns have been standardized by federal rules and the customs of the secondary market for decades.

Consumers of Improved Real Estate. Ultimately, land developers, builders, and investors are all seeking to attract the business of the customers of improved real estate—the businesses, institutions, and individuals that buy, rent, and lease all the buildings that will be constructed as a result of land use approvals. In one way or another, this market includes almost everyone in the country, including large and small business, government and educational institutions, homebuyers, and renters.

Unlike the developers themselves, however, the consumers of improved real estate are not directly involved in the planning process. This leads to a peculiar set of inequities. For example, the residents of a community's existing homes are enfranchised—they vote, they can participate in public hearings, and so on. But obviously the prospective residents of homes yet to be built are not, for the simple reason that they do not yet live in the community.

The only real advocate for this latter group is the developer who wants to build homes that consumers will buy. For this reason, and because they believe they understand what the marketplace wants, developers often claim to represent their own customers in the planning process. Yet this causes a certain awkwardness. Project opponents can dismiss the interests of future residents who are represented at the table only by developers, whom opponents can characterize as greedy. How the planning process can consider the interests of additional residents and businesses that would benefit from new development remains a difficult question, especially in parts of California hostile to growth.

Private Citizen Groups

Over the past 30 years, state and federal laws designed to encourage citizen participation have narrowed the gap between developers and citizens. Environmental impact reports, required of all significant projects under CEQA, provide citizens with a tremendous amount of information on the impact a proposed development is likely to have. The procedural requirements of CEQA and state planning law give citizen groups leverage over developers, and citizen enforcement powers grant them the right to sue if local governments do not follow procedures. The political transformation of many small suburban cities from pro-growth to slow-growth has given citizen groups a voice as well.

On many projects, city governments require an extensive public review process, with lots of citizen participation. If negotiations take place between a developer and a city, citizen groups have a seat at the table. And occasionally, if the project is controversial enough and the citizens have enough leverage, developers will offer citizen groups money to hire their own expert consultants.

Citizen groups come in all shapes and sizes. The most active local groups are usually homeowner or neighborhood associations that seek to protect the interests of their community. Environmental groups are active participants in the planning process and often have ties to statewide and national groups. Many other specialized groups exist, such as historic preservation or arts groups. And, of course, the local Chamber of Commerce and similar organizations will usually be involved in the planning process in order to protect the interests of the local business community.

If citizen groups have the virtue of participating in planning processes to further their own principles, rather than to make money, they often commit the sin of being narrow or parochial in their approach.

NIMBY = Not in my backyard

If citizen groups have the virtue of participating in planning processes to further their own principles, rather than to make money, they often commit the sin of being narrow or parochial in their approach. Many citizen groups are characterized by planners and developers as NIMBYs—people concerned only with promoting a not-in-my backyard agenda. This is not always true, but it is true frequently enough that it can cost these groups their credibility. Homeowner associations (ironically, sometimes established by a developer to manage common areas) often evolve into political organizations dedicated to protecting turf and the status quo. In addition, easy access to both the courthouse and the ballot box gives them a special ability to gain leverage over the process, a fact not lost on public officials or on candidates who need votes.

Though lawsuits and ballot measures are often used responsibly by citizen groups to effect needed change, these tools also provide the opportunity for these same groups to reject the outcome of the normal political process. If they lose in front of the city council, they can either sue or gather signatures to place the issue on the ballot. Once in court or at the polling place, they can either win outright or fight a righteous losing battle. In most cases, under these circumstances citizen groups remain focused on parochial matters, rather than on participating in a broader discussion of planning issues in their community.

Though lawsuits and ballot measures are often used responsibly by citizen groups to effect needed change, they also provide the opportunity for these same groups to reject the outcome of the normal political process.

Chapter 6

The Basic Tools
Part 1—The General Plan

Although planning—that is, guiding the physical development of California's communities—is a task undertaken by myriad government agencies, private companies, and individuals, the core of this task is the planning work done by the state's 478 cities and 58 counties. And for local governments, the day-to-day planning work is achieved mostly through the use of three well-established tools: the "general plan," a comprehensive policy document, and two sets of implementing regulations, the zoning ordinance (often called the development code) and the "subdivision regulations."

Although planning involves many other documents, regulations, and implementation mechanisms, these three tools do most of the work, and no one can truly understand California's planning system without understanding what they are and how they operate. Together they create the policy foundation for local planning and the administrative regulations that carry out that policy.

The "general plan" (required by Govt. Code § 65300 *et seq.*) is California's version of the "master" or "comprehensive" plan. It lays out the future of the city's development in general terms through a series of policy statements (in text and map form).

The general plan is California's version of the master or comprehensive plan.

The "zoning ordinance" (authorized by Govt. Code § 65850 *et seq.*) is, at least theoretically, the beast of burden for the general plan, designed to translate the general plan's broad policy statements into specific requirements of individual landowners. The zoning ordinance divides all land in the city into zones and specifies the permitted uses and required standards in each zone.

The zoning ordinance is designed to translate the general plan's broad policy statements into specific requirements of individual landowners.

The Subdivision Map Act (Govt. Code § 66410 *et seq.*) is a state law that establishes the procedures local governments must use when considering the subdivision of land. The Map Act is intended to ensure, among other things, that adequate public services will be provided to these new subdivisions.

Some overlap exists among the three tools. Generally speaking, however, they are meant to be used together to ensure the orderly development of communities in California. This chapter will focus on the general plan, while the next two chapters will discuss zoning ordinances and subdivision regulations respectively. Later chapters will discuss other tools used to shape and implement planning policy in California.

General Plans

Since the early 20th century, the idea of a comprehensive or master plan guiding a city's future has been an elusive ideal for both planners and local policy makers. Comprehensive plans have gone through many faddish changes during that time. Some have been little more than town-sized "site plans." Others have been policy plans, offering a set of policies to guide future decisionmaking without providing a vision of a community's physical future. And from time to time planners have grappled with the seemingly unanswerable question of whether a comprehensive plan should be a static and hard-to-change document, similar to a constitution, or a living document that can be constantly updated to respond to rapidly changing conditions.

Through all these evolutions, however, one fact has remained constant: Living or static, the comprehensive plan is supposed to be the supreme document guiding the future physical development of a community—the set of policies from which all decisions flow. This has not always been the case in California planning, of course, but over the last 30 years it has become a reality.

The idea of a comprehensive or master plan dates back to 1927, when the California legislature first gave local governments express authorization to form planning commissions.

The idea of a comprehensive or master plan in California dates back to 1927, when the legislature first gave express authorization to local governments to form planning commissions and called upon those planning commissions "to make and adopt a master plan for the physical development of the municipality, or county, and of any land outside its boundaries which, in the commission's judgment, bears relation to the planning thereof." Two years later, adopting the principles contained in the Standard City Planning Enabling Act, the legislature made a master plan mandatory for those cities and counties that created a planning commission.

In succeeding decades, the master plan requirements evolved gradually toward the general plan process we know today. In

1937, the state began requiring all cities and counties to adopt master plans, making California one of the first states in the nation to impose this requirement. Beginning in the 1950s, the state began requiring localities to prepare specific "elements," or sections, of the master plans, with land use and circulation—still the core of most general plans—becoming mandatory first.

In 1937, the state began requiring all cities and counties to adopt master plans.

Finally, in 1965, the state's planning laws were reorganized. The master plan was renamed the "general plan," and localities were authorized to draw up "specific plans" to implement the general plan in specific geographical areas. This general plan may have been intended as the primary document for planning a community's future, but there was no requirement that it be enforceable. As prominent land use lawyer Daniel J. Curtin, Jr., points out in his book *Curtin's California Land Use and Planning Law,* up until 1971 state law even permitted local governments to adopt a zoning ordinance before they adopted a general plan.

In 1965, the master plan was renamed the "general plan," and localities were authorized to draw up "specific plans" to implement the general plan in specific geographical areas.

In 1971, however, the state legislature passed a law requiring counties and most cities to bring their zoning ordinances and subdivision procedures into conformance with their general plans. Ironically, this law was originally drafted with the narrow purpose of controlling second-home subdivisions. Nevertheless, the "consistency law," as it is usually known, became one of the most important planning laws in California history, because it essentially reversed the legal hierarchy of the general plan and the zoning ordinance.

In 1971, the state legislature passed the "consistency law" which essentially reversed the legal hierarchy of the general plan and the zoning ordinance.

In the past, the zoning ordinance usually had the most teeth, but today its legal function is to serve as a tool by which the general plan can be implemented. As one appellate court wrote, the consistency law "transformed the general plan from just an 'interesting study' to the basic land use charter governing the direction of future land use in the local jurisdiction." (The consistency legislation applies only to counties and general law cities. But a later state law specifically required Los Angeles's zoning to be consistent with its general plan, and some legal opinions suggest that other charter cities are subject to the provisions as well. In addition, according to the state Office of Planning and Research, at least 60 of the state's 108 charter cities have local ordinances requiring consistency.) Perhaps the best way to understand the role of the general plan is to think of it, as many court rulings have done, as the "constitution" for the future development of a community. Like the constitution, the general plan is the supreme document from which all local land use decisions must derive.

Like a constitution, it is truly general. The general plan contains a set of broad policy statements about the goals for future development of the city. But usually it does not contain specific implementation procedures. That's why the zoning ordinance and other implementation tools are needed. (Occasionally the general plan and zoning ordinance are combined into one document, but typically the zoning ordinance is written after the general plan has been adopted.)

And like a constitution, the process of drawing up and revising a general plan creates an important forum for debate about the future of a community. Although the state does not establish a specific timetable for updating general plans, a wholesale revision typically occurs about once every 10 to 15 years—usually when the data on which the plan is based become dated, when the growth patterns facing a community have changed, or when the plan is perceived as legally vulnerable. The process of drawing up and adopting these revisions often becomes, essentially, a "constitutional convention," at which many different citizens and interest groups debate the community's future.

There is, however, one important difference between a constitution and a general plan. Unlike a constitution, a general plan is not particularly hard to change—a fact which often undermines its political credibility. General plan amendments, which are usually designed to accommodate a particular development project or tweak the plan in some specific way, are permitted four times per year under state law. But even this restriction does not reflect the plan's true fluidity. Because any number of individual changes may be grouped into a formal amendment each quarter, the plan can essentially change at any time as long as a majority of the city council or board of supervisors deems the action appropriate.

Thus, the general plan in California—though it has more teeth than it once had—often reflects the basic tension between the static and the dynamic that has characterized master planning efforts for the past century. On the one hand, the general plan is supposed to be a stable document providing a consistent vision for the future of a community. On the other hand, it can be easily changed for short-term political gain. By its very nature, the general plan is a document that is at once imposing and malleable.

What the General Plan Contains

General plans come in all shapes and sizes. Some are slick and colorful; others consist of little more than some typewritten text and a couple of rudimentary diagrams.[1] But all general plans share certain characteristics.

Most important, a general plan is supposed to contain a vision of the community's future. At its best, the general plan identifies hopes and aspirations, and translates them into a set of policies laying out the community's physical development. Considering how few restraints the state imposes on general plan content, it is remarkable how rarely a general plan actually contains a thoughtful vision of its community's future.

A general plan is supposed to contain a vision of the community's future.

Most will contain a preamble that includes a set of inspirational comments. But the policies that generate widespread public debate usually revolve around some quantitative measurement of the future: the eventual population, the number of housing units to be added, the amount of commercial square footage that will be permitted. Indeed, as will be discussed in more detail later, this is one of the great weaknesses of community debate about general plans—that they tend to focus on specific numbers, rather than a broader discussion of a community's future. In most general plans, remarkably little attention is given to design, quality of life, and the likely patterns of day-to-day living that will emerge as a result of the plan's policies.

General Plan

- (Preamble)
- (Technical Background Report)
- Land use element
- Circulation element
- Housing element
- Conservation element
- Open-space element
- Noise element
- Safety element
- (Optional additional elements)

Many general plans will also encompass "area plans," which are more specific versions of the general plan dealing with smaller geographical areas. Sometimes known as a community plan, an area plan has the same force of law as a general plan. (It is different, however, from a specific plan, which will be discussed in chapter 12.)

Most general plans will also include a technical background report, consisting of quantitative information about the city's demography, housing stock, economic make-up, and other aspects of the community. This information will be used as documentation to support the policy direction laid out in the general plan. Also important in shaping policy direction for the general plan are the circulation element and the soils, slopes, and seismic subsections of the safety element that are, or should be, the primary determinants of any

1. One important breakthrough in the distribution of county general plans, at least, has been achieved by the California Resources Agency. Working with UC Berkeley, the agency has electronically scanned all county general plans and has made them available on the Internet through California's Land Use Planning Information Network, or LUPIN. The general plans are available on the world wide web at: http://ceres.ca.gov/planning.

LUPIN = Land Use Planning Information Network

limitations on the use of land and on the pattern, location, and character of development. These are the constraints that, if properly identified and mapped, form the reality check around which land use preferences are expressed in the land use element.

The fact that the general plan is the constitution—the supreme local land use document—does not mean it is exempt from state laws.

The general plan also must follow certain state requirements contained in the state Planning and Zoning Law. The fact that the general plan is the constitution—the supreme local land use document—does not mean it is exempt from state laws.

In fact, complying with the California Environmental Quality Act often is an expensive and time-consuming part of a general plan update. Most cities and counties report spending one-fifth to one-third of their general plan budgets on an EIR for the plan.

As one might expect given the state's general approach to land use policy, California's general plan requirements do not require that local governments accept specific policy conclusions. Nor is a city's layout, mix of uses, height limitations, character, economic development, or any number of other matters the concern of the state. Rather, local governments are required to follow certain procedures and cover certain subject areas (called "elements") in the general plan. Similarly, the state does not, generally speaking, review general plans for compliance with state law; such compliance is ensured only through litigation. (The housing element is something of an exception to both of these statements, and will be dealt with in a separate section later in this chapter.)

The state does not review general plans for compliance with state law; compliance is ensured only through litigation.

Under state law, every local general plan must include seven elements, or sections. These include:

- **The land use element,** the most basic part of the plan, which deals with such matters as population density, building intensity, and the distribution of land uses within a city or county.
- **The circulation element,** which must deal with all major transportation improvements. It serves as an infrastructure plan and also must be specifically "correlated" with the land use element—that is, the infrastructure must address the development patterns expected by the land use element.
- **The housing element,** which must assess the need for housing for all income groups and lay out a program to meet those needs.
- **The conservation element,** which deals with flood control, water and air pollution, and the need to conserve natural resources such as agricultural land and endangered species.
- **The open-space element,** which is supposed to provide a plan for the long-term conservation of open space in the community.

- **The noise element,** which must identify noise problems in the community and suggest measures for noise abatement.
- **The safety element,** which must identify seismic, geologic, flood, and wildfire hazards, and establish policies to protect the community.

These seven elements are not etched in stone. The legislature may amend the general plan law to add or subtract required elements whenever it wants. From 1970 to 1984, for example, the state required separate elements to deal with scenic highways and seismic safety, but then folded those requirements into other elements. The legislature has not increased the number of required elements since the 1980s. Instead, lawmakers have mandated that the elements address certain issues. For example, a law adopted in 2002 requires a city or county with a military base to address in the land use element the impacts of urban development on military operations. The law also requires the circulation element to include existing and proposed military airports and seaports.

Individual communities may add any other elements they wish— and most communities do. The specific mix of elements will vary depending on the needs of each community, but many patterns are evident. According to the Office of Planning and Research, parks and recreation, public facilities, and economic/commerce are the most popular optional elements. In Southern California, where smog is a major issue, air quality elements are common, partly because the South Coast Air Quality Management District has provided funding for local governments to prepare the elements. Agriculture elements are popular in rural areas. About 20 counties have adopted agriculture elements, but so have some unlikely cities, such as Rancho Palos Verdes (an extremely wealthy residential community near Long Beach) and San Jose (one of the most densely populated big cities in America). Virtually any area of community concern may be addressed in a separate element, but once an element is included in the general plan, it carries the same force of law as the seven elements required by the state.

It is also permissible to combine elements, and many communities do so. A particularly popular technique is a combined land use and circulation element, because the distribution of land uses and the construction of roads and transit lines are closely related, and because state law requires that they be specifically correlated. As will be discussed later in the chapter, even if they are not combined, these two elements are often developed in tandem.

The Most Popular Optional General Plan Elements

HERE IS A LIST OF the most frequently used "optional" elements of the general plan by cities and counties in California:

- Parks and Recreation (194)
- Economic (123)
- Public Facilities (114)
- Design (113)
- Air Quality (101)
- Seismic (94)
- Scenic Highways (89)
- Growth Management (85)
- Historic Preservation (82)
- Transportation (67)

Source: 2003 Planners Book of Lists, Governor's Office of Planning and Research, Sacramento

Not only must the zoning ordinance and other planning documents be consistent with the general plan, the general plan's provisions must be internally consistent as well.

Perhaps the most important legal principle is that the elements of the general plan must be consistent. Not only must the zoning ordinance and other planning documents be consistent with the general plan, the general plan's provisions must be internally consistent as well. (Under law they are all regarded as equally important.)

The reasons for this requirement are obvious. A city council intent on pleasing all interest groups could be tempted to pass conflicting policies. For example, the city may enact an open-space plan saying that 80 percent of the city's land must be set aside for open space, and at the same time approve a housing element saying that 80 percent of the city's land must be set aside for housing. The internal consistency requirement is meant to assure that the general plan is not only visionary, but also realistic.

It is probably impossible, however, to draw up a general plan that is totally free from internal inconsistencies, meaning that most general plans are, at least theoretically, vulnerable to legal attack. Indeed, the consistency requirements—both zoning consistency and internal consistency—have been a favorite tool for builders trying to strike down growth-control initiatives.

Each element of the general plan has its own story, and a separate chapter could be written for each one. In order to describe the general plan, however, this chapter will primarily focus on the land use element, which often serves as the bedrock of the general plan. The housing element will be discussed in chapter 16.

The Land Use Element

Although the general plan deals with many aspects of a community and its future, perhaps its most basic job is to chart a course for the community's physical development. And for this reason the land use element is the broadest ranging, the most important, and usually the most highly publicized aspect of the general plan.

The land use element must lay out a vision of all the buildings, roads, and public facilities in the city—not only where they are now, but where they will be in the future.

At its core, the land use element must lay out a vision of all the buildings, roads, and public facilities in the city—not only where they are now, but where they will be in the future. Perhaps the most important piece of the land use element is the diagram accompanying the text. This diagram graphically represents the policies laid out in the land use element, and must be consistent with the written text.

Because it looks like a map, the land use diagram often becomes the focal point of discussion. Residents can relate much more directly to the diagram than to the written text. They can identify the part of town where they live and see what the land use element calls for in that area. In many ways, this is good, because it sparks discussion and involves the residents in the process of preparing the land use element. In some ways, however, it is not so good. The diagram and its vivid graphic elements—bright colors, geometric shapes, and so forth—might encourage residents to think that the map's potential will be fully realized, especially if the diagram includes something they don't like.

For this reason, it is important to note that the land use diagram is not necessarily a map, nor is it required to be by law. Unlike a zoning map, it does not have to show the impact of the city's regulations on every single parcel of land. Rather, it is merely a graphic representation of a series of policy statements. The diagram does not say, "We are going to put this building on this parcel." Instead, it says, "Generally speaking, in this part of town we're going to permit and encourage these kinds of developments." The diagram doesn't even have to look like a map; it could be a schematic diagram or even something more abstract, as long as it gets the message across to the citizens.

Unlike a zoning map, the land use diagram does not have to show the impact of the city's regulations on every single parcel of land.

In planning jargon, the land use element is supposed to be concerned primarily with three characteristics of the buildings, facilities, and arrangements of land uses in a given community. These are:

- **Location**. Where different land uses—residential, business, retail, industry, open space—will be located in the community.
- **Distribution**. The geographical pattern, showing how those different land uses are arranged in the community.
- **Density and intensity**. How large the buildings will be and how tightly packed on the landscape.

The general plan law and its accompanying guidelines organize general plan requirements in these areas in a slightly different way. Under the law, the land use element must contain the following information about the use of land in the community:

- **Distribution and location**. State law requires the land use element to discuss the general distribution of some land uses and the specific location of others.

The land use element must address the distribution of:

- **Housing, business, and industry**
- **Open space and agricultural land**
- **Mineral resources**
- **Recreational facilities**

As with the land use diagram, these discussions do not have to identify the specific parcels where these uses are or will be located. Rather, they must reveal general patterns in the community.

However, the land use element must discuss the specific location of certain land uses—mostly those that require the intimate involvement of public agencies. These include:

- Educational facilities
- Public buildings and grounds
- Future solid and liquid waste facilities

When applicable, the land use element must also identify flood plains and areas designated for timber production.

The basic role of the land use element is to lay out the general patterns of development in the community.

The reasons for these requirements should be clear. The basic role of the land use element is to lay out the general patterns of development in the community. If they have to identify the probable future location of public facilities, as well as the current location of flood plains and timber lines, local governments are much more likely to consider whether the broad land use patterns they are establishing bear a relationship to their own public works projects, and to natural barriers to development.

- Standards for density and intensity. The land use element must also lay out standards for population density (how many people per square mile or a similar measurement) and building intensity (how much building space will permitted in relation to the land area involved).

A city does not regulate the actual number of people moving in or out of it. The population density projections are translated into dwelling units per acre.

Many communities deal with population density by including a projected "ultimate" population for the city or county, and perhaps even for subareas as well. A city does not regulate the actual number of people moving in or out of it. Rather, the population density projections are translated into dwelling units per acre.

Each neighborhood is assigned a "standard" in terms of dwelling units per acre (between four and eight, say, in a single-family neighborhood; 35, 50, or even more in a multi-family neighborhood). Then the locality will make some assumptions about household size—that is, how many people will live, on average, in each household. (Average household size typically runs between two and three persons, though it has been rising in some urban areas because of demographic changes.) Collectively, these standards will be used to create both the density and distribution of population called for in the land use element's broad policy statements.

Standards for building intensity are required to avoid the problem of using vague terms in drawing up land use policies. The land use diagram may call for "regional commercial" development along a local freeway, "service and neighborhood commercial" projects adjacent to residential neighborhoods, and "very low-density residential" development on the edge of town. But these general terms must be defined more specifically somewhere in the general plan. For example, while the diagram may earmark an area for very low-density development, a section of the land use element dealing with standards may define "very low density" to mean specifically one unit for every two acres of land.

Interaction With Other Elements

The land use element, of course, must be consistent with all other elements of the general plan, as well as with the general plan's other provisions. Nevertheless, two specific relationships are worth noting.

The land use element must bear a close correlation to the circulation element. Simply put, the circulation element must call for the creation of a transportation system that can handle the traffic created by the community envisioned in the land use element. Though the land use element must be consistent with other elements, the correlation with the circulation element is regarded as particularly important. It would be counterproductive to earmark an area for future development without also identifying the transportation facilities that would be required to accommodate that growth.

The circulation element must call for the creation of a transportation system that can handle the traffic created by the community envisioned in the land use element.

In practice, the land use and circulation elements will be crafted together in an iterative process. Typically, planners will draft a land use element with densities and intensities for the entire community—where jobs, housing, and shopping are likely to be located and in what quantities. Then the traffic engineers will incorporate the draft information into their statistical analysis, translating the land use patterns into a prediction of future traffic patterns.

Through this process, the traffic engineers will identify potential problem areas—road segments, intersections, etc.—which the planners will then use to redraft the policies in the land use element. Generally speaking, the combined land use and circulation analysis will provide decisionmakers with a well-defined set of policy choices. They may have to choose among the following types of policy options:

- **Expand road capacity** in areas where new development is expanded
- **Move new development** to areas which already have excess road capacity
- **Adopt policies to reduce** vehicle trips or encourage car drivers to use other modes of transportation
- **Reduce the total** amount of development permitted

There may be many other options, but these examples illustrate how the land use and circulation elements are developed together to create a coherent strategy for the future development of the community.

The noise element must be used in the land use element to determine what the land use patterns will be.

The land use element must also maintain a close relationship to the noise element. This requirement means that the noise contours and standards developed in the noise element must be used in the land use element to determine what the land use patterns will be. For example, if a vacant district lies next to a freeway, the land use element must recognize that freeway noise will have an impact on the adjacent land. Thus, the land use element might call for industrial buildings or warehouses on the vacant property, or else require that sound barriers be constructed if it is to be part of a residential district. The technical analysis conducted in the noise element will be discussed in more detail later in the chapter.

While the land use element must meet certain general requirements, the specifics are up to each individual community. For example, although requiring that a land use element identify the location of future schools and public buildings, state planning law imposes few standards. The law says that new schools must be at least 500 feet away from freeways, but the law does not say that the schools must be located near the houses where the students will live.

Neither does the law require a city or county to accept the recommendations of the local school district, which is free to ignore the general plan anyway.

This approach is different from that of several other states, notably Oregon and Florida, which review local plans and require strict conformance to state goals and standards. Nevertheless, it is in keeping with California's general attitude toward local planning, which is to set up the process and then stay out of it.

Crafting the General Plan

The legally prescribed process of creating and adopting a general plan is relatively simple. State law imposes only a few procedural requirements—notably one public hearing before the planning commission and one before the city council. But, as is clear from the Office of Planning and Research's General Plan Guidelines, writing a general plan can be a terribly involved process. If the general plan is the constitution for the future development of a community, then the process of writing or revising the general plan is really the "constitutional convention." For most cities and counties, it is a long, expensive, messy, often frustrating, often exciting process.

A wholesale general plan revision is likely to take at least three years and, even for small cities, will cost at least half a million dollars. Technical analysis on specific aspects of the general plan (a process that can dovetail with the environmental impact report) and public meetings and workshops typically consume much of the general plan budget. If a community does not have a consensus about growth, then there is almost no limit to how much the general plan revision can cost in money and time. In 1995, El Dorado County finally adopted a revised general plan after almost seven years of debate and multiple political swings on the board of supervisors. Environmental organizations sued, and four years later, a Superior Court judge threw out the revised plan because the EIR was inadequate. In 2004—15 years and four planning directors after the general plan process began—El Dorado County adopted a new general plan. The plan then barely survived a voter referendum, and the county still had to convince a judge to accept it.

Adopting a general plan is, of course, regarded as a "legislative" act by local government, and in cities with well-organized citizen groups, the general plan process closely resembles the legislative wrangling that goes on in Washington and Sacramento. Elected officials are heavily lobbied on particular issues. Interest groups decide which issues they can compromise on and which they must go to the mat for. In the end, a general plan, like a law or a constitutional amendment, will succeed only if all the important political constituencies are satisfied.

Riverside County Integrated Plan

STATE LAW REQUIRES THAT A general plan be "comprehensive" and "long term." The state Supreme Court has called the general plan the "constitution for future development." So when a county prepares a general plan, transportation plan, and species habitat plan at the same time, it might appear to be the normal practice. Instead, it's the exception.

In 1999, Riverside County began work on the Riverside County Integrated Plan (RCIP), which involved crafting a new general plan for the entire county, and preparing a transportation plan and a multi-species habitat conservation plan for the western part of the county. Oftentimes, cities and counties adopt a general plan first, and then they work with whichever entity is responsible for the transportation plan to ensure that growth outlined in the general plan is accommodated. Whatever territory is left over after those two plans are adopted becomes, by default, open spaces for flora and fauna. Riverside County tried a more comprehensive approach.

Groundwork began in 1996, when county officials saw projections that called for continued rapid growth and worsening congestion on already clogged freeways. Demographers said the western county's population would nearly double to about 2 million people by 2020, so officials talked about preparing a new transportation plan. But they soon recognized that requirements for protecting endangered species could block proposals in a new transportation plan. Thus, preparing a transportation plan and a plan that set aside habitat for rare plants and animals seemed like the way to go. At the same time, the county's 1981 general plan, which had been amended piecemeal hundreds of times, was in need of an overhaul. The RCIP was born.

Initially, county officials set aside $30 million and three years for the RCIP. Those were not enough. After four years, about $35 million, and a name change to the Riverside County Integrated *Project* (to make the effort sound more action-oriented), the county had adopted the general plan and habitat plan. But adoption of the transportation blueprint by the Riverside County Transportation Commission was still a ways off.

Riverside County used a "stakeholder-driven" process, in which representatives of various interest groups, such as developers, landowners, and environmentalists, served on a number of committees that steered the planning effort. There were hundreds of publicly noticed advisory committee meetings with scores of stakeholders joining an army of county planners and consultants. All of the planning was aimed at accommodating growth—not slowing growth or trying to direct it elsewhere. The end result was a general plan that was clearly favorable to homebuilders. Yet the habitat plan designated about 500,000 acres—350,000 acres of publicly owned land and 150,000 acres of private property—for preservation, meaning that nearly one-quarter of western Riverside County would remain off-limits to development. The transportation plan intended to designate broad corridors where the government could build freeways, and possibly rail lines and separate lanes for trucks or busses. The transportation plan also sought to create one new connection each to neighboring Orange and San Bernardino counties.

Many of western Riverside County's 14 cities felt left out of the process. The alienation deepened when county officials told the cities to collect development impact fees to fund transportation projects and habitat land purchases, and to set aside land within their cities as habitat. The penalty for not going along with the county's approach was the loss of future transportation improvements. The cities reluctantly fell into line.

At more than $35 million, the RCIP is likely to be the most expensive local planning effort in the country's history. The cost and scope are similar to state plans adopted in places like New Jersey. Whether the final plans are effective or not will depend largely on implementation. The transportation projects and habitat land purchases are expected to cost more than $10 billion, and no one is certain about the sources of all of that money. Recalcitrant cities are likely to continue quarreling with the county. And environmentalists who are unsatisfied that the plan does not stem urban sprawl adequately have vowed to take their cause to the courtroom.

Planners all over California closely watched Riverside County's experience with comprehensive planning. Thus far, no other county has been willing to try the approach for itself. ■

The Process:
Participation and Politics

A proposed general plan (or general plan revision) usually doesn't leap forward into public hearings fully formed. In most cities, the process begins with two steps: the creation of an advisory task force, often known as the "general plan advisory committee," and the selection of an outside general plan consultant. About half of all cities do their general plans in house. Some cities precede creation of the task force with a "visioning" process, in which the city and community leaders gather public input and attempt to reach a consensus about what sorts of things they want for the city, such as better parks or preservation of an historic district. Sometimes the advisory task force undertakes the visioning process.

A citizen's advisory committee is usually made up of 20 to 30 citizens who represent various neighborhoods, industries, and other interest groups in the city. Membership will vary from city to city, depending on the political climate. In many cities, the real estate industry will be strongly represented. In slow-growth cities, on the other hand, it may be politically difficult to include more than a few representatives from the real estate industry, and the emphasis is likely to be on broad representation from neighborhood and homeowner groups. Architects, planners, engineers, representatives of other government agencies, and other people familiar with the land use process may also participate on the advisory committee.

Over a period of months or even a few years, the consultant or lead staff person and the citizens committee will put together a draft of the general plan. In most instances, the consulting team will provide the committee with technical background and make recommendations, while the committee will make the initial policy choices. After receiving advisory committee approval, the general plan will then move on to the planning commission and the city council. Either or both of these bodies may alter the basic document or even change it completely. Again, this adoption process can last for many months. (As a major policy statement affecting the environment, the general plan also requires that an environmental impact report be prepared before approval. EIRs will be discussed in more detail in chapter 9.)

The rise of citizen power has changed the general plan process considerably, making it longer, more expensive, in some ways more cumbersome, in others more democratic. In many cities, city managers and council members resist broad public participation. They believe that an elite group of decisionmakers will make the most-informed choices and prevent the process from getting bogged down. These city managers and council members say visioning and consensus-building is unrealistic. Leaders in many other cities recognize that organized citizen groups cannot be ignored and welcome their participation.

The rise of citizen power has changed this process considerably in recent years, making it longer, more expensive, in some ways more cumbersome, in others more democratic.

The 2003 version of the General Plan Guidelines for the first time included a public participation chapter. Partly as a method of avoiding future conflicts, the guidelines strongly recommend early, frequent, and broad public participation in workshops, town hall meetings, focus groups, design "charrettes," and other activities.

Typically, an active citizenry is a response to a series of development disputes within a community, when ordinary people feel that their neighborhoods are threatened and organize to protect themselves. Once politicized, these people rarely return to the role of passive citizens. If the members have interest and dedication, the group becomes a permanent part of the city's decision-making infrastructure, monitoring and commenting on the general plan as it proceeds from the advisory committee to the city council. And members of neighborhood groups and citizens committees often graduate to planning commissions and political office on the strength of their newfound exposure.

Generally speaking, it is easier for a smaller city to become highly political about planning issues, and affluent citizens are more likely than poor citizens to become active participants in the debate. This is not always true, of course. San Francisco is one of the state's largest cities and the level of citizen participation is remarkably high. And citizen groups in poor neighborhoods sometimes carry considerable political weight. Nevertheless, political organization is more likely to occur in a smaller community with an affluent and educated populace.

Even in a highly organized city, a political consensus among organized groups does not guarantee the smooth passage and implementation of the general plan.

Even in a highly organized city, however, a political consensus among organized groups does not guarantee the smooth passage and implementation of the general plan. Most citizens are mobilized only by an immediate threat, such as the appearance of a bulldozer on a nearby piece of land. A general plan, by contrast, is an abstract process laying out a broad brush vision of a community's future. Average citizens won't care much about the general plan unless they understand how the process works and how the general plan's provisions will affect the likelihood of a bulldozer turning up in their neighborhood in the near future. Even if a city solicits participation, many citizens simply won't pay attention until a specific development proposal arises, long after the general plan is done. By contrast, developers usually understand how the general plan affects their interests, and are often major participants in both the crafting and hearing processes.

Technical Analysis

As the general plan has grown in importance, so has the role of technical analysis and the consultants who may perform these tasks.

The policies contained in a general plan are supposed to be based not only on a vision of a community's future, but also on data and analysis.

The policies contained in a general plan are supposed to be based not only on a vision of a community's future, but also on data and analysis. That is why the starting point for most general plans is a technical background report—reconnaissance of existing data on myriad aspects of life in the community, including building density and condition, traffic patterns, demographic and population data, information about water and wildlife, discussion of hazards, the community's fiscal condition, assessment of community needs for parks and open space, and so on. As the general plan is drafted, additional technical analysis will be required to test traffic, land use, and air quality scenarios, to examine the fiscal impact of future change, to assess noise problems, and to measure change in many other ways. (Most wholesale general plan revisions are accompanied by an environmental impact report, and much of the technical information will overlap, eliminating the need to collect it twice.)

The most important point to note, however, is that as the general plan has been strengthened as a policy document, both communities and the courts have come to demand a higher standard of technical analysis. In part, this is required to bulletproof a general plan against litigation, which will be discussed later in more detail. At the same time, the analysis provides a foundation of information on which the policy choices contained in the general plan can be built.

A good example of the growing role of technical analysis is the noise element. As noted earlier, the general plan law calls for linkage between the land use element, which identifies the distribution of potentially noisy activities, and the noise element, which is supposed to analyze and mitigate noise levels in a community.

Noise analysis, however, is not a casual affair. Under state law, state guidelines, and case law, noise analysis must be done in a particular manner.

State law (Govt. Code § 65302(f)) requires noise elements to identify and analyze noise problems associated with a broad range of specific activities, including major roads and freeways, railroads, aviation facilities, and industrial plants. The law also requires localities to follow the "Noise Element Guidelines" prepared by the state Department of Health Services (appendix C of the *General Plan Guidelines*).

These guidelines call for a very specific noise analysis process, including identification of noisy activities, the likely impact of future land use patterns on noise, and a strategy to mitigate noise problems. In effect, the state law and the Noise Element Guidelines mandate that local governments use noise contour analysis, especially in conjunction with the land use element. (Noise contours are similar to topographical contours. Noise specialists measure decibel levels in many locations, or predict them, and then map the resulting contours at which those levels occur.)

Local governments who don't undertake technical analysis on issues such as noise are faced with serious consequences, whether the problems being analyzed are large or small. In 1978, two years after the noise element legislation was passed, Mendocino County's general plan was challenged on the grounds that its noise element contained no technical background information about the impact of noise on land within the county.

Mendocino County's response was simply that a detailed technical analysis was not necessary for "a quiet rural county such as Mendocino." Mendocino County may be a quiet place even to a casual observer, but this fact did not let the county off the hook. The court of appeal found the noise element inadequate, saying that the technical requirements in state law were mandatory, not optional, even if local decisionmakers didn't think they had a noise problem. *Camp v. Board of Supervisors,* 123 Cal. App. 3d 334 (1981). As a result of this ruling, the entire general plan was declared legally inadequate and the county was enjoined from issuing development permits until the problems were rectified.

Court Challenges

Had it not revised its noise element, Mendocino County would have been prohibited from issuing any building permits—just as Yuba County at one time was prohibited from approving a large specific plan until it revised its housing element to conform with state law. Because there is no state mandated schedule for revising general plans, communities often undertake needed revisions as a response to, or in order to avoid, litigation.

With a few minor exceptions, no state agencies hold the power to review local general plans and penalize cities and counties if their general plans are inadequate.

As with so much of California planning law, state laws regarding general plans are enforced only by litigation. With the minor exceptions noted above, no state agencies hold the power to review local general plans and penalize cities and counties if their general plans are inadequate. Only a court can do so. For this reason, citizen groups and others with an interest in land use regulations, such as the building industry, hold considerable power over general plans because of their ability to sue. This is why cities and counties have come to fear general plan lawsuits, whether they come from builders, slow-growthers, or affordable housing activists.

A court that finds a local general plan invalid can strip the locality of all of its land use power.

Thus, the planning process depends heavily on citizen enforcement to hold local governments accountable. Typically, if citizen groups or building industry leaders dislike the results of the general plan process (or a general plan amendment), they will sue to have the plan declared invalid. In essence, a court that finds a local general plan invalid can strip the locality of all of its land use power. If the general plan is invalid, a city or county cannot enact a zoning ordinance or approve new developments. It cannot approve a project under its subdivision review procedures. Its environmental impact reports are not binding, and in all probability the city or county may not be able to proceed with public works projects. In other words, the entire planning process can be shut down by the court, at least until the city or county approves a new (or amended) general plan that passes legal muster. In El Dorado County, where a court declared the general plan EIR invalid in 1999, the court allowed the county to continue processing development applications under a decades-old general plan until a new plan and EIR was adopted. But the court could have taken more drastic action against the county. The threat of shutting down a city's planning process (or forcing a city to undertake a costly and time consuming general plan revision) is a powerful incentive for local officials to do things right.

Cities and counties are well aware that a strategic and successful general plan lawsuit could prevent them from acting on an important decision (such as a major development project) in a timely fashion.

A lawsuit challenging the general plan usually challenges one of four areas: consistency with other planning documents, internal consistency, compliance with state laws governing general plans, and adequacy of the EIR.

A lawsuit challenging the general plan usually challenges its consistency with other planning documents, its internal consistency, or compliance with state laws governing general plans.

Consistency with other planning documents. Starting in the 1980s, lawsuits attacked general plans for being inconsistent with the zoning ordinance. The surge of growth-control initiatives that were written as amendments to the zoning ordinance gave rise to this type of litigation.

The first important court case of this sort involved a growth-control initiative in the city of Norco in western Riverside County. The initiative was written as an amendment to the zoning ordinance, but did not seek to change the general plan. The building industry sought to stop the election on the grounds that the initiative would create a zoning ordinance inconsistent with the general plan. *deBottari v. City Council,* 171 Cal. App. 3d 1204 (1985).

This concept was later ratified by the California Supreme Court in a case from Walnut Creek. In 1985, the city's voters approved a growth-control initiative that would limit development in areas with heavy traffic congestion. A prominent landowner sued, claiming the initiative was a zoning ordinance that was inconsistent with the general plan, which called for Walnut Creek to develop into a regional center. The Supreme Court eventually ruled that the initiative was invalid because it was inconsistent with the general plan. *Lesher Communications, Inc. v. City of Walnut Creek,* 52 Cal. 3d 531 (1990).

Because initiative and referendum powers are protected by the California Constitution, the courts accord them great deference. For this reason, judges usually permit a measure to appear on the ballot even when there is a legal challenge, thereby postponing a discussion on the merits of the case until after the election. In the Norco case, however, the court of appeal stopped the election. The court ruled that because the initiative changed the zoning ordinance but not the general plan, the measure would create a zoning ordinance that was, on its face, inconsistent with the general plan.

Because initiative and referendum powers are protected by the California Constitution, the courts accord them great deference.

For this reason, most growth-control initiatives in California are now written as general plan amendments that direct local officials to change other planning documents to retain consistency, or as both general plan amendments and zoning amendments.

It is important to note that the consistency requirement does not apply to California's 108 charter cities, though in practice they often follow the same policy.

Internal consistency. Another favorite legal strategy is to attack the general plan's internal consistency. While most plans do not contain flagrant inconsistencies, general plans are long and complex documents and any judge is virtually certain to find an internal inconsistency if he or she looks hard enough.

The internal inconsistency argument is so fertile that both citizen groups and landowners are likely to rely on it for years to come, especially in the context of growth-related ballot measures. Judges, however, are often reluctant to overturn a voter-approved initiative in its entirety.

Compliance with state laws. A general plan may be the supreme document from which all other local land use policies must flow, but it still must comply with state planning laws. A general plan that does not comply with some aspect of state law may be legally vulnerable.

For example, if a city or county prepares a general plan without including the seven required elements, the plan will surely be struck down as inadequate. Just as important, however, is the fact that a general plan may be legally vulnerable if it does not contain the standards required in state law.

Sometimes even the simplest error can lead to legal problems. In challenging the general plan for the city of Riverside, lawyers for a group of landowners sent one of their clerks to city hall to pick up a copy of the plan. However, the clerk returned empty-handed; the city was unable to produce a current copy of the plan and all its elements under one cover. Because state law requires the general plan to be readily available to the public, the lawyers made the plan's unavailability one of the causes of action in the lawsuit. And the courts subsequently declared the Riverside plan invalid, partly because it was unavailable. *Garat v. City of Riverside,* 2 Cal. App. 4th 259 (1991).

More recently, housing developers sued over Measure D, a growth-restricting initiative that Alameda County voters approved in 2000, claiming that it conflicted with the state housing element law. Specifically, developers argued that because the initiative foreclosed building in North Livermore (where 12,500 housing units had been

The consistency requirement does not apply to California's 80-plus charter cities, though in practice they often follow the same policy.

A general plan that does not include the seven required elements will be struck down as inadequate.

proposed), the ballot measure discriminated against low- and moderate-income housing development and shifted the housing burden to other jurisdictions. The courts rejected the developers' arguments because the county housing element in effect during 2000 did not include the North Livermore project and because prohibiting development in North Livermore did not preclude the county from meeting its housing obligations elsewhere. *Shea Homes Limited Partnership v. County of Alameda,* 110 Cal. App. 4th 1246 (2003).

Tests for an adequate general plan. In *Curtin's California Land Use and Planning Law,* Daniel J. Curtin, Jr., poses several questions to determine whether a general plan is legally adequate. The list is so good that it bears reprinting here:

Curtin's California Land Use and Planning Law *lays out several questions to determine whether a general plan is legally adequate.*

- **Is it complete?** (Seven elements)
- **Is it informational, readable, and public?**
- **Is it internally consistent?**
- **Is it consistent with state policy?**
- **Does it cover all territory** within its boundaries and outside its boundaries that relate to its planning?
- **Is it long-term in perspective?**
- **Does it address all locally relevant issues?**
- **Is it current?**
- **Does it contain the statutory criteria** required by state law as demanded by the courts? For example:
  - Does the land use element identify areas that are subject to flooding?
  - Are noise contours shown for all of the listed sources of noise?
  - Does it contain adequate standards of population density and building intensity?
  - Does the circulation element responsibly list sources of funding for new transportation facilities?
  - Is the circulation element fiscally responsible?
  - Is the circulation element correlated with the land use element?
  - Does the general plan clearly specify allowable uses for each land use district?
  - Are the density ranges specific enough to provide guidelines in making consistency findings where necessary?
  - Does the housing element contain a program to conserve and improve the condition of the existing affordable housing stock?

- Has the city adopted an analysis and program for preserving assisted housing developments as part of its housing element?
- Does the housing element identify adequate sites that will be available through an action program for development of emergency shelters and transitional housing for the homeless?

- **Are the diagrams or maps adequate?** Do they show proposed land uses for the entire planning area? Is the land use map linked directly to the text of the general plan? Are the maps and text consistent?

- **Does it serve as a yardstick?** Can you take an individual parcel and check it against the plan and then know how you can use your property?

- **Does it contain an action plan** or implementation plan?

- **Finally, was it adopted correctly?** Did it receive proper environmental review? Was the draft housing element or amendment sent to HCD for review before adoption?

Strengths and Weaknesses of the General Plan Process

State law focuses heavily on public participation, the approval process, and requirements for technical analysis, but leaves the question of a community's vision to that community.

In assessing the way general plans are crafted in California today, it is important to remember the legal context within which they are prepared. State law focuses heavily on public participation, the approval process, and requirements for technical analysis. But it leaves the question of each community's vision to that community.

This is, perhaps, appropriate. After all, each community knows itself better than anyone else does. But by regulating some aspects of the general plan process and letting others be, the state often sets the priorities for the general plan discussion. The typical general plan process contains a great deal of discussion about densities and population buildouts and noise levels and traffic levels-of-service, but precious little discussion about the vision for a community's future.

This is not always true, of course. Many communities undertake the general plan with an enthusiastic desire to shape their own future. But because of the emphasis on technical analysis, that future is often examined only in terms of the quantitative results—the numbers—that emerge from the technical analysis. And all too often, those numbers are bandied about as a replacement for a discussion of a community's vision.

Take the question of population. Many general plan debates revolve almost entirely around the eventual population—the number of people who will live in the community at the end of the period covered by the general plan. Community leaders, business leaders, planning commissioners, and elected officials often spend many months debating what that number should be. Should it be 120,000? 140,000? 105,000?

Yet these debates are rarely informed by a real world understanding of what the impact of such a population would be. Progrowthers want a big target to shoot at, while slow-growthers use the population number as an organizing principle against more development. Lost in the discussion are countless subtleties—including, for example, the fact that the population figure is based on a host of assumptions about household size and the rate of housing construction which are mostly beyond the control of local government.

At the same time, it is hard to argue that California communities should return to the days when the typical general plan was "just an interesting study" and the real planning—such as it was—was accomplished by "good ol' boys" behind closed doors and executed through incremental zone changes that had nothing to do with the plan sitting on the shelf. Instead, the general plan has changed planning in California by imposing a rational process on communities. That process is sometimes too technical or too oriented around numbers; it is sometimes more procedural than substantive; and, in the end, it creates a document that can be changed all too easily. Yet in community after community, the general plan has also provided a focal point for discussion about what the future really should be—and that, after all, is the point of the exercise.

Chapter 7

The Basic Tools
Part 2—Zoning Ordinances and Development Codes

As the history of American planning (contained in chapter 3) reveals, zoning has traditionally had a strong and somewhat independent place in the land use regulation system. Zoning performs the basic chore of dividing a community into districts and prescribing what can and cannot be built on each parcel *Euclid v. Ambler,* the legal opinion on which most American land use regulations are based, upheld not a comprehensive plan nor a development code but specifically a zoning ordinance. Even communities that perform only perfunctory planning (or none at all) often have a zoning ordinance that divides the community into "use districts."

In California, of course, zoning is supposed to be a tool to implement the general plan. The goals and principles of the plan are supposed to be translated into parcel-specific regulations by the zoning ordinance.[1] And in most cities and counties, the zoning ordinance does, in fact, serve as a beast of burden for the general plan. In some places, however, the zoning ordinance remains the primary tool of land use planning even today, partly because it is more easily bent to meet the political needs of any given moment than the general plan can be. As the previous chapter explained, the general plan has been made much stronger over the past 30 years, and localities are finding it harder and harder to use the zoning ordinance independent of the general plan.

In some places, the zoning ordinance remains the primary tool of land use planning, partly because it is more easily bent to meet the political needs of any given moment than the general plan.

---

1. Zoning ordinances are authorized by Government Code § 65850 *et seq.*

What a Zoning Ordinance Contains

The legal basis for zoning, as for most land use regulations, is the local government's police power. A zoning ordinance must serve to protect the public health, safety, and welfare, and it cannot be, to use a legal phrase, arbitrary or capricious. To meet the constitutional tests laid out in *Euclid v. Ambler*, a zoning ordinance must be both comprehensive and fair. Comprehensiveness means the ordinance must cover every piece of property within the jurisdiction (although some jurisdictions use "unclassified" as a zoning district). Fairness means that while different pieces of property may be assigned to different zones, each piece of property within the same zone must be treated alike.

To meet the constitutional tests laid out in the Euclid *case, a zoning ordinance must be both comprehensive and fair.*

Thus, a zoning ordinance must be a set of parcel-specific regulations intended to implement the policies of the general plan as they apply to every single parcel of land. The zoning ordinance will typically be catalogued as part of the municipal code, along with ordinances covering other typical subjects of local government concern, such as meeting rules, business license taxes, nuisance abatement, and animal control. Often, the zoning ordinance, along with subdivision regulations, design review guidelines, and other planning requirements, will be included in a comprehensive "development code." The development code can run to several hundred pages.

Usually regulations have three dimensions: use, bulk, and what might be called impact or performance.

The typical zoning ordinance is a set of regulations that prescribes or restricts what landowners can do with their property. Usually regulations have three dimensions: use, bulk, and a third dimension that might be called impact or performance.

Use. The use dimension is the most basic characteristic of zoning. Each piece of property falls into a use district, which restricts the type of development that may be built there: single-family residential, multi-family residential, neighborhood commercial, regional commercial, industrial, and agricultural. (See "Use Districts," page 129.)

Every piece of property must be assigned to a district, and the uses permitted in each district must be explicitly spelled out.

But every piece of property must be assigned to a district, and the uses permitted in each district must be explicitly spelled out. It is important to keep in mind that the true purpose of many zoning ordinances remains the protection of the single-family neighborhood from intrusion. (In some cases, the stated purpose is the promotion of economic development in commercial and industrial districts, though, in part, this segregation of uses is also meant to protect single-family neighborhoods.)

Though the use district has been the foundation of zoning for more than 70 years, the remarkable fluidity of today's economy may be making it obsolete. Already, developers who build low-rise suburban business parks rarely do so with a fixed idea of the use it will contain; it could include anything from a warehouse to a research lab to an office center. (Increasingly, we are seeing not one or another but a combination of all three under the same roof.)

For this reason, new commercial and industrial developments are often being built under a flexible "business park" zoning designation that will permit a combination of these uses. As more and more people work at home on a full- or part-time basis, the traditional prohibition on commercial ventures in residential neighborhoods is also beginning to break down; in 1996, the city of Los Angeles finally created a zoning classification that formally recognizes home businesses.

This blurring of the once-bright line between use districts is certainly an accurate reflection of the nature of American society, which is moving away from a segregation of uses. At the same time, it challenges the tradition of establishing a strong set of completely different standards for each zone. Separate parking standards have traditionally been imposed for office, manufacturing, warehouse, and retail use—but what standard should be imposed in a business park that will house an unpredictable combination of these different uses? Does it make sense to require separate parking for each business when some businesses operate primarily at night while others keep 8-to-5 hours? As the economy becomes more fluid, and as real estate in existing cities becomes more valuable, planners will have to grapple with the resulting pressure to break down the traditional barriers between uses.

This blurring of the once-bright line between use districts is certainly an accurate reflection of the nature of American society, which is moving away from a segregation of uses.

In recent years, advocates of the New Urbanism have criticized the low-density, auto-oriented dictates of the traditional zoning code, saying that they prevent innovative developers from building old-fashioned pedestrian- and transit-oriented neighborhoods. Additionally, developers of "lifestyle centers" have found that some of the most popular projects mix ground-floor retail with upper-floor offices and residences. And after the bottom dropped out of the San Francisco Bay Area office market during the dot-com bust, some property owners and housing advocates sought to convert offices to housing in struggling business parks.

In response, more than half of California's cities and counties have adopted "mixed use" zoning ordinances, and many of these jurisdictions also report that they have approved mixed-use projects. Some of these projects are nothing more than offices and a sandwich shop next to a distribution warehouse. But other projects satisfy the New Urbanist desires for traditional, walkable neighborhoods. Sometimes, these New Urbanist-oriented projects are part of downtown redevelopment efforts in which cities seek to bring new life to dilapidated areas. For example, the Mission Promenade project in downtown Pomona fills most of a city block with ground-floor retail, second-floor offices, and condominiums on the top floor. Mission Promenade is across the street from large government offices and on the edge of the Pomona Arts Colony, a lively district with about 20 studios, museums, and art-oriented schools.

And even with mixed-use zoning, planners sometimes still have to make accommodations. For example, the University Village project near the University of California, Riverside, campus mixes offices with nighttime-oriented businesses like a cinema, restaurants, and a nightclub. City of Riverside officials gave the project a significant break in the amount of parking required because they knew that the cinema would not get busy until evening, when the offices would be mostly empty.

Bulk. Zoning ordinances typically also create an "envelope" within which any building must fit. This envelope is created by specifying setbacks, height limits, and sometimes limits on the percentage of a site that may be covered by buildings, other structures, and paving. For example, a typical single-family zone may require a 15-foot front yard, a 20-foot back yard, a 5-foot setback from the property line on either side of the house, and a building height of no more than 25 feet. The landowner must construct a house within the resulting envelope. A commercial property envelope will be dictated not only by height and setback limitations, but also by the square footage allowed under a maximum floor-area ratio.

The floor-area ratio, or FAR, is expressed as a ratio of building square footage to square footage of land—for example, a FAR of 3:1, meaning that for every square foot of land the landowner may build three square feet of building. Thus, a 3:1 FAR on a 10,000-square-foot commercial lot means that the landowner may build a 30,000-square-foot building. But this does not mean the result will always be a three-story building. Because of setback and lot coverage requirements, the landowner might have to build a taller building—four, five, even six stories—to obtain the 30,000 square feet.

Envelopes vary from use to use. Pedestrian-oriented retail districts may not need setbacks; such a district may, in fact, require buildings to run from lot line to lot line and all the way up to the sidewalk.

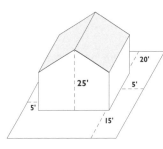

Zoning Envelope

The zoning envelope specifies setbacks, height limits, and sometimes limits on the percentage of a site that may be covered by buildings, other structures, and paving.

FAR = Floor-area ratio

But industrial zones often specify a maximum lot coverage so that factories are buffered from surrounding neighborhoods, and increasingly commercial and multi-family districts have similar requirements.

Many communities have FAR or lot coverage requirements that dictate a low-density, auto-oriented community. For example, the requirements of the city of Simi Valley zoning ordinance call for the creation of office, retailing, and industrial districts with FARs in the range of 0.20 to 0.32—meaning that parking and landscaping on a typical site will take up two to four times as much land area as the buildings themselves.

Impact/Performance. The last set of requirements in the typical zoning ordinance tries to regulate how a building will perform in the context of its neighborhood. Ideally, these requirements seek to minimize the negative side effects a building and its uses will have. For example, virtually no modern zoning ordinance permits the construction of any building without parking. Parking requirements will vary from zone to zone; a single-family residence may require one or two parking places, while an office building may need four spaces per one thousand square feet of space.

The only exception would be the zoning ordinance for a dense urban area with a good transit system. San Francisco, for example, actually discourages the provision of off-street parking places in some parts of the city. (Though, increasingly, developers in San Francisco and densely built sections of Southern California may be required to contribute funds to a parking authority that constructs parking garages serving an entire business district.)

Similarly, in industrial zones, builders may be required to provide heavy landscaping and berms in order to shield industrial activity from public view.

All three types of requirements play an important role in shaping the look of a new development. The use requirement will dictate that a piece of property in a multi-family zone will be an apartment building rather than a store or a factory. Bulk requirements will set the zoning envelope, establishing, in essence, the building's size and shape. And the impact requirements will assure that the building will provide a certain number of parking spaces. Increasingly, however, the impact requirements drive the entire development process—not the use of the project necessarily, but often its bulk and height.

Take the example of a high-density apartment project in an area that's already built-up. Let's say the property is zoned for 30 apartment units per acre. Theoretically, building a 30-unit apartment

Floor-Area Ratio

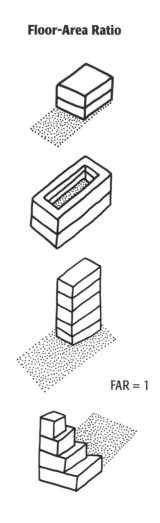

FAR = 1

Use Districts

THE ORIGINAL ARCHITECTS of zoning imagined that zoning ordinances would contain only a few use districts that would segregate major categories of land uses from one another: single-family homes, apartments, retail, factory. Today, most zoning ordinances have at least 20 use districts, a number that is often multiplied with the implementation of overlay zones. The reason for the proliferation of districts is simple: Under *Euclid v. Ambler,* communities may differentiate among parcels by placing them into different use districts, but every parcel in the same use district must be treated alike. In order to subject many different types of parcels to different requirements and still be constitutional, a zoning ordinance must have many use districts.

For example, Los Angeles County is the nation's largest local government unit, and its zoning ordinance must cover myriad situations, ranging from uninhabited desert to urban areas developed to Manhattan-like densities. The L.A. County zoning ordinance contains 39 different use districts, including 6 for residential areas, 3 for agriculture, 7 for commercial, 9 for industrial, and 14 special districts and overlay zoning districts that accommodate a range of special situations such as billboard exclusion, watersheds, open space, arts and crafts, professional offices in residences, and specific plans.

Even smaller jurisdictions have great variety in their use districts. The city of Redding at the north end of the Sacramento Valley is fairly typical of a mid-sized or suburban city that has updated its zoning ordinance in recent years. With a population of 85,000, Redding has grown steadily since the 1970s but has struggled to build a solid economic base. With 45 square miles and several lightly developed areas inside its boundaries, Redding also has some of the attributes of counties and rural towns. The city adopted a new zoning ordinance in 2003 to reflect a general plan update. Because of the zoning ordinance's newness, it contains a bit more flexibility than many older codes. Some cities have a larger number of residential codes to tightly define the number of units allowed per acre in different zones.

The Redding zoning ordinance (chapter 18 of the Municipal Code) contains 15 basic use districts plus eight overlay zones. As an example of how the zones in a typical ordinance are organized, a brief description of each one appears on the following page. ∎

building on a piece of land already zoned for such a purpose should be easy. However, most zoning ordinances require two off-street parking spaces per unit, plus additional parking spaces for guests or visitors (usually one space for every four units). Suddenly, the owner of a one-acre site must build not only 30 apartments but also 68 parking spaces.

This is a much harder task—probably meaning that the developer must forego surface parking and provide spaces within or underneath the apartment building itself. Furthermore, if the area in question has a three-story height limit, the only alternative is to provide underground spaces, which doubles their cost of construction.

A developer boxed in by this kind of zoning envelope—and a substantial impact requirement, such as 2.25 parking spaces per unit—may discover that building the largest project permitted is just too expensive. To cut the cost of providing parking, the developer may have to reduce the size of the project. In this example, the project size is driven by the parking requirement, not by allowable density or the setback requirements.

The landowner is placed in a similar situation when different uses permitted in the same zone—a restaurant and a retail shop, for example—have vastly different parking requirements. A restaurant will usually be required to have far more parking available than a retail shop. The ability of the landowner to open a restaurant will depend not on the zoning, but on the ability to build or secure enough parking. If the parking can't be worked into the project, the landowner may be forced to open a retail shop instead of a restaurant.

Sometimes, performance standards alone dictate the type of building or business a particular parcel of land may handle. Rather than identifying uses, setbacks, or even specific standards, some cities simply require that a building perform to a certain level—for example, producing no more than a certain number of vehicle trips, no matter the use. Sometimes uses may be permitted conditionally only if these performance standards can be met. Performance standards were regarded as a "new wave" of zoning techniques in the 1970s. But they are more difficult and expensive to administer, so most cities still rely on older, more familiar zoning methods.

Recently, New Urbanists have advocated a new approach—the "form-based code"—that focuses on building mass rather than use and performance. (*See* chapter 18.)

Zoning Tools

Within the concept of zoning are many tools that landowners, developers, and cities may use to accommodate projects that otherwise would be unacceptable, or to stop projects otherwise allowed. Traditionally, these tools have permitted developers and elected officials to exert political power

Residential Zones

Rural Lands (RL) Houses on two- or five-acre lots on properties with "relatively extreme topography or…in outlying rural areas."

Residential Estate (RE) Large-lot development of one or two houses per acre.

Residential Single-Family (RS) A variety of suburban environments with two to six units per acre. Duplexes are acceptable.

Residential Mixed Housing Type (RM) Multi-family developments of anywhere from six to 30 units per acre.

Commercial Zones

Neighborhood Commercial (NC) Retail and professional service buildings of up to 30,000 square feet and office buildings of up to 5,000 square feet in a "pedestrian environment."

Shopping Center (SC) Typically 50,000 to 200,000 square feet of retail development with two or more anchor stores. Minimum five-acre development site. A maximum of 75,000 square feet under one roof.

Regional Commercial (RC) "Malls, free-standing retail, power centers, and office and service establishments." Minimum 15-acre site. No maximum building size.

General Commercial (GC) Almost any commercial use. Maximum building size, 60,000-square-feet.

Heavy Commercial (HC) Automobile sales and service, lumber yards, nurseries and wholesale facilities; 60,000-square-foot maximum building size.

Industrial Zones

General Industry (GI) Businesses with a limited impact on adjoining neighbors. Maximum floor-area ratio of 0.40, and minimum 20,000-square-foot lots.

Heavy Industry (HI) "The broadest range of industrial uses," including quarries. Maximum FAR of 0.50 and one-acre minimum lot size.

Other Zones

Open Space (OS) Floodplains, 20 percent slopes and lands subject to open space easements.

Public Facilities (PF) Schools, government offices, hospitals, parks, airports, etc.

Overlay Zones

Airport Environment Overlay (A) Restricts building heights around Benton Airpark.

Floodplain Overlay (FP) Covers land near rivers and streams and is based on Federal Emergency Management Agency flood maps. Prohibits new development within the 100-year floodplain and allows limited development in the "flood fringe" with a conditional use permit.

Mineral Resources Overlay (MR) Restricts housing development to one unit per 40 acres and limits commercial uses to utilities.

Planned Development Overlay (PD) "Where greater flexibility in design is desired to provide for a more efficient use of land." Requires a Planned Development Plan that addresses proposed uses and buildings, topography, development schedule, design concepts, and other details.

Mixed Use Overlay (MU) Can be combined with any residential, offic,e or commercial zone. The City Council "may delete permitted or conditionally permitted uses, may designate conditionally permitted uses as permitted uses, or many require site development permits or use permits for all uses."

Mixed Use Neighborhood (MU-N) In residential zones, 20 to 160 acres. Allows some office and commercial development. Also allows more intense development in a "mixed use core" around a transit stop. Requires building orientations and street design to facilitate walking.

Design Review (DR) Requires a site development permit or use permit for anything except a single-family home on an existing parcel.

Specific Plan (SP) Allows a Specific Plan to supercede the underlying zoning.

over the land use process, whether or not the project in question conforms with local plans. The growing strength of the slow-growth movement and the power of the general plan have made this kind of political manipulation more difficult to achieve, though it still exists. More frequently today, some of these tools (principally discretionary review) are used to make otherwise acceptable projects more difficult to build.

Zone Changes

The most obvious method of permitting a project that otherwise would not be allowed is to change the zoning on the parcel of land in question.

The most obvious method of permitting a project that otherwise would not be allowed is to change the zoning on the parcel of land in question. And, indeed, this is the classic route landowners take. City councils and boards of supervisors have always shown a willingness to change zoning if the project proposed is something they really want built. (This is true not only of projects proposed by developers with political influence, but also of projects desirable for the tax revenue or prestige they would bring to the community.) Zone changes are "legislative" in nature under California law, even if they involve only one parcel of land. This designation means that all zone changes are, essentially, policy statements by the city or county. Therefore, they must be approved by the legislative body—the city council or board of supervisors—after a public hearing, and they are subject to initiative and referendum. They are also subject to the provisions of the California Environmental Quality Act.

In the past, spot zoning was probably the most abused type of zoning change.

In the past, spot zoning was probably the most abused type of zoning change. Spot zoning essentially grants one parcel of land a designation that is incompatible with the rest of the neighborhood, but probably affords the landowner an economic windfall. Spot zoning, for example, might designate one house in a residential area for retail use, or one commercial parcel along a pedestrian-oriented strip for an automobile body shop. In theory, spot zoning is legally vulnerable, because all parcels in a zone have not been treated alike—one has been moved into a new zone, while others have not.

In practice, the strengthened legal status of general plans has made spot zoning and other questionable zone changes much more difficult to achieve. In decades past, the zoning designation on a parcel of land could be changed without much consideration for the general plan. Now, however, a zone change that creates an inconsistency with the general plan is legally vulnerable. Therefore, zone changes and general plan amendments are typically processed together in order to avoid inconsistencies. This practice serves to reduce the number of zone changes (because general plan amendments are restricted to four per year) and can sometimes heighten public awareness of the proposal, especially if the city or county has recently been through a major general plan revision.

Variances

As the name suggests, a variance is a permit that allows a landowner to do something he couldn't otherwise do. Traditionally, zoning has encompassed two types of variances: The so-called "use variance," which permits an otherwise unacceptable use on the property without changing the zone, and the "variance from standards," which permits the landowner to construct a building or open a business without having to comply with the standards required of other landowners in the same zone. Use variances are not permitted under California law, but variances from standards are common. (The legal limitations on variances are contained in Government Code § 65906.)

A variance is a permit that allows a landowner to do something he couldn't otherwise do.

On paper, the variance serves a useful purpose by providing for a "hardship" exemption. It permits a landowner to make use of his property even if something about that property prevents the landowner from fully complying with the zoning ordinance.

But such a hardship should be associated with the land, not the owner. The classic example involves a residential lot that is identical in size and shape to the surrounding lots, but suffers from the presence of a large, immovable boulder. In this instance, a variance waiving ordinary setback requirements may permit the landowner to build a house, even though the boulder makes construction of the house within the normal zoning envelope impossible.

Beyond the geologic impediment, the legal authority for a variance is vague. California court opinions are split on whether a lot with an odd size or shape constitutes a hardship. Under other conditions, variances are not legally acceptable. In particular, economic hardship cannot form the basis for a variance because an economic problem, unlike a geologic problem, is self-inflicted.

Economic hardship cannot form the basis for a variance because an economic problem, unlike a geologic problem, is self-inflicted.

These legal limitations have not prevented many cities and counties from using the variance when it is politically expedient. In all of planning, probably no tool has been more widely abused, simply because it is so tempting. If a zone change would be politically difficult to achieve, a variance is likely to attract much less attention. If a favored landowner can almost (but not quite) meet the standards required in a particular zone, and the city wants the project, then a variance offers a convenient solution. In some pro-development communities, planners may actually encourage variance applications, knowing that moving one through the political process is not difficult.

In the city of Los Angeles, for example, the owner of a gas station just off the Pacific Coast Highway sought a variance so that he could add a car wash. A neighbor fought the proposed variance, yet the variance request passed through the city zoning administrator, the planning commission, and the city council without a single dissenting vote. But when the neighbor kept fighting, a state appeals court found it easy to overturn the variance. Pointing out that the property owner had invested $144,000 in new gasoline tanks shortly before applying for a variance, the court ruled that there was no evidence the zoning conditions imposed a hardship necessitating a variance. *Stolman v. City of Los Angeles,* 114 Cal. App. 4th 916 (2003).

A variance is quasi-judicial, which means that the planning commission's approval is binding (unless appealed to the city council) and that it cannot be placed on the ballot by initiative or referendum.

Whether or not it is difficult to achieve, a variance perverts the process when broadly used. Unlike a zone change, a variance is quasi-judicial, not legislative. This designation means that the planning commission's approval is binding (unless appealed to the city council) and also that it cannot be placed on the ballot, either by initiative or referendum. A variance is quasi-judicial because, at least in theory, it does not deal with policy issues, but, rather, with the application of city policy to one particular case. A variance may be passed by resolution, not by ordinance, which means that it may take effect immediately following a short appeals period. (An ordinance must receive two readings before a city council or board of supervisors, and have a 30-day waiting period before it is enacted.)

A variance that facilitates a use otherwise not allowed is really a zone change in disguise.

A variance that deals with a geologic problem clearly constitutes nothing more than the application of city policy to an unusual case. But any other kind of variance is simply an insidious way of shielding a policy decision from broad public debate. A variance that facilitates a use otherwise not allowed—such as the car wash at the Los Angeles gas station—is really a zone change in disguise. A zone-change decision is clearly a political decision, but at least it is made in an overtly political forum—before the legislative body, with voters having the recourse of initiative and referendum.

Nonconforming Uses

As zoning ordinances change over time, inevitably many structures that don't conform will be left over from previous eras—a corner store in a residential neighborhood, for example. In many traditional zoning schemes, these nonconforming uses were simply permitted to continue indefinitely, as long as they did not expand or change the nature of their business. More recently, zoning ordinances have been less tolerant over the long term, requiring that nonconforming uses be phased out over a period of years. Generally speaking, the courts have permitted this "amortized" approach.

The problem of nonconforming signs, however, has been much more controversial. As more and more local governments have passed strict sign ordinances, the advertising industry has used its clout in Sacramento to restrict the ability of localities to eliminate nonconforming signs. (An indication of the advertising industry's influence in this area lies in the fact that while local government power to restrict signs is located in the Government Code, the limitations on that power are included in the Business and Professions Code (§§ 5200–5486), where laws sponsored by specific industries are typically spelled out.) While their power to restrict signs is broad, local governments usually can't require the removal of a nonconforming sign unless the owner is compensated. Localities can require that a sign be phased out over a period of time without compensation, but the amortization periods are specified by the state. Bus. & Prof. Code § 5412.1.

Local governments usually can't require the removal of a nonconforming sign unless the owner is compensated.

Conditional Use Permits

A conditional use permit, or CUP, represents another tradition in the zoning field that offers a middle ground between a zone change and a variance. CUPs allow a local government the ability to permit specific uses that might not otherwise be allowed, as long as the landowner or business owner meets certain conditions.

CUP = Conditional use permit

Like the variance, the conditional use permit was originally conceived as an escape valve for a property owner, so that the zoning ordinance could pass constitutional muster. Its basic goal is to permit the full range of land uses required for a community to function, while still giving the community some control over individual situations that could cause conflict. In many communities, the CUP constitutes the bread-and-butter work of the planning commission, which holds public hearings and imposes conditions in CUP cases. (In some cities, staff-level hearing officers may also deal with CUPs, with the planning commission as an appeal body.) CUPs are quasi-judicial actions, and therefore the planning commission decision is final unless appealed to the city council or board of supervisors.

The basic goal of a CUP is to permit the full range of land uses required for a community to function, while still giving the community some control over individual situations that could cause conflict.

In a typical case, the CUP process focuses on the type of business being proposed, rather than on the underlying size of the building or location of the property. A CUP will often focus on a business that is similar to one permitted under the zoning ordinance by right, but which has some potential for detrimental side effects. For example, a zoning ordinance may permit a convenience market or neighborhood grocery store on a commercial strip by right, but allow the establishment to sell liquor only with a CUP. The CUP typically imposes additional restrictions, such as those limiting business hours. Other uses subject to a CUP process include sex-oriented businesses, restaurants with liquor licenses, churches, and industrial businesses in close proximity to residential neighborhoods.

Because it is typically used to regulate businesses located close to residential areas, the CUP process can become the battleground for neighborhood disputes.

Because it is typically used to regulate businesses located close to residential areas, the CUP process can become the battleground for neighborhood disputes. In the context of a CUP, the disputes often turn on whether the owner can be subjected to additional conditions once the business is in operation. Thus, CUPs often lead to legal questions about vested rights.

After the 1992 Los Angeles riots, for example, the city of Los Angeles sought to impose conditional use permits on the reconstruction of liquor stores in South-Central L.A., which has a high concentration of such businesses. Liquor store owners sued, claiming that state alcohol control laws took precedence. The liquor store owners lost.

Recent court rulings on the question of CUPs and vested rights have helped business owners.

On the other hand, recent court rulings on the question of CUPs and vested rights have helped business owners. One important case involved the Goat Hill Tavern, a restaurant that conducted business adjacent to a residential neighborhood in Costa Mesa for some 40 years. Though the restaurant was a nonconforming use, a beer garden added in 1970 was subject to a city conditional use permit. After complaints from neighbors, the city extended Goat Hill Tavern's CUP for only three months at a time. But when the city finally denied a three-month renewal, the tavern sued, and the court of appeal found that the longstanding nature of the CUP had established a property right for the owner. Though it had been extended for only three months at a time, the CUP could not be revoked without compensating the tavern's owner. *Goat Hill Tavern v. City of Costa Mesa*, 6 Cal. App. 4th 1519 (1992).

A more recent decision bolstered property owners' rights. During the 1990s, the city of San Diego began requiring new stores that sell alcoholic beverages to get a conditional use permit. Existing stores were "grandfathered," meaning the CUP requirement did not apply. When the state suspended Hilltop Liquor's liquor license for 60 days for selling alcohol to a minor, city officials said the nature of the business changed, meaning the grandfather provision no longer applied and the store would have to apply for a CUP. The store owner applied for a CUP, which the City Council denied. The store owner sued and a court ruled that the store owner had a vested right, and that the city could not revoke that right unless it provided a full hearing and made a decision based on all available evidence. *Bauer v. City of San Diego,* 74 Cal. App. 4th 1281 (1999).

Although usually dealing with the operating conditions of a business, rather than its underlying land use, CUPs are important in California land use planning because they are part of the legal tradition that has permitted the emergence of an important additional tool: discretionary review.

Discretionary Review

Most aspects of the zoning ordinance are designed to yield a "yes" or "no." A landowner may build a house in a residential neighborhood but not a store. A developer may build a 30-unit apartment building on a particular parcel of land if certain requirements are met (setback, parking, etc.), but not if the requirements are not met. In recent years, however, many cities have begun to emphasize one aspect of zoning designed to yield an answer of "yes … if."

Discretionary review is a process that permits local officials, usually the planning commission, to review a specific development proposal and either attach conditions or deny approval. Even a proposal conforming to the paper requirements of the zoning ordinance must be reviewed by the planning commission, which may or may not give its approval. In recent years, many cities have expanded the boundaries of discretionary review to include not just potentially incompatible uses, but essentially all projects over a certain size.

The concept of discretionary review builds on the conditional use permit process, which permits planning commission review of individual cases even if the "use" in question is allowed under the zoning ordinance. This expanded use of discretionary review is not really a logical extension of the 1950s pig-in-the-parlor concept of a conditional use permit. Rather, it's a response to citizen demand for more open decisionmaking, because it opens up for public debate many projects that wouldn't otherwise come before a public body.

A trailblazer in this area has been the city of San Francisco. The San Francisco city charter contains one line permitting the

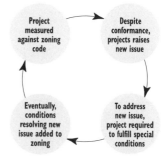

Discretionary Review
to describe what is essentially
a circular process

The concept of discretionary review builds on the CUP process, which permits planning commission review of individual cases even if the use is allowed under the zoning ordinance.

planning commission to review development projects at its own discretion. The commission and the city planning department have not been timid about using this phrase as the legal basis to review a vast array of projects, large and small. Many other cities have followed suit. During times of economic recession, landowners and businesses join with property rights activists and conservative politicians to demand a scaling back of discretionary review, arguing that such review makes a city or county "uncompetitive." Some cities and counties even respond with "streamlined" processes. But few local governments are willing to give up much authority.

CEQA = California Environmental
Quality Act

In many respects, the expanded use of discretionary review has been influenced by the California Environmental Quality Act, which encourages a spirited public debate on the environmental aspects of a project, whether or not it conforms to zoning. CEQA's case-by-case analytical structure has prompted many communities to expand the range of projects they will review with discretion, because the projects will be reviewed individually under CEQA. (For more information on the CEQA review process, *see* chapter 9.)

Of course, local politicians often prefer discretionary review, because the process allows them to approve or reject a project depending on the current political situation, no matter what the local codes say. And, in practice, cities also use discretionary review to gain leverage over a developer. On a complicated project, a conditional use permit may impose several dozen conditions. While some of these are associated with the "conditional use" being considered—a store's hours of operation, for example—others are really exactions, imposed in response to political pressure and perceived planning problems. ("Exactions" are conditions or financial obligations imposed on developers to deal with specific problems arising from the development in question, such as traffic, housing, and open space. Exactions are discussed in detail in chapter 10.)

On a complicated project, a conditional use permit may impose several dozen conditions.

Conditions imposed on a development through discretionary review may call for anything "reasonably related" to the project— the planting of a large number of trees, the construction of affordable housing, the payment of a traffic mitigation fee. Design review (sometimes known as architectural review) also falls under the category of discretionary review, and can lead to a separate set of conditions specifying anything from the placement of dumpsters to the color of the building.

Many times, the discretionary review process is really the beginning of a policy cycle. An issue that pops up during discretionary review will be dealt with on a case-by-case basis at first. But eventually, requirements based on the case-by-case experience are included in the zoning code. Many exactions and impact fees have become established city policy in this way. Partly because of discretionary review, however, the cycle is never-ending: New problems (both planning and political) are always discovered in discretionary review, new conditions are imposed, and eventually new exactions are institutionalized in the zoning ordinance.

Discretionary review provides both the city and its citizens with many opportunities that wouldn't otherwise exist. At the same time, it makes the development process a lot longer and less predictable. Developers don't always know what kind of project they'll wind up with in the end, or how expensive it will be. It's also hard to predict in advance whether any agreement between developers and city staff (or between developers and angry citizens) will hold up in front of the planning commission or city council.

Code Enforcement

As the number of conditions imposed on developers has grown, so has the importance of code enforcement. Yet, historically, code enforcement has been a virtually forgotten area of land use planning. Often, code enforcement officers aren't even in the same division of city government with the planners who craft all the conditions. Rather, they're often attached to the building and safety department, because the bulk of their job consists of responding to citizen complaints about possible code violations—a neighbor who is constructing an addition to his house without a permit, for example.

Findings

ONE OF THE MOST IMPORTANT, BUT ABUSED concepts in planning is the concept of "findings." A set of findings is simply meant to be the rationale that a city council or planning commission uses in making a decision. In the words of the landmark court case on the subject, findings "expose the agency's mode of analysis" and "bridge the analytical gap between raw data and ultimate decision." *Topanga Association for a Scenic Community v. County of Los Angeles,* 11 Cal. 3d 506 (1974). In short, findings should discuss the reasons why a city or county has decided to take a certain action.

The legal purpose of findings is to give judges a way to assess the local government's decision if that decision is challenged in court. With a few exceptions, localities don't need to draw up findings for legislative actions such as zoning ordinances and general plan amendments, because these are presumed to be policy statements. But quasi-judicial decisions must be supported by findings, so that it is clear how a city or county is applying its policy to a particular case. Thus, findings are required for such actions as conditional use permits, variances, subdivision approvals, and other development permits.

State law requires findings for a variety of other actions that are legislative in nature, such as general plan consistency, moratoria on residential construction, and growth-control ordinances. (However, findings are not required for initiatives that control growth.)

Findings are also required under the California Environmental Quality Act when a project is approved through a "statement of overriding considerations"—a statement indicating that the project is needed even though it will have significant environmental effects. In one court case, the court of appeal struck the approval of a development project on Bethel Island in the Sacramento-San Joaquin River Delta because the findings on which the statement of overriding considerations was based referred to the need for "an effective jobs/housing balance" even though no evidence in the record identified such a problem. This was not to say that a jobs/ housing balance wasn't a problem in the Bay Area—the court admitted it was—but merely that the county had failed to include this information in the record. *Sierra Club v. County of Contra Costa,* 10 Cal. App. 4th 1212 (1992).

As the Bethel Island case indicates, findings are supposed to present the evidence a city council or planning commission considered and then explain how that evidence laid the groundwork for the decision that eventually was made. The findings will then be attached to the decision itself as part of the permanent record.

In fact, findings are often poorly written, typically constituting little more than an after-the-fact rationale for governmental action. Most findings are made up of boilerplate material, and rarely will they go on to cover what they're supposed to cover: the evidence on which the decision is based, and the connections between the evidence and the case at hand.

In one situation in Ventura County, the findings attached to a development approval simply restated the county's planning standards in conclusory fashion. The relevant county code sections contained standards that were posed as a series of questions—for example, "Is [it] compatible with the character of surrounding development?" The findings simply turned the question into a statement (adding a negative) and stated: "The proposed development, as conditioned, would not be compatible with the residential character of the surrounding community." Based on these findings, the board of supervisors rejected the project.

Nevertheless, the court of appeal affirmed this approach to writing findings, saying that the facts supporting the decision were clearly incorporated by reference into the decision—precisely what Contra Costa County did not do in the Bethel Island case. *Dore v. County of Ventura,* 23 Cal. App. 4th 320 (1994). ■

To many code enforcement officers, the complicated conditions imposed on a modern development project simply constitute an annoying distraction from their bread-and-butter work. At the same time, however, planners seldom take responsibility for code enforcement; they rarely investigate whether conditions have been met, assuming instead that investigation is the job of code enforcement.

Zoning violations are usually misdemeanors, meaning that a property owner who is cited is thrown into criminal court. Even when code violators are caught and cited, local governments have difficulty motivating property owners to comply with the law. The property owners may pay a fine and promise to clean up their act, but in all likelihood they won't change the way they do business—for two reasons. One is that code enforcement officers are usually overworked, and property owners know it will be a long time before the officers get around to doing follow-up. The second reason is that the threat of further punishment usually doesn't exist.

A retail business—a drive-through restaurant next to a residential area, for example—that is violating conditions of approval by staying open late can probably make more money by continually paying fines than by closing on time. In order to take any more serious action, most cities must depend on the county district attorney to press charges. And a busy district attorney's office concerned with murder and rape isn't going to assign high priority to a neighborhood dispute over a late-night hamburger stand.

Some cities have tried to deal with this problem by "downgrading" zoning violations from a misdemeanor to an infraction. This action permits code enforcement officers to issue tickets, just as a Highway Patrol officer does, and places the burden on the property owner to go into court and defend himself. A few cities have experimented with code enforcement by hiring their own city prosecutor who is empowered to take code enforcement problems to court.

But even then there are problems. A property owner charged with a misdemeanor will usually correct the violation prior to an appearance in court, which will often lead the judge to dismiss the charge. Furthermore, many cities don't regard a violation of conditions imposed via discretionary review as a true violation of the zoning ordinance. If the conditions are construction-related (using a particular type of window, for example), the city can simply withhold the certificate of occupancy, which the landowner needs to occupy the building, until the conditions are met. (Of course, for many structures, certificates of occupancy aren't required.) However, if a condition related to the building's operation is violated (no carpooling program five years later, for example), the city may have no recourse if the violation is not considered a true violation of the zoning ordinance. Compared with neighborhood nuisances and true zoning violations (substandard or unpermitted building construction, improper use for the zone, etc.), discretionary conditions are given low priority indeed—and often they are never implemented at all.

Chapter 8

The Basic Tools
Part 3—The Subdivision Map Act

O
ne of the most colorful chapters in American history is the story of land speculation in the United States—and especially the story of the land swindlers who bought property, subdivided it, and sold it to gullible people who had never seen it. In the 19th century, huge pieces of the Midwest were sold by these swindlers, who promised to build bustling new towns but then disappeared with the profits. By the turn of the century, Middle America had been carved up, and these shady characters turned to exotic resort areas like California and Florida, subdividing mountains and deserts and swamps into lots that existed only on paper—and in the minds of small buyers who dreamed of retiring there.

In the 19th century, huge pieces of the Midwest were sold by land swindlers, who promised to build bustling new towns but then disappeared with the profits.

Up until 1930, land in the mountains and deserts of California was still so cheap that these lots were sometimes given away. The *Los Angeles Examiner,* the flagship of Hearst's great newspaper chain, sometimes gave away lots to new subscribers. Some encyclopedia companies also gave away building lots as an incentive to buy a set of encyclopedias. For decades, people all over the country cherished their 25- by 50-foot "encyclopedia lots," unaware that their parcel might lie on the side of a steep hill eight miles from the nearest road.

From time immemorial, the mere act of subdividing land into smaller parcels has been a profitable enterprise, and that is why, in addition to zoning and general plans, state law requires cities and counties to regulate the subdivision of land.

The Subdivision Map Act was the first land use law ever passed by the state legislature (1907). A century later, the Map Act has evolved into a powerful tool used by local governments to exact

Magic Subdivisions

IN SOME COUNTIES, A SCENE that gave planners fits was played out over and over again: A landowner or his representative would come to the planning counter with an ancient, crinkled map containing an official-appearing county stamp. The landowner would insist that the map represented a subdivision that he intended to act on. The land in question typically was rural and, under modern-day zoning, could be only lightly developed if at all. But with a "certificate of compliance"—in which the government recognizes that separate lots exist—the landowner could pursue his development.

For years, planners in California struggled with how to handle these "magic" subdivisions. But a 2003 ruling by the state Supreme Court provided planners with a great deal of guidance—to the chagrin of property owners and land speculators. The state Supreme Court ruled that maps recorded prior to the first precursor to the Subdivision Map Act in 1893 do not create legal parcels for today's purposes. *Gardner v. County of Sonoma,* 29 Cal. 4th 990 (2003).

The Supreme Court case concerned a map recorded with the county in 1865 for property in Sonoma County, near Sebastopol. In 1996, the Gardner family, which owned 158 acres of hilly, heavily wooded property, presented the map to county planners. The map depicted two complete lots and parts of 10 others on the Gardner's land. They applied for certificates of compliance for 12 lots, but the county refused to recognize the map. So the Gardners sued the county and eventually took the case to the state Supreme Court.

In a previous case having more to do with the Map Act's merger provisions, the court had only nibbled at the edge of the magic subdivision issue. *Morehart v. County of Santa Barbara,* 7 Cal. 4th 725 (1994). But the unanimous *Gardner* decision

many concessions from developers related to what the law calls the "design and improvements" of subdivided land. At the same time, it is also a source of important protections for property owners seeking permission to subdivide their property. Because so much is at stake for both sides, the Map Act is a complicated law full of little traps and protections for both local governments and landowners.

The Subdivision Map Act (Govt. Code § 66410 *et seq.*) is equal parts consumer protection, real property law, and land use regulation. The original intent of the Subdivision Map Act was merely to keep track of the subdivision of land, so that real estate titles would not become clouded. In the 1920s and '30s, it was amended to combat the ill effects of land speculation—especially the problem of "paper" subdivisions, in which a landowner might subdivide and sell property but never provide even the roads required to reach the land.

Whereas the original Subdivision Map Act merely required developers to file subdivision maps so that government could keep track of ownership, a 1929 revision of the law permitted local governments, for the first time, to require subdividers to dedicate land for streets and sidewalks, provide utility easements, and conform their subdivision configurations to major roads.

Beginning in the 1930s, a series of amendments to the Subdivision Map Act gave local governments progressively more power to control the design and improvements of a subdivision. These powers had two purposes: first, to prevent the creation of new subdivided lots that were so small or badly configured that they were essentially unbuildable; and second, to give local governments sufficient legal authority to exact from developers the improvements required to serve a new subdivision. Together, these two powers were supposed to permit local governments to assure orderly patterns of development and prevent sprawling subdivisions, which were expensive for the government to serve.

By the 1970s, the Map Act had been recodified from the Business and Professions Code to the Government Code, and coordination was required between subdivision requirements and general plan requirements.

Unlike zoning or general plan law, the Subdivision Map Act does not apply to all land within a community. Rather, it comes into play only when a landowner seeks to subdivide his property. (It applies to condominium conversions as well as the more conventional subdivision of land.) But the influence of the Subdivision Map Act is remarkably broad. Because subdivision regulations typically govern the physical layout of new development on the ground, it is fair to say that the Map Act affects the physical appearance of a community far more than the zoning ordinance. And because local governments may regulate the design and improvements of a subdivision, the Map Act is an important tool in today's exaction-driven regulatory environment.

The Map

Under the Subdivision Map Act, any time land is subdivided in order to be sold, leased, or financed, the subdivision must be approved by the appropriate local government. For this purpose, each local government must adopt subdivision regulations that comply with the state law. Actions under the Subdivision Map Act are quasi-judicial in nature, which means that they are not subject to initiative and referendum. The quasi-judicial nature of the Subdivision Map Act also means that binding Map Act approvals can be granted by a city or county planning commission. However, some jurisdictions require approval by the city council or board of supervisors as well, and in all cases these planning commission decisions can be appealed to the elected body.

answered the question head-on. Unless the county had a chance to review and approve the map, or unless the lots had been conveyed separately at some point, the subdivision did not exist, the court ruled. Prior to 1893, there was no legal way for counties and cities to review and approve of maps. The maps were simply drawn and recorded at the will of a surveyor. Therefore, the court determined, all pre-1893 maps were invalid as subdivision maps unless the lots had been conveyed separately.

While the court's ruling regarding maps recorded prior to 1893 was unambiguous, the court threw into question the legality of maps recorded from 1893 until 1929. During that period, the Map Act concerned only the technical requirements of what should appear on a map and how it must be drafted. The 1929 revision of the Subdivision Map Act for the first time provided local agencies authority to review a subdivision map's design and improvements. Maps recorded during this period are likely to be the subject of the next round of lawsuits.

Exactly how many parcels are depicted in antiquated subdivision maps is unknown because no one is sure what old maps exist. Some experts estimate California has hundreds of thousands such lots. Some of them are as small as 25-feet-square—about the size of a living room in a new house—and were drawn without regard for topography, access, or public facilities, such as roads and utility lines. The maps are little more than grid lines.

Stretches of land along the San Mateo County coast are covered with these postage-stamp lots from maps that were recorded during the early 20th century. Local government agencies recognize the legality of the parcels, but agencies require new construction to meet current zoning and building regulations. Thus, a builder typically must assemble multiple parcels to have enough land on which to build. ■

Technically, the document being approved by the local government is the subdivision map—a two-dimensional representation of the land in question, showing exactly how the property will be split up and where the lot lines will be. (This requirement goes back to the original intent of the Map Act, which was to make sure the government had a precise record of subdivided lots for title purposes.) If a property is subdivided into two, three, or four parcels, the landowner needs governmental approval for a parcel map, which is not subject to all strict state requirements on subdivisions. However, all subdivisions of five or more lots must go through the full Subdivision Map Act procedures, meaning that landowners must receive approval for both a tentative map and a final map.

In practice, the essence of the Subdivision Map Act is the horsetrading that goes on between the local government and the developer over the design and improvements of the subdivision—that is, the site layout and the exactions required to permit the subdivision project to go forward. In these negotiations, each side brings something to the table and is seeking something in return. The local government wants subdivisions that meet its planning goals—with roads, schools, parks, and everything else on the planning laundry list. Meanwhile, the landowner comes to the table with the presumed financial ability to deliver those goodies—in exchange for an approved Subdivision Map, which will give the landowner the ability to create the lots and sell them off.

These negotiations typically occur while the landowner is seeking approval of a tentative map. Under the Subdivision Map Act, the tentative map is really the crucial document, because under law it virtually guarantees approval of the final map. To smooth out the sometimes rough process of subdivision negotiations, many cities require a "prefiling" conference—that is, a meeting with the landowner even before the tentative map application is filed.

An application for a tentative map is subject to hearing and notice requirements similar to those for conditional use permits, and is also subject to the provisions of CEQA. Once a city or county approves a tentative map, the jurisdiction must approve the final map if the project has not changed substantially in the interim.

How long an approved Subdivision Map can remain in existence is always the subject of a great deal of legal controversy. Under the law, the map has a life of two years and the local government may adopt an ordinance permitting it to last a third year. During real estate busts, when many planned subdivisions are delayed,

All subdivisions of five or more lots must go through the full Map Act procedures, meaning that landowners must receive approval for both a tentative map and a final map.

CEQA = California Environmental Quality Act

the state sometimes extends the life of existing maps. This happened most recently in 1996, when the legislature passed a law extending the life of all subdivision maps that had not expired by May 14, 1996, by one year—meaning the map had a life of up to four years.

Under case law, maps can be extended up to a total of 13 years—10 years if permitted by state law and another three if agreed to by the local government. In most cases, however, market conditions will change so dramatically during a 10- or 12-year period that landowners will probably want to change the plan and seek a new map anyway.

Horsetrading Over Design and Improvements

Over the past 20 years, the Subdivision Map Act has become a powerful tool for obtaining exactions from developers via conditions of approval. The topic of exactions will be dealt with in greater detail in chapter 10, but a general description of the Map Act's power in this area is necessary here.

Because the Map Act permits regulation of design and improvement of subdivisions, the law gives local governments expansive power to require developers to provide land, public facilities, and/or in lieu fees needed for those subdivisions to operate smoothly. These exactions are subject to many legal limitations that will be discussed in detail in the next chapter—most notably the requirement that they be directly related to the project in question. But probably no other state law provides so many ways for local governments to exact conditions of approval from developers.

For example, the Subdivision Map Act contains a long list of exactions and fees that local governments are specifically authorized to collect. Perhaps the best-known exaction of this type is the "Quimby Fee," which permits cities and counties to require that developers either dedicate parkland or pay an equivalent fee that will allow the governmental jurisdiction to buy land for parks. The Quimby Act lays out a specific set of procedures localities must follow if they plan to implement the law's parkland requirements. These procedures include setting standards for parkland (the number of acres required per 1,000 residents, for example) and a specific schedule of how the land and/or fees will be used to develop a park system. Govt. Code § 66477.

The Subdivision Map Act also specifically permits local governments to require that land be set aside for streets, bicycle paths, and public transit lines; fees for drainage and sewer facilities,

Under case law, maps can be extended up to a total of 13 years—10 years if permitted by state law and another three if agreed to by the local government.

The Subdivision Map Act contains a long list of exactions and fees that local governments are specifically authorized to collect.

bridges, and groundwater recharge programs; and easements that will provide public access to rivers and streams. A specific portion of the Map Act also covers fees for schools, a knotty topic that will be discussed in detail later in the book.

EIR = Environmental impact report

Because the Map Act also contains a separate provision requiring environmental review of subdivision projects, the Map Act and CEQA together can provide a powerful legal tool for environmentally related exactions. Essentially, the Map Act forms the legal basis for any exaction required to mitigate a significant environmental effect that has been identified through an environmental impact report. (EIRs are discussed in more detail in chapter 9.)

The Subdivision Map Act provides cities and counties with the legal power to impose exactions required to bring subdivisions into compliance with the local general plan.

Finally, the Subdivision Map Act also provides cities and counties with the legal power to impose exactions required to bring subdivisions into compliance with the local general plan. These provisions broaden the Map Act's exaction power beyond the mere dedication of land for streets and schools. In fact, local governments can require any physical rearrangement of the project—or any fee—necessary to bring the project into conformance with the general plan. For example, in an important piece of case law known as the *Soderling* ruling, the court of appeal ruled that the city of Santa Monica could require that the owner of an apartment building install smoke detectors in order to convert the building to condominiums. The smoke detectors were required to achieve the city's general plan goal of "promoting safe housing for all." *Soderling v. City of Santa Monica,* 142 Cal. App. 3d 501 (1983).

The legal provisions linking the Map Act to the general plan give local governments tremendous power to impose conditions that would otherwise be outside the scope of subdivision review.

According to prominent land use lawyer Daniel J. Curtin, Jr., the *Soderling* case—and, indeed, all the legal provisions linking the Map Act to the general plan—give local governments tremendous power to impose conditions that would otherwise be outside the scope of subdivision review. These conditions include fees for childcare centers and public art, inclusionary housing set-asides, and other exactions not specifically authorized under the Map Act itself.

Denial and Appeal

Under the Subdivision Map Act, a city or county must deny a landowner permission to subdivide property if, in its legal findings, the jurisdiction finds that one or more of the following conditions is present:

- **Environmental damage.** In combination, the Subdivision Map Act and the California Environmental Quality Act give local governments considerable power over subdivisions. If an environmental impact report finds that the subdivision of land may lead to significant environmental damage, the subdivision application must be rejected. As with any action under CEQA, the local jurisdiction may approve the project even under these circumstances if it adopts a statement of overriding consideration with appropriate findings. (For more information on these CEQA procedures, *see* chapter 9.)

- **Inconsistency with local plans.** The subdivision of land must be consistent with the local general plan.

- **Physical unsuitability of the site.** A subdivision must be denied if the proposed project is not suitable for the site. For example, in a leading court case on this topic, a proposed residential project in Carmel Highlands was rejected because the soils in the area were not suitable for the system of septic tanks proposed by the developer. *Carmel Valley View, Ltd. v. Board of Supervisors,* 58 Cal. App. 3d 817 (1976). However, in such a situation, the local jurisdiction may approve a subdivision map on the condition that the density be reduced to a level that may be sustained by the physical characteristics of the site.

- **Conflict with public easements.** Utility or other easements running through the site must not be disturbed by the subdivision. But the subdivision may be approved if the landowner agrees to provide alternative easements.

In 2001, the legislature passed a law that requires a city or county to obtain proof that a sufficient water supply is available for any proposed subdivision with at least 500 lots. If the subdivider proposes to use groundwater for the new homes, the local water agency must evaluate the landowner's right to pump the water. With approval of the 2001 law and a precursor that was approved in 1995, the courts have begun to scrutinize more tightly the evidence that a subdivision will have adequate water. This is especially true when a developer intends to rely on the never-finished State Water Project, which can deliver only about half the water to which customers are entitled. As one appeals court justice wrote while invalidating a subdivision, "The dream of water entitlements from the incomplete State Water Project is no substitute for the reality of actual water the SWP can deliver." *Santa Clarita Organization for Planning the Environment v. County of Los Angeles,* 106 Cal. App. 4th 715 (2003).

Local planning commissions often have binding approval power over subdivision maps, but their decisions may always be appealed to the local city council or board of supervisors. Historically, the only

In 2001, the legislature passed a law that requires a city or county to obtain proof that a sufficient water supply is available for any proposed subdivision with at least 500 lots.

party interested in an appeal has been the landowner, who asked for one if the planning commission turned him down. As their power has grown in recent years, however, citizens have often chosen to appeal subdivision approvals to the legislative body. Appeals can require a fee so large (sometimes a few thousand dollars) that it discourages some citizen groups, but most serious organizations round up the money.

Sometimes, staff planning directors may try to appeal subdivision rulings they dislike. The typical situation occurs when a planning director proposes that a subdivision be denied, or approved only with certain conditions, and the planning commission overrules the decision. The state Attorney General's Office has issued an opinion concluding that planning directors do, indeed, have the legal power to seek an appeal. In a way, such appeals merely ensure that controversial approvals make it to the legislative body, not just controversial denials. However, an appellate court has ruled that a city council member is not an "interested person" eligible to appeal a planning commission approval of a tentative map. *Cohan v. City of Thousand Oaks*, 30 Cal. App. 4th 547 (1994).

An appellate court has ruled that a city council member is not an "interested person" eligible to appeal a planning commission approval of a tentative map.

Vesting Tentative Map and Protection for Landowners

While occasionally subjecting landowners to onerous requirements, the Subdivision Map Act can also be a source of protection. A subdivision map can be denied only for specific reasons, and once approved it remains valid for several years. Most important, however, is the vesting tentative map.

One of the most controversial aspects of planning law in California is the question of vested rights. Under California case law, a developer's right to build becomes "vested"—that is, protected against future growth restrictions or other regulatory reversals—only after a building permit is issued and the developer has made a "substantial investment" in the project. (For a complete discussion of the history of vested rights in California, *see* the section in chapter 12 discussing development agreements.)

In response to this harsh requirement for vested rights, the state legislature has passed two laws that will vest a developer's right to build earlier in the process. The first is the "development agreement," which will be discussed later in the book. The second, adopted in 1984, is the "vesting tentative map" under the Subdivision Map Act. The vesting tentative map is identical to a tentative map except that the words "vesting tentative map" are printed on it. By law, when the local jurisdiction approves this map, the developer has received the vested right to build the project laid out in the tentative map.

The law also specifies that a city or county cannot deny a subdivision proposal simply because a vesting tentative map is sought. However, local governments can—and usually do—ask for more detailed information about the project at the tentative map stage if vesting is requested. In fact, some localities have established an approval procedure for a vesting tentative map that is completely different from, and far more difficult than, approval of a simple tentative map. At the same time, under an important appellate case, the local government has a different responsibility: It cannot impose new standards or conditions on a vesting tentative map application that were not in place at the time the application was deemed complete. *Bright Development Co. v. City of Tracy*, 20 Cal. App. 4th 783 (1993).

Permit Streamlining Act

To prevent local governments from sitting on development applications indefinitely, the state has passed the Permit Streamlining Act—a law that sets important deadlines for local government action, especially in connection with the Subdivision Map Act.

Crossing the (Lot) Line

FEW PIECES OF PRIVATE PROPERTY in California are as treasured by the public as the Hearst Ranch. The newspaper family's spread in San Luis Obispo County covers 82,000 acres, including 18 miles of spectacular coastline along Highway 1. The Hearst family for years has tried to develop a portion of the property, but overwhelming public opposition stymied the landowners. So the family indicated it would use Subdivision Map Act loopholes that other developers had learned to exploit.

The Map Act allows a landowner or potential buyer to seek a "certificate of compliance" for a lot, which is essentially the local government's stamp of approval that the lot exists legally. (The certificate of compliance, however, does not grant a development right.) The Map Act also allows landowners to adjust lot lines for adjacent parcels. Recognizing that local governments have minimal discretion over applications for certificates of compliance and lot line adjustments, creative developers and speculators put these two tools together. They would locate maps from the late 19th or early 20th century for desirable tracts of land, seek certificates of compliance for the lots, and then use a series of lot line adjustments to configure the parcels for the greatest development potential. Essentially, they were re-subdividing the property without the government's review. For a time, San Luis Obispo and Sonoma Counties saw as many new parcels created through certificates of compliance followed by lot line adjustments as through the normal process of subdividing land.

In 2001, the Hearsts produced an antiquated subdivision map depicting about 200 lots in the backcountry portion of the property. The Hearsts indicated they would seek certificates of compliance for the parcels and would then use the lot line adjustment process to move the parcels to the coast, where development would be far more valuable.

Because of the property's sensitivity, the Hearst plan stirred a hornet's nest and became exhibit A for Subdivision Map Act abuse. The 1976 amendment permitting lot line adjustments had been intended to enable two adjoining property owners to alter their lot lines without going through the subdivision process. At the time, no one envisioned the serial lot line adjustments that became common during the 1990s. The legislature responded by approving a bill that limits lot line adjustments to no more than four lots. Wholesale changes like those proposed for Hearst Ranch were forbidden—and a developer's dream method of carving up land vanished. ▪

The Permit Streamlining Act (Govt. Code §§ 65920–65963.1) applies only to quasi-judicial actions, meaning that it covers Map Act approvals, variances, and conditional use permits, but not general plan amendments or zone changes. Under the law, the clock starts ticking when a local government "deems" a development application complete. But even here there are time restrictions: The locality must determine within 30 days whether an application is complete and, if not, give the applicant a detailed explanation of what else is needed.

Once the application is deemed complete, a whole new set of deadlines is triggered that requires the locality to take final action on the project within six months if the application requires a negative declaration under the California Environmental Quality Act and one year if the application requires an environmental impact report.

If the local government misses the deadlines, the development is deemed approved under the Permit Streamlining Act. Though it is not common, the "deemed approved" action has been upheld by appellate courts in several specific cases.

Chapter 9

The California
Environmental Quality Act

The general plan, the zoning ordinance or development code, and the Subdivision Map Act all play basic roles in local land use planning. But there's one other important component in the local land use process that is not, strictly speaking, a planning law: the California Environmental Quality Act, commonly known as CEQA.

Since its passage in 1970, CEQA has easily had as much influence on land use patterns in California as any planning law. To understand its full significance, just imagine what land use planning in California would be like without it.

General plans and zoning ordinances could be written and revised without much consideration for environmental consequences. In reviewing a tall office building or a huge suburban subdivision, local planners would concern themselves only with zoning matters and perhaps the site planning questions that emerge under the Subdivision Map Act. Some projects might be constructed with hardly any review at all, because the trend toward discretionary government review is a result, in good measure, of the approach CEQA takes to development. The same is true of exactions, because our current concept of the purpose and broad use of exactions (to mitigate a project's impact, in CEQA jargon) is derived directly from CEQA. Environmental impact reports (EIRs), lengthy review processes, expensive mitigation measures, even the concept of a broad-based public debate over a particular development project—all are attributable in large part to CEQA's role in local land use planning.

Although its impact has been undeniable, there is vigorous debate throughout California as to whether CEQA has been a

CEQA = California Environmental
Quality Act
EIR = Environmental impact report

EIRs, lengthy review processes, expensive mitigation measures, even the concept of a broad-based public debate over a particular development project—all are attributable to CEQA's role in local land use planning.

uniformly positive influence. Indeed, CEQA is probably the most hotly debated planning-related law in California. Its supporters must constantly defend its usefulness and value against opponents who claim that it is nothing more than a "paper tiger" that slows down the land use approval process and makes California uncompetitive compared with surrounding states, none of which have a similar law. Especially in the recession of the early 1990s, CEQA became a scapegoat—rightly or wrongly—for the state's sluggish inability to turn itself around. While CEQA's scope and influence have not appreciably expanded in recent years, neither have they been significantly reined in. For all the law's shortcomings, state lawmakers and mainstream interest groups have not even proposed an overhaul of CEQA in more than a decade. In short, CEQA is a permanent and important part of the California planning landscape.

Unlike zoning or general plan laws, CEQA is not concerned with overarching urban planning issues. Rather, CEQA is a single-issue law concerned with one aspect of public policy—environmental protection—that overlaps with planning.

CEQA is the product of the first wave of environmental consciousness that swept the United States in the late '60s. Enacted in 1970, CEQA is patterned after a federal law, the National Environmental Policy Act, which was enacted by Congress the previous year. (According to some accounts, NEPA is actually patterned after CEQA, which was written first but passed second.) Fourteen other states and the District of Columbia also have CEQA-type laws. Many of them have looked to CEQA for guidance; in fact, the New York State law, which went into effect in 1978, used CEQA as its foundation. However, most state laws outside of California apply only to public development projects, and only New York and the state of Washington have environmental review activity that approaches the level of CEQA. No other state matches California's mandate for detailed, project-specific review.

Because CEQA is concerned solely with the environment, rather than broader land use planning issues, its regulatory scheme is different from traditional planning and, in fact, turns many of those principles upside down. Whereas traditional zoning and planning schemes treat all property as similarly as possible, CEQA treats each property and each proposal uniquely. Often, this approach creates conflict with traditional planning processes. Just as often, however, the CEQA approach has rubbed off on local planners, who have undertaken more project-specific review within the context of traditional planning tools.

At the same time, the relationship between CEQA and the basic planning process is often a murky one. Members of the public and even local officials sometimes confuse environmental review with discussion of a project's actual merits. Most of the time, the two processes move along parallel tracks—sometimes in harmony and sometimes in confused conflict.

CEQA's Role

Contrary to popular perception, CEQA's primary function is not to improve California's environment directly. CEQA does not usurp local authority over land use decisions or establish a state agency to enforce the law. CEQA does not even require local governments to deny all projects that would harm the environment.

Rather, CEQA's role is primarily informational, and in fact the act is sometimes referred to as a "full disclosure law." By law, CEQA has four functions:

- **To inform** decisionmakers about significant environmental effects
- **To identify** ways environmental damage can be avoided
- **To prevent** avoidable environmental damage
- **To disclose** to the public why a project is approved even if it leads to environmental damage

CEQA's role is primarily informational, and the act is sometimes referred to as a full disclosure law.

In carrying out these functions, the CEQA process is meant to unearth information about the likely environmental consequences of any "project"—from general plan adoption to permit approval— and make sure that those consequences are debated by the public and elected officials before a decision is made.

The CEQA process is meant to unearth information about the likely environmental consequences of any project and make sure that those consequences are debated by the public and elected officials before a decision is made.

As we will discuss in much greater detail later, this process begins with an assessment of whether a specific project is subject to CEQA's provisions at all. Then local government planners conduct an "initial study" of the probable environmental consequences of a project. If those consequences are likely to be significant, then an "environmental impact report" must be prepared, specifying the environmental damage and laying out ways to "mitigate" that damage. The initial study and the EIR form the basis for public discussion of the project.

In this sense, CEQA is not unlike many state planning laws, such as the general plan law. It lays out a process but does not dictate an outcome. CEQA does not absolutely require that environmentally harmful projects be rejected, nor does it even specify how to minimize environmental damage. These decisions are left up to local governments, which operate with relatively little interference from the state.

CEQA does not absolutely require that environmentally harmful projects be rejected, nor does it even specify how to minimize environmental damage.

Do-It-Yourself EIRs

FOR YEARS, ENVIRONMENTALISTS complained about the practice of some cities and counties to allow a developer to submit his own environmental impact report. Environmentalists and other opponents of development projects contended this practice set up a conflict of interest. In 2001, they found what appeared to be a prime example of the conflict.

Consultants hired by the Newhall Land & Farming Co. to prepare an EIR for the 21,000-home Newhall Ranch project near Santa Clarita had been advised to search for the San Fernando Valley spineflower. The plant, previously thought extinct, was rediscovered in 1999 on similar land in the Santa Monica Mountains. The biologists found one stand of spineflowers along a dirt road at Newhall Ranch, and several other stands of what they suspected were members of the same species. Newhall then instructed the biologists it had hired to stop searching, and reminded the consultants that they were bound by a confidentiality agreement that barred them from disclosing what they had found to anyone outside the company. The suspect plants were never sent to a lab for testing, and at some point the site where the plants were found was plowed up.

When Newhall released the EIR, it reported only a single confirmed stand of spineflowers along the road, and concluded that a fence could protect the plants from development. Environmentalists and

⇢

As with general plan law, the Governor's Office of Planning and Research and the Resources Agency are required to prepare guidelines for CEQA on a regular basis. While the General Plan Guidelines are truly advisory, however, the CEQA Guidelines are binding on local governments, and courts often give as much weight to the Guidelines as to the law itself. These guidelines have grown from about 10 pages when they were first written, in the early '70s, to more than 200 pages today.

Updating the Guidelines, however, is politically difficult, with developers, local governments and environmentalists advocating very different amendments. The Wilson administration did not complete an update until three months before it left office, while the Davis administration finished an update only weeks before Davis left office. Environmentalists sued over some of the Wilson administration changes, and the courts ultimately threw out some of the most substantive changes. The Davis administration changes were mostly technical amendments.

How CEQA Has Evolved

CEQA's procedural nature has made it perhaps the most litigated environmental or planning law in the state. Even environmental law experts agree that CEQA's procedural requirements are so broad, and so expandable, that virtually any CEQA document could be challenged in court. Also, no state agency holds the administrative power to enforce CEQA; it is meant to be enforced by citizens through litigation. However, the state attorney general can file lawsuits to force CEQA compliance. Attorney General Bill Lockyer, for example, sued some counties in the San Joaquin Valley that were permitting the construction of large dairies with little or no environmental review. Still, Lockyer's lawsuits filed on behalf of the state were exceptions.

CEQA's litigious nature has had two consequences. First, citizen groups (environmentalists, homeowners, and so forth) have used the threat of CEQA litigation to obtain leverage over land use planning and, especially, over the review of particular development projects. Second, the litigation has given the courts an unusual opportunity to shape the law and how it is used throughout the state. Since its passage in 1970, CEQA has generated more than 250 published appellate court decisions, the vast majority of which have expanded CEQA's scope and requirements. According to planner/lawyer Ronald Bass, these court rulings fall into four general categories.

- **Whether CEQA applies.** Especially in the early days of CEQA, developers and local governments often argued that certain projects were exempt from CEQA review altogether. Even in recent years, a few important cases have revolved around this question.

- **Whether an EIR should be prepared.** This is perhaps the most common area of litigation. Citizen groups often challenge a project's negative declaration, which declares that an EIR is not necessary. Over the years, whenever a question in this area has arisen the courts have usually ordered the EIR to be done. This line of cases has greatly expanded CEQA's scope by requiring EIRs on a broad range of projects.

- **Whether the EIR is adequate.** Another common legal tactic is to challenge the adequacy of the EIR, arguing that some particular aspect of the discussion is incomplete. Again, over time the courts have greatly broadened the scope of EIRs themselves by requiring more complete discussions of potential environmental damage.

- **Whether procedures were followed.** CEQA contains a broad array of procedural requirements, from hearings to findings to review processes. Generally, the courts have protected these procedural safeguards zealously.

Though CEQA has been the subject of more than 250 appellate cases, one has far more importance than the rest of the cases: the *Friends of Mammoth* case in 1972, in which the California Supreme Court ruled that CEQA applies to private development projects as well as public projects. *Friends of Mammoth v. Board of Supervisors of Mono County,* 8 Cal. 3d 247 (1972). No other case has had a broader impact on the everyday use of CEQA in the planning field—nor does any other case illustrate the expansive attitude the courts have brought to CEQA cases.

California Department of Fish and Game investigators—whom Newhall had refused to allow on the site—were suspicious, so they contacted the Los Angeles County District Attorney's Office with allegations that Newhall was covering up the presence of additional stands of the endangered plant. After the district attorney started investigating, Newhall acknowledged having found additional stands of spineflowers. But the company said that the destruction of endangered plants took place during the course of routine agricultural operations and was therefore lawful. The company subsequently filed new environmental documents disclosing the additional spineflower populations.

The district attorney did not prosecute, but state lawmakers took up the cause. A bill introduced in 2003 would have prohibited cities and counties from allowing a developer to hire his own EIR consultants. Under the proposed law, only a lead agency or consultants hired by the lead agency could prepare an EIR. The building industry, business interests, and even the California Chapter of the American Planning Association waged a successful war on the bill, and it died.

Cities and counties defend their practice as a pragmatic approach to CEQA. Planners say they do not have the resources to manage all of the environmental reviews on projects proposed within their jurisdiction—a tacit admission that they do not even try to learn everything about development within their city or county. ■

After CEQA was passed in 1970, the law was applied only to strictly governmental projects—the construction of buildings, public works facilities, and other projects in which the government was a direct participant. (As with many other aspects of CEQA, this practice was derived from the way the federal government implemented NEPA.) In the *Friends of Mammoth* case, however, environmentalists and the state Attorney General's Office argued that CEQA should apply to all private projects that must receive some sort of governmental approval in order to build.

At the time, CEQA said that local governments had to undertake environmental review "on any project they intend to carry out...." In strict legal terms, then, the California Supreme Court had to determine whether a private development proposal constituted a "project" under CEQA, and whether a local government's issuance of development permits constituted "carrying out" a project.

The court concluded that the term "project" did indeed include "the issuance of permits, leases, and other entitlements." And after reviewing the legislative history of CEQA (which at one time included the phrase "any project or change in zoning they intend to carry out"), the Supreme Court concluded that if "project" encompassed development permits, then certainly issuing such permits constituted a "carrying out" of those projects. Suddenly, one day in 1972, CEQA applied not just to public building projects but to all private building projects as well. It has been a major element in local land use planning ever since. (The state legislature subsequently amended CEQA to make the meaning of the *Friends of Mammoth* decision clear in the law itself.)

Suddenly, one day in 1972, CEQA applied not just to public building projects but to all private building projects as well. It has been a major element in local land use planning ever since.

The courts' aggressive expansion of CEQA's role continued into the early 1990s. By then, most of the basic questions—when does CEQA apply? when must an EIR be prepared?—had been answered, and a more conservative state Supreme Court was frowning on the use of CEQA as a weapon to stall or kill projects.

More recently, the courts have concentrated on applying the details of CEQA to particular situations, and the California Supreme Court has shown little interest. From 1997 until 2005, the state's high court decided only one CEQA case involving the narrow question of whether a city-sponsored ballot measure was subject to CEQA. In *Friends of Sierra Madre v. City of Sierra Madre*, 25 Cal. 4th 165 (2001), the answer was yes.

The legislature has never undertaken a comprehensive reform of CEQA. The recession of the early 1990s caused business and development interests to press for CEQA reform, and Governor Wilson promoted a similar agenda as part of his never-adopted statewide growth management package. But the reformers did not get far. The most significant legislative change, passed in 1993, was a measure encouraging the use of "master EIRs" or "program EIRs" for broad plans or programs, which are followed by "focused" or "tiered" EIRs for specific projects. The bill also codified the mitigated negative declaration, a tool that was widely used by not recognized in law.

The lack of CEQA reform is due largely to the strong presence of the environmental lobby, and, maybe more so, to the leading role played by environmentalist state lawmakers. For about a decade, all CEQA legislation needed the blessing of Palo Alto Democrat Byron Sher, one of the most environmentally oriented lawmakers of recent times. Sher held so much power that even proposals for large-scale CEQA reform became rare. Term limits forced Sher from the legislature in 2004, but other liberal lawmakers are willing to carry the CEQA torch.

One result of the legislature's hands-off approach to CEQA is to magnify the role of litigation in CEQA's development, which is been both a blessing and a curse. On the one hand, the court rulings have expanded the discussion of environmental factors far beyond the modest expectations of the legislators who originally passed the bill more than 30 years ago. Probably nowhere else in the world are the environmental consequences of development projects so broadly—and openly—debated as in California.

At the same time, however, CEQA's ever-broadening requirements sometimes make it difficult for planners to determine how much environmental review is enough. Whenever the adequacy of environmental review is challenged, the appellate courts' response is usually that more environmental analysis should have been done. A local planner in Southern California once called the CEQA process "Kafkaesque." "These things go to court," he said, "and the judges tell us how we're wrong. But they don't tell us how we can be right." In practice, the result is one of two very different attitudes toward projects under CEQA. Cautious local governments suffer from paralysis by analysis because they fear litigation. By contrast, localities hoping to push an important project through are often tempted to cut corners under CEQA by underestimating likely environmental damage and therefore avoiding the EIR process altogether; or by trying to minimize delays and too much public scrutiny by determining that a project warrants only a negative declaration.

CEQA's ever-broadening requirements sometimes make it difficult for planners to determine how much environmental review is enough.

The Three-Step Process

Under the state CEQA Guidelines, local governments must follow a three-step process in applying CEQA to a particular development project. Depending on the size and likely impact of the project, the result of this analysis can be anything from no further environmental review at all to a full-blown EIR. If more than one public agency is involved in the environmental review, the agency with the greatest responsibility for reviewing the project will be designated the "lead agency."

If more than one public agency is involved in the environmental review, the agency with the greatest responsibility for reviewing the project will be designated the lead agency.

Step 1. Is the action in question a "project" under CEQA?

Generally speaking, any discretionary action involving the physical environment is a "project" subject to CEQA, ranging from the approval of a general plan to the issuance of grading permits for major projects. Ministerial actions, on the other hand, are not projects because their issuance does not involve any discretion. Similarly, many local ordinances not related to land uses (an increase in water rates, for example) don't qualify as projects.

Traditionally, the classic example of a ministerial action exempt from CEQA has been the issuance of a building permit. In fact, some building permit processes may contain enough leeway to qualify as discretionary actions, but in general this is a good example. Once you have obtained land use approvals, the building permit is more or less automatic: Pay your money, follow the conditions included in the approval, and the local government must give you your permit.

Even if an action is discretionary, sometimes it may be exempt from CEQA review anyway. Both the state legislature and the secretary of the state Resources Agency have identified specific types of projects that are exempt. Sometimes these exemptions reflect the fact that such projects are unlikely to create environmental damage; sometimes they merely attest to the lobbying power of a particular interest group. Statutory exemptions (those exemptions determined by the legislature) include demolition permits, adoption of coastal and timberland plans, and some mass transit projects. In 1996, for example, the legislature passed a statutory exemption for all actions taken by transit agencies to reduce their budgets.

In recent years, the legislature has added exemptions for certain types of small infill and affordable housing projects in urban areas. But those exemptions have raised concerns from environmental

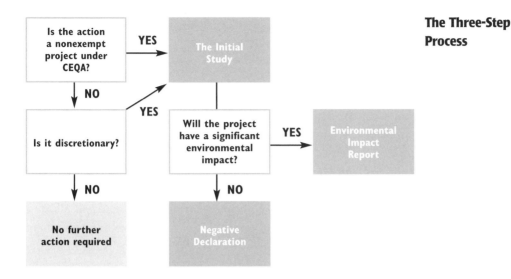

Is the action a nonexempt project under CEQA? — YES → **The Initial Study**

NO ↓

Is it discretionary? — YES ↗ **The Initial Study**

NO ↓

No further action required

Will the project have a significant environmental impact? — YES → **Environmental Impact Report**

NO ↓

Negative Declaration

justice advocates, who say CEQA should not be weakened in poor and inner-city areas.

Categorical exemptions (those exemptions specified by the Resources Agency) are divided into some 32 categories, but they include building projects of under 10,000 square feet, projects of three homes or fewer, projects that will result in "minor alterations on the land," and the transfer of land ownership in order to create parks. (A complete list of the exemptions is included in Article 19 of the CEQA Guidelines.)

Step 2. The Initial Study

If a development proposal is found to be a project under CEQA, and is not exempt, the local government then moves on to the next step: an assessment to determine if the project may produce "significant" environmental effects.

To a great extent, significance is in the eye of the beholder. Unlike most other states with similar laws, California does not establish formal thresholds of significance in different areas of environmental impact. The state does include a list of significant effects in the CEQA Guidelines—for example, any project that would have a major impact on the aesthetic quality of an area; "substantially diminish" a habitat for fish, wildlife, or plant life; or displace a large number of people is considered significant. But the Guidelines do not define any of these terms.

Unlike most other states with similar laws, California does not establish formal thresholds of significance in different areas of environmental impact.

Instead, the determination of what's significant is left to each local government and, more frequently, to the professional judgment of the consultant or staff member doing the CEQA analysis. Many consulting firms that routinely conduct CEQA analysis have a large database of information for the geographical areas where they typically work, and they may have their own formal or informal thresholds of significance. With its 1998 amendments to the CEQA guidelines, the Wilson administration attempted to increase the use of thresholds of significance as a way of making CEQA more predictable. A threshold might be, for example, 500 vehicle trips per day; therefore, any project that generated more than 500 trips per day would be said to have a significant impact. However, the courts struck down the thresholds of significance amendment because it allowed an agency that had adopted thresholds of significance to rely on them solely, and not to have to consider a "fair argument" that an impact was potentially significant. The court said the fair argument standard remained in place. *Communities for a Better Environment v. California Resources Agency,* 103 Cal. App. 4th 98 (2002).

In the initial study, a local planner or consultant uses a checklist to assess all the environmental factors and determine if the project may have significant environmental impacts.

Significance determinations are usually made with the assistance of an initial study. In the initial study, a local planner or consultant uses a checklist to assess all the environmental factors and determine if the project may have significant environmental impacts. This checklist usually includes a long list of possible areas of environmental damage that government agencies should review—geology, air pollution, damage to plant and animal life, and so on. In the past, many cities have used such a checklist in stripped-down form, checking "yes," "no," or "maybe" with no further explanation. Though widely used in the '70s and '80s, the so-called "naked checklist" is now illegal as the result of a court of appeal ruling in 1988.

If the initial study reveals that the project will have no significant environmental effects, then the local government prepares a negative declaration.

If the initial study reveals that the project will have no significant environmental effects, then the local government prepares a document known as a "negative declaration," a simple declaration that no further environmental review is needed. Sometimes, if a developer can eliminate all significant environmental effects by changing his project or adopting mitigation measures, the local government will prepare what is known as a "mitigated negative declaration"—meaning certain steps must be taken but no further environmental review is necessary. (*See* "Mitigated Negative Declaration," page 166.) Environmental lawyers argue that it is often used as a means of short-circuiting environmental review.

The case that outlawed the naked checklist involved both a checklist problem and problems created by a mitigated negative declaration. A private developer proposed building a sewage treatment plant for a small development project along the Mendocino County coast. In conducting the initial study, Mendocino County planners checked "no" for 38 of the checklist's 43 questions and provided a boilerplate answer for the other questions, where environmental problems had been identified. The permit was approved, with a mitigated negative declaration requiring approval from regional air pollution and water quality boards, as well as a plan for sludge disposal.

This skimpy environmental review up front led to problems later on. As it turned out, the Regional Water Quality Control Board found hydrological problems. The county then required the applicant, Harold K. Miller, to submit drainage studies. Miller then proposed a drainage solution, and the board of supervisors approved the project.

The county's environmental review did not hold up in court. In the *Sundstrom* case, the court of appeal in San Francisco wrote: "The initial study... displayed only a token observance of regulatory requirements. In the case of several questions marked "no," evidence clearly disclosed that the project would disturb existing conditions, e.g., change present drainage characteristics and alter local plant conditions." *Sundstrom v. County of Mendocino,* 202 Cal. App. 3d 296 (1988). The court went on to say that a naked checklist did not satisfy CEQA's goal of providing the public with detailed information about the environmental impact of a project.

Therefore, a "no" on the checklist now must be accompanied by a short explanation of why there will be no environmental impact. Longtime CEQA lawyer Dallas Holmes (now a Riverside County Superior Court judge), who coined the term "naked checklist," likens the requirement to the tenth grade math teacher's admonition that students show their work. Being required to show one's work discourages cheating or guessing—a goal of both tenth grade math teachers and California judges reviewing CEQA cases.

The *Sundstrom* case also ended the common practice of approving projects contingent on the results of subsequent environmental studies. An appellate court based in Fresno built on this theme in a case involving the Diablo Grande resort in the hills of Stanislaus County west of Interstate 5. The court said Stanislaus County could not approve part of the project while deferring an analysis of water supply for the entire project. *Stanislaus Natural Heritage Project v. County of Stanislaus,* (1996) 48 Cal. App. 4th 182.

The Sundstrom *case ended the common practice of approving projects contingent on the results of subsequent environmental studies.*

The Mitigated Negative Declaration

ONE OF THE REALITIES of environmental law is that when a particular requirement begins to take so much time and money that the businesses being regulated balk, environmental practices are made more flexible to minimize the cost and annoyance to them. Despite CEQA's consistently bad press, this axiom is just as true for CEQA as it is for the Clean Air Act or the Endangered Species Act. Take, for example, the mitigated negative declaration.

When CEQA was passed in 1970, no one contemplated the emergence of the mitigated negative declaration. The second step of the three-step process would lead to one of two results: a negative declaration or an EIR. Since early EIRs were thin and cheap—more like today's initial studies—this distinction wasn't a big problem. But in the late '70s and early '80s, things began to change.

As the courts expanded CEQA requirements, the time and cost required to prepare an EIR grew exponentially. EIRs ran to hundreds and sometimes thousands of pages, and even just responding to comments on draft EIRs was an enormous chore. The distinction between a negative declaration and an EIR became a chasm. And it was clear that in many cases, the potential "significant impact" of a particular project was confined to a few specific areas of concern.

So in the early 1980s, some CEQA practitioners devised the idea of a "mitigated"

➡

Step 3. The Environmental Impact Report

If the initial study reveals that the project may have a significant environmental impact, the local government must prepare an environmental impact report. EIRs are prepared for only the small minority of projects which, according to the initial study, "may" produce significant environmental effects. But, as many courts have pointed out, the EIR is the heart of CEQA—a broad-ranging document meant to provide lots of information to the public about the environmental effects of a big project.

In many ways, only the EIR can satisfy CEQA's requirement of informing the public. Even an annotated initial study will provide relatively little information about a project's environmental effects. That is why the courts, when presented with the question, usually have ruled that EIRs should be prepared on large projects.

Because of ever-broadening court directives about what it must contain, however, the EIR has become expensive and time-consuming. The typical EIR costs around $50,000 to $100,000 and takes months to prepare; the team of consultants typically includes planners, geologists, biologists, even paleontologists. On very large projects, EIRs often go through several rounds, take several months (or years), and cost more than $1 million.

Developers often fight the preparation of an EIR for several reasons. The most obvious reason is the cost, which they must bear. In more than 100 cities and counties, developers are allowed to hire environmental consultants directly to prepare the EIR. The city or county then adopts the EIR as its own, but the most that the local government has done is review documents the developer submitted. In most cities and counties, the planning department hires the EIR consultant, and payment is funneled from the developer through the local government to ensure greater objectivity.

The direct cost of the EIR may be the least of the developer's concerns however. Far more important is the time that preparing and debating an EIR takes. If an EIR takes six months and $200,000 to prepare, the cost to the developer is far more than $200,000, because in all likelihood the developer is "carrying" the property—making option or interest payments each month that could amount to several hundred thousand dollars on a large parcel of land. A lengthy environmental review process can kill a project if a developer does not have deep pockets. Furthermore, the EIR is likely to greatly increase the cost of building a project, because the developer will be responsible for "mitigating" (minimizing or eliminating) any likely environmental damage identified in the EIR.

Types of EIRs

EIRs come in all shapes and sizes, and the distinctions are important. Sometimes they are prepared for specific development projects, sometimes for larger planning processes. Sometimes a series of EIRs is prepared on large projects; other times EIRs are added to or supplemented as new information arises. Here is a rundown:

Development-specific EIRs. The most common EIR deals with a specific development project—an office building, a hotel, a subdivision, a road-building project.

General plan EIRs. A city's general plan is also a project and, thus, extensive EIRs are usually prepared in conjunction with the preparation or revision of a general plan and/or its elements. The general plan revision and its EIR are often prepared simultaneously, sometimes even as part of the same document.

Master EIRs and tiering. Master EIRs and tiering are used to encourage efficiency in environmental review. CEQA encourages local governments to use master EIRs to deal with a series of related actions that may occur under one program. But program EIRs do not necessarily eliminate the need for more detailed environmental review on each specific action.

Tiering is a similar concept used in dealing with very large projects that will be reviewed and built over a long period of time, as with an extensive road-building program. For example, tiering was used to build three toll highways in Orange County. Initially, a broad EIR was prepared to examine the environmental impact of various proposed corridors. When the alternative corridors were narrowed to about three, a more detailed EIR on the specific environmental impact of those three alternatives was prepared. Finally, when a route corridor was selected—when, in the

negative declaration. A mitigated negative declaration is simply a negative declaration with a set of mitigation conditions attached to it. The idea was that in those cases where the potentially significant impact was limited to just a few areas, the impact could be reduced to an insignificant level, and an environmental impact report would not be necessary. The mitigated negative declaration was thus conceived as "middle ground" between a traditional negative declaration and an EIR.

The mitigated negative declaration was not recognized as a valid device in CEQA practice at first. However, it was upheld as legitimate by the Third District Court of Appeal in 1982 in *Perley v. County of Calaveras,* 137 Cal. App. 3d 424. Once a court had signalled its approval, the practice become more widespread. A few years later, the mitigated negative declaration was acknowledged in the CEQA Guidelines as legitimate. However, it was not recognized as part of the CEQA law itself until the reform legislation of 1993, more than a decade after the *Perley* decision was handed down.

Today mitigated negative declarations are an important part of the CEQA landscape. As one survey revealed, more than half of all negative declarations in the state are "mitigated" negative declarations. For years, mitigated negative declarations received scant attention in CEQA literature and textbooks. Since the mid-'90s, however, CEQA experts have been providing planners with ➡

guidance on when to use mitigated negative declarations.

An advisory paper on mitigated negative declarations published by the Office of Planning and Research in 2004 lists three prerequisites for adopting a mitigated negative declaration:

1. The lead agency must make a good faith effort to determine whether the project would have a significant impact.

2. Project revisions or mitigations must be incorporated into the project to alleviate potential impacts before the public review process begins.

3. There must be evidence to support the lead agency's determination that there will be no significant impact as a result of the mitigated project.

Additionally, the Office of Planning and Research makes clear that the project proponent must accept the project revisions or mitigations prior to the public review process. This makes the mitigated negative declaration far different from the EIR, in which mitigations often result from the public review process.

Of course, the temptation to use the faster and cheaper mitigated negative declaration, rather than an EIR, has led to trouble for some cities and counties. In a number of cases, courts have told a local government that its mitigated negative declaration was inadequate under CEQA, usually because there was evidence that not all impacts were being offset. ■

words of one lawyer who worked on the project, the decision boiled down to "which trees to fell"—a project-style EIR was produced.

On the one hand, tiering provides more environmental information earlier in the process than a standard EIR produced after the planning work has been done; on the other hand, if the entire process takes several years, the initial EIR's information may be out of date.

Some practitioners say that tiering is tricky business, and that neither the law itself nor the CEQA Guidelines make Master EIRs and tiering a truly efficient approach to environmental review. Additionally, an appeals court in 2002 threw out a tiered EIR for a proposed water transfer because the Master EIR had been invalidated earlier by a different court. *Friends of the Santa Clara River v. Castaic Lake Water Agency*, 95 Cal. App. 4th 1373 (2002). The court ruling made some practitioners that much more wary of the approach.

Additions, supplements, etc. Over time, the project in question might change, or new information may come to light about its environmental consequences. If so, further review under CEQA may be necessary. The extent of that review, however, depends on the scale and significance of these changes.

Technical corrections that do not involve substantive changes can be included in an addendum. If only small changes are required, a supplemental EIR will suffice. If the project has been substantially changed, however, a subsequent EIR may be necessary. Unlike a supplemental EIR, which need deal only with the changes in the project, a subsequent EIR is really an entirely new EIR, subject to the same notification and review requirements of the original EIR.

In practice, local governments often prepare a supplemental EIR when a subsequent EIR is called for—especially if there is political pressure to push the project through. The reasons for doing so are obvious. A supplemental EIR is far less costly and time-consuming, and it does not open up the entire environmental review process for discussion. Also, in many cases, city approvals may be based on the certification of a previous EIR and neither city officials nor applicants want to jeopardize that approval.

Draft and final EIRs. The last important distinction must be made between the draft EIR and the final EIR. The draft EIR is the original document, with all environmental analysis, prepared by the local government staff or consultant. The draft is circulated to a vast array of individuals and organizations, including citizen groups, lobbying organizations, public utilities, and state and federal agencies. These people then comment on the draft and the staff or planning consultant must respond to all the comments. The comments and responses are then incorporated into the final EIR. If additional environmental information is revealed after the draft EIR is circulated, that information must also be circulated for comment.

The draft EIR is circulated to a vast array of individuals and organizations, including citizen groups, lobbying organizations, public utilities, and state and federal agencies.

Contents and Preparation of EIRs

Both CEQA and the CEQA Guidelines contain requirements governing the organization and content of an environmental impact report. In keeping with CEQA's reputation as a complicated, procedurally oriented law, however, any one of these requirements can be used (or abused) to shape the scope of environmental review.

Both the CEQA law and the Guidelines contain requirements governing the organization and content of an environmental impact report.

For example, the EIR must contain a project description which includes, among other things, a statement of the project's objectives. At first this requirement may sound straightforward and innocuous. But its wording can alter the entire CEQA process regarding the project—especially the discussion of alternatives to the project, which is becoming a significant part of environmental review. Take, for example, a proposed highway. If the description states that the project's objective is to improve the flow of vehicle traffic, then the alternatives are likely to include a narrow range of alternative routes, configurations, and sizes. If, on the other hand, the project's objective is stated to be the fast and efficient transportation of people, then the alternatives will be much broader: buses, light rail, high occupancy-vehicle lanes, perhaps even a monorail. A highway is almost certain to be more environmentally significant than the transit alternatives, but if the transit alternatives do not meet the project's objectives, they will not even be considered under CEQA.

The EIR also must contain two elements designed to make it easy to read and understand. First is a table of contents or index. Second is a summary of its contents, written in understandable language, that does not exceed 15 pages. As EIRs become longer and more technical, these provisions become more important in achieving CEQA's goal of public information and debate.

The EIR must contain a table of contents or index and a summary of its contents, written in understandable language, that does not exceed 15 pages.

The EIR also must contain discussion of several important items relating to the environmental impact of a project. They are:

- **Significant** environmental effects
- **Unavoidable** environmental effects
- **Significant irreversible** environmental change
- **Alternatives** to the proposed project
- **Cumulative impact** that the project might have in combination with other projects
- **Growth-inducing impact** of the project
- **Mitigation measures** that will minimize the environmental effects

The first three items (significant, unavoidable, and irreversible effects) are usually combined into a lengthy "impact analysis" compiled by environmental scientists, traffic engineers, and other experts. The next three items (alternatives, cumulative impact, and growth-inducing impact) have traditionally been called "back-of-the-book" items and have been given only the most cursory treatment in EIRs. Mitigation measures have always received considerable attention in the CEQA process, but until recently little attention has been paid to whether they are actually carried out.

Mitigation measures have always received considerable attention in the CEQA process, but until recently little attention has been paid to whether they are actually carried out.

Impact Analysis

The impact analysis usually constitutes most of the EIR. It is, in essence, a more detailed version of an initial study's checklist. In the EIR, any item checked "yes" or "maybe" will receive its own detailed discussion: air quality, water supply, traffic, plant and animal life, and so forth. A typical format is to divide the impact analysis section into four parts: the current environmental setting (which is required by law), the impact analysis, a list of mitigation measures, and a final description of the environmental setting after the project has been built and the mitigation measures have been implemented.

These sections are typically written by specialists, such as traffic consultants, biologists, and archaeologists. (Sometimes these specialists are on the staffs of the planning consultants that do EIRs, and sometimes they are sub-consultants.) Some of this specialized material is gathered specifically for the project in question, but most EIRs rely heavily on databases in common use.

Traffic consultants, for example, may make counts of current traffic near the site. But to forecast the impact, they will almost certainly use the so-called "trip tables" from the Institute of

Transportation Engineers to determine how many vehicle trips are likely to be generated from the construction of a certain number of houses or a certain amount of office space. Similarly, biologists will walk the site to survey plant and animal life. But they will also use a state database of plants and animal life, and compile their own databases if they do many environmental surveys in the same area. At its best, this material can be insightful and useful. At its worst, it is true "boilerplate." In fact, some of the information is so easily transferable from one document to another that occasionally EIRs or their technical background reports will contain accidental references to another city or another project.

The adequacy of these scientific inquiries may, of course, always be challenged in court. And if something important is overlooked by a technical expert, or by a planning consultant summarizing the technical expert's work for the EIR, the EIR may become legally vulnerable and the project may be in jeopardy. The last-minute discovery of an endangered species on the property, for example, is almost certain to kill or delay a project. In recent years, however, the scientific analysis in the EIR has not been the source of legal challenge and controversy. Most of the attention has been focused on the back-of-the-book items and on the effectiveness of mitigation measures.

If something important is overlooked, the EIR may become legally vulnerable and the project may be in jeopardy.

The Back-of-the-Book Items

Traditionally, the back-of-the-book items—cumulative impacts, growth-inducing impacts, and alternatives—have received very little attention, often as little as a page or two in an EIR. Partly this is because the methods of analysis required have not been well developed. But in part this cursory review of back-of-the-book items has come from a desire to keep EIRs short and inexpensive. These items were simply not considered as valuable as the objective scientific information gathered by specialists. However, as growth and growth control have loomed larger as political and legal issues in California, agencies have been under considerable pressure to give these sections equal time.

Additionally, more and more litigation focuses on back-of-the-book items, possibly because environmental attorneys have come to recognize the traditionally weak treatment provided to these issues. As a result, EIRs today provide a fuller discussion of cumulative impacts, growth-inducing impacts, and alternatives analysis than EIRs of 10 or 20 years ago.

Cumulative Impact

The main purpose of the cumulative impact requirement is to make sure that a community does not approve a series of small projects without considering the overall effect of these actions on the environment.

The main purpose of the cumulative impact requirement is to make sure that a community does not approve a series of small projects without considering the overall effect of these actions on the environment. (Similarly, the cumulative impact requirement should make it harder for developers to slice large projects up into smaller pieces in order to avoid a full CEQA review.)

Cumulative impact was given little attention until 1984, when the court of appeal in San Francisco forced the city of San Francisco to rewrite EIRs on four downtown skyscrapers because cumulative impact had not been considered adequately. *San Franciscans for Reasonable Growth v. City and County of San Francisco,* 151 Cal. App. 3d 61 (1984). Specifically, the court said the San Francisco Planning Commission should have taken into account the likely construction of several additional office projects. (Some had already been approved, some were in the pipeline, and others, while they had not yet been formally proposed, were the subject of wide discussion.) "The only reason we can infer for the commission's failure to consider and analyze this group of projects was that it was more expedient to ignore them," the court said.

The San Francisco case was a good example of both the weaknesses and the strengths of CEQA. The EIRs were routinely redrafted and recertified with hardly any fanfare, so the opinion had no effect on the construction project. Moreover, the buildings were almost finished by the time the court handed down its ruling. Yet the slow-growthers who brought the suit used the court ruling as another piece of evidence in their frankly political (and ultimately successful) struggle to curb office construction in downtown San Francisco. And, of course, once the court of appeal ruling was on the books, planners in San Francisco and elsewhere in the state had to pay attention to it.

The cumulative impact requirement got another boost four years later in the California Supreme Court's ruling in the *Laurel Heights* case. Though it has received more publicity for its discussion of alternatives under CEQA (which will be explained in detail below), this case also discouraged developers from cutting a project up into phases in order to avoid a tough cumulative-impact analysis. The University of California, San Francisco, had proposed moving its medical laboratories to the Laurel Heights neighborhood. Though UCSF clearly planned to move all its labs to Laurel Heights eventually, the EIR dealt only with the initial phase of the move. The

Supreme Court struck down this approach, saying an EIR must deal with all "reasonably foreseeable future uses" associated with the project. *Laurel Heights Improvement Association v. Regents of the University of California,* 47 Cal. 3d 376 (1988).

Although the *San Franciscans for Reasonable Growth* and *Laurel Heights* opinions were issued during the 1980s, practitioners' understanding of how to treat cumulative impacts has not improved. The appeals court decision striking down some of the Wilson administration's CEQA Guideline amendments added to the confusion. The court invalidated a new guideline allowing planners to determine that a project's contribution to a cumulative condition (usually poor air quality) was "de minimis" and, therefore, not deserving of further study. The court said that the "one molecule rule" was inappropriate, but also that comparisons and ratios were not proper either. Instead, the court ruled, "[T]he lead agency shall consider whether the cumulative impact is significant and whether the proposed project's incremental effects are cumulatively considerable." The opinion was met with a collective scratching of heads.

Growth-Inducing Impact

Unlike cumulative impact, the question of growth-inducing impact has not been the subject of landmark court rulings. And the analytical methods available for a growth-inducement study have been weak. Typically, a growth-inducement section will include a page or less of general information about the relationship of the project to the region's growth generally. For example, the growth-inducement section of a draft EIR prepared years ago for a 1.5-million-square-foot office building in downtown Los Angeles was only three paragraphs long. It described the number of jobs that would be created by the construction of the project, stated in vague terms that migration to the region might result, and concluded by saying that the project was consistent with L.A.'s policy objective that the downtown area serve as a "regional center."

As "growth control" and "growth management" have become the main buzzwords of planning in California, however, the concept of "growth inducement" is likely to become more important as well. In Orange County, for example, the growth-inducing impact of the new toll highways became a major issue. Supporters said the highways would simply relieve current traffic congestion. Opponents said the highways had the backing of developers because they would open up new areas for development.

Unlike cumulative impact, the question of growth-inducing impact has not been the subject of landmark court rulings, and analytical methods available for a growth-inducement study have been weak.

Making such distinctions is not easy. It is not hard to understand that the construction of a new road is likely to induce growth in a localized fashion—encouraging the construction of gas stations, motels, and convenience stores at critical interchanges. But regional growth depends on a whole range of economic forces that are local, national, and international in scope. Furthermore, it is hard to assess the growth-inducing impact of new facilities in an already urbanized area.

Alternatives

The CEQA Guidelines state that an agency should not approve a project if there are feasible alternatives available that would substantially lessen any significant effects.

The CEQA Guidelines state that an agency should not approve a project "if there are feasible alternatives... available that would substantially lessen any significant effects." For this reason, EIRs must discuss a range of "reasonable" alternatives. An environmentally preferable alternative must be selected unless it is "infeasible." In recent years, the courts have greatly broadened the required alternatives analysis.

Traditionally, an EIR's alternatives analysis discussed only variations on the proposed project. For example, turning once again to the proposed office tower in downtown Los Angeles, the alternatives included a smaller project; concentrating development on one part of the site or another; using the site for public facilities instead of private offices (because the site was publicly owned); and constructing no project at all. (The "no project" alternative is required under California case law.) Alternative sites have usually not been considered, because landowners typically own only one site.

EIR Alternatives Analysis

In 1988, however, the California Supreme Court ruled in the *Laurel Heights* case that alternative sites must be extensively examined in an EIR, at least when public projects are involved. The UC Regents had argued that little discussion of alternatives was necessary because the university had concluded that all alternatives were infeasible. But the Supreme Court said that the purpose of alternatives analysis is not just to inform decisionmakers but also the public: "Without meaningful analysis of alternatives, neither the courts nor the public can fulfill their proper roles in the CEQA process."

But two years later, the Supreme Court declined to extend the alternative site requirements to all private projects. Ruling in a case commonly known as *Citizens of Goleta Valley*, the court said that alternative sites need not be considered if the private landowners involved don't have a feasible chance of purchasing the land. The case involved a proposal to build a large Hyatt Hotel on a beachfront property near Santa Barbara. The court of appeal had ruled that many alternative sites should have been seriously analyzed—even those that did not lie within Santa Barbara County's jurisdiction—because CEQA is designed to serve the public, not the landowner. But the Supreme Court concluded that there is no point in analyzing alternative sites if the landowner in question won't be able to use them for the proposed project. However, the court did say that when feasible alternative sites are available, an EIR should consider them even if the project is private. *Citizens of Goleta Valley v. Board of Supervisors,* 52 Cal. 3d 553 (1990).

The 1998 update to the CEQA Guidelines tried to clarify things, but kept open the door for plenty of arguments. The Guidelines state that an EIR "must consider a reasonable range of potentially feasible alternatives that will foster informed decisionmaking and public participation. An EIR is not required to consider alternatives which are infeasible." So far, so good. But the Guidelines continue, "there is no ironclad rule governing the nature or scope of the alternatives to be discussed other than the rule of reason." Guidelines § 15126.6(a).

Public projects have continued to be at the forefront of battles over alternatives, especially the "no project" alternative. In 2000, the court of appeal invalidated an EIR for an enormous State Water Project plan for allocating water, in part because the EIR's no project alternative did not consider that existing water contracts could be interpreted in a variety of ways. *Planning & Conserv. League v. Department of Water Resources,* 83 Cal. App. 4th 892 (2000). In a different case, the court rejected an EIR for a Russian River water project because the EIR did not address alternatives that might be required based on cumulative impacts of the project and an unrelated hydroelectric project involving the same water. If the cumulative impacts were significant (the court also rejected the cumulative impacts analysis), the court held that the EIR would have to provide alternatives. *Friends of the Eel River v. Sonoma County Water Agency,* 108 Cal. App. 4th 859 (2003).

Public projects have continued to be at the forefront of battles over alternatives, especially the "no project" alternative.

Governmental Action and Mitigation

If an environmental impact report prepared under CEQA does identify "significant environmental effects," then the governmental agency reviewing the project has four options:

- **Deny the project.** The discovery of significant environmental effects is, in and of itself, sufficient legal grounds to turn down a development project altogether.

- **Approve an environmentally preferable alternative** to the project, as identified in the EIR.
- **Approve the project,** but only if "mitigation measures" are adopted to lessen the environmental impact.
- **Approve the project in spite of** environmental effects and adopt a statement of overriding considerations, usually outlining the project's economic benefit.

The statement of overriding considerations is the escape valve which permits a local government to approve a project in spite of environmental damage.

In practice, the first two actions (denial and approval of alternatives) rarely occur, while the third and fourth (mitigation and overriding considerations) are used in most instances. The statement of overriding considerations is the escape valve which permits a local government to approve a project in spite of environmental damage.

It is this provision which places the final environmental decision in the hands of local officials, instead of making it an inevitable outcome of environmental investigation and review. As one CEQA lawyer put it: "The EIR could show the most horrendous environmental consequences of a particular activity. And a planning commission or city council could approve the project by saying, 'Yes, we know about all these horrendous environmental effects; however, there are overriding considerations which permit us to approve the project anyway.'"

For example, an EIR for an 11,000-housing unit project in the Central Valley city of Lathrop identified unmitigated impacts on traffic, air quality, agricultural resources, mineral resources, public services and utilities, and fisheries. But in 2003 the Lathrop City Council overrode those impacts because the project, known as River Islands, would provide jobs and a diverse mix of housing.

In theory, a statement of overriding considerations may be adopted only if it is supported by information on the record; findings are required to explain how this conclusion is drawn. In practice, overriding considerations are often used when a project's environmental damage is significant but local officials have other reasons (usually tax benefits but sometimes political reasons as well) for wanting to see the project approved. In many cases, the required findings are skimpy because the environmental damage is well documented but the supposed benefits of the project are not.

Perhaps the most common route is to approve a project, but require the developer to implement mitigation measures to lessen its environmental impact. In fact, without a statement of overriding considerations, a project with significant environmental effects can be approved only if the developer agrees to perform feasible mitigation measures.

Mitigation can mean anything from replacing destroyed trees to a mandatory carpooling program. If a project is subject to discretionary approval, CEQA-identified mitigation measures often form the basis for the conditions of approval; in cities with an active environmental community, these conditions can sometimes number 100 or more. No matter how many mitigation measures are required, however, local governments are faced with the difficult question of figuring out how to make sure the measures are actually carried out.

Mitigation can mean anything from replacing destroyed trees to a mandatory carpooling program.

As conditions of approval have proliferated because of CEQA's mitigation requirements, lack of follow-up has become a more significant problem. And as these conditions have become more performance- or service-oriented, their implementation has become harder to check. It is not difficult to determine whether trucks are loading and unloading only at certain hours during construction. It is much more difficult to determine whether an ambitious carpooling program is still working five years after the project is built.

A study by the University of California, Davis, revealed that only 27 percent of the state's cities always make site visits to monitor mitigation measures. (For counties the figure was 54 percent.) The same study revealed that more than half of all local agencies never even receive a follow-up letter from developers regarding mitigation measures, though in this case the cities did better than the counties. Other surveys have found widespread lack of compliance with requirements for conservation easements and ride-sharing programs.

A study by the University of California, Davis, revealed that only 27 percent of the state's cities always make site visits to monitor mitigation measures.

In fact, the problem of monitoring mitigation measures became so significant that in 1988 the legislature took the rare step of amending CEQA to deal with the negligence. The law, AB 3180, requires local governments to establish a program to monitor the mitigation measures they require of developers. (Public Resources Code §21081.6) The law is very short and not very specific, and different local governments have implemented it in different ways. Some are calling on building inspectors and zoning administrators to add environmental monitoring to their duties. Others have hired environmental experts in the planning department to run monitoring programs. Many have asked their regular EIR consultants to fold mitigation monitoring programs into their other work.

Protector of the Environment or Paper Tiger?

CEQA can be such an emotional issue to participants in the land use planning process that it is often difficult to determine how effective a tool it has been in protecting the environment. There is no question that CEQA has achieved its goal of informing the public and generating public debate on the environmental consequences of building projects. Reams of environmental information are now available on virtually every large project, and the debate among citizens and local elected officials usually takes place on a sophisticated and informed level.

CEQA calls on local governments to establish many processes designed to make developers and public agencies accountable for the environmental impact of their projects, but frequently the processes are reduced to rote exercises.

On the other hand, CEQA can easily be viewed as a paper tiger, which generates a tremendous amount of material—at tremendous cost—but doesn't necessarily safeguard the environment. CEQA calls on local governments to establish many processes designed to make developers (and public agencies) accountable for the environmental impact of their projects. Frequently, however, those processes are reduced to rote exercises. The analysis in an environmental impact report becomes cut-and-paste boilerplate material, for example, or the checklist in an initial study becomes automatic and unthinking. So then the courts or the legislature will impose a new requirement meant to make up for the emptiness of these processes: requiring annotations in the checklist, for example, or a plan to monitor otherwise meaningless mitigation measures. Soon enough, however, these new requirements become empty exercises as well, as EIR consultants develop boilerplate material for checklist annotations, and prepare monitoring plans that are no more likely to be implemented than the mitigation measures they're supposed to be monitoring.

A mid-1990s analysis of CEQA by researchers at UC Berkeley and the University of Illinois is probably the most comprehensive look at the law ever undertaken. The researchers' conclusions and recommendations provide a useful benchmark for understanding how CEQA could be changed for the better. These conclusions boiled down to three different points:

- **Broader issues are not well integrated into the CEQA review process.** The participation of state and regional agencies is spotty, and it is much harder to consider issues of cumulative impact than issues specific to the project at hand.
- **Alternatives analysis isn't very useful.** Despite the knock-down, drag-out fight over alternatives in the courts since the mid-1980s, there is still no effective way to deal with alternatives analysis, especially for private projects.
- **CEQA review by both local governments and judges is not consistent or predictable enough.** This is the nub of most CEQA criticism. Once you get into the CEQA loop, you're never quite sure when or how you'll get out of it.

These problems are perhaps inherent in a process-oriented state law such as CEQA, which does not impose environmental values on local decisionmakers. A community's values remain the same, CEQA or not. If political forces drive a city or county in a certain direction—whether it's an overall pro-development policy or the approval of a specific project—CEQA is not going to change that direction. That is why local governments all over the state are constantly approving, for example, land-consuming, auto-oriented real estate projects in spite of the undeniable environmental degradation involved.

A community's values remain the same, CEQA or not. If political forces drive a city or county in a certain direction, CEQA is not going to change that direction.

On the other hand, one of CEQA's overarching goals was to foster an environmental consciousness in California, and clearly the law has succeeded in this respect. CEQA inevitably provides a lot of environmental information to anyone who cares to pay attention, and the sum total of CEQA's processes over 35 years—empty and rote as any individual process may be—has encouraged many people to pay attention. And that is exactly what the legislators who drafted the bill had in mind.

Local Planning: Advanced Techniques and Backlash

Chapter 10

Exactions

In 1988, businessman Richard K. Ehrlich decided to try to build condominiums on a piece of land he owned in the Los Angeles suburb of Culver City. Ehrlich had owned the property for several years, but had a hard time making profitable use of it. A private tennis club located on the site had gone out of business years before, and he later approached the city about an office building, but then abandoned the idea.

When Ehrlich applied for a zone change and general plan amendment for the condos, the city imposed a $280,000 "recreation fee." The money was meant to mitigate the community's loss of the four tennis courts at the club, even though the club was private and had been closed for several years.

Given the contentious nature of California land use planning, it was not surprising that Ehrlich sued the city, claiming that the recreation fee was so unfair that it amounted to an unconstitutional taking of his property. What is surprising is that six years later, the California Supreme Court didn't agree. Though suggesting that $280,000 might have been too much, the court concluded that "the city has met its burden of demonstrating the required connection or nexus between the rezoning...and the imposition of a monetary exaction to be expended in support of recreational purposes as a means of mitigating that loss." *Ehrlich v. City of Culver City*, 12 Cal. 4th 854 (1996).

The *Ehrlich* case remains a legal cornerstone. But Culver City's recreation fee on the Ehrlich property is only one example of the lengths to which local governments in California are willing to go to impose "exactions." The concept of exacting concessions from

Given the contentious nature of California land use planning, it was not surprising that Ehrlich sued the city, claiming that the recreation fee was so unfair that it amounted to an unconstitutional taking of his property.

developers in exchange for permission to build is generations old. But since the passage of Proposition 13 in 1978, it has become a major instrument of planning policy in California.

The reason for this change is obvious. Proposition 13 dramatically reduced local government property tax revenue and made it much more difficult for cities and counties to issue infrastructure bonds. The passage of Proposition 13 also coincided with the decline of state and federal grant programs that had once provided a good portion of the infrastructure money localities needed to finance growth. During years of big public works projects prior to Proposition 13, the state would fund up to 80 percent of the cost of highway projects (with much of the state's portion being a pass-through of federal dollars). Twenty-five years later, highway projects are more likely to be 50-50 state-local efforts. Thus, when fast-growing Riverside County drew up a plan that called for two new transportation corridors and other major highway improvements, the county and 14 cities began charging developers $6,650 for every new house to pay for the highway construction.

Proposition 13 dramatically reduced local government tax revenue and virtually eliminated the ability of cities and counties to issue infrastructure bonds.

Increasingly, local governments have called upon growth to pay for itself—in other words, for developers to hold the community financially harmless for any problems that new growth might create. Since the approval of Proposition 13, cities and counties in California have become highly skilled at using land use planning and approval processes to obtain these exactions from developers. And they have become more creative in dreaming up exactions that may or may not be directly related to the project in question. Political pressure to have developers solve all community problems is great, especially given general taxpayer reluctance to pay for past "deficits" in community facilities. Just as quickly, landowners and developers have struck back. As part of the property rights movement (described in more detail in chapter 20), they have sought to rein in the exactions movement and make it more accountable.

Since approval of Proposition 13, cities and counties in California have become highly skilled at using land use planning and approval processes to obtain these exactions from developers.

Legal Basis for Exactions

In general, the power to exact concessions from developers is part of a local government's police power. Exactions, if proper, further a legitimate governmental (public) interest. Because it is an exercise of the police power, the process of exacting concessions from developers can be derived from the general plan and zoning ordinance. Probably the oldest arena for exactions, however, is the subdivision approval process. Because subdivision review emphasized the need for responsible site planning, the process recognized that developers had to account for the consequences of their projects. For example, they would have to build roads and sidewalks within the subdivision, or at least set aside the land required. At first even these modest requirements were challenged. A landmark case from the 1950s addressed whether a "taking" occurred if a city required developers to provide curbs, gutters, and storm sewers. (The city's view was upheld.) *Petterson v. City of Naperville*, 137 N.E.2d 371 (1956).

At first exactions were permitted only when there was a direct relationship—a direct "nexus" in legal terms—between the exactions required and the project in question. For example, if a locality required developers to dedicate land for streets within new subdivisions, or even to build those streets, the direct nexus was clear; without the subdivision, the streets would not be needed.

At first exactions were permitted only when there was a direct relationship between the exactions required and the project in question.

In time, the legally acceptable definition of nexus expanded, especially in California. A developer required to dedicate land for streets, because the residents of the subdivision would use them, surely could be required to dedicate land for a new school, because children from that subdivision would need a school. Similarly, a developer could be required to set aside land for a park to serve the new subdivision.

Soon, the idea of exactions expanded to include not just the provision of land or facilities, but also the payment of funds "in lieu of" the land and facilities. For example, during the 1960s the legislature specifically authorized both dedication of land and payment of in lieu fees for parks in the Quimby Act. Govt. Code § 66477. (To this day, these fees are commonly referred to around the state as "Quimby fees.")

During the 1970s, the requirement of a direct nexus was broken, and localities emerged with a great deal more legal power in exacting concessions from developers. In a 1971 case known as *Associated Home Builders*, the California Supreme Court ruled that an indirect relationship between the project in question and the exaction required was legally acceptable. *Associated Home Builders, Inc. v. City of Walnut Creek*, 4 Cal. 3d 633 (1971). Subsequently, the Attorney General's Office concluded that the 1971 consistency legislation, combined with *Associated Home Builders*, gave local governments a great deal more power to exact concessions. In essence, any exaction could be imposed, so long as it furthered the implementation of the city's general plan and bore at least an

In the 1970s, the direct nexus requirement was broken, and localities emerged with a great deal more legal power in exacting concessions from developers.

indirect relationship to the development project being proposed. 59 Ops. Cal. Atty. Gen. 129 (1976).

After Proposition 13 passed in 1978, local governments began leaning more heavily on the broad powers they had acquired in the preceding few years. Fees for child care and public art became popular in certain cities, including Culver City, which imposed an arts fee as well as a recreational fee on the Ehrlich project. A few cities even imposed fees on office developers to pay for new affordable housing supposedly necessary to accommodate the new office workers. These "linkage fees" were aggressively challenged in court but never overturned. Linkage fees—which top $5.00 per square foot in some cities—regained popularity during the late 1990s, when job growth soared while housing production remained sluggish.

The breadth of governmental power in the field of exactions permitted suburban jurisdictions to piece together a capital improvement program by requiring each developer to pay for a small piece of the overall pie.

Other types of development fees were not limited to a narrow political spectrum, however. The breadth of governmental power in the field of exactions permitted suburban jurisdictions to piece together a "capital improvement program" by requiring each developer to pay for a small piece of the overall pie. This practice was based on a simple extension of the concept, originally contained in subdivision regulations, that development ought to "pay its own way."

If a developer could be required to build all the streets inside a new subdivision, then surely that same developer could be required to build the new freeway interchange nearby—the theory being, again, that if the subdivision weren't built, the interchange wouldn't be needed. Similarly, that same developer could be required to pay a fee into a highway fund, because the car trips generated by his subdivision would contribute to the need for additional freeway lanes.

Some cities quantified their capital needs down to the last penny. As part of its growth-management program, Carlsbad estimated the need for all public facilities over a 20-year period, and then determined how much each housing unit and each commercial or industrial building would have to contribute to the capital fund. Those calculations became the basis for the development fee structure. In 1986 the state legislature authorized local school districts to impose development fees (originally up to $1.50 per square foot on residential projects, 25 cents per square foot on commercial and industrial projects) as part of an overall statewide school construction finance program. Lawmakers overhauled the school fees laws in 1998, and the cap on per-square-foot fees has continued to rise to considerably more than $2.00 per square foot. Govt. Code § 53080 and §§ 65995-65998; for more discussion of school facilities, *see* chapter 21.

There is little argument that fees and exactions can add considerably to the cost of new development. But there is shockingly little uniformity in fees due to the level of public facilities provided and because of the local political climate. In some rural and growth-hungry parts of the state, impact fees remain minimal. In 2004, for example, development impact and utility connection fees for one new house in unincorporated Tehama County totaled only about $2,200. But a new house of roughly the same size might get charged $40,000 in the city of Santa Rosa, and close to $100,000 in the city of San Ramon. In a hot real estate market, builders have simply passed this cost on to home buyers. When the real estate market slumps, builders have swallowed at least some of this cost in order to lower the price of their houses.

There is shockingly little uniformity in fees due to the level of public facilities provided and because of the local political climate.

Builders have also objected to what they regarded as a cavalier attitude toward fees on the part of many local governments. Not all cities were like Carlsbad; some plucked development fee figures out of mid-air and then simply dropped the proceeds into the general fund. This generated a sharp reaction from builders, who demanded, if not lower fees, then at least greater accountability. Between the mid-'80s and the mid-'90s, all these factors led to a backlash that has, in fact, led to far more accountability in the use of exactions.

The *Nollan* Case

During the 1970s and early '80s, the California courts granted local governments tremendous leeway in imposing exactions on development. However, property rights lawyers kept hammering away, hoping to prove that California-style exactions could be so broad as to constitute a "taking" of private property without compensation. Not surprisingly, they got nowhere in the California courts—but in 1987 they managed to persuade the U.S. Supreme Court to hear what became a landmark case on the law of exactions. *Nollan v. California Coastal Commission*, 483 U.S. 825 (1987).

The case involved a dispute between the California Coastal Commission and the Nollan family, which owned a small piece of beachfront property near Ventura. The Nollans wanted to tear down their small house and replace it with a two-story house that would have the same "footprint" on the ground. The Coastal Commission, which has land use authority over beachfront areas, agreed to approve the new house, but only if the Nollans would grant an easement permitting public access along the beach in front of their house. The Nollans built their house anyway (the access issue did not affect site or construction plans) and sued the Coastal Commission.

The Coastal Commission didn't treat the *Nollan* case any differently than it had hundreds of other permit cases up and down the California coast. One of its major charges is to maximize public access to the beach, and so the commission had required public access easements in exchange for many coastal development permits. In fact, more than 40 of the Nollans' neighbors in the Faria Beach area of Ventura had agreed to this same condition. (The commission wanted to create a "public trail" along the beach connecting two neighboring public beaches.) But the Nollans argued that there was no reasonable relationship, or "nexus," between the construction of a taller house and access along the beachfront.

The local judge in Ventura sided with the Nollans, but the court of appeal sided with the Coastal Commission, and the California Supreme Court chose not to take the case. The U.S. Supreme Court, however, was filling up with conservative Reagan appointees, and the high court agreed to hear the case. The result was a bitterly divided 5 to 4 ruling that signaled an important change in the world of exactions. Writing for the court, Justice Antonin Scalia called the Coastal Commission's policy "an out-and-out plan of extortion." Scalia said that no nexus, or relationship, existed between project and exaction. "When that essential nexus is eliminated," he added, "the situation becomes the same as if California law forbade shouting 'fire' in a crowded theater, but granted dispensations to those willing to contribute $100 to the state treasury."

Though it struck down the Coastal Commission's ruling in the particular case of the Nollan property, the Supreme Court hardly outlawed exactions in the *Nollan* ruling. Rather, the court merely reimposed the requirement that a direct nexus be established between the project proposed and the exaction required. In fact, Scalia specifically stated in his ruling that the Coastal Commission would have been well within its rights to require the Nollans to build a public viewing deck on their small lot, because such a condition would have been directly related to government's interest in the project.

California Exactions After *Nollan*

Coincidentally, the same year that the *Nollan* ruling was issued, the California legislature passed a law designed to hold local governments that imposed development fees accountable.

AB 1600 (Govt. Code § 66000 *et seq.*) requires that, before a development fee is imposed, a city or county must identify the purpose of the fee and the use toward which it will be put. The locality must document the relationship between the fee and the project on which it is being imposed. The law also requires local governments to segregate fee revenue from other city funds, and refund fees if they are not spent within five years for the purposes originally identified, unless the government can make specific findings about how and when the money will be spent. (Drafted before *Nollan*, AB 1600 also contained the "reasonable relationship" test from the *Associated Homebuilders* ruling, rather than the "essential nexus" language of the *Nollan* case.)

AB 1600 requires that, before a development fee is imposed, a city or county must identify the purpose of the fee and the use toward which it will be put.

The *Nollan* case and AB 1600 did not discourage local governments from imposing exactions and fees on development projects. Rather, the combination of the *Nollan* case and AB 1600 ushered in an era of what is often called "green-eyeshade planning." The era of open-ended exactions and dumping the revenue into the general fund has passed. Instead, before imposing exactions or conditions—either as part of a broad general plan or on a particular development project—local governments now hire fiscal or economic consultants to conduct a "nexus" study. The purpose of the study is to document the link between the project being considered and the exaction being imposed. A nexus consultant might, for example, project the number of vehicle trips a new project will create and translate that number into the cost to build additional roadways and other transportation infrastructure, thereby devising a traffic mitigation fee for each development project.

The purpose of a nexus study is to provide the link, or nexus, between the development project being considered and the exaction being imposed.

Even after *Nollan* and AB 1600, California courts proved reluctant to second-guess the judgment of local governments in imposing exactions. So long as some kind of nexus study was done, the exactions were generally upheld in court. For example, in 1988, the California Supreme Court upheld San Francisco's $5-per-square-foot transit impact fee on office development. *Russ Building Partnership v. City and County of San Francisco,* 44 Cal. 3d 839 (1988). In 1991, the Ninth U.S. Circuit Court of Appeals scotched the hopes of the building industry by upholding a housing fee on commercial and industrial development in Sacramento. *Commercial*

Builders of Northern California v. City of Sacramento, 941 F. 2d 872 (9th Cir. 1991).

The fee was based on the assumption that new jobs in Sacramento were driving up the cost of housing, creating an impact that had to be mitigated through an exaction. The builders argued that the real-life situation was exactly the opposite: Demand among businesses for commercial and industrial space was strong in Sacramento, they insisted, because home prices there were so much lower than they were in the Bay Area. But the Ninth Circuit declined to second-guess Sacramento's nexus study, relying on the reasonable relationship test contained in the *Associated Homebuilders* case. In short, so long as local governments attempted to prove a nexus by hiring a nexus consultant, usually the exactions and fees were upheld in court.

So long as local governments attempted to prove a nexus by hiring a nexus consultant, usually the exactions and fees were upheld in court.

By the early 1990s, local governments began to feel whipsawed on the issue. On the one hand, they felt more financial pressure than ever before, especially after a property tax shift in 1992 and 1993 left them with less property tax revenue than before. Because of local government cutbacks, there was increasing political pressure in many communities to force new development to pay for itself. On the other hand, during the recession of the early '90s, local governments felt political pressure to roll back fees and exactions in an effort to stimulate more growth.

The dynamic changed again with the long-running real estate boom that began during the late 1990s. As home prices appreciated by 15 to 25 percent annually in many places, with no reduction in the number of units sold, many developers toned down their criticism of fees and exactions. Builders wanted to cash in on the boom, so instead they focused on getting their projects approved as quickly as possible. In hopes of making their projects more appealing to local governments and potential project opponents, some developers in desirable towns were even willing to sign development agreements that called for fees far greater than would normally be allowed. After all, if a new tract home in Orange County could sell for $600,000, what would another $10,000 added to the sales price to pay for roads and parks matter?

Refining Accountability in Exactions: *Dolan* and *Ehrlich*

In the 1990s, the legal trend in the field of exactions began to build on *Nollan* and AB 1600, requiring more accountability and a strong direct relationship between exactions and the projects in

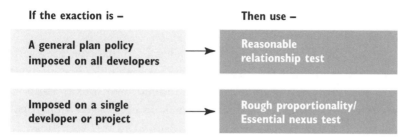

If the exaction is –	Then use –
A general plan policy imposed on all developers	Reasonable relationship test
Imposed on a single developer or project	Rough proportionality/ Essential nexus test

Reasonable Relationship vs. Rough Proportionality

question. In general, these trends have led to more green-eyeshade planning as a way to bulletproof exactions from legal challenge.

Seven years after *Nollan*, the U.S. Supreme Court refined its approach to exactions in a case from the Portland suburb of Tigard, Oregon. *Dolan v. City of Tigard*, 512 U.S. 319, 114 S.Ct. 2309 (1994). The result of *Dolan v. Tigard* reinforced the green-eyeshade planning approach, but also put more pressure on California courts to resolve how direct the nexus needs to be for an exaction to be valid. This pressure, in turn, led to the California Supreme Court's 1996 ruling in *Ehrlich v. City of Culver City*.

The result of Dolan v. Tigard *reinforced the green-eyeshade planning approach, but also put more pressure on California courts to resolve how direct the nexus needs to be for an exaction to be valid.*

Dolan v. Tigard emerged from a dispute between the city of Tigard and the owner of a downtown Tigard appliance store. Florence Dolan sought city permission to build a larger store and expand the parking lot on her 1.67-acre downtown parcel, which was located partly in the floodplain of Fanno Creek. As a condition of approval, Tigard required Dolan to dedicate approximately 10 percent of her property to the city for a bike path and public greenway. The city wanted the greenway as a buffer between the river and the downtown in case of flooding. The intent of the bike path (to be constructed in the greenway) was to promote bicycle use and reduce vehicle traffic in the downtown.

The U.S. Supreme Court ruled against the city. First, the court said, Tigard had not proven why deeding over the greenway, as opposed to merely providing an easement, was necessary for flood control. More important, however, the court found that Tigard had not proven a strong relationship between the additional traffic the store would cause and the need for the bike path

In making this last point, the court laid down a new and important rule. Not only must local governments show a nexus between the project and the exaction, but the exaction must have a "rough proportionality" to the impact the project is creating. "No precise mathematical calculation is required, but the city must make some sort of individualized determination that the required dedication is related both in nature and extent to the impact of the proposed development."

In other words, *Dolan* provided a legal test that coincided with the nexus study approach many California communities had adopted as a result of *Nollan* and AB 1600. Indeed, with nexus studies, many communities had sought to make a precise mathematical calculation. On that score at least, *Dolan* did not significantly change California planning practice but rather reinforced the trend toward accountability.

But the *Dolan* ruling did raise an additional legal question: whether *Nollan* and *Dolan*, taken together, had created a new legal standard that went far beyond the reasonable relationship standard contained in the *Associated Homebuilders* case.

Ever since the *Nollan* case was handed down, property rights lawyers had argued that the legal standard for an exaction should reflect *Nollan's* language requiring an "essential" or "direct" nexus, as opposed to the reasonable relationship requirement. Municipal lawyers continued to argue that, nexus studies aside, *Nollan* did not overturn the reasonable relationship test; an indirect connection, they claimed, was still legally valid. This was the reasoning used by the Ninth Circuit in the fee case from Sacramento.

After *Dolan*, however, the property rights lawyers had a stronger argument. It was a long way from a "reasonable relationship," implying that an indirect connection was sufficient, to a requirement demanding both an "essential nexus" and "rough proportionality." It was this dispute that the California Supreme Court chose to take up in the *Ehrlich v. Culver City* case.

The *Ehrlich* case was on appeal to the U.S. Supreme Court at the time the *Dolan* ruling was handed down. The high court set aside the court of appeal ruling upholding the recreation fee, and then sent the case back to the court of appeal for reconsideration in light of the *Dolan* ruling. After the court of appeal again upheld the fee, Richard Ehrlich appealed to the California Supreme Court, setting the stage for that court's first important exactions ruling in many years.

In the *Ehrlich* ruling, the state Supreme Court fashioned a new test for exactions in California which combined elements of both reasonable relationship and rough proportionality/essential nexus. Interestingly enough, the resulting test strengthens the power of the general plan vis-à-vis individual project decisions.

The reasonable relationship test is sufficient for exactions that are imposed on all developers as part of a broad policy scheme. But

With nexus studies, many communities had sought to make a precise mathematical calculation. On that score at least, Dolan *did not significantly change California planning practice but rather reinforced the trend toward accountability.*

In the Ehrlich *ruling, the state Supreme Court fashioned a new test for exactions in California which combined elements of both reasonable relationship and rough proportionality/ essential nexus.*

the stricter rough proportionality/essential nexus test should be used when exactions are imposed on a single developer as a result of the expected impact of a single development project. The court also clarified that these same standards apply whether the exaction comes in the form of a monetary fee, dedication of land, or construction of facilities. (The big difference in *Ehrlich* was that Culver City passed the rough proportionality/essential nexus test, while Tigard and the Coastal Commission failed the test.)

Thus, under *Ehrlich*, it is easier for cities and counties to impose exactions if they are part of a policy contained in their general plans. Such exaction plans do not require a direct nexus, nor even the rough proportionality called for in the *Dolan* case. It is more difficult to impose exactions loosely in the case of individual development projects, because such exactions must be closely tied to a project's impacts identified through a traffic study or other impact analysis through CEQA. This theme was amplified in a more recent state Supreme Court decision that upheld the city of San Francisco's conditions for approving the conversion of a residential hotel to tourist use.

Under Ehrlich, *it is easier for cities and counties to impose exactions if they are part of a policy contained in their general plans.*

In 1981, San Francisco adopted a hotel conversion ordinance, which the city later amended, that prohibited the conversion of residential units to tourist use unless hotel owners replaced the converted units with new affordable housing or paid a mitigation fee. The ordinance was approved at a time when affordable housing was scarce and city officials were trying to preserve residential hotels as a low-cost housing option.

When the owners of the 62-unit San Remo Hotel sought a conditional use permit to convert their building to tourist use, city officials said the owners would have to provide replacement units or pay $9,000 per unit (a total of $567,000). The owners paid the fee in protest but fought back in court, all the way to the state Supreme Court, where the hotel owners argued that the conversion fee amounted to a taking of private property. In a 4 to 3 ruling issued in 2002, the court ruled that because the policy requiring a mitigation fee or replacement units applied to all residential hotels, the regulation qualified for a deferential review in court. Under that standard, the court could strike down the regulation only if it was arbitrary, which the court determined it was not. *San Remo Hotel v. City and County of San Francisco*, 27 Cal. 4th 643 (2002). The court said San Francisco's exaction was unlike the "ad hoc" condition imposed in the *Ehrlich* case.

In writing for the majority, Justice Kathryn Mickle Werdegar specifically rejected the idea that the "heightened scrutiny" called for by *Nollan* and *Dolan* should apply to an ordinance of general applicability. Extending the essential nexus and rough proportionality tests to such an ordinance would invite the sort of second-guessing on policy decisions courts have long sought to avoid, Werdegar wrote.

The state Supreme Court's *San Remo* decision received a minor boost in 2004 when the Ninth U.S. Circuit Court of Appeals refused to consider the hotel owner's arguments. The federal court concluded that the hotel owners had already received their day in court. One year later, the U.S. Supreme Court unanimously upheld the Ninth Circuit's decision, ruling that property owners have no guaranteed right to have their local takings claims tried in federal court. *San Remo Hotel v. City and County of San Francisco*, 545 U.S. __ (2005).

The state Supreme Court's most recent ruling regarding development fees suggested just how arcane this field is.

The state Supreme Court's most recent ruling regarding development fees suggested just how arcane this field is, partly because the court ruled that the charge in question was not technically a development fee.

The case came from the Shasta Community Services District, which provides a water system and fire protection for a rural residential area west of Redding. *Richmond v. Shasta Community Services Dist.*, 32 Cal. 4th 409 (2004). Beginning in 1994, the district began to levy on landowners a "capacity charge" for connecting to the water system and a "fire suppression charge" to fund firefighting equipment. Both charges, according to the district, were based on the cost of providing services to new homes. Four property owners filed a lawsuit claiming that the charges were subject to Proposition 218, a 1996 initiative that sought to close loopholes in Proposition 13. The district had adopted the fees without any public vote, which the property owners said was a violation of Proposition 218.

In upholding the charges, the state high court ruled that the charges were neither "fees" nor "charges" within the meaning of Proposition 218, so no vote was required. But the court also ruled that the charges were not development fees either. The water capacity charge "is similar to a development fee in being imposed only in response to a property owner's voluntary application to a public entity," Justice Joyce Kennard wrote, "but it is different in that the application may be only for a water service connection without necessarily involving any development."

Local government agencies searching for revenue took heart from the *Richmond* decision. But it is unclear whether *Richmond* will have broader implications in the world of development fees, whatever they might be called. Instead, the *Nollan/Dolan/Ehrlich* line of cases provides guidance for individual exactions by requiring a strong link between the government's demand and the project's impact, while *Ehrlich* and *San Remo* give the government more leeway to decide on exactions that are part of broader public policies.

Chapter 11

Traditional Growth Management

Growth has been a constant for California ever since the Gold Rush—and resistance to it has been a constant for almost as long, or so it seems. In the midst of the postwar boom almost a half-century ago—when California had less than half as many people as it has now—the first citizen activists began to fight growth and sprawl throughout the state. The group "Cry California" first expressed concern about the environmental damage of growth in the late 1950s, and at that same time residents of San Francisco rose up successfully against the completion of the Embarcadero Freeway.

Ever since then, individual communities in California have sought to repel, control, and/or manage growth through a wide variety of sophisticated planning techniques that fall generally under the headline of "growth management." When California cities first adopted growth management techniques in the 1970s—focused mostly on the timing and sequencing of development—the state was clearly ahead of the national curve. As the California Environmental Quality Act became the predominant tool in the state during the 1980s and '90s, however, California fell behind many other states, including Oregon, Washington, Florida, and Maryland, in growth management innovation.

CEQA = California Environmental Quality Act

Only in the last few years has California begun to catch up, as many individual communities have adopted "smart growth" policies, largely in response to both changing circumstances and changing attitudes about growth. It is probably too soon to say for sure just how much these "smart growth" policies will change the landscape of California communities. (smart growth is discussed in much more

It is probably too soon to say for sure just how much these "Smart Growth" policies will change the landscape of California communities.

detail in chapter 16.) However, one thing is clear: Even as they adopt "smart growth" policies, most of California's communities—especially those in coastal areas—are not abandoning traditional growth management tools. These tools remain strongly in place in most of the locations where they were adopted in the '80s and '90s.

The Origins of Growth Management

Traditional land use regulatory schemes such as zoning still had, basically, only two dimensions: "use" and "bulk."

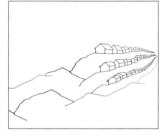

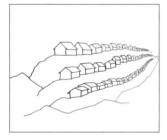

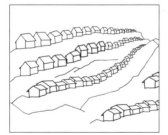

Even when they were subject to the twists and turns of political manipulation, traditional land use regulatory schemes such as zoning still had, basically, only two dimensions: "use" and "bulk." All the land in a community was divided into use districts, and then height, bulk, and setback standards were devised for each of those use districts. The concept of "growth management," as defined by prominent land use lawyer Robert Freilich, added two new dimensions to the land use regulatory picture. In addition to use and bulk, growth-management schemes also regulate the "timing" and "sequencing" of development—especially residential development—within a community.

Today, close to 40 years after Freilich drew up the first growth control ordinances—and more than 30 years after they found their way to California—most growth-management systems throughout the state still try to accomplish their goals by managing timing and sequencing.

The type of growth management system so common in California was actually first created by Freilich for a suburb of New York that was experiencing similar suburban-era pressures, most notably a rapid increase in housing development. Even though they did not take place in California, Ramapo's growth-management plan and the subsequent legal challenge merit discussion because they established the patterns and ground rules that growth-management systems in California still follow today.

Between 1960 and 1970, Ramapo's population more than doubled. Under the guidance of Freilich, now one of the nation's most prominent growth-management experts, Ramapo devised a multi-faceted program that included several important components:

- **Timing and sequencing.** The town placed all development in Ramapo on a timing and sequencing schedule that forced some landowners to wait up to 18 years to develop their property. The town did not restrict growth to a certain number of building permits per year, as California growth-control pioneer Petaluma did, but, rather, granted permits to development proposals that garnered the highest number of points (which was similar to Petaluma's plan, described below).

- **Linkage between timing/sequencing and the capital improvement program.** The linkage was built into the point system described above. Developments providing sewer systems, rather than septic tanks, received higher scores. Similarly, more points were awarded to developments in close proximity to parks, arterial roads with sidewalks, and fire houses.

- **Integration of planning, zoning, and the capital improvement plan.** This is equivalent to "consistency" in a modern-day California general plan, with zoning and the infrastructure construction program reinforcing the growth-management concepts contained in the plan.

- **Lower taxes for some undeveloped land.** The plan called for the purchase of development rights from owners of undeveloped land, a practice that has since become popular among environmentalists. Most important, landowners who had sold their development rights would be taxed at a much lower rate than those who had not.

This growth-management system was upheld in 1972 by the New York Court of Appeals, New York's equivalent of the California Supreme Court. *Golden v. Planning Board of Town of Ramapo*, 283 N.E. 2d 291, appeal to the U.S. Supreme Court dismissed, 409 U.S. 1003 (1972). According to Freilich himself, the Ramapo system was able to withstand constitutional challenge largely because of its 18-year time limit. This permitted Ramapo to argue in court that the growth-management plan did not shut off a landowner's development possibilities forever, but rather permitted "reasonable use" of a landowner's property within a "reasonable period of time."

Ramapo argued in court that the growth-management plan did not shut off a landowner's development possibilities forever, but rather permitted "reasonable use" of a landowner's property within a "reasonable period of time."

At the time, many California communities were being drawn into the suburban orbit by the opening of new freeways—and, like Ramapo, they were experiencing a rapid increase in suburban-style residential development. So it is not surprising that Freilich's ideas made their way to California before long—along with the legal challenges to those ideas.

Many California communities were being drawn into the suburban orbit by the opening of new freeways—and, like Ramapo, they were experiencing a rapid increase in suburban-style residential development.

The test case came from Petaluma, a small community in Sonoma County some 40 miles north of San Francisco. When Highway 101 first opened in 1969, residential development grew from 300 homes a year to 600 in 1970 and then to 900 in 1971. The result of this explosive growth was a pattern of events recognizable in fast-growing areas throughout California today: double-session schools,

Do Numerical Caps Work?

WHEN THE FAMOUS PETALUMA "point system" was upheld in the courts more than 30 years ago, it touched off a wave of interest in similar growth-management schemes. But over time, these restrictions have come under considerable criticism, and even Petaluma itself has changed and simplified its system.

Here's how the system worked—

The city was divided into four geographical areas, each of which was allocated an equal number of building permits. Of course, demand for permits was not the same in all four areas of the city, so the net effect was to encourage developers to move from one part of town to another in order to avoid competition for permits. In the first year of the allocation system, for example, there were 505 applications for the 125 permits in one quadrant of the city, and only 59 applications (all of them obviously approved) in another quadrant.

The point system involved a matrix through which projects were rated in two broad categories (public services and design/amenities).

The public service portion of the matrix was worth 30 points, with up to five points being awarded for such criteria as drainage, the sewer system, fire prevention, and impact on schools. The design/amenities portion of the matrix was worth 80 points, with 10 points each being awarded for architectural quality, landscape, bike paths, infill development, and affordable housing.

The highest scores didn't automatically win. A certain score was required to make the cut; and a city board then made the final decisions.

Three important points must be understood about this kind of matrix.

➡

an overloaded sewer system, and political pressure to restrict growth.

The city responded by imposing the first "growth management" restrictions in California history: a cap of 500 housing units per year and an allocation system that awarded those units to builders who met criteria for both aesthetics and public services. Three years later, the U.S. Ninth Circuit Court of Appeals upheld Petaluma's growth restrictions as a proper exercise of police power. (*Construction Industry Association, Sonoma County v. City of Petaluma*, 522 F.2d 897 (9th Cir. 1975).)

Since that time, more than 60 cities in California have adopted some version of the Petaluma plan in order to slow and/or manage growth in their communities. Many have instituted growth "control" by actually limiting the amount of real estate development. Some have restricted growth through a Petaluma-like ordinance that permits only a certain number of housing units per year. Others have restricted commercial growth to a certain amount of square footage per year. More recently, some cities have restricted growth by tying development in their communities to the availability of roads and other infrastructure.

Many other cities have tried to manage growth by directing new developments into certain geographical locations, and by taking other steps that seek to ensure that new growth does not run too far ahead of needed infrastructure even if development is not restricted on an annual basis. Many cities (and a few counties) have tried to use control and management mechanisms together. And, increasingly, growth restrictions have come about as the result of initiatives or referenda placed on the ballot by disgruntled local citizens.

Growth Management Trends in California

Though caps on population and housing typically receive the most publicity, they represent only the tip of the iceberg when it comes to local growth management. Extensive research on growth management—initiated almost 20 years ago by UCLA researchers Madelyn Glickfeld and Ned Levine and later refined by Solimar Research Group—has found that growth management tools fall into six general categories.

Housing and Population Caps

Population growth caps establish a population growth limit or restrict the level of population growth for a given time period. These are usually implemented by restricting the number of housing units permitted for construction, as in Petaluma. Housing permit limitations restrict the total number of residential building permits in a given time period. Although population growth caps purport to control the actual number of people in a community, in point of fact both population and housing caps seek to manage growth by restricting and controlling the number of housing units in a community. (Population caps limit housing construction through the use of assumptions about how many people, on average, will live in each housing unit.) Population and housing caps were popular in the 1970s and 1980s but they have not spread to very many new communities since 1988.

Commercial and Industrial Caps

These are the nonresidential equivalents of the population and housing controls described above. They seek to limit the overall square footage or size of commercial and/or industrial buildings permitted in the jurisdiction. Implicitly, of course, these types of measures restrict the built space available for employment and retail transactions, just as limiting housing construction limits population. Although many communities in California have adopted controls on population and housing, relatively few have adopted restrictions on the amount of nonresidential development. (Many have

First, the criteria chosen (and the weight given each one) are not objective, but, rather, serve as a reflection of the community's values. Thus, in Petaluma, bike paths were given twice the weight of good sewers. Second, while the matrix appears quantitative, in actuality it's merely the sum total of a series of subjective judgments, which again reflect the values of the community (or at least the planning staff). And third, a point system can lead developers to build large-scale projects and/or more expensive homes, because they need both economies of scale and an extra profit margin in order to build all the amenities required to win the competition.

In the years since Petaluma adopted this system, both research and practical application have raised important questions about the value of numerical caps. A study conducted by Berkeley planning professor John Landis found that numerical caps often make little difference. The caps are typically imposed at a time when the real estate market is hot, so the cap is set at a very high number. And when he compared cities with caps to similar cities without caps, Landis found that the overall growth patterns weren't very different. Far more important than the cap itself, he concluded, was the political attitude of the community toward growth. A community that wants to restrict growth will find a way to do it with or without numerical caps.

Petaluma's experience reflects the Landis research. Once the initial wave of freeway-related growth had swept over the city, the 500-unit cap proved high. Over the past decade, the average number of residential permit requests has averaged around 380. And Petaluma's planners eventually scrapped the point system, calling it tedious and subjective. Now, builders wanting priority must meet broad community goals instead. ■

adopted height limits.) The tool most often used to restrict non-residential growth is the floor-area ratio or FAR.

Urban Growth Boundaries

Urban growth boundaries and related tools have become increasingly popular in the last 10 years, especially in certain counties in the Bay Area and along the coast. Simply put, these boundaries seek to limit urban growth to specific geographical areas through regulatory restrictions and/or limitations on infrastructure expansion. They have become closely identified with the "smart growth" movement and have been especially popular with voters since the ruling in *DeVita v. County of Napa* (1995) 9 Cal. 4th 763, which held that voters could create growth boundaries at the ballot and require them to be amended only with a subsequent vote.

Infrastructure

APFO = Adequate public facilities ordinances

FAR = Floor-area ratio

LOS = Level of service

This technique goes by many other names: adequate public facilities ordinances (APFOs), level of service (LOS) requirements, or concurrency requirements. (The term "concurrency" is derived from the Florida Growth Management Act and is not widely used in California.) In general, these measures prohibit the construction of new development unless the public infrastructure is in place to support it. Usually, infrastructure adequacy is measured by predicting the impact on "levels of service"—that is, specific standards for virtually all public infrastructure, including roads (congestion levels), schools (capacity and crowding), parks (acres per person), and police and fire services (response times).

Upzoning and Downzoning

Zoning is, of course, the most basic land use regulatory tool. One of the most common tools in California growth management is simply to alter the zoning (and usually the land use designation in the general plan as well) to permit only less intense uses—for example, rezoning commercial land to residential use, or "downzoning" residential property so that it can accommodate fewer units per acre than it could before.

General Controls

This category includes a variety of miscellaneous approaches to managing growth in California communities. Perhaps the most important is the growth management Element, which has become

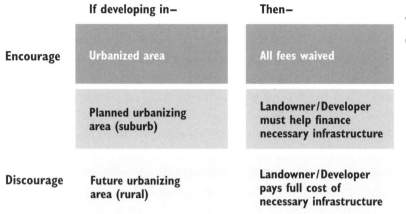

	If developing in—	Then—
Encourage	Urbanized area	All fees waived
	Planned urbanizing area (suburb)	Landowner/Developer must help finance necessary infrastructure
Discourage	Future urbanizing area (rural)	Landowner/Developer pays full cost of necessary infrastructure

Tiered Approach to Growth Management

increasingly popular in the last 20 years as a means of incorporating the community's growth management goals into the comprehensive context of the general plan. It can contain a wide range of tools within it, but most often it contains some kind of long-term restriction on the amount of housing and nonresidential space, along with some kind of infrastructure finance and monitoring plan.

No matter which approach they take, most California growth-management ordinances contain the basic elements of the Ramapo method—especially if they were crafted by the local city council, rather than through the initiative process. The most carefully constructed growth-management ordinances typically follow the pattern set by the Carlsbad ordinance, which was discussed in chapter 10.

The Carlsbad ordinance does not have an annual cap on the number of building permits. It sets out the ultimate number of dwelling units that will be constructed in the city (by the year 2010); describes where they will be located; and then permits development only when the infrastructure is constructed concurrently. In this way, the ordinance allows for ups and downs in the market over a 20-year period, rather than tightly constricting annual growth. The Carlsbad ordinance also contains a fiscal component, which imposes fees on developers to raise the money required for the infrastructure. It should be clear from this description how neatly a well-thought-out growth-management ordinance fits into a city's general plan.

While they may control the timing of development, building caps do not always control the sequencing—that is, they do not control the sequence in which different areas of the city are developed. And, while metering the rate of growth can be important to avoid over-burdening infrastructure and schools, the sequencing of

No matter which approach they take, most California growth-management ordinances contain the basic elements of the Ramapo method.

development can be even more important. Under traditional "two-dimensional" zoning, a developer could build a subdivision adjacent to the existing city or 10 miles away, if he could obtain the proper zoning. From the city's point of view, this "leapfrog" subdivision was probably not a good deal. Because of its location, the subdivision was expensive to serve with infrastructure and public services, and its approval would probably lead to land speculation all around. But the principle of comprehensive "use districts" was upheld.

Broad-based growth-management systems deal with sequencing, as the Ramapo system did, by tying new development to the construction of infrastructure and then strictly controlling its location and timing. As the Ramapo case proved, this approach can survive a legal challenge if the sequencing rules are clear, and if development is permitted in all areas of the city within a foreseeable time frame. (Of course, what's "foreseeable" to the planner may not be foreseeable to the developer; hence the ongoing legal challenges surrounding these ordinances.)

But other techniques have emerged to reinforce the sequencing aspect of local growth-management programs. Perhaps the most innovative is the "tiered" approach, which specifies areas where development is encouraged and/or discouraged—and backs up these designations with financial incentives. One tiered growth-management plan was implemented with Freilich's help in San Diego. This plan divided the city (and areas likely to be annexed to the city) into three categories: urbanized area, planned urbanizing area, and future urbanizing area—or, to put it more simply, urban, suburban, and rural areas. To encourage infill development, fees were waived in the urban area. To discourage development in the rural area, developers were required to pay the full freight of all infrastructure, and were offered tax breaks under the state's Williamson Act farmland preservation law if they kept the land in agricultural use. In the suburban areas, landowners helped finance infrastructure and public facilities through a mandatory assessment district.

The process worked well—too well, in fact. When the tiers were adopted in 1979, only 10 percent of San Diego's growth constituted infill development in the already urban area. Throughout the '80s, however, the urban areas received 60 percent of the growth, with only about 30 percent going to suburban areas and a smattering to rural areas. The result was that the infrastructure in the urban areas was soon overloaded, and the city did not have the capital funds to solve the problem; after all, 60 percent of the developers had not paid any fees. Faced with an infrastructure crisis, San Diego had to revise its growth-management program and begin imposing fees on infill development.

Despite this remarkable success, San Diego's growth-management scheme was not tough enough to endure the slow-growth environment that emerged in the city during the building boom of the 1980s. In 1987, threatened with citizen initiatives, the city council also imposed an annual cap on residential building permits (8,000) and began an overhaul of the growth-management system in order to tie all of its elements together.

Legal Constraints on Traditional Growth Management

By and large, managing growth falls within the broad discretion of local governments to engage in whatever form of land use planning they deem most appropriate for their community. Yet cities and counties in California do not have unlimited power to restrict growth through growth-management systems.

Cities and counties in California do not have unlimited power to restrict growth through growth-management systems.

As always when they are exercising their police power, local governments must prove that their actions further a legitimate governmental (public) interest and bear a reasonable relationship to the public welfare. The courts have been especially receptive to the idea that growth-management ordinances should not restrict the housing supply. Over time, the builders' legal firepower on this particular point has expanded greatly. But so far the builders have not been able to deliver a knockout blow to municipal growth management and growth control in the courts.

According to prominent land use attorney Daniel J. Curtin, Jr., in the 1976 case of *Associated Home Builders, Inc. v. City of Livermore*, 18 Cal. 3d 582, the California Supreme Court said that local growth-management systems must be addressed in light of three questions:

- **What is the probable** effect and duration of the ordinance?
- **What are the competing** interests affected by the ordinance (for example, environmental protection versus the opportunity of people to settle where they choose)?
- **Does the ordinance,** in light of its probable impact, represent a reasonable accommodation of these competing interests?

Furthermore, the court said that the "public welfare" must include the welfare of all people who would be affected significantly by the ordinance, and not just those who live within the boundaries of the city or county enacting the measure. This aspect of the court's

Ballot Box Zoning

ONE OF THE MOST CHERISHED RIGHTS of California citizens is the right of initiative and referendum—the right, in essence, to circumvent elected legislators and place pieces of legislation on the ballot (state or local) for a direct vote of the people. Though initiative and referendum has been more widely used on the state level, it has emerged in the last 20 years as a potentially powerful tool in local planning as well.

After a modest beginning in the 1970s and early '80s, "ballot-box zoning," as the use of initiative and referendum in the planning arena has come to be known, is now a widely used technique, especially in coastal metropolitan areas. According to statistics maintained by California Planning & Development Report and Solimar Research Group, more than 600 growth-related measures appeared on local ballots in California from 1986 through 2000, most of them in communities located close to the coast.

In many communities, ballot-box zoning has brought widespread attention to the debate over a community's future in a way that a typical general plan revision could never do. At the same time, the practice created a scattershot approach to land use planning in many cities by focusing the public's attention on one project or one issue, rather than the overall planning process. But simply by moving a planning decision to the voting booth, ballot-box zoning has made planning decisions more political than ever.

Any legislative act—that is, any action by a city council or county board of supervisors acting in its legislative capacity—may be placed on the ballot, because such actions set a local government's policy. No quasi-judicial act is eligible to be placed on the ballot, either as an initiative or a referendum, because such acts involve the simple application of existing policy to a specific situation. Thus, a zoning ordinance or a general plan amendment may be placed on the ballot as an initiative or a referendum, but a conditional use permit or a variance may not. (An initiative is a legislative action initiated by voters, rather than the legislative body; a referendum is a vote on whether to accept or overturn an action already taken by a legislative body.)

ruling is especially important because so many growth-management ordinances deliberately restrict the availability of housing in a given city.

In the *Livermore* case, the court essentially said that cities which restrict housing must take into account the regional impact of their actions. The Livermore test is potentially devastating, because growth-management systems, almost by definition, restrict construction and therefore limit the regional supply of housing. Subsequent to the *Livermore* case, the California legislature adopted Evidence Code section 669.5, which established a legal presumption that growth-management ordinances harm regional housing supply and placed the burden of proof on the city or county to show otherwise. But in a 1986 case, the California Supreme Court ruled that this provision does not apply to initiatives.[1]

Traditionally, local governments have had great leeway to enact growth-control ordinances that restrict the supply of housing, especially if the ordinances are adopted by initiative. In one notable example, the court of appeal upheld an open-space ordinance in the town of Moraga, even though the justices acknowledged that the ordinance would have a detrimental effect

---

1. *Building Industry Association v. City of Camarillo*, 41 Cal. 3d 810 (1986). Because so many contentious and high-profile growth-management ordinances were enacted by initiative, many of the most important court cases in the growth-management field deal with initiatives rather than ordinary ordinances, meaning the legal issues associated with growth management have become intertwined with the legal issues associated with initiatives. In general, the courts have given initiatives far more deference than council- or board-adopted growth-management ordinances, as the *Camarillo* ruling indicates.

on the supply of housing in the Bay Area. *Northwood Homes, Inc. v. Town of Moraga*, 216 Cal. App. 3d 1197 (1989).

For growth-management opponents, the most important legal victory so far came in 1994, when the court of appeal in San Diego ruled that Oceanside's growth-management system violated state housing law. *Building Industry Association v. City of Oceanside*, 27 Cal. App. 4th 744 (1994). Oceanside's Proposition A was a voter-approved initiative that restricted the number of residential units permitted each year in the city. Despite the traditional deference to local initiative powers, the court of appeal found that the restriction violated three sections of the state housing element law that call for and promote the construction of affordable housing.[2]

The Oceanside case would appear to weaken the legal underpinnings of the 60 or so growth-management ordinances in California that rely on numerical caps to restrict housing. However, many of these ordinances provide priority or exemptions for low- and moderate-income housing—a mitigating factor which may comply with the Oceanside ruling. In any event, there is no question that in the future cities and counties adopting growth-management ordinances will have to pay much more attention to the impact of those ordinances on the supply of housing.

2. The three provisions are Government Code section 65008(c), which prohibits land use policies that discriminate against low- and moderate-income residents in need of housing; section 65913.1, which calls upon municipalities to zone vacant land to accommodate low- and moderate-income housing; and section 65915, which requires localities to provide density bonuses for projects that are 100 percent affordable.

Ballot-box zoning began on a small scale in the 1970s, mostly in Northern California. Throughout the '70s, communities in the Bay Area skirmished over ballot-box zoning, and developers went to the courts to try to stop growth measures from being placed on the ballot. Many legal experts argued that a general plan amendment or a zone change was a quasi-judicial decision and therefore not eligible for the ballot. In 1980, the California Supreme Court clarified the legal issues by ruling that even the rezoning of a small amount of land (in this case, 68 acres held by three landowners) was a legislative act and therefore could be placed on the ballot. *Arnel Development Company v. City of Costa Mesa,* 28 Cal. 3d 511 (1980).

The *Arnel* decision was a landmark. Although subdivision review, conditional use permits, and the like remained quasi-judicial, the court ruled, in effect, that virtually any zone change and general plan amendment could be placed on the ballot.

Arnel opened the floodgates for ballot-box zoning in California. Growth-related ballot measures have appeared regularly ever since. Although the number fluctuates based on the real estate cycle, somewhere between 20 and 50 measures have been voted on almost every year since 1986. Recent analysis by Solimar Research Group has found that these measures are concentrated in certain parts of the state—especially in certain coastal and metropolitan counties, such as Sonoma, Alameda, Ventura, Orange, and San Diego Counties. This trend is so strong that it is fair to say that the state has split into two political cultures—a coastal culture where residents routinely vote on important land use matters and an inland culture where they do not.

The growth management tools used in ballot-box zoning are no different than those used by elected officials. The six or seven growth management tools presented above are common on ballot measures as well. In part, this is driven by the fact that initiatives must mimic the legislative process and alter general plans or zoning ordinances in similar fashion to an ordinance passed by elected officials.

No matter how they are constructed, however, ballot measures regarding land use often redound to the benefit of those on the slow-growth side. This varies from year to year and place to place, but generally speaking, citizens who promote a slow-growth vision usually win at the ballot box. In some cases—especially in smaller cities—local officials who place an alternative measure on the ballot do succeed. In those rare instances when developers go straight to the ballot, they typically lose. In 2000, a developer who went to the ballot to expand the Sacramento County Urban Services Area lost 69–31 even though he promised senior housing. In 2002, landowners who went to the ballot in the city of Ventura for a similar purpose lost 70–30, even though they promised 3,000 acres of open space. In each case the developer spent well over $1 million on the campaign.

Oftentimes, initiatives have served as a harbinger of political change in a community. If an initiative gains widespread support, that support is an indication of dissatisfaction with the current political regime—and, therefore, suggests the possibility of a political shift. An initiative's drafters often run for city council in the same election that residents are voting on the initiative, hoping to ride the initiative's popularity into office. If dissatisfaction with the city's current growth policies is widespread, these candidates often win. But because of the difficulty of organizing a grassroots campaign on a mass scale, initiatives have been much more successful in small cities than in geographically large counties.

This relationship to political change in a community is important to note. Despite the widespread publicity ballot measures receive, the vast majority of growth-management measures in California—perhaps as much as 85 percent—are enacted by local city councils and boards of supervisors, not via ballot-box zoning. In most communities, ballot-box zoning indicates lack of consensus or roiling discontent rather than a permanent way of doing business.

In some California communities, however, ballot-box zoning has become the norm rather than the exception—a way of doing business rather than a way of expressing political discontent. These communities have generally been located on or near the coast, and they have passed measures that require subsequent voter approval for certain types of general plan amendments. For example, the city of Escondido, in northern San Diego ⇒

More recent court cases have reinforced this idea. In 1995, the court of appeal in San Diego struck down a longstanding growth-control ordinance in the city of Oceanside, saying that it violated the state's housing element law. *Del Oro Hills v. City of Oceanside*, 31 Cal. App. 4th 1060 (1995). Officials at HCD do not allow local governments to use growth control initiatives as an "excuse" for not planning to meet the fair share housing requirement.

Does Traditional Growth Management "Work"?

As always in the arena of land use planning, that depends on your definition of "work." Most of the growth-management schemes have, in fact, slowed growth within the boundaries of a particular city and/or channeled growth into certain areas of the city where the streets, sewers, and other infrastructure could handle it. Just like growth itself, however, growth management has unpleasant side effects—some of which are predictable and most of which are inevitable given the constraints under which local governments work.

The most common complaint from the building industry is that growth restrictions drive up the cost of housing and other development. Obviously, there is some truth to this claim, especially in a high-demand situation. The whole point of a growth-management system is to tinker with the private market, and in the case of an annual cap on construction, the local government is blatantly replacing the private market with governmental rationing. But the true impact of a growth-management scheme on real estate prices depends on many factors, including the underlying market demand, the actions of neighboring local governments, and the amount of speculation occurring in the market. If a market is really hot, prices may go up with or without growth restrictions.

Second, while they may, in fact, preserve the "character" of a community by limiting development, growth-managing systems can also change the character of a community by encouraging development of a different type and scale. Point systems such as those used in Petaluma encourage developers to build larger, more expensive houses, in order to finance all the amenities they must offer to win the competition for building permits. Point systems also work to the advantage of large development companies that sit on large tracts of land because their financial power gives them the ability to hold land for the long-term and provide up-front amenities.

Third, because growth management emerged from residential suburbs, often the systems focus too much on restricting only residential development, and therefore create an imbalance with too little housing and too many jobs. In the late '60s and early '70s, this was an understandable response; suburban towns like Petaluma and Ramapo were inundated by residential builders almost exclusively. But nowadays, most office and industrial development also occurs in the suburbs, even though many growth-management schemes (and most growth-control measures) still deal only with residential growth.

In large part, this continuing emphasis on residential restrictions is a reflection of the prevailing political ethic. Most

County, adopted a measure in 1998 requiring voter approval to change the general plan to increase residential densities or change residential zoning to industrial or commercial zoning. The City Council subsequently put out a call to all property owners interested in making such changes and then put eight of them on the ballot in 2000. All involved small properties—together the changes would have added 700 units and 150,000 square feet of commercial space to the general plan's buildout—and they all failed.

The institutionalization of ballot-box zoning in many communities was hastened along by the California Supreme Court's 1995 ruling that local general plans can be amended via the initiative process. *DeVita v. County of Napa,* 9 Cal. 4th 763 (1995). A property owner in Napa County had challenged the county's longstanding policy requiring voter approval for conversion of agricultural land to urban use. The property owner argued that subjecting general plans to the initiative process "frustrates the basic purposes of the planning law"—namely, flexibility and ability to adapt to changing circumstances. But the state Supreme Court disagreed, concluding that the state elections law specifically permits general plans to be amended via the initiative process.

Despite tenacious lobbying by the building industry, local initiatives remain exempt from the California Environmental Quality Act. A city council or board of supervisors may, however, hold a proposed initiative for 30 days while studying its impact. This doctrine was reaffirmed by the California Supreme Court in the *DeVita* case.

The *DeVita* case led not only to the Escondido situation, but also to an intense—if narrowly focused—effort to promote urban growth boundaries via initiative in certain parts of the state. Following *DeVita,* more than 20 UGB measures appeared on ballots in California, and virtually all of them passed. But most of these measures appeared on the ballot in only three counties—Alameda, where slow-growth activists and developers duked out growth issues on the ballot several times; Sonoma, where the Greenbelt Alliance promoted a countywide UGB strategy by

➡

placing initiatives on city ballots one by one; and Ventura, where the *DeVita* case stimulated a countywide movement for voter-imposed UGBs.

The genesis of the Ventura County movement involved a roiling growth debate in the city of Ventura that happened to be ongoing at the time the *DeVita* case was handed down. Objecting to the city's plans to trade a park site to a developer who planned to build houses, local residents—supported by some current and former elected officials—placed an initiative on the ballot requiring a vote prior to rezoning any land designated for agriculture in the city's general plan. The measure, dubbed "Save Our Agricultural Resources," or SOAR, passed narrowly.

Three years later, the SOAR movement went countywide, culminating in a series of citywide UGB measures and a countywide measure prohibiting the rezoning of any agricultural or open space land without a vote. The movement was renamed slightly to reflect these broader priorities—"Save Open-space and Agricultural Resources"—but all the measures passed overwhelmingly. Ventura County has the most comprehensive system of voter-created UGBs in the country—in general, they cannot be changed without a vote. Attempts to alter the boundaries have met with mixed success.

Alameda and Sonoma Counties have also been active in the voter-approved UGB arena. So far, the SOAR movement has remained confined to Ventura County. Attempts to pass SOAR-like measures in other counties have largely failed, and ballot-box zoning has remained a mixed bag around the state—largely the function of local political cultures and combustible planning situations. The state is somewhat bifurcated on ballot-box zoning: It's very common in most coastal communities but uncommon in most inland areas such as the Central Valley and the Inland Empire, where traditional suburban-style growth still abounds. But that doesn't mean ballot-box zoning won't migrate inland eventually. Polls from the Public Policy Institute of California have consistently found that residents all over the state—including in the Central Valley—believe they should be able to vote on major planning and land use issues. ∎

polls show that local voters see no connection between residential development and economic growth; often, they want to restrict housing construction, yet they oppose restrictions on other types of growth. The San Diego Association of Governments once issued a report pointing out that all of the cities in the San Diego area that had imposed residential building caps nevertheless continued to subsidize the county's economic development efforts—efforts which, presumably, attracted new residents to the area.

Most important, municipal-level growth-management efforts can't really succeed because, as recent research has shown, they are really local political solutions to problems associated with regional economic and population growth.

UCLA researchers Ned Levine and Madelyn Glickfeld have found that growth management is usually a response to regional problems such as population growth, traffic congestion, and economic expansion. When new houses are built in Petaluma, or new offices are built in downtown San Francisco, this construction is seeking to meet the regional demand of the entire Bay Area, not just local demand. Similarly, traffic con-gestion is a regional problem that spills across municipal boundaries.

But California's voters and politicians have been unwilling to try to grapple with growth management at a regional or statewide level. The only political solution available to angry residents is at the local level. So citizens and their elected representatives seek to meter residential development or tie new growth to the alleviation of traffic congestion.

Chapter 12

Doing the Big Deals: Specific Plans and Development Agreements

Despite the increased significance of general plans during the last 35 years, much of California's growth still remains driven by large development projects. In California—and especially in Southern California and the Central Valley—most large tracts of undeveloped land are held in the form of huge ranches, usually several thousand acres in size. This form of ownership dates back to the Spanish and Mexican periods, and also to the 1860s and '70s, when the state and federal governments permitted large accumulations of land.

When large development companies decide to go forward with a project, they usually seek approval for the entire tract at once and then schedule its development in several phases, each phase taking several years. This practice has led to a two-step approval process. In step one, the developers seek local government approval for the overall land use plan, including a broad-brush physical plan, an infrastructure finance plan, and a proposed schedule of construction, often requiring 10 to 20 years. Once the overall plan is approved, the developers move to step two: processing tentative tract maps for each phase under the Subdivision Map Act.

Both developers and local governments like the two-step approval process. Developers want local governments to approve the plan so that the whole development can be planned at the outset, making it easier to arrange financing. But developers want to delay applying for subdivision tract maps, which usually expire within three to five years, until they are ready to build. Local governments like this process because plan approval can mean influencing a project's character and design and extracting a greater commitment

When large development companies decide to go forward with a project, they usually seek approval for the entire tract at once and then schedule its development in several phases, each phase taking several years.

The need to do large-scale planning has led to the creation of several planning tools that are more flexible than traditional zoning and subdivision regulations.

from the developer to provide infrastructure. Local governments also want the flexibility that a tract map approval offers down the road. It is not uncommon for a developer to propose dramatic changes in a plan during a 10- to 20-year development permit. The project might even change hands or go in and out of bankruptcy before it is built out.

In some of the more growth-friendly cities and counties, developers will seek approval for vested tract maps at the same time that government officials consider the land use and infrastructure plans. These vested maps often do not expire for 10 to 20 years, providing the developer or landowner with rock-solid entitlements that are attractive to financers or potential buyers of the project.

The need to do large-scale planning has led to the creation of several planning tools that are more flexible than traditional zoning and subdivision regulations. In particular, most large-scale plans require the use of both the specific plan and the development agreement.

Specific plans permit local governments and developers to write planning policies and development codes specifically for one particular geographical area. Development agreements allow for more negotiation between localities and developers, creating a more flexible environment for implementation. Both specific plans and development agreements are often created in conjunction with an infrastructure financing system and a general plan amendment. With few exceptions, all of the state's large-scale, high-profile development projects of the last two decades have come about with specific plans and development agreements.

Specific Plans: The Basics

A specific plan is, in essence, a special set of development standards that apply to a particular geographical area.

A specific plan is, in essence, a special set of development standards that apply to a particular geographical area. Like planned unit developments (a precursor to the specific plan), the specific plan gives cities and developers the flexibility to create zoning standards appropriate to the site and the project in question. Cities and counties often use specific plans to deal with a planning problem in a particular area, especially if citizens are demanding action. Developers often use the specific plan as part of a package of planning documents used to lay out development of large new tracts in the suburbs.

One of the amusing ironies of California planning law is that the legal requirements for general plans are quite specific, while the legal requirements for specific plans are very general. The skimpy code sections simply state that after a general plan is adopted, a local government may "prepare specific plans for the systematic implementation of the general plan for all or part of the area covered by the general plan." The code then requires specific plans to cover the same kind of material (distribution, location, standards, etc.) as the general plan must cover. Legal requirements for specific plans are contained in Government Code §§ 65450–65457. Essentially, the rules governing specific plans are skimpy, and most of the few rules that do exist do not apply to charter cities.

A specific plan is not part of the general plan. Cities and counties can prepare "mini" general plans for specific areas, but these documents are usually called "area" or "community" plans. Such documents are incorporated into a community's overall general plan, and they carry the same legal force as the general plan. Legally, the specific plan is more akin to a zoning ordinance—and, especially, to the planned unit development. Despite these bare-bones requirements—or perhaps because of them—the specific plan has become one of the workhorses of California land development.

Legally, the specific plan is more akin to a zoning ordinance—and, especially, to the planned unit development.

At bottom, as state law indicates, the specific plan is an implementation document—a document designed to implement the general plan (or an area plan) within a certain area. And perhaps the most important part is the set of development standards the specific plan contains, which is typically spelled out in great detail. Nevertheless, it is a hybrid in the sense that a specific plan may also contain statements of planning policy, so long as they are consistent with the community's general plan. This flexibility is very attractive to both developers and communities, which accounts for its popularity.

Specific plans are used in many different contexts, and may be initiated by either the local government or the developer. Specific plans have covered areas as large as 30 square miles and as small as one-third of an acre. Specific plans can be policy-oriented, regulatory-oriented, or both.

OPR has prepared a set of Specific Plan Guidelines to assist local governments. These guidelines are similar in tone and approach to the General Plan Guidelines but, because specific plans are such a flexible tool, they are not comprehensive.

OPR = Governor's Office of Planning and Research

The Guidelines, last updated in 2001, describe how to create a specific plan and offer a model specific plan outline. They are especially helpful for understanding consistency requirements

CEQA = California Environmental Quality Act

between specific plans and other planning documents, including the general plan, and understanding how to approach CEQA analysis of specific plans. The Guidelines make clear that even though the statutory requirements for specific plans are minimal, many plans fail to meet the requirements. The plans often fail to map or describe major infrastructure components, especially energy and trash facilities, do not discuss implementation measures, do not address infrastructure financing, and do not explain how the specific plan carries out the general plan.

In a blunt introduction to the Guidelines, OPR states, "Although specific plans are being used for projects ranging from 'new towns' to manufacturing and warehouse developments, there remain many basic uncertainties about what a specific plan is, how it functions, its relationship to the implementation of the general plan, and the extent of its powers."

Types of Specific Plans

Specific plans will typically be used when a single large landowner wants to create a master-planned development on a very large parcel of land.

Specific plans are used in all kinds of situations around the state. In general, they can be separated into three categories:

- **Master-planned developments.** Specific plans will typically be used when a single large landowner wants to create a master-planned development on a very large parcel of land. Perhaps the classic specific plan for a master-planned development is the San Joaquin County Specific Plan for the Mountain House development, a free-standing "new town" planned to accommodate about 44,000 people near Tracy. In large-scale land development situations, the specific plan will typically lay out the overall development scheme, establish the specific development standards the project must follow, and identify the public facilities and capital infrastructure required to support the project.

- **Multiple-owner properties.** In many cases, a city or county will be concerned about rapid growth in a newly developing area, and will respond by requiring landowners to cooperate with each other in a specific plan for the entire area. This ensures that a coordinated development and infrastructure plan will be created (and hopefully followed) as the area is developed. The Evergreen Specific Plan, adopted by the city of San Jose in 1991, is a classic example of a plan for an area with multiple property owners. The plan not only coordinated development among different landowners, but also linked the 865-acre specific plan area with surrounding subdivisions. More recently, the cities of Ontario and Chino have adopted specific plans for intense redevelopment of about 14,000 acres in the San Bernardino County Dairy Preserve. Another good example of a multiple-owner specific plan is the Milpitas Midtown Specific Plan, which seeks to bring nearly 5,000 new housing units to the suburban town's neglected core.

- **Specific urban problems**. Many cities (and counties as well) use specific plans to address specific urban problems. A specific plan prepared under these circumstances is likely to include development standards permitting new development, but constraining their size and shape very specifically in response to neighborhood political pressure. A specific plan might also serve to persuade or coerce property owners into solving a problem together, either by acting jointly or by paying fees enumerated in the policy portion of the specific plan. Good examples of specific plans dealing with specific urban problems are San Luis Obispo's Railroad District Plan, which sought to improve conditions for motorists, pedestrians, and cyclists in the city's increasingly congested core area; the Sunset Boulevard Specific Plan, which sought to attract new business onto the Sunset Strip by identifying specific parcels of land on which larger office buildings could be constructed.

Specific Plans for
Master-Planned Developments

The specific plan is ideally suited for doing large-scale planning of a "new town" or "master-planned development"—a large development project, usually on raw land owned by a single developer.

Because the law contains few standards or guidelines, it is difficult to generalize about how to write a specific plan for a master-planned development. Perhaps the best way is to show how one is used in a specific case.

The Mountain House project is a proposed new town to be located on nearly 7.5 square miles (about 4,700 acres) on the San Joaquin-Alameda county line between Livermore and Tracy. The project has been controversial because it is proposed in unincorporated territory and would have spillover effects in Alameda County, Contra Costa County, and Tracy. However, the developer, Trimark Communities, proposed a project that would, at least theoretically, be a "self-contained" new town including a balance of jobs and houses.

The Mountain House project was so big that it caused San Joaquin County to change its entire approach to processing large

The specific plan is ideally suited for doing large-scale planning of a new town or master-planned development— a large development project, usually on raw land owned by a single developer.

projects. The county amended its general plan to permit a "new community" designation. A new community project requires the county to process a general plan amendment, a master plan, a public financing plan, and a specific plan.

San Joaquin County and Trimark processed Mountain House as a "new community." The overall planning document was the master plan, which in Mountain House's case became a "super-specific plan" that covered the entire 7.5 square miles and served as a device to implement the general plan amendment. The master plan included an overall land use plan with density and intensity standards not unlike those contained in a general plan. The master plan also included:

- **A requirement that** commercial development be timed to accompany residential development so that Mountain House would not become simply a residential suburb
- **Location and standards** for neighborhood centers in each of 12 neighborhoods
- **A jobs/housing program,** including an economic development incentives plan, to ensure a mixture of jobs and housing
- **An affordable housing program** designed to ensure that housing is available for people who work in the Mountain House community even if the private market cannot provide it
- **A design review manual** providing design standards and guidelines for all developments
- **A policy delineating** community buffers to separate Mountain House from all surrounding development
- **A community services program** covering education, childcare, libraries, police protection, fire protection, potential site hazards, and parks and recreation
- **A management plan** to deal with the impact on endangered species, including the Swainson's hawk and the kit fox
- **A transportation plan** covering both regional and local roadways
- **Water and wastewater plans**

Because Mountain House is such a large project, expected to be constructed over a long period of time, the key to its implementation is monitoring, as well as preparation of subsequent plans and program. The Mountain House master plan calls for the preparation of some 22 subsequent plans and programs.

When Mountain House was approved in 1994, the board of supervisors approved the master plan, the public financing plan, the development agreement, the first of several specific plans for particular geographical areas within Mountain House, a general plan amendment, and changes in zoning. Trimark began constructing Mountain House's infrastructure and community facilities in 2001, and houses in 2002.

However, Mountain House also exemplifies some of the pitfalls in the long-term, master-plan approach. Because plan adoption and the start of construction took so many years, market conditions had changed radically by the time the first homeowners started moving into Mountain House. The price of the average house had more than doubled from an expected price of about $150,000 to actual prices in the neighborhood of $350,000 to $400,000. The price run-up placed a new focus on the project's affordable housing component, which suddenly appeared inadequate. When county supervisors rejected a proposal to strengthen the affordable housing program—largely by charging builders of market-rate homes a fee to subsidize affordable housing development—Mountain House's promise of being a self-contained community with housing for everyone faded away.

Because plan adoption and the start of construction took so many years, market conditions had changed radically by the time the first homeowners started moving into Mountain House.

Specific Plans for Multiple-Owner Properties

One of the most valuable uses for a specific plan is to encourage (or coerce) multiple property owners into a single, coordinated planning process. Cities and counties frequently encounter a situation where a new area is likely to be developed—or redeveloped—but the area is broken up into small land ownerships. In these situations, coordinating land planning among the many property owners is difficult, unless a specific plan is used.

One of the most valuable uses for a specific plan is to encourage (or coerce) multiple property owners into a single, coordinated planning process.

The Milpitas Midtown Specific Plan is a good example of a multiple-property-owner plan that was adopted to encourage redevelopment of a neglected area, and adopted at a time when developers were starting to eye the district.

The plan, adopted in 2002, covers about 940 acres (divided into 384 parcels with 220 different owners) in an L-shaped area that had been the South Bay community's original core. During the 1970s, '80s. and '90s, the city paid little attention to the area because houses and shopping centers were rising in the new part of town, which was separated from midtown by railroad tracks. While not completely dilapidated, midtown became a low-rent district with an abundance of auto repair shops and car washes, and a mish-mash of housing. However, Milpitas voters in 1998 approved a tight urban growth boundary that essentially halted the town's outward growth. Infill quickly became the best development option, and city officials wanted to steer that infill to the midtown district.

The city undertook a two-and-a-half-year planning process that was heavy on public participation. The result was a specific plan that called for 4,860 housing units, 720,000 square feet of office space, lesser amounts of commercial and retail space, 48 acres of parks, and an extensive system of pedestrian and bicycle paths. The plan:

- **Provides an overview and history** of the area that helps put the specific plan in context
- **Tackles the issues of land use,** traffic circulation, community design, and utilities and public services much like a general plan would, with goals, objectives and detailed implementation policies for each topic
- **Creates a mixed-use, pedestrian-oriented** district along two north-south thoroughfares
- **Focuses high-density housing** around two new light-rail stations and a proposed BART station
- **Contains 39 pages worth** of development standards and design guidelines, including numerous photos and drawings that provide examples

Although the plan does not contain specifics on infrastructure financing, it does discuss infrastructure needs and financing options. And after adopting the specific plan, the city went to work on a tax-increment financing plan to pay for streetscape improvements, putting utility lines underground, conversion of an old grammar school into a library, and acquisition of 35 acres of land owned by Santa Clara County where the specific plan envisioned hundreds of new housing units.

Specific Plans for Specific Urban Problems

Although best known for their use in "greenfield" projects, specific plans are often adapted to deal with particular urban problems.

Although best known for their use in "greenfield" projects, specific plans are often adapted to deal with particular urban problems. Because they are flexible and action-oriented, specific plans are well suited for this task.

One good example of a specific plan's application to an urban problem is the Sunset Specific Plan, which seeks to deal with the particular problems associated with the lively and colorful portion of the city of West Hollywood known as the Sunset Strip.[1]

West Hollywood is a two-square-mile sliver of land containing about 40,000 residents sandwiched in between Beverly Hills and the Hollywood section of Los Angeles. Ever since its incorporation in 1984, West Hollywood has struggled with the question of how to plan the future of the Strip—retaining its distinctive character, protecting surrounding residential neighborhoods, and still providing enough room for economic growth.

Ever since its incorporation in 1984, West Hollywood has struggled with the question of how to plan the future of the Strip.

The need for the Sunset Specific Plan emerged after residents of the city's crowded neighborhoods began to oppose large development projects, especially in areas—like the Strip—where office towers and noisy nightclubs rub elbows with apartment buildings. This new attitude caused a problem for the city's economy. Without large, modern buildings to accommodate them, the Strip's core of entertainment-oriented businesses—such as talent agencies and small record companies—began fleeing further west to Beverly Hills, Century City, and Santa Monica.

The planning problem was to reinforce good urban design, protect the neighborhoods, and still provide several good locations for new office buildings. The solution was to draw up a plan that actually called for less development than would be permitted under the city's general plan, but focus it on a few target sites.

In structure, the Sunset Specific Plan sets policies, standards, and guidelines in five different areas: economic development, density and height, urban design, open space and streetscape, and use mix. It also creates a separate development application process for projects that would conform to the plan.

The Sunset Specific Plan sets policies, standards, and guidelines in five different areas: economic development, density and height, urban design, open space and streetscape, and use mix.

The plan calls for about 1.1 million square feet of commercial development along the Strip over 20 years—a figure that is actually about 50 percent lower than was anticipated in the city's general plan, adopted during the real estate boom of the 1980s. But most of this development is expected to be concentrated on at least some of the 13 target sites the plan identified.

Some of the buildings constructed on the target sites might be up to 10 stories high—much higher than most current development, but still considerably lower than the few landmark towers already

---

1. In the interest of full disclosure, it must be said Bill Fulton was a charter member of the West Hollywood Planning Commission in 1986, later served as its chair, and still later served as a consultant to the city on economic development issues that later led to the Sunset Specific Plan. However, he did not work on the Sunset Specific Plan itself.

Vested Rights

COMPENSATION FOR A taking of property is not the only issue of concern to developers and others in the property rights movement. Equally important over the last 30 years, at least in California, has been the concept of "vested rights."

A vested right to build is the irrevocable right of a property owner to develop his or her property—a right that cannot be changed by local government permitting agencies or a slow-growth initiative. In 1976, the California Supreme Court issued a ruling that made it very difficult for California developers to obtain vested rights. Since then, two new tools have emerged that are used in most cases to lock in vested rights.

The so-called *Avco* case arose out of the passage of Proposition 20, the coastal initiative, in 1972. At the time, Avco Community Developers, a large homebuilder, had spent more than $2 million planning and grading a subdivision site in Orange County that had already been approved by local officials. Even though grading had already begun, the brand-new Coastal Commission claimed it had the power to review the project because Avco had not yet established a vested right to build. When the case went to court, the state Supreme Court agreed: California developers could obtain vested

➡

in existence. And the plan establishes competition among the target sites. Not all 13 sites can be built out to their maximum potential; the landowners who come forward first will be allowed to build. The remaining target sites will be developed with smaller buildings.

The Sunset Specific Plan also had to deal with the vexing problem of the Strip's nationally renowned billboards. Since incorporation, the city's planners and political leaders had struggled with the question of the landmark billboards along the Strip, considering everything from protecting them as historic structures to forcing the owners to tear them down. In general, the Sunset Specific Plan seeks to maintain some existing large billboards along the Strip and permits some new ones through what has been dubbed the "creative billboard process." New billboards will be permitted if they don't affect views, are "well integrated into the urban context," and enhance the architectural elements located on a particular site.

Development Agreements

Often used in conjunction with a specific plan, the development agreement is a contract between a city or county and a developer. The intent of the DA is to provide security for both sides. The local government gets a legally binding promise that the developer will provide infrastructure and/or pay fees required by a new project. In return, the developer gets a legally binding promise that he or she can build the project, even if the locality later passes a growth-control initiative. Like specific plans, development agreements cover projects of all types and sizes, from new towns with shopping centers and thousands of homes, to single buildings.

Development agreements were authorized by the legislature in 1979 in response to the California Supreme Court's decision in 1976 that made obtaining vested rights much more difficult. (The development agreement statute is Government Code §§ 65864–65869.5.) The law originally envisioned that developers would be willing to make huge up-front infrastructure investments in exchange for vested rights to build, especially on a long-term, multi-phase project. But, as written, the law permits virtually open-ended bargaining between developers and local governments. Theoretically, DAs must conform with local general plans. But in practice, everything is thrown open for discussion—especially because DAs are often processed concurrently with general plan amendments and specific plans. There might be more backroom negotiating over development agreements than about anything else related to planning and development. Still, the law specifically classifies DAs as legislative, so they are subject to initiative and referendum. And they have, on occasion, been turned down by the voters.

Uses of Development Agreements

Many of the provisions included in development agreements could be dealt with through other regulatory agreements such as the specific plan. But developers find the vested rights available through development agreements to be very attractive, especially if they are expected to make large front-end investments in infrastructure. The risk on a multi-phase project without such vested rights is too great. One good example came in the Ventura County city of Moorpark, where Urban West Communities, a homebuilder, negotiated a 10-year DA for a 2,500-home subdivision called Mountain Meadows. Relying on the agreement, Urban West made infrastructure investments it valued at $28 million. But in a controversial election, voters rejected the DA, while imposing a growth cap of 250 homes per year for the entire city. Claiming it had a vested right to build, Urban West went to court. The company eventually won the vested rights case on other grounds, but the project was held up for years in the process and easily could have lost in court.

Development agreements have been popular in rapidly growing areas such as Riverside, Orange, and San Diego Counties, where large developers own huge tracts of land on which they are processing specific plans. These DAs have represented the institutionalization of development fees—with cities and counties extracting far more in fees and/or infrastructure than they would have obtained under traditional processes. Local governments may extract these extraordinary concessions because DAs are exempt from the post-*Nollan* nexus requirement and *Dolan*'s rough proportionality test. Development agreements are specifically

rights only after getting building permits and investing substantial expenditure. And Avco's $2 million investment wasn't enough, the court said. *Avco Community Developers, Inc. v. South Coastal Regional Commission,* 17 Cal. 3d 785 (1976). Over the next decade, the legislature responded with two new techniques that permit builders to obtain earlier vested rights by following alternate processes.

The first was the development agreement law, which permits developers and local government to, in essence, sign a contract for a development proposal. In a development agreement situation, developers typically agree to provide infrastructure beyond what would be permitted under normal exactions in exchange for a guaranteed right to build. Although development agreements are legally suspect (local governments may not contract away their police power), they are widely used in conjunction with specific plans to process large development projects.

The other is the vesting tentative map process, which permits property owners to seek vested rights for a tentative map under the Subdivision Map Act. Vesting tentative maps, which are usually used for single subdivisions that are too small for development agreements, are discussed in more detail in chapter 8. ■

exempted from the provisions of AB 1600 because they serve as a voluntary alternative to normal regulation.

In Orange County, development agreements were the cornerstone of the Foothill Circulation Phasing Program. Large landowners such as The Irvine Company, Mission Viejo Company, and Rancho Santa Margarita Company planned to build tens of thousands of homes in the area. But traditional sources of funds were inadequate to pay for the arterial roads the new developments required. So 19 Orange County developers agreed to provide more than $200 million in exchange for a vested right to build their projects. The vast majority of the funds came from bond issues, and the DAs—guaranteeing that the houses will receive governmental approval—were vital in marketing the Orange County bonds on Wall Street.

Cities and counties also use these agreements to deal with tricky problems involved with timing and sequencing, to lock in assurance that a particular mix of development will occur, and to bring together small developers to fund large public improvements. More recently, development agreements have been used as tools to broker a deal between developers and neighbors or other slow-growth forces. In exchange for the right to develop part of its land, the development company agrees to dedicate other parts for open space, parks, or farms. The developer might even help pay for maintenance of the land that will not be developed.

For years, local governments and developers relied on development agreements even though the constitutionality of DAs was uncertain. Not until 2000 did an appellate court publish a decision specifically upholding the constitutionality of the state development agreement statute. That case also provided a good example of the sort of horse-trading behind many DAs.

The Santa Margarita Ranch was a huge chunk of farmland, pasture, and hills in a desirable area between San Luis Obispo and Paso Robles. Developers were eager to build, but area residents and San Luis Obispo County officials opposed large-scale development. So a development company called Santa Margarita Limited uncovered an antiquated parcel map and insisted the county recognize the map. The county refused, so the developer sued the county to determine the number of legal parcels that could be developed (*see* chapter 8 for a discussion of antiquated subdivision maps). Rather than let a court decide, the county, the developer, and a slow-growth group (the smartly named Santa Margarita Area Residents Together) negotiated a settlement that became a development agreement. The DA designated 1,800 acres for development of 550 homes, plus a golf course, lodge, and equestrian center. The agreement set aside 8,400 acres for permanent open space, and made the remaining 3,600 acres subject to a long-term contract for agricultural production. These were the same designations made in the Salinas River Area Plan, which the county adopted before signing the development agreement.

The county agreed to freeze those land use designations for five years, which was a common move. The Santa Margarita Ranch DA was unusual in that it called for the developer to follow up with a specific plan, a vesting tentative map, an environmental impact report, and a second development agreement. Typically, the county would approve those items prior to, or at the same time as, the development agreement itself. Members of SMART, who were dissatisfied with the deal, jumped on the unusual process and sued, claiming that the county signed the DA too early. An appellate court, however, ruled that a development agreement was appropriate "as soon as the government and the developer are required to make significant financial and personnel commitments to a project." *Santa Margarita Area Residents Together (SMART) v. San Luis Obispo County Board of Supervisors*, 84 Cal. App. 4th 221.

More importantly, the court rejected a second argument from SMART—that the county had improperly surrendered its police power by signing a DA that froze the zoning for a prescribed period of time. The argument over the surrendering of police powers was one that development opponents elsewhere had tried before in court. But the appellate court in the Santa Margarita Ranch case ruled that the DA—as well as the development agreement statute—did not conflict with the county's regulatory responsibilities. "This type of action by the county is more accurately described as a legitimate exercise of governmental police power in the public interest than as a surrender of police power to a special interest," the court ruled.

The Santa Margarita Ranch DA was unusual in that it called for the developer to follow up with a specific plan, a vesting tentative map, an environmental impact report, and a second development agreement.

The appellate court in the Santa Margarita Ranch case ruled that the DA—as well as the development agreement statute—did not conflict with the county's regulatory responsibilities.

Problems With Development Agreements

Despite their popularity throughout the state, development agreements do raise three significant issues. First, the negotiations between the local government and developer may unfairly lock out citizen groups—or may even constitute an attempt to circumvent their efforts. Second, in many cases, renegotiation may be necessary, but both developers and local officials are often afraid to try it for fear that they will lose more than they gain. And, third, some cities have become known for using DAs to strong-arm developers.

Development agreements in Orange and Riverside Counties raised questions about citizen participation. In both counties, slow-growthers placed growth-control initiatives on the ballot in 1988, causing the boards of supervisors to rush through DAs prior to the election. The result was quick approval—and vested rights—for 60,000 units in Orange County and about 100,000 units in Riverside County. Many of these projects had already received all other governmental approvals. Some were partially built. On other projects, the counties were able to exact additional concessions from developers in exchange for the DAs. Nevertheless, the projects protected by DAs are immune from any future growth measure or change in political sentiment.

The second question, regarding renegotiation, naturally did not arise until after development agreements had been around. The law's drafters did not really contemplate renegotiation, although they did specify that DA amendments should be subject to the same notice-and-public-hearing process as the original agreement.

Renegotiation, which is common in long-term private real estate contracts, seems inevitable in the case of 15- to 30-year development agreements.

But renegotiation, which is common in long-term private real estate contracts, seems inevitable in the case of 15- to 30-year development agreements. For developers, market and financial circumstances change; for cities and counties, the political climate might change, as might the cost of public facilities required to service a project. And, recognizing a DA's vested rights as currency, many developers sell the projects before they are built—bringing in new owners who may want to change things around. A few cities have responded by building a process for renegotiation into the original agreement.

Strong-arm tactics rose to prominence during the real estate boom that started during the late 1990s.

The third issue—strong-arm tactics—rose to prominence during the real estate boom that started during the late 1990s. Cities in which developers badly want to build essentially give developers two options: accept a development agreement or go through the "normal" process. If the developer goes the DA route, he is much more likely to win approval for the project, but at the price of big fees or extraordinary dedications of land for public purposes. If a developer opts against a DA, he might get a cool reception at City Hall and find himself bogged down in a bureaucratic and uncertain process. In other words, city officials know they are in the driver's seat. Developers eager to build expensive houses while the market is hot have little choice but to accept the conditions and exactions that the city includes in a DA. If a town has a slow-growth reputation, the city's position at the bargaining table only strengthens.

Although developers and building industry leaders seethe over some cities' strong-arm approach to DAs, developers have been unwilling to challenge the cities publicly or in court. Because development agreement haggling typically occurs behind the scenes and with an incomplete paper trail, city officials may easily disavow any allegations of extortion. They were simply watching out for the best interest of their constituents! Even if a developer were to win a lawsuit, the victory could take years to achieve; meanwhile, the real estate market might have changed drastically, making the victory a hollow one.

Although developers and building industry leaders seethe over some cities' strong-arm approach to DAs, developers have been unwilling to challenge the cities publicly or in court.

Chapter 13

The Consequences of Regulation
Land Use Regulation and Property Rights

Over the past 30 years, all the rules and regulations discussed in the preceding chapters have made life much more difficult for landowners and developers all over California. The easy permit approvals that developers once counted on have disappeared. The planning and pre-development costs they must figure into their pro formas have escalated dramatically. Because of ever-shifting general plans, zoning, and subdivision policies, many developers have found it difficult to figure out just exactly what they are permitted to build. Many have designed projects that comply with existing land use regulations, only to be confronted with lengthy hearings under discretionary review ordinances or CEQA—and then asked to scale down their projects and carry a heavy infrastructure burden as the price of approval. Many more have made it all the way to project approval—even obtained building permits—only to be thwarted by the discovery of an endangered species, a new slow-growth initiative, a less sympathetic city council, or some other change in local political attitudes.

CEQA = California Environmental Quality Act

All developers, whether they have confronted such problems or not, have watched public opinion turn against them. When they were building huge neighborhoods for the returning war veterans and young families during the late 1940s and '50s, these developers were seen as heroes. Today, they are often the objects of public scorn. This derision is due partly to poor public relations and partly to some developers' failing to deliver as promised. The poor public relations stems from most developers' wariness of the news media. Like many private business executives, developers are often unwilling to answer reporters' questions. At the same time, project

All developers, whether they have confronted such problems or not, have watched public opinion turn against them.

opponents usually are happy to talk to the press. Thus, news stories often cast a negative light on developers and their projects. Additionally, if a high-profile project does not live up to expectations or overburdens a community's infrastructure, local public opinion can turn against all developers.

But since the late '70s, California landowners and developers— and, especially, the well-organized and politically powerful home-builders—have been fighting back. They have fought back, with limited success, in the arena of public opinion. They have tried to fight back, with a touch more success, in the legislature. And they have also fought back in the courts, and here they have succeeded.

Members of the property rights movement have scored a series of court victories.

Members of the property rights movement—a loose-knit but committed collection of landowners, developers, and individuals who have a strong ideological commitment against property regulation— have scored a series of court victories. Their chief weapon in the war against land use regulation is a legal concept known as the regulatory taking, which derives from the Bill of Rights. As a result of these victories in court, landowners and developers changed the balance of power in local land use planning in California. But the fights are far from over, and the legal issues and court rulings are so complex that it is not always easy to determine which side is winning the overall battle.

The Property Rights Movement and the Regulatory Taking

The Fifth Amendment to the U.S. Constitution promises that no property shall be taken from a private individual by the government unless the government pays just compensation to the property owner.

The Fifth Amendment to the U.S. Constitution promises that no property shall be "taken" from a private individual by the government unless the government pays "just compensation" to the property owner. The origin of this portion of the Bill of Rights is obvious: It was to protect the citizens of the new United States of America from a capricious government such as the British monarchy, which had regularly commandeered private houses and property before and during the Revolutionary War.

Over time, this constitutional provision was extensively interpreted to include a taking of property by "physical occupation." For example, if the government built a freeway or a reservoir on your property—thus rendering it useless to you—the government had committed a taking by physical occupation and therefore owed you compensation. When it wanted to take your property by physical occupation, the government typically filed an eminent domain lawsuit (sometimes known as a condemnation lawsuit) against you in court, and the fair market value of the property was determined through the court proceeding.

From the dawn of zoning, however, property owners and their lawyers made the argument that a land use regulation could be so restrictive that it also created a taking of property, just as if that property had been taken by physical occupation. This concept of a "regulatory taking" was first acknowledged by Justice Oliver Wendell Holmes of the United States Supreme Court in 1922. In a case involving coal-mining restrictions in Pennsylvania, Justice Holmes wrote that if a land regulation was so restrictive that the landowner was robbed of all economically viable use of his land, the regulation constituted a "taking" under the Fifth Amendment. *Pennsylvania Coal Company v. Mahon*, 260 U.S. 393 (1922). The government was required to pay just compensation to the landowner, just as if the landowner's property had been taken by eminent domain. Relying on due process and equal protection grounds instead, property lawyers did not rely heavily on the takings concept in *Euclid v. Ambler* and subsequent challenges to zoning.

However, during the 1970s, when land use regulations in California first became burdensome to developers, the concept was revived. Many builders began to claim that a regulatory taking had occurred, and they filed what became known as "inverse condemnation" suits. In one sense, these suits were identical to traditional eminent domain suits because they sought to establish the just compensation due the landowner by the government under the Fifth Amendment. In another sense, these lawsuits were the opposite—the inverse—of a traditional condemnation suit because they were filed by the landowner, not the government. The most important court ruling on

The Great Buyout

ALTHOUGH COURT RULINGS HAVE NOT always provided clear guidance, it is evident that regulation cannot be used to stop all development on a piece of private land. In order to preserve private land solely for scenic or environmental purposes, the government must compensate the landowner in some fashion.

This fact, among others, has led to a resurgence in interest in having government agencies actually buy property in order to protect it from development. Alternatively, many local land trusts and government agencies choose to buy the "development rights"—essentially, the speculative value of the property for real estate development—rather than the land itself. With farmland, this concept has evolved into the now-common practice of establishing an "agricultural easement." The landowner sells the easement to a land trust or government agency, and the easement restricts use of the land to farming.

The first evidence of this political shift was the passage of Proposition 70, a 1988 statewide ballot initiative that authorized a $770 million bond issue to establish a state land acquisition program. The brainchild of California environmentalists, Proposition 70 was the first bond issue in more than 70 years to reach the ballot via the initiative process.

Proposition 70 was sometimes called the "park barrel" initiative—a play on the legislative slang phrase "pork barrel"—because of the way the signatures were gathered. Local environmental groups helped gather signatures to place the measure on the ballot; in return, the groups' pet land acquisition projects were specifically included in the initiative. The initiative led to some crucial land conservation efforts, including the purchase of 2,700 acres of land near South Lake Tahoe and a 700-acre tract that connected the city of Glendale's park system with Angeles National Forest.

The success of Proposition 70 spurred local environmentalists and local governments around the state to consider similar bond programs. Soon, voters in many counties were approving bonds to fund land acquisition programs to provide public parks and preserve natural habitats. Over time, the acquisition of land and development rights became linked to broader conservation programs such as regional habitat plans. Oftentimes, builders are required to help fund these efforts.

In the year 2000, the idea of buying sensitive land—sensitive environmentally or politically—took off when California voters approved Proposition 12, the $2.1 billion "Safe Neighborhood Parks, Clean Water, Clear Air, and Coastal Protection Bond Fund." Two years later, voters passed the even larger Proposition 40, the $2.6 billion "California Clean Water, Clean Air, Safe Neighborhood Parks and Coastal Protection Fund." These bonds, plus three other resources bonds approved from 1996 to 2002 and worth a combined $6.4 billion, have provided something of a slush fund for state and local officials looking to buy land.

The recent resources bonds have funded some of the most politically charged buyouts of recent years. The state paid $140 million to acquire or preserve (through the acquisition of development rights) 550 acres of the Ballona wetlands in Los Angeles, in part to rein in the controversial Playa Vista housing and commercial development. The state spent $135 million to acquire 2,800 acres in Ventura County where a locally unpopular housing project had been approved. And the state used bond funds to buy beaches and secure a conservation easement at Hearst Ranch on the Central Coast.

All of these purchases were made with the understanding that simply imposing regulations to block the development was neither practical nor legal. The purchases also emboldened other landowners who said that if people wanted to enjoy looking at open space, the people would have to pay for it. ▪

inverse condemnation in this era—and, indeed, the ruling that California homebuilders spent a decade trying to overturn—involved a five-acre parcel of land in Tiburon owned by Donald Agins and his family.

Agins had bought the undeveloped parcel during the late 1960s, drawn by its spectacular views of San Francisco Bay. At the time, the Agins' zoning called for one-acre lots, meaning Agins could build five houses. During the early '70s, however, the town of Tiburon downzoned the property to permit only one house on the entire five acres. (Tiburon's action took place at about the same time that the nearby city of Petaluma enacted its famous growth-management ordinance. The Bay Area was growing rapidly, and suburban citizens, for the first time, were flexing their political muscles to restrict growth.)

The Agins family filed an inverse condemnation suit, claiming that their property had been taken by the downzoning and demanding $2 million in damages as just compensation. The California Supreme Court disagreed. In the *Agins* decision, the court essentially outlawed inverse condemnation suits in California. The justices said that because a regulation can be changed easily, then, by definition, no regulation can create a taking for which the landowner must be compensated. If a regulation is so restrictive that it might create a taking, the court ruled, then the legal remedy is not to pay compensation to the landowner, but to invalidate the regulation so the landowner can build. *Agins v. City of Tiburon*, 24 Cal. 3d 266 (1979).

The *Agins* ruling was merely one of several "anti-landowner" rulings handed down by the California Supreme Court in the late '70s and early '80s. It was issued only three years after the *Avco* case, which made vested rights very difficult to obtain, and just a year before the court opened the floodgates for ballot-box zoning in the *Arnel* case. Eager to see the *Agins* case overturned, the building industry quickly appealed it to the U.S. Supreme Court. But the court ran into the difficult question of when a legal challenge to any regulation is ripe for review by the courts.

Courts are not supposed to review a plaintiff's complaint unless the plaintiff has "exhausted" all administrative procedures—that is, until the plaintiff has done everything he or she can do outside of court to resolve the issue. Because regulations can be changed at any time, the question of when administrative procedures are exhausted is a very tricky one. If a developer tries, and fails, to have the city council change a regulation, has he exhausted all administrative remedies? If the developer has applied for a zone change once and been rejected, does that satisfy the question of ripeness?

Because regulations can be changed at any time, the question of when administrative procedures are exhausted is a very tricky one.

In Tiburon, the *Agins* family had never formally applied to the city to rezone the property back to the one-house-per-acre zoning that had been in place when the land was purchased. Thus, the U.S. Supreme Court ruled in 1980, the *Agins* case was not "ripe" for judicial review. *Agins v. City of Tiburon*, 447 U.S. 255 (1980).

From 1980 through 1986, the U.S. Supreme Court heard three more cases on the question of regulatory takings. Two of the cases, like the *Agins* case, were from California, because California was one of the few states in the country where the state courts had ruled that a landowner could not obtain monetary compensation for a regulatory taking. Each time, the U.S. Supreme Court found some similar reason that the case was not ripe for review. In a 1986 case from the Davis area, for example, the Supreme Court ruled that a constitutional challenge to a land use regulation is ripe only after the local government has rejected a specific development plan and also denied a variance. *MacDonald, Sommer and Frates v. County of Yolo*, 477 U.S. 340 (1986).

In a 1986 case from the Davis area, the Supreme Court ruled that a constitutional challenge to a land use regulation is ripe only after the local government has rejected a specific development plan and also denied a variance.

At the time, many land use lawyers—and even the justices themselves—were frustrated by the court's inability to get past the ripeness question. There appeared to be enough votes on the court to overturn on constitutional grounds the *Agins* rule that a regulation cannot be a taking that deserves compensation. In the context of the ripeness issue, however, the *Agins* rule did make a certain amount of sense. Clearly, there is a difference between a landowner whose land is subject to severe restrictions, which can be changed, and a landowner whose land has been taken for construction of a freeway. The first landowner may not be able to use his property now, but he may be able to use it in the future. Thus, it is hard to argue that a "permanent" taking has occurred.

The *First English* Case

In 1987, the U.S. Supreme Court found a case that permitted the Agins *rule to be overturned.*

Finally, in 1987, the U.S. Supreme Court—by this time bearing the imprint of Ronald Reagan, who had appointed three justices—found a case that permitted the *Agins* rule to be overturned.

Once again the case was from California. Specifically, it involved Los Angeles County's decision to prohibit reconstruction of a church camp in Tujunga Canyon after a fire and a flood. In 1977, a fire had denuded the canyon; the following winter, partly because the trees were gone, a flood washed away the retreat owned by the First English Evangelical Lutheran Church of Glendale. The board of supervisors then passed an ordinance prohibiting reconstruction of most buildings in the flood zone, including the church retreat. At first the prohibition was temporary, but later the county made it permanent.

Claiming its property had been taken, the church filed an inverse condemnation suit against the county, seeking damages under the Fifth Amendment. Not surprisingly, the church didn't get very far in the California courts because the *Agins* rule essentially prohibited such lawsuits. The court of appeal in Los Angeles ruled that such a case could not be filed in California, and the California Supreme Court declined to hear the case.

At this point, property rights advocates saw the opportunity to make the *First English* case into the test case they had been seeking. The facts of the case were strong, and the circumstances surrounding this incident had good publicity value. (The retreat was not merely a church camp, but a camp for disabled children.) Represented by Los Angeles attorney Michael Berger, one of the nation's top property rights lawyers, the church appealed to the U.S. Supreme Court, which agreed to hear the case. The court's intent was not to decide whether a taking had occurred at the First English camp. (Such a determination is typically made only after a trial.) Rather, the Supreme Court simply wanted to address the question of whether a landowner who claims a taking has occurred is entitled to just compensation, rather than simple invalidation of the ordinance in question, if a taking had occurred.

By a 6 to 3 vote, the Supreme Court overturned the *Agins* rule and decided that a landowner whose property has been taken by regulation is, indeed, entitled to money damages. As for the vexing question of how takings can occur if a regulation can be changed, the court introduced the concept of a "temporary" taking. Even if a confiscatory regulation is overturned or changed, the court said, the government still must compensate the landowner for the loss of his property during that interim period. Noting that the future of the First English camp had been in litigation for almost a decade, Chief Justice William Rehnquist said: "The United States has been required to pay compensation for leasehold interests of shorter duration than this." Therefore, he added, "(i)nvalidation of the ordinance or its successor ordinance after (a) period of time, though converting the taking into a 'temporary' one, is not a sufficient remedy to meet the demands of the just compensation clause." *First English Evangelical Lutheran Church of Glendale v. County of Los Angeles,* 482 U.S. 304 (1987).

Sixty-one years after *Euclid v. Ambler,* the building industry had finally managed to reverse the trend toward giving local governments greater leeway in land use regulation. Property owners have rights, the Supreme Court was saying, and while land use regulations protect the public welfare (and sometimes even public health and safety, as in *First English*), they must protect the private property owner's rights as well.

The *First English* ruling is important not only for what it did, but also for what it did not do. The Supreme Court did not decide (and never intended to decide) whether a taking had occurred with regard to the

Exactions and Takings

IN TRYING TO WIN LEGITIMACY for the legal concept of regulatory takings, the property rights movement has really targeted two somewhat different aspects of land use regulation: compensation and exactions.

Compensation and exaction cases have followed a parallel track and have often been litigated by the same property rights lawyers, who see both ideas as aspects of the same movement. The compensation cases have focused on the question of whether and when the government owes compensation to property owners for overly restrictive regulation. The exaction cases have focused on the question of when exactions become so burdensome that they constitute a taking of property.

The exactions cases are discussed in detail in chapter 10, but they are important to understand in the takings context as well. In all the leading exactions cases, the property owners made the legal argument that the exactions were so onerous that they constituted a taking of property and the government should compensate them accordingly. (These cases include *Nollan v. California Coastal Commission, Dolan v. City of Tigard,* both decided by the U.S. Supreme Court, and *Ehrlich v. City of Culver City,* decided by the California Supreme Court.)

Nollan, Dolan, and *Ehrlich* have all refined the allowable boundaries for exactions in California. Exactions must be related to the projects in question under any circumstances; if they are project-specific, rather than part of a broad policy, they must be directly related and roughly proportional to the impact the project creates. But the cases also established another principle: An excessive exaction can be a form of regulatory taking. An exaction that goes too far clearly diminishes a property's value and therefore the property owner has the right to sue for compensation. Whether or not a property owner is entitled to compensation, of course, depends on the specific circumstances of the case—just as it does in any other takings situation. ■

church camp. That job, the court said, was more appropriately left up to lower courts examining the specific facts of the *First English* case. (In a controversial decision, the state court of appeal subsequently ruled that the facts of the First English case, taken on their face, showed that no taking had occurred and therefore no trial was needed. *First English Evangelical Lutheran Church v. County of Los Angeles,* 210 Cal. App. 3d 1353 (1989).

The *Lucas* Case

Once the First English *case had established that an excessive regulation can constitute a taking and that property owners have the right to sue, the next big question was: When is a regulation so excessive that it constitutes a taking?*

Once the *First English* case had established that an excessive regulation can constitute a taking and that property owners do have the right to sue, the next big question was: When is a regulation so excessive that it constitutes a taking? The U.S. Supreme Court immediately began searching for cases that would provide an answer to that question, and in the 1991–92 term, the court found a case from South Carolina that seemed to offer the right opportunity.

The case involved David Lucas, who owned two beachfront lots on the Isle of Palms off the South Carolina coast worth approximately $1.2 million. In 1988, the state passed the Beachfront Management Act, a law regulating property development in South Carolina beachfront areas. The law contained a strict formula to protect beachfront areas from erosion. Under the law, Lucas was prohibited from building on his lots, even though neighboring property owners with similar lots had been permitted to construct homes prior to the passage of the law.

After Hurricane Hugo in 1989, in which many property owners were wiped out, the law was changed to permit hardship exemptions. But Lucas chose to continue litigating. The South Carolina Supreme Court upheld the Beachfront Management Act as a proper exercise of the state's police power. In 1992, the U.S. Supreme Court overturned the South Carolina court, but used legal reasoning that no one anticipated.

Instead of laying down rules to determine when a taking does and does not occur, the court chose to address the question of whether the state had the right to impose a new regulatory scheme on Lucas's property after he owned it. In an opinion written by Justice Antonin Scalia, a conservative jurist who essentially invented the *Nollan/Dolan* tests for weighing exactions, the court concluded that South Carolina could restrict Lucas's property development only by identifying "background principles of nuisance and property law" that support the goals of the Beachfront Management Act.

In other words, the state could not impose new restrictions on Lucas's property without compensation unless Lucas's proposed construction could be viewed as a public nuisance. *Lucas v. South Carolina Coastal Council,* 505 U.S. 1003 (1992).

The *Lucas* case occasioned a great deal of comment among legal scholars. Those who favor property rights declared a victory, saying it was an important step forward in restricting the government's power to impose regulations. Those who favor land use regulation saw the decision as an odd one, which focused on arcane points of "common law" (like nuisance law), rather than addressing head-on the question of when a taking occurs.

The Supreme Court sent the *Lucas* case back to the South Carolina Supreme Court, where the state's lawyers argued unsuccessfully that beach erosion was a public nuisance. Subsequently the state purchased the property from Lucas and—in the ultimate embarrassment—put it on the market, seeking a buyer who would be willing to build on the lots.

The *Lucas* case clearly reduced the government's power to impose land use regulations, and, like *First English*, had an important psychological impact on both public planners and private landowners, who both perceived that the pendulum had swung back in the direction of the landowners once again. However, the *Lucas* court chose not to provide an answer to the question on everyone's mind: When is a regulation so extreme that it creates a taking of property?

The Holy Grail:
A Firm Takings Standard

"In 1922," legal affairs writer Kenneth Jost observed a while back, "the U.S. Supreme Court declared that landowners may be entitled to compensation for a governmental 'taking' of their property if a land use restriction 'goes too far.' But more than 70 years later, the justices have yet to define how far is too far."

Since Jost made that observation, the Supreme Court has handed down three more takings rulings that build on *First English* and *Lucas* to some extent. But rather than defining "too far," the Supreme Court has continued to employ case-by-case analyses on which not even the nine justices can agree.

The first of the rulings came during 1999 in yet another case from California. At issue was the potential development of 37 acres along the beach in north Monterey. The developer, Del Monte Dunes

The Lucas *decision stated that the state could not impose new restrictions on Lucas's property without compensation unless Lucas's proposed construction could be viewed as a public nuisance.*

The Supreme Court sent the Lucas *case back to the South Carolina Supreme Court, where the state's lawyers argued unsuccessfully that beach erosion was a public nuisance.*

at Monterey, Ltd., filed no fewer than five applications and 19 site plans for the property. Even though the property was zoned for residential development and the plans included successively fewer units, the city of Monterey rejected every proposal. After a rejection in 1986, the developer sued, alleging that the city had denied any "economically viable use" of the land and, therefore, had taken the property in violation of the Fifth Amendment. The company also alleged the city had violated the company's right to equal protection of the law under the Fourteenth Amendment.

A judge determined that a jury should render a decision on major parts of the lawsuit—a terrifying thought to government regulators who feared that 12 lay people would be inclined to favor an aggrieved landowner over bureaucrats explaining the intricacies of land use planning and policy. In the *Del Monte Dunes* case, the jury determined that the city's continual denials amounted to a temporary taking and a violation of the developer's equal protection rights. The jury then awarded the developer $1.45 million.

In the Del Monte Dunes *case, the jury determined that the city's continual denials amounted to a temporary taking and a violation of the developer's equal protection rights.*

The case made its way to the U.S. Supreme Court, which upheld the developer's right to a jury trial and the jury's award of damages. *Monterey v. Del Monte Dunes at Monterey, Ltd.,* 526 U. S. 687 (1999). Many government lawyers feared the decision permitting jury trials would make it easier for developers to obtain a large judgment in a takings claim. But the court was bitterly divided (the ruling was 5 to 4), and *Del Monte Dunes* appears to have had a limited impact. Maybe the most important aspect of *Del Monte Dunes* for planners is the implication that a city cannot simply say no to a developer again and again. At some point, the city has to say what project it will approve.

The court's next crack at setting a firm takings standard came in Palazzolo v. Rhode Island.

The court's next crack at setting a firm takings standard came in *Palazzolo v. Rhode Island,* 533 U.S. 606 (2001). However, the facts of case were muddled, and the court was again deeply split. The *Palazzolo* court did make two important decisions. First, the court ruled that Anthony Palazzolo—a retired auto wrecker who owned 18 acres of wetlands in coastal Rhode Island—could pursue a takings claim even though government officials contended they had never made a final decision on what Palazzolo could or could not build. The state's Coastal Management Council had rejected two applications to fill wetlands. The Supreme Court said those rejections were enough and the council had made clear it would prohibit any development activity on the wetlands. Thus, the court ruled 6 to 3 that Palazzolo's claim was ripe. Second, the court ruled

TDR = Transfer of Development Rights

5 to 4 that the landowner could base his claim on a regulation that took effect before he acquired his property. In this case, the Coastal Management Council was enforcing wetlands protection statutes that had taken effect before Palazzolo acquired sole possession of the property in 1978. Still, exactly what the court meant regarding pre-existing regulations was unclear, partly because two of the five justices in the majority filed concurring—yet contradictory—opinions.

Like *Del Monte Dunes, Palazzolo* again stood for the proposition that the government may not simply say no. The government must indicate what development it will permit. But had the state regulation taken Palazzolo's land? Not necessarily. It was clear that Palazzolo had the ability to construct at least one house on his land, so the court unanimously agreed that a "total taking" had not occurred. The question of a partial taking was sent back to state court in Rhode Island.

While *Del Monte Dunes* and *Palazzolo* shed little light on exactly what regulation constitutes a taking, the Supreme Court's most recent takings decision helped define what sort of regulation is not a taking. In *Tahoe-Sierra Preservation Council, Inc., v. Tahoe Regional Planning Agency*, 535 U.S. 302 (2002), the court considered the fairly straightforward question of whether a 32-month building moratorium amounted to a temporary taking. The bi-state Tahoe Regional Planning Agency (TRPA) had imposed the moratorium during the 1980s while the agency prepared a regional land use plan to protect the lake's clarity from urban runoff. Hundreds of landowners represented by a property rights organization argued that the moratorium amounted to a temporary taking under *First English*.

But in a 6 to 3 ruling, the high court called temporary moratoria "an essential tool of successful development" and said no taking had occurred. The court ruled that the case was unlike *First English* because in *First English* the court did not determine whether the regulation in question actually amounted to a taking, only that a regulation could be a taking. In *Tahoe-Sierra*, the court used the "*Penn Central* test" to decide that the

Transferring Development Rights and Obligations

BECAUSE MOST GOVERNMENT agencies cannot afford to purchase development rights, they are often attracted to the concept of "transferring" such rights. The "transferable development right," or TDR, concept holds the potential to achieve land use planning goals while holding property owners harmless financially. But TDR systems have proven difficult to administer in practice, and have recently been the subject of a legal attack by the property rights movement.

The TDR concept is simple. A landowner may have the right, under zoning, to build six houses per acre on a parcel of land. But the government agency may want to preserve the property as undeveloped. So the government grants the landowner permission to transfer his right to build those six houses to another nearby parcel—allowing the construction of 12 houses per acre on the new parcel, rather than only six. Most of the time, the "receiving" parcel will be owned by a different landowner, and the owner of the "sending" parcel will recoup his land investment by selling his TDRs to the other landowner.

TDR programs have been implemented in such diverse locations as the urban core of downtown Los Angeles, the fragile ecosystems of the Tahoe basin, and the rural canyons of the Santa Monica Mountains. But TDR programs are difficult to implement successfully. Sending and receiving zones must be separate enough to achieve public policy goals, but close enough to assure that the process is not abused. There must be an ample supply of buyers and sellers, so that no one can corner the market on development rights in the area and drive the price up or down significantly. And the government agency must be able to assure that TDR buyers will be able to gain approval for their projects quickly and without unnecessary hassle. (This means that residents of the receiving zone must accept the idea of higher densities in their area—never an easy political task in California.)

Planning consultant Madelyn Glickfeld, who has drawn up several TDR programs in California, has written that a successful program "requires planning conditions and a level of political commitment to implementation that does not exist in many localities." A TDR program only works if conditions are right, and even then functions best "not as the sole strategy to mitigate the effects of harsh regulations, but as one of several different positive strategies to avoid takings." In other words, despite its seductive appeal, a TDR program by itself can't solve all planning problems any more than restrictive regulation can.

Even with these caveats, TDR programs are popular in California and likely to become more popular in the future, as planning goals collide with property rights. A recent study conducted by TDR expert Rick Pruetz and Solimar Research Group found that more than 20 percent of all TDR programs in the country are in California jurisdictions. And unlike other parts of the nation—where farmland protection

➥

TRPA regulation was not a taking. Under *Penn Central Transp. Co. v. New York City*, 438 U.S. 104 (1978), the court evaluates a takings claim based on the purpose of the government action, the economic impact on the landowner, and the effect on "reasonable investment-backed expectations."

The *Tahoe-Sierra* decision was a clear defeat for property rights advocates, who had argued for a categorical rule that would have prevented government agencies from blocking development with long-term or multiple moratoria. Still, Justice John Paul Stevens, writing for the majority, refused to say a moratorium may never in any case be a taking: "In our view the answer to the abstract question whether a temporary moratorium effects a taking is neither 'yes always' nor 'no, never;' the answer depends upon the particular circumstances of the case."

Other Fronts in the Takings War

Even after the U.S. Supreme Court struck down the *Agins* rule, state courts in California have maintained a reputation as hostile to property owners' takings claims, and with good reason: Developers and landowners who argue that government regulation has taken their property usually lose in state court, and the actual awarding of damages is almost unheard of. Much of this litigation has been over local rent control and affordable housing ordinances. For the most part, courts have given great deference to the decisions of public officials.

One notable exception involved a long-running dispute between a Los Angeles landowner and the city. In 1988, a fire nearly destroyed the Ferraro Hotel. The owner, Syed Mouzzam Ali, then sought permission to demolish the burned-out structure. The city rejected Ali's application because, city officials said, the hotel was a single-room occupancy (SRO) hotel, and city ordinances prohibited the demolition of such affordable housing unless the building could not be repaired or the owner provided replacement units. Ali protested that the Ferraro was not an SRO, and, after some administrative and legal proceedings, the city concluded the owner was correct. Nineteen months after filing his application, Ali received the demolition permit.

Ali then sued the city. In an early phase of the litigation, an appellate court ruled that the city's delay violated a state law regarding rental housing. In a second round of litigation, Ali contended that the 19-month delay and the city's actions—the city had hired security guards to prevent further damage to the hotel and billed Ali—amounted to both a regulatory taking and a physical taking of private property. A Los Angeles judge agreed and awarded Ali $1.2 million, plus interest, in damages. An appellate court upheld the decision. The city's actions, the court ruled, violated state law, were arbitrary, "not in furtherance of any legitimate governmental objective, and for no other purpose than to delay any development other than for an SRO hotel. Therefore, the delay in demolition of the hotel was a temporary regulatory taking requiring compensation." *Ali v. City of Los Angeles*, 77 Cal. App. 4th 246 (1999).

The award of damages was remarkable, in part because it appeared to conflict with a state Supreme Court decision regarding permit delays. But the *Ali* decision is an exception that has not proven to be the property rights boon that either side predicted in the immediate aftermath.

With so much uncertainty in the courts, property rights advocates have, from time to time, attempted to create a firm takings definition via legislation. Some proposed federal legislation and regulatory rulemaking has sought to compensate landowners when a regulation diminished property value by a certain percentage However, no substantive takings legislation has ever passed in Congress or in the California legislature, no matter which political party was in power.

Property rights advocates also have tried the direct democracy approach. In Oregon, property rights proponents wrote a statewide ballot initiative that would have required the government to compensate a landowner for any regulation that diminished the value

is a major goal—most TDR programs in California seek to protect environmental goals.

Perhaps fearing the rise of TDR programs after *First English* and *Lucas,* property rights lawyers have recently targeted the TDR concept for legal challenge. In *Suitum v. Tahoe Regional Planning Agency,* 520 U.S. 725, 1672 (1997), the property rights movement launched a direct attack on the TDR program in the Lake Tahoe area, claiming that there is no real market for the sale of development rights and insisting that the entire idea is a sham. The court issued a narrow ruling in favor of the property owner without resolving the larger constitutional question of TDRs.

But the concept of trading a development "right" is really only half the story. Increasingly, developers in California are being asked to buy and sell what might be called development "obligations" as well. In exchange for developing environmentally sensitive land, developers often must provide "mitigation" by paying for the acquisition or enhancement of other environmentally sensitive land. These requirements have led to a brisk business in mitigation and conservation "banking," in which nonprofits or for-profit businesses buy and maintain open land, then sell "credits" for that effort to developers in search of mitigation. Indeed, some of the TDR programs in California—especially lot-retirement programs in the Santa Monica Mountains and motel retirement programs in Lake Tahoe—function more like mitigation banking than TDRs. In the future, there is reason to expect more fusion between these two concepts. ∎

of property. Although Oregon has a reputation for aggressive land regulation, voters approved Measure 7 in 2000, in part because of the initiative's innocuous wording. Oregon state courts prevented the measure from ever taking effect, and the state Supreme Court ultimately decided that Measure 7 violated the state's prohibition against initiatives that address more than one subject. However, four years later, Oregon voters passed a similar, though differently worded, property rights initiative known as Measure 37.

The Oregon elections have buoyed property rights believers. In 2002, they took their case to voters in Nevada County, a semi-rural county in the Sierra Nevada Mountains. Again, the tool was a brief, apparently innocuous ballot initiative. But backers of Measure D conceded they had a broad goal, namely, to give greater rights to property owners who, backers said, were "impotent" within the current legal system. With a 30-year history of polarized growth politics and a large base of conservative voters, Nevada County appeared to be an ideal venue for property rights activists, and Measure D supporters spent heavily on the campaign. Planners nationwide eyed the election as a potential precedent setter. But Nevada County voters surprised many pundits by rejecting Measure D, and people who favor government regulation breathed a sigh of relief.

Part Four

Urban Development

Chapter 14

Economic Development

Californiaʼs miraculous growth since World War II has not come about merely because millions of people have moved here. In large part, the miracle has occurred because the state's economy has been able to provide for all of these extra people—and then some.

For example, between 1940 and 1970—a period covering wartime mobilization and rapid postwar expansion—California's population almost tripled, but the number of jobs in the state kept pace by almost tripling as well. Between 1970 and 1990—a more troubled economic period when millions of women entered the work force for the first time—the state's population increased by half. But the number of jobs in the state grew twice as fast as the population.

The recession-wracked early and mid-1990s tell a different story, however. Between 1990 and 1995, the state's population grew by almost three million people—a 9 percent increase. But, largely because of devastating cuts in aerospace and defense, the number of jobs in the state actually dropped. In 1990, the state had almost five jobs for every 10 residents. Only five years later, that figure had dropped to only a little more than four jobs for every 10 people. The trend reversed starting in about 1994 (the reversal was slower to begin in Southern California) and California saw huge job gains during the second half of the decade. The technology and Internet boom of the late 1990s produced many new, well-paying jobs, especially in the Bay Area and San Diego regions.

During the period of the late 1990s, Silicon Valley was adding seven new jobs for every new house. The growth came to a rapid

Between 1970 and 1990, the state's population increased by half, but the number of jobs in the state grew twice as fast as the population.

In 1990, the state had almost five jobs for every 10 residents. Five years later, that figure had dropped to only a little over four jobs for every 10 people.

halt during 2000, with tech again leading the curve. From 2001 through 2003, the Bay Area lost almost 9 percent of its jobs. During that same period, Santa Clara County led the nation in job losses–about 220,000 jobs (one in five) disappeared in only three years. Southern California also struggled, but generally experienced only minor jobs losses.

Up until the recession of the 1990s, most cities and counties in California took economic growth for granted.

This recent, unstable history of boom and bust helps explain why economic development has grown prominent in California planning. Up until the recession of the early 1990s, most cities and counties in California–especially in the large metropolitan areas in Southern California and the Bay Area–simply took economic growth for granted. Even temporary economic downturns were not as severe in California as elsewhere. By and large, California was considered recession-proof, so the state never created a comprehensive economic development strategy. The state's programs were scattershot at best, mostly providing subsidies for redeveloping downtrodden districts and communities. Local officials, rather than focusing on fostering economic expansion and creating jobs, had the luxury of "skimming the cream." In crafting their economic development strategies, these local officials were able to choose which type of economic growth they wanted and then pursue it.

Especially for many smaller suburban jurisdictions, this luxurious position meant a city could go after–and often subsidize–developments such as shopping centers that would add big dollars to the city treasury. The future success of the shopping center was taken for granted because overall economic growth in the metropolitan area assured a ready market.

California's new emphasis on economic development–whether for the sake of sales tax revenue or stable jobs–has had a significant impact on the practice of local planning throughout the state.

During the recession of the early 1990s, however, things began to change, especially in and around Los Angeles and Orange County, which were hit hardest by aerospace and defense cutbacks. Many local communities remained focused on retail stores and other new development projects that would improve their sales tax revenue, but, because of that recession, many California cities and counties, especially larger ones, have emphasized basic economic growth in areas such as manufacturing, technology, and tourism. As the "global economy" has become more of a reality, California cannot take economic development for granted. This new emphasis on economic development–whether for the sake of sales tax revenue or stable jobs–has had a significant impact on the practice of local planning throughout the state.

The Different Roles
of Economic Development

As the discussion above suggests, the definition of economic development depends upon whom you ask and why. For some practitioners, it is the task of fueling general economic expansion. For others, it involves fostering growth in certain types of jobs and businesses targeted to the needs of a particular community and its labor force. For still others, as most planners are well aware, economic development has nothing to do with jobs or businesses—and everything to do with increasing sales tax revenue and balancing the local government's budget.

Of course, where you stand on the question of economic development depends on where you sit. If you're a city manager, luring an auto dealership or big-box retail store definitely qualifies as economic development. But if you're the governor, this sort of economic development may mean nothing, especially if the retailer has only relocated from one town to the next or has put existing stores out of business. In fact, if the city has used subsidies to attract the retail business, the state may lose money on the deal. Many economists argue that one city's increased retail development does almost nothing for the larger economy because the retail business does not bring new money to the region, as do manufacturing and technology enterprises. In fact, big retailers send their profits out of town, not to mention the fact that retail jobs are among the lowest paid of any sector.

In general, the work of economic development can be defined as local and state governments cooperating with the federal government to ensure a healthy mix of many different types of jobs and a diversified tax base. In practice, economic development in a given agency is typically defined more narrowly. The actual role played by practitioners of economic development will be closely linked to the types of development their agencies desire. Economic development efforts can be broadly divided into two different approaches, which often come into conflict with one another.

First are the broad regional and statewide efforts often promoted by the state and federal governments and by regionwide business consortiums. These efforts usually promote general economic growth without concern for the benefits or burdens that growth may impose on any particular neighborhood or jurisdiction. They often promote expansion of high-growth industries, such as technology, and creation of regional economic infrastructure, such as airports, ports, highways, and data transmission facilities.

In general, the work of economic development can be defined as local and state governments cooperating with the federal government to ensure a healthy mix of many different types of jobs and a diversified tax base.

The Alameda Corridor

ALTHOUGH IT OPENED FOR business in the 21st century, when everything high-tech is supposed to rule the world, the Alameda Corridor is a classic public works project that is intended to feed the local, regional, and even national economies. It is a public investment with economic development at its very heart.

The Alameda Corridor is quite simple. It is a 20-mile long rail line connecting the Los Angeles and Long Beach port complex with the rail yards just east of downtown Los Angeles, where the transcontinental railroad begins. The central feature of the corridor is a 10-mile long trench that is 50 feet wide and 33 feet deep. At either end of the trench is a series of bridges, overpasses, and underpasses. The purpose of the corridor is equally simple—to speed the transport of freight to and from the port by slicing through an intensely congested area. Trains began hauling cargo on the Alameda Corridor in 2002.

Of course, no large project carved into an existing urban area is truly simple. It took 20 years of planning, litigation, politicking, and construction to complete the project. The Alameda Corridor cost $2.2 billion, making it one of the most expensive public works projects to date in the United States. The two ports, the state, and the federal government provided funding.

The project was intended to aid the growth of the port complex, which is the third largest in the world and is expected to see a quadrupling of cargo over a 25-year period. The port is considered vital to the health of transportation, manufacturing, and importing/exporting businesses, especially those in Southern California. Analysts say at least half a million Southern California jobs are connected in some way to the port. The two dozen "Gateway

The second approach to economic development, often promoted by local governments and neighborhood-based organizations, typically involves a narrowly focused effort to solve certain economic problems in a particular jurisdiction or geographical area. These local efforts often seek to bring business investment into distressed areas or to maintain and improve the tax base of a local government, whether distressed or not.

Obviously, both types of efforts are closely tied to land use planning, but planners themselves are typically more involved in local economic development simply because they usually work for local government.

The Role of State and Federal Government

The state and federal governments play an important role in both the "regional" and the "local" approaches to economic development, but their role in the regional approach is far more direct.

The state often chooses to finance big-ticket infrastructure items or provide tax breaks or other subsidies for specific industries. As with federal projects, these state projects tend to be highly political—brought about either by high-level deal making in the state legislature or by the governor's desire to make headlines. For example, when Governor Gray Davis introduced the $5 billion Traffic Congestion Relief Program in 2001, a number of the projects to be funded were intended to support specific development projects, such as an Indian casino and shopping mall on Interstate 10 near Palm Springs. The program's investment decisions, which were made outside the normal transportation planning process, appeared to be based largely on the promise of ribbon-cutting photo opportunities and the desires of Davis backers, such as Silicon Valley businesses and Indian tribes. (The program was intended to be funded with "surplus revenues" that disappeared as soon as Davis rolled out the program. The program ended up getting scaled down and then suspended, leaving some of the chosen development projects in the lurch.)

Both the state and federal governments play an important supporting role in the local approach to economic development, too. In addition to directly funding regional big-ticket items, the state and the feds also create and maintain a variety of programs that local economic development agencies use in their work. Many of these programs target distressed areas and have a close relationship to local planning.

For example, both the state and federal governments have some type of enterprise zone program. The concept of an "enterprise zone"—which first became popular during the Reagan years—is simply that regulatory and tax burdens should be loosened in distressed areas to stimulate private investment in these areas. In the 1980s, the state passed two separate enterprise zone programs that provided state tax breaks to businesses locating in specified distressed areas. After Bill Clinton became president in 1993, the federal government initiated a somewhat similar "empowerment zone" program providing large sums of federal money for distressed urban areas.

The state also provides economic development grants to cities and counties, which then loan the money to businesses for things like land and equipment acquisitions. In exchange, the businesses must provide a certain number of jobs. However, these programs are not self-executing at either the state or federal level. Rather, they are designed to help local governments carry out their own economic development plans. In both the state and federal enterprise zone-style programs, local governments must first seek designation as an enterprise zone or an empowerment zone before being eligible for their benefits.

Cities" in the vicinity of the corridor had identified the Alameda Corridor project as an important component in their economic development strategy. This strategy has attempted to turn around local fortunes after the aerospace cutbacks of the 1980s and 1990s hammered the cities.

Although most local politicians eventually ended up praising the project, the Alameda Corridor is a classic example of the typical tension between regional and local approaches to economic growth. The project's importance to the regional and national economies is unquestionable, yet the project generated vigorous debate about increased air pollution, noise, and danger from rapidly moving trains in the communities that were sliced in half by the rail line. There also was plenty of argument about whether the corridor was the best way to spend $2.2 billion—especially whether the money could have been better spent to aid the ailing Gateway Cities more directly.

Although some environmental justice advocates never stopped fighting, most local politicians in the end saw that the impacts would be minimal—a fast-moving train generates less air pollution than a line of trucks stuck in freeway traffic—and accepted the project as a winner for everyone. The fact that about 1,300 local residents were employed during the five years of construction did not hurt public opinion either.

The Alameda Corridor is now considered a vital part of Southern California's economic infrastructure, but as soon as it was complete and in operation, the discussion turned to the potential investment in a similar corridor that would speed the movement of freight eastward, out of the L.A. Basin, and avoid the numerous street crossings along the current rail system. A repeat of the Alameda Corridor's local impact versus regional gain debate is assured. ■

Local Economic Development: The Focus on Tax Revenue and the Link to Planning

When crafting an economic development strategy, individual local governments are often hampered by their own geographical boundaries from doing anything useful in a broad economic sense. In today's world, the scale of most economic growth is simply not the same as the scale of political subdivisions, especially in the suburbs. Labor markets are regional, as workers will usually commute 45 minutes to an hour to get to their jobs. Retail markets, with shopping malls and big-box power centers as their bases, seek to attract shoppers from a similar distance. To lure these shoppers, retail centers have grown ever larger, to the point where they now contain 20, 30, or even 40 football fields worth of shopping opportunities.

With a few exceptions, the typical California city stretches no more than 10 miles from end to end. In metropolitan California, a labor market or a retailing market can encompass 3, 5, 10, or even 20 cities.

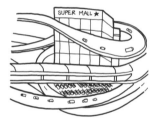

With a few exceptions, the typical California city stretches no more than 10 miles from end to end. In metropolitan California, a labor market or a retailing market can encompass 3, 5, 10, or even 20 cities. Given these limitations of scale, what can a single city do to stimulate economic activity with a political payoff?

The answer, typically, is to abandon broader efforts to encourage economic growth and focus instead on one of two highly parochial goals:

- **Drawing investment into** distressed urban or rural areas that otherwise would not thrive

- **Increasing the city's tax revenue,** rather than jobs or general economic growth

Both of these goals require the creation of particular types of business activity in specific locations. For this reason, they are closely related to land use planning.

Of course, most economic development practitioners are not planners. Some are schooled in redevelopment or public administration, while others come to economic development from backgrounds in marketing and private entrepreneurship. Yet they often understand what planners may overlook—that the use of land and the planning processes that determine that use lie at the heart of the economic development process for local governments.

The use of land and the planning processes that determine that use lie at the heart of the economic development process for local governments.

In this way, economic developers—whether they work for nonprofit agencies or for local government directly—become, in effect, real estate developers. They promote the use of particular pieces of land for particular purposes associated with economic growth. In so doing, these economic developers—and the politicians they work for—place tremendous pressure on planners and the planning process to produce the political results that they desire.

The Fiscalization of Land Use

Ask the typical city manager in California for a definition of economic development, and the answer will likely be "the pursuit of tax revenue," or, more specifically, "the pursuit of sales tax revenue."

This intense focus on tax revenue as economic development is the result of two things. First is the general belief—valid until recently—that local governments in metropolitan California can take basic economic growth for granted. Second is the scarcity of tax revenue created by Proposition 13 and its tax-cutting offspring.

In traditional California thinking, local governments need not concern themselves with attracting industry or jobs. In the post-Proposition 13 environment, local governments can no longer assume that a healthy balance of growth (houses, apartments, stores, offices, factories, etc.) will mean a healthy balance in the budget. That is why cities and counties throughout the state have used planning—and, in particular, economic development—to pursue tax revenue.

In the post-Proposition 13 environment, local governments can no longer assume that a healthy balance of growth (houses, apartments, stores, offices, factories, etc.) will mean a healthy balance in the budget.

Most cities and counties in California receive the vast majority of their tax revenue from two sources: property tax and sales tax. (Subventions from the state and the federal government, usually passed through the state, often provide the largest shares of city and county general fund revenue.) Prior to the passage of Proposition 13 in 1978, property tax was the most important source of local government revenue. However, since Proposition 13 placed restrictions on property tax rates, sales tax revenue has become the key source of revenue for local government. In many communities, sales tax revenue actually exceeds property tax revenue.

Under Proposition 13, property tax rates are limited to one percent of a property's assessed value. Generally speaking, the rate cannot be increased except when approved by a two-thirds vote of the local residents—a difficult task, but achievable for construction of police stations, libraries, and other highly popular items. Furthermore, property may not be reassessed except when it is sold or when new construction occurs. If property is not sold, assessed value may rise by no more than two percent per year, no matter how rapidly the market value is rising.

Property tax revenue, though collected by counties, is typically divided among city, county, school district, and special districts. Under complex formulas that are determined by the state and are different for every county, school districts typically get 50 to 60 percent of property tax revenue. Usually, cities each get about 15 percent of property tax revenues, while counties get about 25 percent.

The stated purpose of Proposition 13 was to protect longtime homeowners who had bought houses for low prices but could not afford rapidly escalating property taxes. (Another motive was to constrain local governments from liberal spending practices.)

Proposition 13 has led to well-publicized inequities among property owners. One homeowner who purchased a home last year may pay $4,000 per year in property taxes, while the longtime owner of an identical house next door may pay only $400. It's less often mentioned—but equally true—that these same inequities exist among owners of commercial and industrial property, who might be the biggest beneficiaries of Proposition 13.

Because property tax revenue after Proposition 13 bears little relationship to the cost of providing a property with public services, some developments are clearly winners and some are clearly losers for local government. An office building or shopping center pays a lot of property tax, but takes up relatively little land compared with a subdivision, requires minimal police and fire protection, and produces no children who must be educated by the local schools. A subdivision of single-family homes stretches across the landscape, requires extensive police and fire protection, and generates a vast number of children who must be educated. But the subdivision produces relatively little property tax revenue and no sales tax revenue. For most cities and counties, the subdivision is a direct money loser.

The sales tax structure permits even more blatant manipulation. The permanent state sales tax is 6 cents for every dollar of retail sales. Of that 6 cents, the state government keeps 5 cents and gives 1 cent to local government. (An additional 1.25 cent sales tax is given to local governments for public safety purposes under the terms of Proposition 172.) Counties can increase the sales tax rate but only with a public vote—two-thirds approval is required—and only for specified purposes such as transportation.

Furthermore, that one cent is returned to the local governments based on the location where the retail sale occurred. Thus, if a resident of Walnut Creek buys a watch at Macy's in San Francisco for $100, San Francisco gets $1 in sales tax revenue and Walnut Creek gets nothing.

It is not too difficult to see that this tax structure leads many financially strapped local governments to "fiscalize" their land use policies. Many localities use both their legal powers and their financial resources to clear out the losers and replace them with projects that will jack up tax revenue. In many cases, the traditional concern for a balanced community that will provide its citizens with everything they need—a variety of housing types, jobs, shops, culture—has been replaced by an overriding desire to increase the local sales tax base.

In recent years, the debate over the fiscalization of land use has evolved from arguments over whether the problem exists, to questions of what to do about it. A 1999 study by the Public Policy Institute of California found that city managers ranked new sales tax revenue as the single most important factor in land use decisions. Not surprisingly, the provision of affordable housing was among the lowest considerations. Although there may not have been a direct correlation, within weeks of the PPIC report's release, the state legislature passed the first law that attempted to prevent cities from using subsidies—such as tax "rebates," discounted real estate, or low-interest loans—to steal a neighboring city's large retail stores or automobile dealerships. Since then, the state law has gotten tighter and tighter, to the point that only the most creative—or brazen—cities even attempt to lure a neighbor's stores. Still, there are few restrictions for subsidizing brand new retail development. So when a big-box retailer such as Wal-Mart or Costco proposes opening a new store in a region, the retailer may play one city off another in attempting to get the best deal.

But there are more subtle implications, as well. For example, because they are unable to increase property tax rates (at least for general fund purposes), local governments can realize higher property tax revenue only when property changes

Revenue Benefits of Retail Development

Shopping center	vs.	Single-family home subdivision
Pays higher property taxes on less land		Pays lower property taxes on more land
+		+
Generates sales tax revenue		Generates NO additional revenue
+		+
Requires minimal fire and police protection		Requires extensive fire and police protection
+		+
Generates no new children to be educated		Generates many new children to be educated
=		=
Revenue PRODUCING Project		Revenue DRAINING Project

Wal-Mart Wars

BECAUSE OF THE INCREASED IMPORTANCE of sales tax as a local government revenue source, many cities and counties view the development of big-box retail stores (Wal-Mart, Costco, The Home Depot, etc.) and power centers (collections of national retailers in a large strip) as economic development projects. Once constructed, these projects usually thrive, but success in the marketplace does not necessarily mean the projects are politically popular.

For one thing, big-boxes and power centers often cannibalize existing businesses. Countless cities with shiny new big-boxes and power centers also contain empty or under-used buildings that formerly housed Montgomery Ward, Kmart, Home Base, or a grocery store. Older commercial strips or downtowns dominated by mom-and-pop businesses almost always suffer when big-boxes and their inexpensive merchandise come to town. Another factor is the wages paid by big-box retailers. Most stores pay minimum wage or slightly more, and benefits are sparse. Plus, retailers do not bring "new money" to a community, like a factory does. Instead, retailers extract money, sending profits to corporate offices and manufacturing plants located far away. Traffic generated by big-boxes and power centers is also an issue.

Still, there is no denying that cities and counties need sales tax revenue, and those cities that resist retailing trends fear getting left in the dust. Thus, many cities provide incentives for big-box stores and power centers in the form of discounted land, infrastructure, and even direct subsidies based on the amount of sales tax a store generates. Thus, the tension is obvious—subsidized, low-paying employment that harms existing businesses versus retail leakage that cuts into local government coffers.

This tension has risen to the surface most often when a Wal-Mart store is proposed, particularly a Wal-Mart supercenter. A supercenter is a big-box on steroids—up to 250,000 square feet (more than four football fields) containing a full-sized Wal-Mart and a giant grocery store all under one roof. Wal-Mart has thousands of supercenters across the nation but did not bring the idea to California until recent years. The proposed stores have created an enormous stir in a number of cities, with opposition driven by grocery store clerk labor unions. Wal-Mart "associates" are not unionized and typically make about half as much as California's mostly organized grocery store employees. Other

➡

hands, or when new, more valuable development is constructed. Thus, many cities and counties use their powers to encourage the sale or redevelopment of valuable property, and many communities zone vast tracts of land for tax-rich commercial and industrial development even though they are in dire need of more housing. The tax issue gives many cities—especially suburban cities—yet another reason not to pursue housing policies that will provide units for below-market buyers and renters.

Since the late 1990s, numerous academics, planners, independent and state-appointed committees, and even the Legislative Analyst's Office have urged state lawmakers to overhaul the government financing system. While not everyone has agreed on the proper approach, nearly everyone has concluded that the current fiscal incentives for local government are warped and inhibit the development of balanced communities. State lawmakers have approved a few regional pilot programs intended to help with certain communities' jobs-housing balance and have made available some grants and loans to jurisdictions that approve their shares of housing projects. Still, the overall system has remained unchanged.

One reason the flawed system remains in place is that there is virtually no public outcry. Even well-educated taxpayers who pay attention to state and local politics—a small minority of Californians—have trouble understanding how local government gets its money. Plus, almost no significant overhaul is possible without tinkering with Proposition 13, which remains as popular as ever among voters. Thus, when a proposal to overhaul the system is made, the constituency behind the proposal is small. When a proposal meets resistance, which is assured, there is little political force to overcome the opposition.

Furthermore, cities are divided over whether to change the system at all. Cities that have profited from the existing system by building huge retail bases or by becoming redevelopment havens—such as Cerritos in Southern California, Emeryville in the Bay Area, and Roseville in the Sacramento region—have lobbied strongly against any changes. Plus, nearly all cities are leery of any systemic overhaul endorsed by state officials.

Stimulating Economic Growth in Distressed Communities

Quite apart from the quest for tax revenue, many local governments often use planning tools to stimulate investment in distressed communities. Though this is a worthy goal, it is one which the planning process is apparently not capable of achieving—at least not all by itself.

One of the sad facts of current American life is the geographical separation of rich and poor—a division that is often made worse by fragmented local government, which permits affluent communities to seal themselves off physically and economically from poor communities.

opposition comes from existing business owners, slow-growth advocates, and community activists worried about Wal-Mart's potential for inducing urban decay.

In response, some cities and counties have declined to rezone land for big-box development or have adopted big-box ordinances. These local laws either limit the size of a retail store or cap the amount of space a big-box may devote to nontaxable items, namely groceries. The latter ordinances specifically target Wal-Mart supercenters. For example, the city of Turlock in the San Joaquin Valley adopted an ordinance during 2003 that prohibits stores of 100,000 or more square feet from dedicating more than 5 percent of floor area to nontaxable merchandise. Turlock officials feared that a planned supercenter would force two or three existing grocery stores to close, leading to the demise of the commercial centers anchored by the grocery stores. Wal-Mart contested the ordinance in court, but the city won.

The argument that Wal-Mart supercenters cause urban decay—by triggering store closures then the abandonment of existing commercial areas—received a boost in late 2004. The Court of Appeal ruled that environmental impact reports for two proposed supercenters in Bakersfield had to consider the potential for the supercenters to induce decay. *Bakersfield Citizens for Local Control v. City of Bakersfield,* 124 Cal. App. 4th 1184 (2004).

Wal-Mart is not accustomed to losing, so it has taken its case directly to voters. These direct appeals have met with mixed success. In 1999, city of Eureka voters rejected a Wal-Mart initiative to rezone land for a proposed store. Five years later in a local election in which Wal-Mart and labor unions spent millions, voters in the city of Inglewood rejected a 71-page initiative that would have forced the city to approve a shopping center anchored by a supercenter. But Wal-Mart has had successes, too. In both Contra Costa County and the city of Lodi, voters repealed big-box ordinances that barred supercenters.

Perhaps the most intense battle has been in the city of Los Angeles, where a City Council with strong ties to labor unions approved an ordinance that prohibits supercenter-type stores in most parts of the city. In Los Angeles, the stated reason for the ordinance was that new supercenters could harm existing commercial areas in which the city has invested heavily with infrastructure and incentives. ▪

Planning Tools Used in Economic Development

BECAUSE PLANNING AND economic development are so closely related, many common planning tools are used to establish and pursue economic development goals. To put it another way, plan making and plan implementation are intertwined with economic development all the way down the line.

Indeed, economic development often holds a favored status in the planning apparatus of the typical local government. Metropolitan communities may shun residential growth, fearing a political backlash by residents who don't want more traffic in their neighborhoods. But those same communities will aggressively pursue commercial and industrial development. These projects often bring considerable tax revenue and require few city services. They permit city residents to work locally, and can be located in burgeoning freeway corridors where the traffic impact on the rest of the community is likely to be minimized.

Economic development goals are usually considered part of the planning process, and are sometimes called out separately as part of the general plan. They will be deeply embedded in the land use element, which will call out specific geographical areas for commercial and industrial development likely to improve the city's economic condition. As pointed out in chapter 6, economic development ranks only behind public facilities as a popular topic for an optional element in the general plan. Much of a local planner's implementation effort will also be focused on economic development goals.

These unfortunate divisions have always been with us, but they were accelerated by suburbanization, which permitted the affluent and the middle class to remove themselves from older neighborhoods. The ghettoization of the poor has been made even worse in the last decade by several trends. These include the shift of many job centers to the suburbs, a lack of private investment in distressed communities, and foreign immigration, which has concentrated large populations of poor people in crowded, older neighborhoods. The housing price increases of recent years have compounded some of these problems. Middle-income workers, especially singles and those without children at home, have returned to some older, distressed neighborhoods because they offered housing at affordable prices. This gentrification, while welcome in some respects, sometimes priced out the poor people who had been living in the community. Though distressed urban neighborhoods receive the most publicity, it is equally true that rural communities often have similar problems, especially in California's farming regions.

For 50 years at least, it has been a basic tenet of public policy in America to use the planning process to try to revive inner-city neighborhoods. By any objective measure, this effort has not succeeded. During this period, poor neighborhoods have only become poorer, as more working- and middle-class people have fled and little economic investment has occurred.

But it is hard to say whether these revitalization efforts have been a complete failure. Perhaps they have made a marginal difference in some neighborhoods. Perhaps things would have been even worse if these efforts had not been undertaken. In any event, revitalization of distressed neighborhoods remains a basic goal for many communities, especially older central cities, such as Oakland and Los Angeles, and rural counties where poverty is common.

Since the advent of urban renewal more than 50 years ago, urban planning has been viewed, rightly or wrongly, as a key to the revitalization of distressed neighborhoods. In large part, this is because the "blight" in these neighborhoods is usually reflected in their physical appearance—rundown houses, potholed streets, vacant storefronts. Therefore, many of the public policy efforts in this area have been directed toward improving the physical design and appearance of these neighborhoods. Most of these efforts have involved bringing public funds into these neighborhoods, though some have also sought to provide incentives for private businesses and to cut red tape for private investments.

A few of the most commonly used planning tools in distressed neighborhoods have been:

- **Targeted public improvements.** A city or county may use either local redevelopment funds or federal Community Development Block Grant funds, which can be used to repair streets, improve infrastructure, and make other investments in what might be called the public domain.

- **Location of public facilities in distressed neighborhoods.** Government agencies are often huge employers that can stimulate other private investments, so the government's own real estate decisions can help turn a neighborhood around. For example, the California Department of General Services has a longstanding policy of placing state offices in downtown areas, especially those in distress. This is why many state offices in the Bay Area are located in downtown Oakland. An executive order signed by Governor Gray Davis further encouraged this selection of downtown areas for state offices.

The mere placement of government offices in distressed areas doesn't always solve problems. Downtown Riverside, for example, is a regional center of government, with numerous city, county, state, and federal office buildings and courthouses. However, the concentration of "8 to 5" government offices has done little to entice private investment in downtown, and city officials have had to use other incentive

Among the plan-making and plan implementation tools typically used to pursue economic development goals are the following:

- **Visionary Planning Direction.** In drawing up its general plan or its vision for the future, a city or a county will likely place great emphasis on fostering economic growth. An affluent community may seek to restrict residential growth but attract upscale businesses. A poor community may deliberately pursue high-end houses in order to change its image among corporate honchos. A community on the suburban fringe may try to bring in more jobs in order to reduce out-commuting by its residents and stem the outflow of retail sales. All of these goals will be included in the general plan—and in its land use element, which will identify specific locations in the community where these activities will take place.

- **Targeted Public Improvements.** A community's economic development plans will likely be closely linked to its infrastructure planning. In order to attract commercial and industrial development, communities must make sure that the proper infrastructure is in place—roads, sewers, electric utilities, and so forth—to accommodate the new development. In many cases, communities will create assessment districts or special taxing districts so that the property owners pay for those improvements. (For more information, see Part Five, Infrastructure Finance.)

- **Financial Subsidies to Desired Businesses.** Providing financial subsidies for specific businesses can be a controversial proposition, because it raises the specter of welfare

➡

for the rich. Nevertheless, giving tax breaks or using public funds to pay for infrastructure are common practices, especially when attracting or keeping a particular company is an extremely important goal. California cities and counties are sometimes at a disadvantage in providing financial subsidies. Proposition 13 and other tax-cutting laws have reduced the overall amount of revenue local governments have to play with in this area. Also, in contrast to other states, California localities are constitutionally prohibited from providing property tax "abatements" as a way to retain or attract businesses.

- **Redevelopment.** For all of the reasons described above, redevelopment has emerged as probably the single most important economic development tool that local governments have at their disposal in the economic development arena. Redevelopment funds—which are, in essence, property tax funds diverted from use by counties, school districts, and other public agencies—can be used for a wide variety of economic development purposes.

Most commonly, redevelopment subsidies are used to install infrastructure and other public improvements, and to "write-down" the cost of land—in effect, subsidizing land cost to make the deal more attractive to prospective businesses and developers. A much more extensive discussion of the use of redevelopment in economic development is contained in chapter 15. ∎

programs in an attempt to revitalize what was a thriving district during the early 20th century.

- **Subsidies for individual businesses and developers.** Especially through redevelopment and Community Development Block Grants, cities and counties may sometimes build infrastructure or provide land for businesses they hope to lure into distressed neighborhoods. Odd as it may seem, distressed neighborhoods often have very high land prices because land is divided into small parcels and property owners often own the land debt-free, meaning they have little incentive to reduce the price in order to sell it.

- **Tax credits and regulatory streamlining.** The enterprise-zone approach, which became popular during the 1990s, seeks to encourage private investment in distressed neighborhoods by lowering taxes and reducing regulation.

Though enterprise zones may be a good idea in theory, they have not really been put to the test, especially in California. In the late 1980s, the state created two different types of enterprise zones—one supported by Democrats and one supported by Republicans. Both types of zones give businesses a tax break for investing and expanding inside their boundaries. The Democratic zones require the businesses to hire local residents in order to qualify for tax credits. But the zones provide tax breaks only on state taxes, which are not nearly as important to businesses as federal tax breaks. (The federal Empowerment Zone program provides some tax breaks in highly selected circumstances.)

While tax breaks have been popular, regulatory streamlining has been much harder to achieve. Advocates of environmental justice and their supporters have effectively halted any attempt to streamline the use of the California Environmental Quality Act and other regulations in distressed areas, arguing that inner-city residents should have the same environmental protections as suburbanites.

Typically, different economic development tools are used in combination with one another in distressed areas to increase the likelihood of effectiveness. For example, the state usually requires enterprise zones to overlap with redevelopment project areas. Sometimes, these combined efforts make a difference. More often, the sad slide of distressed areas continues.

Much of the reason for these continued problems has to do with the fact that planning cannot solve underlying social problems such as crime and poor education. Effective police protection in a distressed neighborhood is probably far more important than any planning tool for the simple reason that people who have choices will not live or invest in neighborhoods they perceive to be unsafe.

Another endemic problem is the fact that many planning tools designed for distressed neighborhoods are not targeted to those neighborhoods. Redevelopment, CDBG, and other tools permit great flexibility for local governments, which are eager to use them as broadly as possible. This is probably a political inevitability; after all, a Congress and a legislature dominated by suburban interests can hardly be expected to support expensive programs that can be used only in inner-city areas. Perhaps this flexibility will come in handy in the future. As traditional efforts to stimulate urban revitalization have failed, the problem of urban blight has spread to older suburbs now facing the same problems that their inner-city counterparts have been grappling with for decades.

Conclusion: The Link Between the Economy and Planning

Economic development straddles an odd set of paradoxes in local government. On the one hand, economic growth in California is mostly the result of private business activity, which is, by design, decentralized, responsive to the marketplace, and impossible to control completely. Planning, on the other hand, is meant to be a process by which a local community exerts almost complete control over the use of its land—and, by extension, all the residential and business activity that occurs on that land. Just as the state has no overarching land use plan for California, the state also has no broad economic development plan, either.

Thus, economic development is a process by which local governments seek to use planning to guide private investment and business activity toward the goals the local government wants to achieve. However, no local government can truly control all of the business activity within its borders, and, as this chapter has pointed out, local governments often have a conflicting set of desires. Many

Another endemic problem is the fact that many planning tools designed for distressed neighborhoods are not targeted to those neighborhoods.

Just as the state has no overarching land use plan for California, the state also has no broad economic development plan, either.

communities, for example, restrict growth inside their borders while at the same time participating in regional efforts to attract growth to their area. Also, more than a few jurisdictions take a sales tax *über alles* view, which leads to immediate gains for the local government's treasury but very little real economic growth.

Chapter 15

Redevelopment

In all of California planning, there is probably no more controversial tool than redevelopment. Originally designed to revitalize struggling inner-city neighborhoods, redevelopment has been transformed by local governments around the state into dozens of different mutations to serve whatever political ends seemed important in a particular place at a particular time.

Redevelopment has been used to clear slums, to build hotels and convention centers, to lure auto dealers and other retailers across municipal boundaries, to construct both low-income and luxury housing, to provide basic stores to inner-city neighborhoods that needed them, to build City Halls, schools, and other public facilities, to solve flooding problems on horse trails, and even to build golf courses on raw land. Not all of these activities are currently legal under redevelopment law; in fact, a number of them are specifically outlawed because of the way redevelopment has been used by particular localities. But the sheer breadth of these activities suggests why redevelopment is at once so popular and so despised.

Redevelopment is a popular tool among local governments—especially cities—because it permits them to manipulate private real estate markets to the cities' own financial advantage, and to engage in a broad range of economic development activities. Redevelopment has a strong core of loyal supporters within the redevelopment establishment—the government professionals who run the redevelopment programs and the consultants, lawyers, and financial wizards who assist them. It is also supported by many community nonprofit organizations who receive redevelopment money for local housing and commercial projects. It is often opposed by other

Redevelopment is a popular tool among local governments—especially cities—because it permits them to manipulate private real estate markets to the cities' own financial advantage, and to engage in a broad range of economic development activities.

Redevelopment is not inherently a tool for social change, but a financial tool designed to facilitate real estate investment in targeted areas.

government agencies, such as counties and school districts, who perceive themselves to be financial losers under its provisions. And it is demonized by a small but vocal group of opponents who believe redevelopment is nothing less than a conspiracy between big government and big business to squeeze out the little guy. Amid all the vested interests and inflated rhetoric it is sometimes easy to forget what redevelopment is supposed to accomplish, and the limitations inherent in redevelopment as a planning tool.

The most important point to remember about redevelopment is what it is not. Though its mission is to revitalize struggling urban neighborhoods, redevelopment is not inherently a tool for social change. It is, rather, a financial tool designed to facilitate real estate investment in targeted areas. It permits local governments to designate the targeted areas, to make special investments in the areas in hopes of stimulating real estate investment, and to "take" property by eminent domain if necessary.

Given this narrow purpose, redevelopment cannot by itself hope to solve California's urban problems. It cannot prevent crime. It cannot eradicate drug abuse. It cannot keep troubled kids in school and give them the training they need to become productive citizens.

Furthermore, redevelopment is complicated and technical. The Community Redevelopment Law takes up more than 200 pages in the state's code books. Administering it properly requires legions of accountants and lawyers. And because the basic concept of redevelopment is financial in nature, the whole orientation of the redevelopment community is toward financial mechanisms. Because bonds are usually used by redevelopment agencies to pay for community investments, the redevelopment field has become enshrouded in a "culture of debt"–dominated by government number-crunchers and Wall Street bond salesmen. The typical redevelopment conference devotes far more time to arcane legal and financial requirements than to the problem of improving economic and social conditions in struggling neighborhoods.

Because bonds are usually used by redevelopment agencies to pay for community investments, the redevelopment field has become enshrouded in a culture of debt.

Throughout its history, the legislature has reined in the redevelopment establishment whenever the cynical use of redevelopment as a financial tool has gotten out of hand. The most recent wrist-slap came in 1993, when–under intense pressure from the state–the redevelopment agencies reluctantly agreed to a moderate set of reforms in redevelopment practice.

During the 1980s, cities openly used redevelopment as a way to gain advantage in the endless financial shell game among government agencies that emerged after Proposition 13. In 1992 and 1993, the state government felt this financial pinch, and the state Department of Finance began pressuring the legislature to force redevelopment agencies to give up some of their funds. At the same time, redevelopment agencies had received widespread publicity for the practice of using their powers to lure auto dealers and other big retailers into their municipalities. The 1993 reforms tightened up the definition of a "blighted" area, placed time limits on the existence of redevelopment zones, and prohibited the use of redevelopment to attract sales tax producers. At the same time, the legislature transferred some property tax funds away from redevelopment agencies to schools. Those transfers were supposedly "one-time-only" measures, but lawmakers have renewed the shift of property tax revenue from redevelopment agencies to schools every year since 2002.

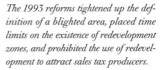

Though the redevelopment establishment went along with the '93 reforms, redevelopment agencies in some cities have chafed under, or run afoul of, the reforms. When combined with the tough real estate market in place during most of the 1990s, the reforms put a damper on new redevelopment activities. New project areas became harder to create and finance, and redevelopment tax revenues dropped, making it more difficult for projects to pencil out financially. But these difficulties were mostly temporary. Redevelopment agencies have figured out how to live with—or, in some cases, get around—the reforms. The requirement for sharing tax increment with schools and counties is now seen as just another rule, not the death knell that some people feared. And the real estate market turned around, even in some truly blighted areas. Thus, redevelopment remains one of the most powerful tools available to local governments, and it will continue to play an important role—sometimes for the better, sometimes not—in local planning throughout the state.

The Roots of Redevelopment: Urban Renewal

The roots of redevelopment lie in the old and now unfashionable concept of "urban renewal." After World War II, the federal government embarked on a major program of slum clearance, giving cities huge sums of money to raze slum neighborhoods. Such areas were considered health and safety hazards—breeding grounds for disease and social disorder. The federal urban renewal program encouraged cities to bulldoze problem areas and start over again by building

The roots of redevelopment lie in the old and now unfashionable concept of urban renewal.

The 1993 Reforms

IN 1993, THE STATE passed the broadest set of redevelopment reforms in almost 20 years. While these reforms did not constitute a wholesale revision of the redevelopment process, they created substantial changes in the way redevelopment in California works.

The reforms were initiated by the state Department of Finance, which was then desperately seeking ways to balance the state's tattered budget. The Finance Department estimated that redevelopment cost the state general fund some $400 million per year. (This estimate is based on the amount of money that the state must "backfill" to local school districts to make up for property tax money the school districts must yield to redevelopment agencies around the state.) At the same time, redevelopment critics were also arguing that cities around the state had abused the redevelopment process in order to shield property tax funds and lure large retailers inside their borders.

Faced with mounting pressure, the California Redevelopment Association agreed to a series of reforms designed to weed out the worst abuses while still permitting local redevelopment to function. These reforms were contained in AB 1290, a legislative bill carried by then-Assemblyman Phil Isenberg, D-Sacramento, who spearheaded the reform effort.

AB 1290's most important provisions took the following steps:

public housing projects, playgrounds, commercial areas, and the rest of a community's infrastructure.

To complement the federal program, California adopted the Community Redevelopment Law in the early 1950s. (Because its goal was to protect public health and safety, the law was placed in the Health and Safety Code, where it remains today at § 33000 *et seq.*) From the beginning, California redevelopment, like federal urban renewal, sought to solve the problems of troubled urban neighborhoods by attacking the physical conditions of those neighborhoods.

In laying out redevelopment's mission, the state law makes this orientation clear by stating that redevelopment must attack neighborhoods where blight is so substantial that "it constitutes a serious physical and economic burden on the community which cannot reasonably be expected to be reversed or alleviated by private enterprise or governmental action, or both, without redevelopment."

To help achieve a physical restructuring of unprecedented scope, the redevelopment law granted cities and counties two powers of immense importance. First, they were granted the power to acquire property by eminent domain, even if private development projects were planned for the site. (Traditionally, eminent domain could be used only for a purely "public" use such as a park, school, freeway, or jail.) Second, cities and counties were given the power to create "tax-increment financing" districts, which permitted them to bond against the future property tax increases inside the redevelopment area. In short, the redevelopment law gives local governments (1) the power to rearrange private land ownership patterns; and (2) the financial resources to subsidize private development projects deemed to be in the public interest. There is simply no other planning tool in California that gives local governments such sweeping power to operate pro-actively.

In the 1950s and '60s, many California cities used redevelopment to acquire and raze huge properties in depressed areas, usually near decaying downtowns. (Most of the land acquisition costs were paid for out of federal urban renewal funds, which dried up by the end of the 1970s.) Beginning in the '70s, however, redevelopment began to fall out of fashion for two reasons. First, many of the most prominent redevelopment sites sat vacant for a decade or more, because private developers simply did not want to take them on. (Perhaps the most prominent examples were the Yerba Buena project in San Francisco and the Bunker Hill area in Los Angeles, both of which took many years to get rolling but which thrived eventually.) Second, community organizers and anti-poverty activists began agitating against the use of redevelopment, which they claimed razed neighborhoods unnecessarily and displaced the very people redevelopment was supposed to help.

When Proposition 13 passed in 1978, experts throughout the state predicted that redevelopment would become even less popular among local governments, because the drastic cut in property taxes would make it very difficult for tax-increment financing deals to pencil out. In fact, the opposite occurred.

In the decade after the passage of Proposition 13, redevelopment became more popular than ever. And the reason was money. Within redevelopment's vague and flexible requirements lay an opportunity for cities to manipulate the use of land and the division of tax revenue for their own financial benefit.

In most cities, there is little difference between the city government and its redevelopment agency. Except in Los Angeles, San Francisco, and a few other large cities, the city council also serves as the board of directors of a redevelopment agency. The city manager or an assistant city manager usually serves as executive director of the redevelopment agency, and often a portion of his or her salary is paid for by redevelopment funds.

In many cases, once a redevelopment project area was created, all or most of the subsequent increases in property tax revenue within that area went to the redevelopment agency's treasury. The city did not have to share those funds with the county government, school districts, and special districts.

In extreme cases, cities were able to shield virtually all of their property tax revenue from other government agencies. The classic examples are industrial cities around

1. Established specific property tax set-asides for counties and school districts. Previously, counties and school districts had negotiated their share of post-redevelopment property tax revenue on a case-by-case basis through the fiscal review committee.

2. Established time limits on redevelopment projects and debts. The redevelopment establishment had received bad publicity because of the fact that no redevelopment project area had ever been terminated. AB 1290 established time limits—generally 30 to 40 years—on redevelopment projects and debts.

3. Tightened the definition of blight. Among other things, AB 1290 prohibits redevelopment agencies from using the problem of inadequate public infrastructure as the sole basis for finding blight. The law also prohibits the use of social blight as the basis for a blight finding.

4. Repealed the ability of agencies to receive sales tax revenues. Previously, agencies had the authority to create sales tax increment deals; this authority was repealed.

5. Tightened finding requirements for disposition of land and financing of public improvements.

6. Created a "death penalty" for agencies that failed to use their housing funds. Most agencies are required to set aside 20 percent of redevelopment revenue for low- and moderate-income housing, but getting agencies to actually spend those funds has been a problem. Under AB 1290, agencies that do not take steps to spend these funds can be shut down, although that has never happened.

Los Angeles, such as Industry and Irwindale—communities that have few residents to please and a great deal of blighted property to redevelop. Such cities have used their redevelopment funds for an endless game of economic development. By using their tax-increment funds to provide land and infrastructure, they can induce new industries to locate in their redevelopment areas; and the new industries then provide huge amounts of tax-increment funds, which will be used to lure yet more industries into town.

Even in ordinary cities, however, the temptation to use redevelopment as a financial weapon was considerable. Because it limited increases in property tax rates, Proposition 13 created a kind of shell game among local government agencies for property tax funds. The only way to obtain more funds was to take them from another agency. Redevelopment proved to be one of the most powerful mechanisms for gaining an advantage in the shell game. This was a major reason for redevelopment reform in 1993.

Proposition 13 created a kind of shell game among local government agencies for property tax funds. The only way to obtain more funds was to "take" them from another agency.

How Redevelopment Works

Cities and counties that undertake redevelopment must follow a carefully prescribed set of procedures.[1] Typically, the redevelopment agency will select a large survey area and hire a consultant to examine which parts can be classified as blighted and, therefore, may be included in a redevelopment project area. After this initial reconnaissance, the agency selects a proposed project area and a redevelopment plan is prepared.

After the initial reconnaissance, the agency selects a proposed project area and a redevelopment plan is prepared.

By law, the redevelopment plan must contain certain pieces of information, such as a map of the project area, development standards within the project area, a financing scheme, and a plan to involve property owners in the redevelopment process. An environmental impact report is prepared; property owners are notified; public hearings are held. If the project includes residential areas, a so-called "project area committee," made up of citizens within the project area, must be created. Finally, the city council must adopt the plan. The redevelopment plan must be consistent with the city's general plan, but, of course, a general plan amendment can easily rectify any inconsistencies.

But plan adoption is not the end of the redevelopment process. Typically, the redevelopment plan will cover from 30 to 40 years,

1. It is not the intent of this chapter to provide a step-by-step guide toward redevelopment plan adoption and implementation. These processes are covered more exhaustively in other references, including Solano Press Books' Redevelopment in California (third edition, 2004), by David Beatty and others.

laying out an ambitious series of projections about what new development will be attracted into the area, what inducements the city will provide to developers, and how needed infrastructure will be paid for. Once the plan is adopted, the city will try to find developers willing to build the specific projects called for in the redevelopment plan.

The deal that is struck between the city and the developer depends on market conditions and each side's bargaining position, but generally speaking such a deal (called a "disposition and development agreement," or "DDA") will involve several elements. Often the city has already assembled a large parcel of land via eminent domain or by acquiring property from willing sellers. Typically the city will agree to a land "write-down"—meaning that the city will sell the property to the developer at a loss. This is a crucial inducement for private investors. (The loss is usually covered by tax-increment funds.) The developer will agree to a specific program and very detailed development standards. The city may agree to build infrastructure, and both sides will agree on a schedule.

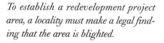

DDA = Disposition and development agreement

Stripped to its bare essentials, redevelopment consists of three elements—eminent domain, tax-increment finance, and the concept of blight. In recent years, two other factors have become important as well: the role of the project area committee and the responsibility of redevelopment to provide housing.

The Finding of Blight

The whole purpose of the California Redevelopment Law is "to protect and promote the development and redevelopment of blighted areas." Thus, to establish a redevelopment project area, a locality must make a legal finding that the area is blighted. But as one legal commentator pointed out four decades ago: "A slum area is usually also a blighted area, but 'blight' has a broader meaning than 'slum.'" The legal definition of blight has traditionally been so expansive that blight has been in the eyes of the beholder—and local governments eager to make use of redevelopment power are likely to behold blight all over the place. One of the major goals of the 1993 reforms was to tighten its legal definition.

To establish a redevelopment project area, a locality must make a legal finding that the area is blighted.

The original definition of blight talked about buildings that are "conducive to ill health, transmission of disease, infant mortality, juvenile delinquency," and so on. But under California's redevelopment law, the term "blight" is expansive, opening the door for redevelopment lawyers to find blight where most people wouldn't

Reforms in Court

WHILE STATE LAWMAKERS HAVE attempted multiple times over the years to crack down on redevelopment abuses, what has truly gotten the attention of local officials is a series of court rulings. Four times from 1998 through 2002, the appellate court threw out redevelopment projects because cities included land that was not blighted under the 1993 definition of "blight." Three of the cities also included land that was not "substantially urbanized," as required by reforms from the 1980s.

The first case was in the city of Murrieta, a rapidly growing suburb between San Diego and Riverside. The city created a redevelopment area of 3,700 acres. However, the city adopted boilerplate language regarding blight and offered "little concrete evidence of actual conditions of blight," the court determined. *County of Riverside v. City of Murrieta,* (1998) 65 Cal. App. 4th 616. A report that identified 41 structures out of 1,100 in the project area as unsafe or unhealthy did not satisfy the court, nor did assertions of incompatible, nonstandard and nonconforming uses, functionally obsolete buildings, and inadequate parking. Repeatedly, the court said the city did not prove how the conditions met the legal definition of blight.

The court also threw out the Murrieta plan because the territory was not substantially urbanized (at least 80 percent urban). The city claimed that 81 percent of the land was urban, but 600 acres that the city declared to be urban were zoned for residential lots as large as 2.5 acres and allowed the growing of livestock and crops.

The next city to get shot down in court was Diamond Bar, a fairly well-to-do suburb in the hills east of Los Angeles. *Beach-Courchesne v.*

expect it. For years, raw land could be declared blighted under certain circumstances—if it was prone to flooding, for example, or if it had been divided up into "paper subdivisions" with unusable lots. This provision explains how places like Indian Wells, a golf course resort town near Palm Springs, and Hidden Hills, an equestrian-oriented gated community near the San Fernando Valley, could find blighted areas inside their city limits.

The legislature banned the practice of declaring raw land blighted in 1984. Thereafter, any land inside a redevelopment project had to be at least 80 percent urbanized. Even this definition did not halt abuses, however, because the definition remained broad. Blight could be found wherever there were irregular lots, economic dislocation or disuse, or loss of population. A 1998 court case from Murrieta concluded that half-acre suburban lots with equestrian privileges were rural, not urban, and for this reason a redevelopment project area failed the 80 percent test.

It is not hard to see how these definitions could be applied broadly. In the early '90s, several cities—desperate to assist their struggling local school districts—sought to declare their entire cities blighted in order to provide redevelopment funding for construction of new schools. Hemet, for example, took this step even though 20 percent of its land was vacant and 40 percent was in agricultural use. San Jacinto (coincidentally a neighboring city) sought to expand an existing redevelopment project by adding 2,400 acres of farmland, including 1,700 protected by the Williamson Act, on the argument that this land could be included because it was integrally linked to adjacent urban areas and was improperly subdivided.[2]

The 1993 redevelopment reforms sought to tighten the definition of blight so that redevelopment

2. The Hemet case took place before the passage of AB 1290. The San Jacinto case took place in late 1993, apparently as an effort to beat the clock before AB 1290 took effect. Both efforts were later dropped.

agencies could better target their actions to truly blighted areas. According to one legislative committee analysis of the new blight definition, the definition includes the following characteristics:

- **The blighted area must be predominantly** urbanized.
- **Blight conditions must be prevalent** and substantial.
- **The blight conditions must cause** both a physical and an economic burden to the community—not just one or the other. These burdens must be defined by meeting specific conditions contained within the law (four for physical conditions, five for economic conditions) that are much more stringent than they used to be.

The definition of blight remains one of the most important issues in redevelopment. It is the idea of blight that serves as a dividing line between redevelopment as a powerful tool for general economic development—its most common use by local governments—and redevelopment as a specific tool to target decaying neighborhoods—its original purpose. Without a strong and clear definition of blight, redevelopment can be used for a range of purposes far beyond those originally envisioned by the drafters of California's redevelopment law.

Eminent Domain

As the chapter on the Subdivision Map Act explained, land is virtually impossible to piece back together once it has been subdivided. But the redevelopment of an older area will almost always require reassembling land into large parcels under single ownership. Thus, redevelopment agencies have unusual power to use eminent domain in assembling land, even if the ultimate landowner will be a private entity.

Typically, a redevelopment agency will use eminent domain to assemble land and then sell it at a much lower price—a land "write-down"—to a private developer who will build a project that fits the redevelopment plan. Thus, through redevelopment, a city might pay $30 million in an

City of Diamond Bar, 80 Cal. App. 4th, 388, (2000). Again, the court took the city to task for its "bald conclusions" regarding blight. The city argued that tiny parcels, small buildings, and incompatible uses in the 1,300-acre redevelopment project area hindered economic development. Essentially, the city argued that its commercial area was obsolete in an age of large retail "power centers." But the court found this argument disingenuous. First, the city's redevelopment plan proposed no new power centers. And second, the project area contained undeveloped parcels of 24, 35, 36, 41, and 47 acres—all large enough for a modern-day power center.

The court also pointed out that the redevelopment plan's contention that the project area lacked sufficient infrastructure directly conflicted with the city's general plan, which said the city had fairly new infrastructure. Redevelopment, the court said flatly, "is not simply a vehicle for cash-strapped municipalities to finance community improvements."

Only three months after the *Diamond Bar* ruling, an appellate court threw out a redevelopment plan for the town of Mammoth Lakes, a resort community on the eastern side of the Sierra. *Friends of Mammoth v. Town of Mammoth Lakes Redevelopment Agency,* 82 Cal. App. 4th, 511 (2000). Once again, the court rejected the city's blight findings and determination that 80 percent of land was urbanized. The town, for example, had counted all 76 acres owned by a community college as urbanized, even though only two acres were actually developed.

"The facts of this case exemplify the misuse of redevelopment power the legislature sought to curb," the court said in a blunt ruling. "The Town sought to include in the Project Area undeveloped and obviously non-blighted land which is planned and approved for extensive private development."

The final case in the string of four was in the city of Upland, another suburb not far from Diamond Bar. *Graber v. City of Upland,* 99 Cal. App. 4th 424 (2002). The city had created a new redevelopment project, and, at the same time, moved 77 acres from an old project area to the new one. Yet again, the court rejected the city's conclusions regarding blight and urbanization, with the court specifically finding that a rock quarry, a garbage dump, and a flood-control basin did not qualify as "urban."

There was one other interesting aspect of the Upland case. The 77 "moved" acres had actually lost value since the creation of the first project area, meaning that the land generated no tax-increment. By placing the land in a new redevelopment project area, the 77 acres would get a new—lower—"base year" assessment. In redevelopment, the lower the base year value, the more tax increment a city gets. The court ruled that the city's maneuver was illegal manipulation.

Cities reversed their losing streak late in 2002 when the appellate court upheld San Francisco's renewed blight findings for an amendment to the Yerba Buena Center redevelopment project. *San Franciscans Upholding the Downtown Plan v. City and County of San Francisco,* 102 Cal. App. 4th 656 (2002). Still, the four stinging defeats made clear that even if city officials could muscle their way past political opponents, courts were not going to be easily convinced. ▪

eminent domain proceeding to unwilling sellers in order to assemble a large parcel. But then the city will sell the property to a developer for $20 million, or $1 million—or even $1, depending on how badly the city wants a particular developer involved in a particular project, and what it can afford, both financially and politically.

Traditionally, local governments could exercise their eminent domain powers only for schools, roads, and other publicly owned projects. In recent years, however, the courts have stated that eminent domain may assist a public purpose even if the land ultimately ends up in private ownership. In a landmark case, the U.S. Supreme Court ruled that "it is not essential that the entire community, nor even any considerable portion... directly enjoy or participate in any improvement in order [for it] to constitute a public use." *Hawaii Housing Authority v. Midkiff,* 467 U.S. 229 (1984). In a controversial decision two decades later, the Supreme Court affirmed that cities may use eminent domain to facilitate private development. *Kelo v. City of New London* (2005).

But the notion that a city government can use the power of eminent domain to reshape land ownership patterns has many opponents—especially small business owners and longtime homeowners of modest means. The end result is that local jurisdictions are becoming more and more reluctant to actually use eminent domain powers, or even to grant this power to the redevelopment agency. In fact, some of the most recently created redevelopment agencies and project areas were approved with a specific prohibition against the use of eminent domain, at least in regards to existing homes. City officials have made this concession to decrease political opposition to redevelopment.

The prospect of eminent domain can be frightening for a homeowner or a small merchant. Such people might eventually get a fair market value for their property, but only after months—or years—of court disputes and lawyers' fees in the eminent domain action. If they are strongly rooted in the neighborhood where they live or do business, they'll probably also object to the idea that their property is blighted, and that it should be part of a redevelopment effort in the first place.

The typical property owner first learns of a redevelopment project when he or she receives a small notice in the mail saying that the property "may be subject to eminent domain." Understandably this often leads to an apoplectic response. The first public meeting on a proposed redevelopment project is often filled with dozens or even hundreds of enraged property owners who fear that "redevelopment" means they will lose their homes.

In recent years, these local residents have combined with a group of anti-redevelopment activists in California to oppose—and occasionally kill—several redevelopment projects throughout the state. The activists, who have worked in many different communities, are motivated by a strong libertarian belief that a redevelopment project using eminent domain constitutes an unchecked alliance of big government and big business that will squeeze out the little guy. As one anti-redevelopment activist put it: "Redevelopment is a political tool to get rid of property owners you don't like."

Anti-redevelopment activists scored several high-profile victories during the '90s. With the rallying cry of "The Mouse Wants Your House," activists defeated a proposed 4,000-acre redevelopment project that included Disneyland in the city of Anaheim. Although the city said it was targeting seedy commercial strips near Disneyland, anti-redevelopment activists and residents believed the whole project was a ruse to subsidize an expansion of Disneyland into nearby residential areas. Faced with more than a thousand angry residents, the Anaheim City Council withdrew the plan. In Ventura, anti-redevelopment activists joined with city residents and small business owners to force a referendum of a redevelopment project in the city's midtown district. Opponents complained about the potential use of eminent domain and public debt in the service of large corporations. Although the project area included two aging boulevards, it also contained a shopping mall owned by a national company and anchored by the likes of Sears, Macy's, and Robinsons-May. The fact that the mall was already undergoing a city-subsidized renovation only fueled the public discontent. When city officials discounted the anti-redevelopment leaders as ill-informed troublemakers, the opposition galvanized and voters rejected the project area.

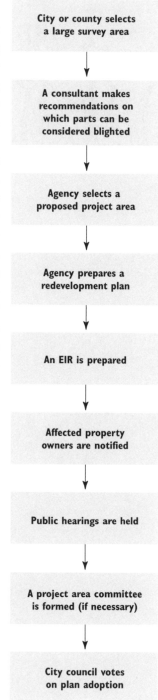

How a Redevelopment Project Gets Started

City or county selects a large survey area

↓

A consultant makes recommendations on which parts can be considered blighted

↓

Agency selects a proposed project area

↓

Agency prepares a redevelopment plan

↓

An EIR is prepared

↓

Affected property owners are notified

↓

Public hearings are held

↓

A project area committee is formed (if necessary)

↓

City council votes on plan adoption

The anti-redevelopment lobby's success in Anaheim, Ventura, and elsewhere has made officials even more reluctant to include eminent domain in their redevelopment plans.

The anti-redevelopment lobby's success in Anaheim, Ventura, and elsewhere has made officials even more reluctant to include eminent domain in their redevelopment plans.[3] This trend is both good and bad. On the one hand, overly aggressive redevelopment officials are much less likely to intrude unnecessarily into the lives of average citizens. On the other, loss of eminent domain removes one of redevelopment's great advantages—the ability to rearrange property ownership to suit the community's redevelopment goals. Combined with limitations on tax-increment financing, this trend has weakened redevelopment in California.

Tax-Increment Financing

Since the passage of Proposition 13 nearly 30 years ago, the most alluring aspect of redevelopment for many local governments has been the power to engage in tax-increment financing, which permits a city to gain control of property tax revenues that otherwise would be split with other government entities.

The concept of tax-increment financing is to use the future growth in property tax revenues generated within a redevelopment area to finance the redevelopment program itself. In most cases, redevelopment agencies issue bonds against this property tax "increment" to pay for public investments inside the redevelopment area, including infrastructure and land write-downs. The theory is that the redevelopment agency is entitled to this tax increment because, without redevelopment activities, the property tax revenues wouldn't go up.

But under Proposition 13, tax-increment financing has a profound influence on local government finance—so much so that cities are highly motivated to create redevelopment areas and set the tax-increment process into motion.

From a fiscal point of view, the most important aspect of the tax-increment system is that it takes this revenue out of the regular property tax stream and allocates it in a different way that usually favors the city that formed the redevelopment area.

Because of Proposition 13, each local government agency with property tax authority (city, county, school district, special district) does not impose its own property tax rate. Instead, these agencies must share a pool of property tax revenue. The formula for this

3. In the interest of full disclosure, it should be noted that Bill Fulton is a member of the Ventura City Council as of the writing of this book. However, the redevelopment referendum occurred four years before his election.

allocation varies, depending largely on how much property tax revenue each agency was receiving in 1978, when Proposition 13 took effect. But school districts and counties combined typically receive about 80 percent of property tax revenue. Under the state redevelopment law, however, incremental growth in property tax revenues is divvied up differently than regular property taxes. How the money is split up depends on the age of the redevelopment area, because reform efforts have forced redevelopment agencies to share revenue with other government entities. But older redevelopment projects have been grandfathered. Thus, the oldest redevelopment projects receive all of the growth in property tax revenue inside their boundaries and do not have to share.

Redevelopment projects set up in the 1970s and '80s usually have to pass through a percentage of their tax increment to counties and school districts, because during that period state law required a negotiated settlement among all these local government agencies. Obviously, the percentage varies from city to city. New project areas created after the redevelopment reforms of 1993 must abide by a set formula. In general, 25 percent of a redevelopment agency's tax-increment funds must be turned over to other local governments.

Redevelopment projects set up in the 1970s and '80s usually have to pass through a percentage of their tax increment to counties and school districts.

The impact of the tax-increment system on local government and local planning in California has been profound. At least $1.5 billion in property tax revenue is diverted each year into redevelopment agency accounts—a figure representing close to 10 percent of all the property tax in the state. Not surprisingly, diverting so many dollars to redevelopment has created a lot of resentment on the part of the other government agencies that see themselves as financial losers—principally counties, which need property tax funds to provide basic social services, and the state, which must make up the difference when local school districts lose money to redevelopment.

How Cities Use Redevelopment to Gain a Financial Advantage

Tax-increment revenues grow when the assessed value of property within the redevelopment area grows. In California today, assessed value can grow only two ways: if a new project is constructed and if a property is sold, which triggers a reassessment under Proposition 13.

Tax-increment revenues grow when the assessed value of property within the redevelopment area grows.

For example, a dilapidated commercial building may be assessed for $100,000. Such a building would produce $1,000 per year in property tax revenue, divided among the city, the county, and the local school district. However, as part of a redevelopment plan, a city[4] may build new roads or sewers, or it may subsidize the construction of a new building nearby. These efforts may improve the commercial market in the neighborhood, leading the building's owners to tear down the old building and replace it with a new building assessed at $1 million. Under Proposition 13, the new building will generate $10,000 per year in property tax revenue. But still only $1,000 would go into the fund divided among county, city, and school district. The other $9,000 would go into the coffers of the city's redevelopment agency. (In newer redevelopment areas, some of these funds would be shared with other agencies, but the city would still come out ahead by at least $6,000.) If all goes according to plan, the money will already be accounted for. The redevelopment agency will have anticipated this increase in value, and will use the funds to help pay off the redevelopment bonds that were used to improve the area in the first place.

That's the way tax-increment financing is supposed to work. But the system provides a number of loopholes that permit cities to use tax-increment financing as a tool of financial manipulation.

The most obvious loophole has to do with the sale of property. Under Proposition 13, property is reassessed only when it is sold. Thus, the assessed value of almost any property is artificially depressed until a sale occurs, and a property tax "windfall" occurs after the sale. Ordinarily, all the governmental entities share in this tax windfall. But inside the boundaries of a redevelopment area, the chief beneficiary is the city's redevelopment agency.

The prospect of such a large potential windfall leads many cities toward a very obvious piece of manipulation: gerrymandering redevelopment boundaries to include a piece of property that is already likely to be sold or redeveloped privately in the near future.

For a city undertaking a new redevelopment effort, the most important task is finding sources of tax increment in the early years of the project. Without a big tax-increment generator inside the project area, the city will have a hard time selling its redevelopment bonds, because Wall Street investors won't have much confidence that the project is financially feasible. And if the project does fall on its face in the first few years, the city treasury will have to make

---

4. Counties also have the power to create redevelopment project areas, and many do. Unlike cities, they do not have the same financial incentive to create property tax increment streams in order to shield their funds from others. In most cases, a county redevelopment project would simply keep money from flowing into the county general fund—an outcome most counties are not eager to pursue.

30-year old shopping center assessed at $10 million	City buys it for $20 million and sells it for $12 million ($8 million write-down)	Redeveloped Mall assessed at $32 million
produces:		produces:
$100,000/yr property taxes $200,000/yr sales taxes	Developer invests $20 million	$320,000/yr property taxes $400,000/yr sales tax

$100,000/yr property taxes shared with county, schools, etc.	**Using the Development Process to Increase Sales Tax Revenue**	most of $220,000 additional, goes to pay off write-down

Net Gain to City: $200,000/yr in sales tax

up the deficit. Thus, the soundest financial move a city can make for a fledgling redevelopment area is to include a significant property that's about to be sold or redeveloped privately—even if that sale or private redevelopment has nothing to do with the city's own pending redevelopment efforts.

The second important financial loophole in redevelopment has to do not only with property tax, but also with sales tax. Because Proposition 13 cut property tax rates so dramatically, sales tax is now more important than ever as a source of revenue for local government. Also, cities receive a one percent cut of the 7.25 percent state sales tax on retail sales occurring inside the city limits, and they do not have to share that revenue with counties or any other governmental entities. (In 2003, state lawmakers approved the "triple flip," which cut cities' shares of the sales tax to 0.5 percent. But the state "backfilled" the lost sales tax revenue with property tax revenue that the state directed away from school districts. And under the triple-flip, current and future local tax revenue is based on sales tax receipts. Essentially, the triple flip is a giant accounting maneuver that was performed to satisfy investment houses that purchased bonds to finance the state's budget deficit. The bottom line remained unchanged: Cities' revenues are tied to the amount of retail sales within the city limits.)

The temptation of sales tax leads cities to a second rather obvious piece of manipulation: using property tax funds under a tax-increment financing scheme to bring in businesses that produce a lot of sales tax revenues. Say, for example, that a city creates a redevelopment project area that includes a 30-year-old shopping center. The shopping center may be assessed at $10 million, which means it generates $100,000 per year in property

Because Proposition 13 cut property tax rates so dramatically, sales tax is now more important than ever as a source of revenue for local government.

San Marcos
Makes Its Mark

DEPENDING UPON ONE'S point of view, the city of San Marcos is either a city that has worked hard to control its destiny, or it has abused its powers to fill city coffers. Either way, San Marcos has been aggressive about getting the sort of development that city officials want, and redevelopment has been one of their tools.

A city of approximately 65,000 people in North San Diego County, San Marcos remained a rural backwater until well into the 1980s, even while neighboring cities blossomed. But during the 1980s, the city courted California State University, eventually agreeing to provide $17 million worth of redevelopment-funded infrastructure for a new campus. CSU San Marcos opened in 1990 and the city has moved full-speed on housing, retail and light industrial development ever since.

Besides trying to attract a university, during the 1980s the city also created three redevelopment project areas. Years later, city officials conceded they could never have created the projects if the 1993 reforms had been in place earlier. But city officials offer no apologies. San Marcos receives only 7.5 percent of property tax generated within the city limits, which is roughly half what many cities get. So San Marcos leaders figure the tax increment generated by redevelopment offsets the city's low tax allocation.

It's the sort of offset that any city official would love. By 2003, the city was taking in $25 million a year in tax increment—about ➡

tax revenue that is split among city, county, and school district. And the shopping center may produce $20 million per year in retail sales—bringing the city $200,000 per year in sales tax revenue under the 1 percent split.

The city probably recognizes the redevelopment potential of the shopping center—and, especially, the likelihood that a new or renovated shopping center could really boost the city's sales tax revenue. A typical redevelopment deal would probably go something like this: The city would buy the shopping center for $20 million and then sell it to a private developer for perhaps $12 million, taking an $8 million hit on the land write-down. The developer then invests $20 million to rebuild the shopping center, which is now expected to produce $40 million per year in retail sales.

Now take a look at the resulting tax situation. The shopping center will now be assessed at $32 million instead of $10 million, meaning it is producing $320,000 per year in property tax revenue instead of $100,000. Most of the additional $220,000 goes to the city redevelopment agency—presumably to help pay off redevelopment bonds used to cover the $8 million land write-down. Now take a look at the resulting sales tax situation. Instead of $200,000 per year, the city is getting $400,000 for the general fund.

The city has used the redevelopment process to invest property tax funds, which are restricted in use and would otherwise have to be shared with other governmental entities, in a venture that has led to a $200,000-a-year increase in sales tax revenue, which can be used for any purpose and does not have to be shared with the county or the school district. When written, the redevelopment law simply did not anticipate that sales tax would be such an important revenue source. (Tax-increment financing schemes may be set up with sales tax revenues, but this technique is rarely used.)

Cities often manipulate the redevelopment law to generate hotel "bed tax" revenue in the same fashion. A tax-increment financing scheme may be created to finance the construction of a new hotel inside a redevelopment project area. But the hotel will throw off huge amounts of local bed tax revenue—and unlike sales and property taxes, the bed tax rate is determined by the local government, not by Sacramento.

Redevelopment
Finance After AB 1290

Clearly, these financial games are far removed from slum clearance and the revival of blighted areas. But they take place in the redevelopment arena because of the financial pressure that local governments feel.

A major impetus for the passage of AB 1290 was the perception that cities used redevelopment mostly for financial gamesmanship rather than urban revitalization. A major force in lobbying for reform at the time was the state Department of Finance, which estimated that redevelopment cost the state general fund some $400 million per year—the amount of money the state must provide to local school districts to make up for property tax revenue lost to tax-increment flows inside redevelopment areas. As a result, AB 1290 contained a series of reforms designed to cut down on financial manipulation. Overall, an analysis by the Public Policy Institute of California estimated that redevelopment project areas recoup only half the tax-increment funds invested in them by cities; the remainder is subsidized by counties, school districts, and other taxing entities whose property tax revenue is diverted to redevelopment efforts. In an attempt to discourage sales tax wars, the legislation prohibits redevelopment agencies from funding auto dealerships and other large projects that will generate primarily sales tax revenues. This has cut down on the use of redevelopment to lure retailers into a city. But in many cases, the result has simply been to cause cities to find other creative ways outside the redevelopment process to assist retailers, including "rebating" a portion of sales tax revenue back to auto dealerships, malls, and large stores.

AB 1290 also sought to limit the financial advantage of city redevelopment agencies by creating the mandatory pass-throughs to other local government

six times the amount of property tax the city receives.

The city has plowed that tax increment into numerous road, drainage, sewer, and other basic infrastructure projects. And over the course of about 10 years, the city used its redevelopment agency to increase San Marcos's affordable housing inventory by about 2,500 units, a remarkably high number for a city of its size. The city used redevelopment to pay for new affordable housing development, rehabilitation projects, and conversion of market-rate mobile home parks to rent-restricted parks.

San Marcos has also used its redevelopment powers to help boost its sales tax revenues. The city has not provided real estate at a discount, as many cities do. But, for example, to lure a Fry's electronics store, the city locked up the land for Fry's and provided $2.5 million worth of infrastructure for a portion of the city that included the Fry's site.

Using its redevelopment powers and provisions in the city charter, San Marcos also has gone directly into the real estate development business. The city developed a recreational vehicle mall and then attracted dealers and accessory businesses. The city has constructed retail buildings and then leased the buildings to businesses such as Best Buy and Staples. A city-owned 60-acre civic center includes not only city hall and government offices, but also land that has been leased to private developers for construction of office and retail buildings. Even half of the city hall building is leased to other government entities or to private businesses. ■

Redevelopment and Housing

REDEVELOPMENT HAS BEEN ATTRACTIVE to cities largely because it permitted them to pursue economic development goals—construction of hotels, office buildings, auto malls, shopping centers, industrial parks, and other development that would either improve the tax base or create job opportunities.

Lurking underneath this rush to economic development, however, have been the requirements of the California redevelopment law regarding housing. These requirements have been in the law since the 1970s, but historically there have been so many loopholes and escape clauses that most cities have been able to avoid them. But as California's affordable housing situation has become more and more bleak, the legislature has closed more and more loopholes. The result is that redevelopment agencies are now pressured to focus more on housing and less on economic development.

The redevelopment law's basic requirement is the 20-percent set-aside. According to this requirement, every redevelopment agency must set aside 20 percent of its tax-increment revenue for low- and moderate-income housing. (As with most housing programs, low-income housing is defined as housing affordable to households with less than 80 percent of the county's median income, while moderate-income housing means housing affordable to households with an income of between 80 and 120 percent of the median.) The money can be spent on housing projects anywhere in the city, not just in redevelopment areas.

But affordable housing—especially low-income housing—is politically unpopular in cities all around the state. In many cases, local politicians have supported redevelopment projects for the purposes of economic development or revenue enhancement, only to run into the politically sticky problem of public housing. So cities around the state have taken advantage of

➡

agencies such as counties and school districts. Those pass-through payments have come to consume about one-sixth of redevelopment agencies' property tax revenues. Thus, there is no question that the mandatory pass-through has made redevelopment a less attractive financial weapon to cities and reduced litigation with counties, although by locking in specific pass-through percentages, AB 1290 has reduced the flexibility of local governments in responding to unusual local situations.

AB 1290 also forced local officials to put time limits on their project areas, making the oldest agencies stop issuing bonds by 2004 and go out of business altogether by 2009 (although they could continue to repay bonds until 2019). As the year 2004 got nearer, decades-old agencies in San Francisco, Oakland, and Sacramento began looking for exemptions from the AB 1290 deadline. San Francisco's wily politicians—namely, then-Mayor and former Assembly Speaker Willie Brown and then-Senate President Pro Tem John Burton—managed to get an extension for that city, even though some of the city's redevelopment projects were already more than half a century old. But lawmakers decided they did not want to deal with exceptions one-by-one. So in 2001, the legislature approved SB 211. The law permits an agency to extend its time limits for another 10 years. However, the agency must make a new finding of blight based on AB 1290's tighter definition, and must increase the amount of tax increment dedicated to low- and very low-income housing.

The legislature began reforming redevelopment law in 1977, and SB 211 was only the latest significant reform. It was one more attempt to force local redevelopment agencies to remain true to the original concept of redeveloping downtrodden neighborhoods.

Does Redevelopment Work?

The answer to the question of whether redevelopment works depends on your idea of what redevelopment is supposed to do. Clearly, redevelopment motivates hundreds of cities around the state to take aggressive action in order to pursue goals they think are important. But the very flexibility that makes redevelopment popular also makes it difficult to measure success.

The biggest question about redevelopment is simply whether it is supposed to be used as a tool for general economic development or as a way to revitalize urban neighborhoods. There is no question about what the spirit of the law conveys: Redevelopment is supposed to be used to alleviate blight in decaying urban areas. But the redevelopment law is so powerful that it serves as a temptation to almost any city seeking to promote general economic revenue—or simply growth in its own revenue. This blurring of purpose has been furthered by the redevelopment lobby in Sacramento, which often argues that redevelopment should be protected because it is the state's largest economic development program.

There can be no doubt that redevelopment is, in fact, the state's largest economic development program. With a price tag approaching $3 billion per year, including an estimated $1 billion from the state general fund, redevelopment dwarfs all the marketing campaigns, enterprise zones, and tax-credit programs in comparison. In addition, agencies' assets have grown rapidly in recent years to about $9 billion, with many of those assets in the form of real estate that generates huge sums of lease and rental payments. But the redevelopment law's many loopholes regarding the housing set-aside.

For example, when first passed in 1977, the housing set-aside requirement applied only to new redevelopment projects, and it exempted projects already in existence. Needless to say, the older projects generate the most tax increment, so the exemption substantially reduced the funds available. Furthermore, if more than 80 percent of a redevelopment project's tax increment is set aside to pay off bonds, then the city does not have to set aside the whole 20 percent for housing. This loophole has encouraged many cities to float more bonds in order to push their bond debt up above 80 percent. Finally, up until 1993 any city could choose not to set aside any funds for housing if the city made a finding that the funds were not needed. Many cities, for example, made findings that other efforts, such as community development block grant programs, were sufficient to meet the city's affordable housing needs. The end result of these loopholes is that in the typical year, somewhat less than 20 percent is set aside statewide.

The biggest loophole of all, however, concerns the set-aside money itself. Although redevelopment agencies are required to set aside for housing, until the 1990s, no state law actually required them to spend that money. Faced with the question of building politically unpopular low-income housing or simply letting the housing money sit in the bank, many cities chose to put the money in the bank. During the state budget crisis of 2003, state officials looked jealously at the $630 million that redevelopment agencies had sitting in their low/mod housing accounts. Questioning why the redevelopment agencies had accumulated so much money, especially during a time of rapidly rising housing prices, the Department of Finance tried to take the low/mod money. Redevelopment agencies protested that most of the money had been earmarked for projects that simply had not come to fruition yet, and, in the end, the state left the low/mod housing bank accounts alone.

Indeed, it can take years to put together affordable housing developments. Thus, it may appear that redevelopment agencies are hoarding money when in fact they are diligently putting together financing, working with developers, acquiring land, and doing other necessary background work before actual construction may commence. And there is no question that cities do provide units. The city of San Jose is often cited as a model. Using redeveloping housing set-aside and other monies, San Jose built 6,100 new units of affordable housing during a five-year period ending in 2004.

But San Jose's may be an exception. The state legislature has passed at least three bills attempting to close loopholes in the low/mod housing requirement and has threatened to impose financial penalties on violators. Auditors at the Department of Housing and Community Development have continued to finger cities that do not meet their low/mod housing obligations.

For example, the city of Corona's redevelopment agency spent nearly three-quarters of a million dollars over three years to purchase and run emergency shelters instead of putting the money toward permanent housing, as required by state law, according to an audit by the state Department of Housing and Community Development. Corona also spent as much as half of its low/mod housing on planning and administration—a questionable practice commonly identified by HCD auditors. The auditors also found that the city of Baldwin Park spent $1.3 million of housing set-aside money on projects other than housing, the city of Concord spent $840,000 of housing money on a general code enforcement program, and the city of Santa Ana spent more than two-thirds of its housing money on either planning and administration, or on off-site improvements such as streets and sidewalks. Cities often protest that their actions are within the letter of the law and complain that HCD does not understand local programs and conditions. But dozens of HCD audits have identified a clear trend: Many cities would rather do anything with their housing set-aside money than actually build housing units. ▪

there is danger in this argument. The largest program is expected to deliver demonstrable results, which redevelopment does not (and, indeed, cannot) always do. And the largest program will also be expected to deliver on statewide economic development goals that are not always the same as the goals of the cities that are using redevelopment. The state is typically concerned with basic economic issues such as job growth and industrial expansion, not with auto malls and downtown hotels.

These are some of the reasons why redevelopment has become such a target in Sacramento. It vacuums up an enormous amount of tax money and distorts the entire system of local government finance. Yet it does not consistently deliver on its basic mission of reviving urban communities—nor is it even used for that purpose much of the time. Healthy, middle-class suburbs are oftentimes great beneficiaries of redevelopment, while some of the state's most notorious slums—such as Hunter's Point in San Francisco and Los Angeles's South Central district—continue to struggle.

It would be far better to find ways to separate out the general economic development tools available to local governments, so they are not tempted to see blight on every street in order to tap into the power of eminent domain and tax-increment financing. Until that distinction is made, however, cities will continue to use redevelopment in ways that the law may or may not intend because redevelopment is by far the best tool available to cities.

Chapter 16

Housing

House for house, California is the most expensive state in the nation to live in. Home prices here are double the national average, and since the 1980s the "match" between incomes and home prices has gotten worse. For most Californians, incomes have risen slowly, yet home prices have increased dramatically.

Especially since the last round of housing price inflation began in 1999, this mismatch has, more than ever before, put housing affordability "front and center" as a planning issue. The older voters who tend to dominate local politics are mostly homeowners, and for that reason many communities have not been aggressive in dealing with housing issues, even as prices have skyrocketed. But to California's emerging populations—mostly working- and middle-class, mostly Latino and Asian, and very focused on upward mobility—housing price inflation has become a core issue. For this reason, housing has become a major issue in many communities where these emerging groups hold political influence—and also in Sacramento, where mostly Latino politicians have joined forces with homebuilders and affordable housing advocates in pursuing legislative changes on housing policy.

Especially since the last round of housing price inflation began in 1999, this mismatch has, more than ever before, put housing affordability "front and center" as a planning issue.

Housing has been a significant issue since the mid-1970s, when the first dramatic run-up in housing prices transformed California from an inexpensive place to an expensive place to live. Home prices doubled in only a few years in the '70s—one of the reasons voters passed Proposition 13 in 1978, which limited property taxes. Prices doubled again in the real estate boom of the 1980s, when growth restrictions collided with the roaring demand created by the wealth boom and population growth of the time.

Housing prices doubled yet again from 2000 to 2004, for several reasons that are important to understand. First, a decade of sluggish housing production had followed the real estate boom of the late 1980s—at about 100,000 dwellings per year, half the amount that experts said was necessary. Second, the Internet boom created vast wealth that had to be invested somewhere—especially in the Bay Area. Third, there was a mismatch between what was being built and was what needed. Almost all new construction came in the form of single-family dwellings, while the demand more than ever included nontraditional households such as busy couples without children. The growing expense of single-family homes was also not well matched to the state's emerging populations, many of whom worked at low-wage jobs.

By 2004, the state's median home price was well in excess of $400,000, compared to an average of about $180,000 nationwide.

By 2004, the state's median home price was well in excess of $400,000, compared with an average of about $180,000 nationwide. Buying the median home required a household income of more than $100,000 per year—and more than $150,000 in most coastal areas, where the average home price was close to $600,000. Price differentials between jobs-rich coastal areas and jobs-poor inland areas were so great that more people than ever commuted one to two hours in order to buy a house. Lower-wage families tended to double- and triple-up—not just to rent a house but often to buy one as well, thus accepting overcrowding as part of the price of the American dream. Although prices leveled off in late 2004 and early 2005, it seemed unlikely that they would ever drop back to the levels of the 1990s. Ironically, the sharp increase in home prices occurred at the same time that housing production was finally going up. By 2004, the number of new housing starts in the state was at last approaching 200,000 units—the figure experts say is required.

Over the past two decades, the state and its communities have greatly expanded their capacity to produce "affordable housing." Yet providing enough housing of the right type at the right price is a greater problem now than ever before.

All of these trends have made housing a more pressing issue in California than ever before. To be sure, over the past two decades, the state and its communities have greatly expanded their capacity to produce "affordable housing." Yet providing enough housing of the right type at the right price is a greater problem now than ever before.

California's Housing Policy Framework

California has been in a "housing crisis" for so long that housing is the one area of planning in which the state has pre-empted much local authority. The state has declared housing to be a matter of statewide concern, and for this reason has a wide variety of programs and policies aimed at stimulating and producing housing. The state Department of Housing and Community Development (HCD) operates a wide variety of programs—mostly financing programs—designed to encourage the production of more housing units.

COG = Council of governments
HCD = Department of Housing and Community Development
SCAG = Southern California Association of Governments

In the housing element, each local government is supposed to assess the community's needs, consider the state-imposed goal of providing housing opportunities for all segments of the community and all income groups, and then establish policies to ensure that these needs are met. These policies are supposed to include the identification of sites available for low-income housing, as well as programs to provide housing specifically targeted for low- and moderate-income residents. (Whether the housing element is supposed to be primarily a "policy" document or a "program" document is one of the law's many confusing aspects.)

The "needs assessment" portion of this requirement begins with a discussion between HCD and the state's demographers. Based on demographic and economic trends, they estimate how many housing units will be required in the next five years—divided by income groups such as very low, low, and moderate income. HCD then allocates this "housing need" among the different regions in the state.

At this point, the housing needs assessment process is turned over to the regional councils of governments (COGs), such as the Southern California Association of Governments or the Association of Bay Area Governments. These agencies allocate the estimated housing need among the cities and counties in their region—although, occasionally, they dispute HCD's total estimate. This happened in 2000, when SCAG challenged HCD's estimate of the region's housing need and eventually sued HCD, partly as a result of dissension among SCAG's own cities and counties on how to divide the need within the region.

Local governments are not required to adopt this fair-share figure, however. Cities and counties may also conduct their own assessment to determine the extent of their low- and moderate-income housing needs. They may adopt the COG figures, but they can also select a different (usually lower) figure if they believe their own research justifies it. Because state goals are involved, the Department of Housing and Community Development holds some review power over local housing elements. All cities and counties must submit draft housing elements to HCD for analysis and comment. Yet even when HCD specifically identifies housing elements that do not comply with state law, local governments are

Cities and counties may adopt the COG figures, but they can also select a different (usually lower) figure if they believe their own research justifies it.

not required to make any changes based on that analysis. In theory, if a housing element is inadequate, a local government's power to approve any development project can be suspended by a judge until the housing element is revised. In practice, however, this has occurred in only a few instances.

On a visceral level, probably no area of state planning law arouses so much passion and anger as the housing element requirements. Local elected officials—and, indeed, ordinary citizens—are often outraged at the idea that the state government can "tell us how much housing we need to build." And, indeed, local governments do have considerable leeway to enact growth-control ordinances that restrict the supply of housing, especially if the ordinances are adopted by initiative. In one notable example, the court of appeal upheld an open-space ordinance in the town of Moraga, even though the justices acknowledged that the ordinance would have a detrimental effect on the supply of housing in the Bay Area. *Northwood Homes, Inc. v. Town of Moraga*, 216 Cal. App. 3d 1197 (1989).

Local elected officials—and, indeed, ordinary citizens—are often outraged at the idea that the state government can "tell us how much housing we need to build."

But more recent court cases have made this strategy more difficult. In 1995, the court of appeal in San Diego struck down a longstanding growth-control ordinance in the city of Oceanside, saying that it violated the state's housing element law. *Del Oro Hills v. City of Oceanside*, 31 Cal. App. 4th 1060 (1995). Officials at HCD do not allow local governments to use growth control initiatives as an "excuse" for not planning to meet the fair share housing requirement.

During the 1990s, the Wilson Administration aggressively sought to increase local compliance with the housing element law.

During the 1990s, the Wilson administration aggressively sought to increase local compliance with the housing element law. The Department of Housing and Community Development emphasized rezoning property to higher densities, provided technical assistance to local governments, and commended local communities for good housing elements. Partly for this reason, compliance with housing element law increased dramatically during this period—from less than half in 1990 to more than 80 percent by 2000.

During the Davis administration, HCD used the housing element process to prod cities and counties to plan for more housing of all varieties. Some councils of government, cities and counties argued that HCD was overstating their ability to provide housing, at least in a particular area. That argument played well with local growth opponents, but it received a cool reception in Sacramento, where policymakers heard regularly about the state's lack of housing supply. So the legislature began making some minor amounts of state funding for local governments dependent on the local entity adopting an HCD-certified housing element. Additionally, a new jobs-housing balance program provided new grants to cities that actually approved—rather than simply planned for—low- and very low-income housing units.

It is very difficult to show that a good housing element will actually lead to more housing—especially more affordable housing—being built in a community. If they are done well, housing elements can be very valuable documents for local planning—documenting the nature of local housing problems and cataloguing policies, programs, and possible sites that can be used to help alleviate those problems. But a report from the Public Policy Institute of California in 2003 concluded that there was no correlation between housing element compliance and actual housing production. During the 1990s, when housing element compliance was rising dramatically, housing production remained low. The PPIC and other analysts have pointed out that the housing element law started out in 1969 as a way to ensure the equitable distribution of housing for poor people. But over the years, the law became the state's tool to encourage overall housing production. This confusion about goals has made it more difficult to focus the housing element law on results.

Housing elements can be very valuable documents for local planning, but a report from the Public Policy Institute of California in 2003 concluded that there was no correlation between housing element compliance and actual housing production.

The Legislative Analyst's Office has recommended suspending the housing allocation process until lawmakers reform it because the law is so ineffective. Attempts to reform the law, however, have failed repeatedly in the face of opposition from local governments, environmentalists and, sometimes, the building industry itself. Proposals to overhaul the fair-share allocation process have failed to gain a consensus. Bills to fine cities and counties that do not have certified housing elements have failed to pass the statehouse. Bills to mandate that cities and counties approve affordable housing and bills that dictate local adoption of certain housing policies—such as requiring developers to build a percentage of affordable units—also have failed.

The Legislative Analyst's Office has recommended suspending the housing allocation process until lawmakers reform it because the law is so ineffective., but attempts to reform it have failed.

The problem is not a lack of ideas or even a lack of desire to change the law. The problem is that, at bottom, all those with an interest in housing element reform do not agree that the law should exist. It is protected in Sacramento largely by low-income housing advocates and by the homebuilding industry, both of which believe the state should play a strong role in forcing local governments to address the issue. It is attacked by local governments, who, obviously, don't want to be strong-armed by the state. As long as this gridlock exists, the housing element will remain

CUP = Conditional use permit

Inclusionary Housing and Housing Setasides

ONE OF THE MOST OFT-DEBATED techniques in the California housing discussion is the concept of "inclusionary" housing. Inclusionary housing seeks to ensure that a certain percentage of all new housing is set aside for low- and moderate-income households. Its advocates say it is one of the only ways to make sure that at least some new housing is affordable to ordinary folks. Its critics say it does not solve the problem and only drives up the cost of housing that is not subsidized.

The term "inclusionary" housing is a play on the term "exclusionary" housing or zoning—a phrase discussed in chapter 7—that is used to describe zoning techniques designed to keep a jurisdiction's home prices high and therefore "zone poor people out." Inclusionary housing is the opposite. It requires all homebuilders to set aside some percentage of their units—usually somewhere between 10 percent and 20 percent—for specific income groups, such as low- and moderate-income residents.

Inclusionary housing programs work in many different ways. In some cases, developers contract with affordable housing specialists to construct and manage the "affordable component" of their projects (*see below*); in other cases the developers do both the affordable and market-rate portions of the project. Some inclusionary projects focus on rental units, usually for low-income residents; while others focus on home ownership opportunities, usually for moderate-income residents.

Inclusionary programs clearly highlight one of the most fundamental debates in California planning about how to solve the housing problem—allocation versus supply.

➡

ineffective—bureaucratic and annoying for local governments, yet not strong enough to produce real results.

In the face of this gridlock, however, homebuilders and affordable housing advocates have successfully promoted a more aggressive state policy in two seemingly minor but potentially important areas: density bonuses and granny flats.

For many years, a state law has been on the books that requires local governments to give developers a 25 percent density bonus in exchange for setting aside 20 percent of their units for low- or moderate-income residents. Under the law, passed largely at the urging of the building industry, if a builder offers to construct a project that meets specified standards for affordability, the city must grant a density bonus. Govt. Code § 65913.4 and §§ 65915–65918. In other words, if land is zoned for 100 units, and a developer agrees to designate 20 percent of new units for low- or moderate-income residents, the developer may use a density bonus to build 125 total units. However, a city may deny the density bonus after making written findings that the bonus isn't needed to ensure affordable housing

Housing advocates have long argued that local governments have undercut this policy by placing stringent requirements on housing developers generally—for example, parking requirements that prevent developers from maximizing the allowed densities. Thus, a regular housing project might be built at only 75 to 80 percent of allowed density, meaning that the density bonus would bring the project back up to 100 percent of allowed density. Some research suggests that this is the case.

In 2002, the law was strengthened to permit developers not only to get a density bonus in exchange for affordable housing, but also to select—at their choice—an incentive or concession from the local government. The biggest incentive, of course, would be reduced parking requirements. Two years later, the law was strengthened to provide developers with a greater range of choices. In exchange for providing up to 35 percent affordable units, developers can select three incentives or concessions. Depending upon the type of affordable or senior housing provided, developers could qualify for a density bonus of up to 35 percent.

A similar evolution has occurred with "granny flats"—accessory housing units in single-family neighborhoods. Local governments have long been required to permit accessory housing units, but many have used a conditional use permit (CUP) process and imposed strict standards—again, such as parking ratios—that could discourage construction of accessory units.

In the same bill in 2002 that dealt with density bonuses, the state also changed the law to eliminate the CUP option. Local governments could still set standards for accessory units, but they could no longer subject such projects to a special permit. They were required to grant permits for accessory units ministerially. The number of accessory-unit applications statewide increased dramatically. Nevertheless, many cities and counties strengthened the requirements for accessory units.

It is unclear what the impact of these changes will be, but the fact that these pro-housing laws were passed in both 2002 and 2004—and signed by two different governors—suggests that Sacramento's balance of power on housing may be shifting away from environmentalists.

How Affordable Housing Is Financed and Implemented

Cities and counties are responsible for documenting the need for affordable housing—and planning to provide it—under the housing element section of their general plans. But the local governments themselves rarely serve as the developer

Many housing advocates argue that the housing problem is so severe that only an allocation system such as inclusionary housing will ensure that low- and moderate-income residents have housing opportunities. Indeed, many such advocates seem to view inclusionary housing as the only way to ensure that at least some housing will be produced for people of specific income groups, and supporters of inclusionary view the idea as a success. According to a recent study by the California Coalition for Rural Housing and the Nonprofit Housing Association of Northern California, about one in five local governments in the state have an inclusionary housing program—a 50 percent increase since the mid-1990s—and over the past 30 years these programs have produced 34,000 affordable housing units.

Opponents of inclusionary housing, on the other hand, argue that it is counterproductive and gets in the way of market-based solutions to the housing problem. Another recent study—this one from the market-oriented Reason Public Policy Institute—took this view. The Reason report, which focused on Southern California only, concluded that inclusionary housing programs are expensive, produce relatively few units, and make other housing more expensive because those houses must subsidize the affordable units. The Reason study also did a statistical analysis concluding that the cities adopting inclusionary requirements saw a decline in housing production the following year.

Even so, it is clear that inclusionary housing programs are on the rise. In reviewing local housing elements, HCD often encourages or requires such programs—as well as requiring strategies to increase supply such as upzoning. And especially in coastal areas where housing is now very costly, the inclusionary trend is likely to continue. ▪

or owner of this affordable housing. Instead, they usually provide financial and technical assistance to nonprofit (or sometimes for-profit) organizations that are in the business of developing and owning affordable housing. These organizations, in turn, typically use affordable housing as the cornerstone of their economic development efforts in a given neighborhood.

Affordable housing is typically defined as housing that is priced to be affordable to specific segments of the population—usually the poor and working poor, who cannot afford housing created by the market. "Affordable" rent and price levels for any given area are determined by the U.S. Department of Housing and Urban Development based on the median income of that area. ("Very low" income households have incomes of 50 percent or less of median income; "low" income households have incomes that are 51–80 percent of median income; while "moderate" income households have incomes that are up to 120 percent of median income.) In some parts of California—particularly inland areas, where land is cheaper—the private real estate market can deliver affordable housing with no governmental assistance. But in most areas, government assistance is required.

Affordable rent and price levels for any given area are determined by the U.S. Department of Housing and Urban Development based on the median income of that area.

Up until the 1970s, most government-assisted affordable housing was "public" housing. These are the infamous "projects," usually built to high density in poor neighborhoods, that are owned and operated by Public Housing Authorities. (Public Housing Authorities are local government agencies funded almost entirely by HUD.) Public Housing Authorities continue to exist, and in California and elsewhere continue to manage thousands of housing units mostly for people of low incomes.

When public housing was discredited, however, public agencies turned to alternative methods of providing affordable housing. For this reason, most new affordable housing today is owned and operated by private nonprofit and for-profit organizations.

Most new affordable housing today is owned and operated by private nonprofit and for-profit organizations.

Many private nonprofit housing developers have grown out of churches and neighborhood groups with a history of activism in distressed neighborhoods. In the 1960s and '70s, these groups concluded that simply agitating for political change was not enough to pull their neighborhoods out of poverty. So they actually went into the business of building housing for the poor and working poor in their communities.

The nonprofit developers typically work closely with local governments and redevelopment agencies.

More recently, nonprofit housing development corporations have been created in virtually every part of the state—often with outside impetus. Many cities or redevelopment agencies have essentially set up or nurtured nonprofit housing developers. In some cases, Public Housing Authorities have spun off such entities. In Los Angeles, major national organizations—such as the Local Initiative Support Corp., which raises equity funds for affordable housing projects—have essentially set up nonprofit housing groups in specific neighborhoods. Some of these housing companies are thinly staffed and marginal. Others are robust. For example, BRIDGE Housing Corp., a San Francisco-based nonprofit, is one of the largest homebuilders in the state, constructing more than 1,000 dwellings per year.

To put their development projects together, nonprofits usually must draw upon several sources of funding. Some money comes from private banks. But typically, most of the funding comes from various public sources, including redevelopment housing set-asides, federal Community Development Block Grant funds, and federal and state low-income housing tax credits. Because every deal must be pieced together with funds from various sources, transaction costs are high—meaning the actual cost of affordable housing can sometimes exceed the cost of housing produced by the private market. (Sales and rental prices will remain low because of public subsidies.)

To put their development projects together, nonprofits usually must draw upon several sources of funding. Some money comes from private banks, but typically, most of the funding comes from various public sources.

The tax credits have made investing in affordable housing an attractive alternative to other investments. For this reason, many for-profit syndicators and developers—some of them respectable and some of them sleazy—also operate in the affordable housing arena. In addition, senior-citizen housing also qualifies as affordable in many communities; basic Social Security is not enough to lift someone out of poverty. And elderly individuals are often viewed with more political favor than poor families. As a result, in some communities, the supply of affordable housing has been skewed toward senior citizens.

The tax credits have made investing in affordable housing an attractive alternative to other investments. For this reason, many for-profit syndicators and developers also operate in the affordable housing arena.

There is little question that the affordable housing sector is a big improvement over the public housing authorities, which were often rife with political corruption. It remains to be seen, however, whether affordable housing provides a useful base for other economic development efforts in a distressed community.

Community-based nonprofit organizations typically construct and own affordable housing projects because the need is great and many public subsidies are available. These projects then provide an ongoing revenue stream, allowing the organizations to pursue retail and business ventures in distressed neighborhoods as well. But commercial development projects are far riskier than affordable housing projects and don't always work out. And some argue that, while they do provide an infusion of investment into a particular neighborhood, affordable housing projects also seal that neighborhood's fate by retaining poor residents permanently.

Administering affordable housing projects permanently can be difficult because residence is income-restricted. Many affordable housing developers specialize in low-income rental projects. This means the organization itself retains ownership of the housing project. If they undertake their task responsibly, it is not a difficult task to screen residents each year to document their eligibility. Sometimes this task is done in conjunction with the local public housing authority, which usually maintains waiting lists of low-income residents.

Affordable ownership projects are more difficult to administer. In an inclusionary project, a certain percentage of houses or townhomes are set aside for purchase by moderate-income residents.

Affordable ownership projects are more difficult to administer. In an inclusionary project, a certain percentage of houses or townhomes are set aside for purchase by moderate-income residents. For example, a project that sells townhomes for $400,000 will be required to sell some of those townhomes for a much lower price—perhaps $275,000—to people of specific incomes. There is also probably a deed covenant stating that those owners cannot re-sell the townhome at a market price, but must sell it to a moderate-income buyer for a particular price.

This raises two problems: First, assuring that the original buyer qualifies; and, second, that the property is subsequently sold to a qualified buyer at a specified price. A mere deed covenant is not guaranteed to make sure that these rules are followed—especially if the project developer is a for-profit entity not accustomed to dealing with income restrictions. And the idea that homebuyers cannot sell their homes at full market value meets resistance in many quarters. During the recent rapid run-up in home prices, many owners of moderate-income restricted units obtained home equity loans that exceeded the price they are permitted to sell the unit for because the banks did not read the deed restrictions very carefully.

The Middle-Income Housing Crisis

As we stated above, California's housing policy is based on the assumption that households with incomes more than 120 percent of the local median income can afford to buy or rent residences in the private marketplace. Median income varies from place to place, but generally this cutoff point is somewhere between $50,000 and $80,000 per year. This income translates into a sales price of somewhere between $230,000 and $370,000, depending on down payment and interest rates, and a rent of between $1,250 and $2,000 per month.

In some parts of the state, the private market can still deliver housing to consumers at these prices. Since the most recent run-up in housing prices began in 1999, however, this has become less and less true. In inland areas—especially the Central Valley and the Inland Empire—the starter home market still thrives. In other areas, however, it is almost impossible for people at 120 percent of median income to buy a house or sometimes even rent an apartment. Median home prices in the Bay Area and coastal Southern California can run anywhere between $500,000 and $1 million, depending on the community. As home prices have gone up, so have rents.

In some parts of the state, the private market can still deliver housing to consumers at these prices. Since the most recent run-up in housing prices began in 1999, however, this has become less and less true.

And at the same time, economic changes have made middle-class incomes harder to maintain, and more and more people—even in the expensive coastal metros—work for low wages. Condo construction has increased significantly since 2000, which provides more housing opportunities for average folks. Everybody else either gets a big downpayment from their family or their employer, commutes long distances, or lives in an overcrowded situation. In a market where median home prices are considerably more than $400,000, a middle-class income of $80,000, $90,000, or even $100,000 won't cut it.

The consequences are clear: No longer is the "housing crisis" in California a problem confined to low- or even moderate-income residents. A crisis is emerging even among the middle class. In expensive areas, public servants such as teachers, nurses, and public safety officers can't afford to live in the communities where they work. In many communities, a "double-bounce" effect is driving up prices beyond the means of people who work locally. High housing costs in the Silicon Valley, for example, have driven many high-tech workers to buy homes 50 miles away in Salinas, the county seat of Monterey County. This trend prices the county's own employees out of the Salinas market—pushing them farther south to Soledad, Greenfield, and King City, where they drive up prices beyond the reach of local residents (such as farmworkers), who must double up or commute as well.

In many communities, a "double-bounce" effect is driving up prices beyond the means of people who work locally.

Just since 2003 or so, California has seen the emergence of a whole new set of developers—middle-income affordable developers who target households with incomes between 120 percent and 200 percent of median income, or roughly $80,000 to $110,000 a year. These developers seek to build high-density projects—townhomes and condominiums—designed for middle-class families that in the past would have gravitated toward starter single-family homes. Rather than seeking financial subsidies, the developers seek upzonings, shorter processing times, and other nonfinancial incentives that will allow them to deliver a 1,200-to-1,700-square-foot unit to homebuyers for $400,000 or less.

There are very few precedents in American history for the middle-income housing program in California today. One of them, however, is in New York City, where land constraints and high home prices drove both public agencies and private corporations toward high-density development and subsidized middle-income housing a century ago. In the 1950s and '60s, the state created a program that stimulated construction of more than 100,000 co-op and rental dwellings by private developers. The carrots were low-interest mortgages and tax incentives. The quid pro quo was a limited equity return for building housing targeted at nurses, teachers, public safety officers—the same service class that is getting priced out of California today. So far, California has not embarked on a middle-class housing subsidy program. But assuming that prices remain high—and there is no reason to believe they will not—both the state and local governments will face increasing pressure to increase densities and expedite entitlements to make such projects work.

Conclusion: A Different Kind of Housing Policy

The housing crisis might seem like a tough issue for California planning already, but demographic and economic trends suggest that it is only the tip of the iceberg.

The housing crisis might seem like a tough issue for California planning already, but demographic and economic trends suggest that it is only the tip of the iceberg. Sometime between 2010 and 2015, the huge Latino baby boom of the 1980s and '90s will reach adulthood—going through college, looking for jobs, and entering the housing market. During this period, both the planning assumptions and the political realities of housing policy in California are likely to change significantly.

Some of this demand will be soaked up by continued suburban development in the Central Valley and the Inland Empire. Increasingly, however, this problem will have to be solved in the state's mature population centers—the Bay Area, Los Angeles, Orange County, and San Diego. This is where most population growth is occurring, as Latinos and other nonwhite populations seek to find housing close to their home neighborhoods, churches, jobs, and community institutions.

The traditional political equation in California would suggest that efforts to build more housing in these areas would crash on the rocky shoals of no-growth sentiment. In most communities, the local voting population consists of older homeowners—often disproportionately white—who see little advantage in permitting more growth generally and more housing in particular. These constituencies cling to traditional growth management tools such as numerical caps on housing. In addition, the use of the California Environmental Quality Act to resist community change has spread even to mostly Latino communities, where many activists fear being overburdened by new growth that more affluent areas are rejecting.

The traditional political equation in California would suggest that efforts to build more housing in these areas would crash on the rocky shoals of no-growth sentiment.

Yet it is clear that sometime before 2015, something will have to give. There is an emerging urban constituency for more infill housing—and, indeed, more infill housing is being constructed, though not nearly enough. There is growing pressure to amend CEQA so that infill housing projects do not have to run the typical gauntlet of environmental review—though both traditional environmentalists and some urban activists oppose CEQA process breaks for infill development. And while they may level off in the short run, home prices are likely to continue going up in the long run. It is likely that, over the next decade, California and its communities will have to provide deeper subsidies for low- and moderate-income housing, and higher densities and easier entitlement processes for housing that is targeted to the middle class.

There is an emerging urban constituency for more infill housing—and, indeed, more infill housing is being constructed, though not nearly enough.

Chapter 17

The Emergence of "Smart Growth"
and Infill Development in California

O ver the past decade, no single concept has caught on faster in California than the concept of "smart growth." Unheard of in the early '90s, this term is now a buzz phrase used in communities throughout the state every day. There is a smart growth caucus in the legislature. Dan Walters, the state's leading political columnist, has written about it. Smart growth partnerships exist all over the state, and innovative cities claim to be pursuing smart growth strategies. Indeed, the idea has become so common that—true to form—both builders and environmentalists have attacked smart growth as being simply a "Trojan Horse" for the other's ideas.

Sometimes it seems that the concept of smart growth contains so many different elements that it's hard to know what it really means. But the most common definitions do not differ from most of the ideals of "good planning" that the profession of city and regional planning has held for decades. Among other things, smart growth policies call for compact, diverse, and walkable neighborhoods; alternatives to the car; protection of open land and natural resources; and an integration, rather than a separation, of housing types and prices.

There are two reasons that smart growth has gained so much currency in the last decade. The first is good marketing. Building on the publicity for "The New Urbanism," smart growth has been aggressively marketed by its advocates as a new set of ideas whose time has come. The second is a factor that is an underlying theme of this entire book—the shift in California from a suburban to an urban society.

Smart growth policies call for compact, diverse, and walkable neighborhoods; alternatives to the car; protection of open land and natural resources; and an integration, rather than a separation, of housing types and prices.

As was explained earlier in this book, the land use planning system in place in California was devised mostly in the '60s and '70s for a burgeoning middle-class suburban society. Because of its middle-class affluence, this society was sprawling, low-rise, and auto-oriented. At the same time, an increasing number of California residents became concerned about quality of life and environmental protection—essentially, the fear that treasured aspects of both the natural and built landscape would be lost. These are the forces that led to the original concerns about growth in the late '50s and early '60s—and led to the rise of the traditional growth management techniques described in chapter 11.

As that chapter describes, these growth management techniques were mostly regulatory in nature—designed primarily to restrain market forces at the local level. In most cases, they sought to restrict the overall amount of development or direct it geographically; in other cases, they required new development to cover the cost of infrastructure and other impacts. In a way, of course, even the California Environmental Quality Act is a traditional growth management technique—it seeks to identify the impacts that suburban-style development creates on the emerging landscape and require developers to reconfigure projects or otherwise minimize the impact.

CEQA = California Environmental Quality Act

In many ways, smart growth is not fundamentally different in its goals. Like many traditional ideas of "good planning," smart growth seeks to concentrate development into centers—both to protect open space in fringe areas and to provide transportation alternatives and more vibrant neighborhoods in areas that are developed. But smart growth is different from traditional growth management in at least one fundamental way—it is focused on the design and form of development rather than the quantity.

Smart growth is different from traditional growth management in at least one fundamental way: It is focused on the design and form of development rather than the quantity.

Traditional California growth management emerged from the political crucible of the suburbs in the '60s and '70s, where residents were feeling overwhelmed by the amount of residential growth brought by newly constructed freeways. The core goals of traditional growth management usually involved restricting the amount of residential growth, metering the pace of residential development, and tying new residential development to infrastructure capacity.

At least in its purest form, smart growth has different goals. Although it often seeks to restrict the outward geographical expansion of growth, it does not usually seek to restrict the overall amount of development. And metering is not as important as form. Smart growth seeks to create "centered" neighborhoods and districts that are diverse in their activities, walkable, and potential nodes in a regional or subregional transit system. This is a huge difference from traditional growth management, which accepted traditional suburban form as a given and gave scant consideration to altering that form.

Because traditional growth management—and its cousin, CEQA—is so deeply embedded in the California land use system, smart growth ideas were slow to catch on. Many other states—including Maryland, Washington, and Florida—saw more aggressive smart growth efforts during the '90s. But increased traffic congestion, housing costs, and land prices since the late '90s have changed both political and economic reality in California. Smart growth strategies do not always overturn pre-existing growth limits contained in planning policies, but they do seek to move the discussion away from "how much" development to "what kind" and "where."

What Is Smart Growth?

Almost a decade ago, when he was casting about for a snappy way to sell a package of legislation on land use reform, Governor Parris Glendening of Maryland hit upon the idea of calling his ideas "smart growth." His reasoning was that anybody opposed to his legislation—principally the homebuilders—would have to defend themselves in public as favoring "dumb growth."

Almost a decade ago, when he was casting about for a snappy way to sell a package of legislation on land use reform, Governor Parris Glendening of Maryland hit upon the idea of calling his ideas "smart growth."

That's the legend, anyway. The result in Maryland was a legislation package that will be discussed below. In the broader world of planning, however, the result has been, at the very least, a revolution in terminology.

Since the term first came into common usage in the late 1990s, it has been appropriated by practically everybody in the planning and development business to mean whatever they want it to mean. Even the National Association of Home Builders has a smart growth policy statement, which understandably focuses on building more housing.

Since the term first came into common usage in the late 1990s, it has been appropriated by practically everybody in the planning and development business to mean whatever they want it to mean.

Recently, Smart Growth America—a coalition that includes a wide range of advocacy groups as well as prominent people in the field such as now-former Governor Glendening himself—laid out "Ten Principles of smart growth," which are increasingly used by communities throughout California as "the definition of smart growth." These principles are:

1. **Create a Range of Housing** Opportunities and Choices
2. **Create Walkable Neighborhoods**
3. **Encourage Community** and Stakeholder Collaboration
4. **Foster Distinctive, Attractive Communities** With a Strong Sense of Place
5. **Make Development Decisions Predictable,** Fair, and Cost Effective
6. **Mix Land Uses**
7. **Preserve Open Space, Farmland,** Natural Beauty, and Critical Environmental Areas
8. **Provide a Variety** of Transportation Choices
9. **Strengthen and Direct Development** Toward Existing Communities
10. **Take Advantage of Compact Building Design**

Most of the smart growth principles have been on the "best practices" list for planners—if not for developers—for decades.

This is not exactly a revolutionary set of planning concepts. Most of them have been on the "best practices" list for planners—if not for developers—for decades. Indeed, in a review for the Fannie Mae Foundation, Rutgers University Professor Robert W. Burchell and his colleagues found that while some techniques may be new, all of the goals of smart growth can be found in previous generations of planning policies.

One thing that does distinguish smart growth from more traditional planning concepts, however, is the way it is implemented. Many smart growth ideas are put into place through traditional land use policy mechanisms such as regulation. The form-based code, discussed in chapter 18, is one example of a regulatory mechanism used to implement smart growth. So too is the urban growth boundary, a traditional regulatory tool described in chapter 11.

But smart growth advocates have been more aggressive than traditional growth management advocates in using infrastructure investment and open space acquisition to promote their agenda, and also in combining financial and regulatory tools to achieve smart growth goals.

The use of government investment money to promote smart growth began with Glendening in Maryland. Traditionally, state-level land use policy focused on a statewide system of regulatory reforms—as in Oregon, where metropolitan regions must create urban growth boundaries under state law, and in Florida, where all local governments in each county must submit their Comprehensive Plans to the state simultaneously for review and approval. In California, the Coastal Commission was a variation on this theme.

By the 1990s, there was little political appetite for such strong state-level regulatory tactics anywhere in the nation.

Seeking an alternate approach, Glendening turned to financial incentives rather than regulatory reform as a way to promote his notion of smart growth. In 1997, he engineered the passage of two laws that sought to manage growth by the way state funds were directed. The first created "Priority Funding Areas" in existing urban and suburban areas and directed state infrastructure funds to those areas. The second created a "Rural Legacy" program and directed state land conservation funds to specific areas targeted for conservation. Local governments could direct growth wherever they pleased, but they could not get state infrastructure funds outside the Priority Funding Areas, and the Rural Legacy program meant that the state might purchase lands that local governments were thinking of developing. "We decided to use our budget as a $15 billion incentive for smart growth," Glendening said.

In 1997, Glendening engineered the passage of two laws that sought to manage growth by the way state funds were directed.

Although much of the momentum for smart growth in Maryland petered out after he left office in 2003, Glendening's policies did make a difference. He cancelled all the highway bypasses in the state, for example; and in a matter of a few years he increased the percentage of school construction money built inside the Priority Funding Areas from around 40 percent to around 80 percent. The state also began to measure the number of acres developed and conserved each year; the conservation effort soon exceeded the development effort.

How California Is Moving Toward Smart Growth

California is not Maryland or Oregon or even Florida. It is the largest state in the nation, where a uniform set of state laws must apply in vastly different growth and development contexts from urban Los Angeles to rural Susanville. It is, as we have seen, a state with a long history of vastly complicated planning and development laws and practices. It also has a vast planning infrastructure. For example, 20 percent of the nation's practicing urban planners live in California. Most of these planners have an orientation toward traditional growth management, which was the predominant planning trend in the state from the 1970s well into the 1990s.

Twenty percent of the nation's urban planners live in California, and they have an orientation toward traditional growth management, which was the predominant planning trend in the state from the 1970s well into the 1990s.

All of these factors played a role in California's slow embrace of smart growth principles during the late 1990s. Since 2000, however, the pace has picked up considerably, for several reasons.

Perhaps the single most important fact is the maturing of the state's older suburbs. The planning principles that guided the suburbanization of California up until 1980 simply didn't envision that there would be ongoing growth and change once "buildout" occurred. However, these older suburbs—mostly in Los Angeles, Orange County, and the Bay Area, are now receiving additional population growth and lots of new economic activity even though they are running out of land. In order to accommodate these changes—and do so in a way that enriches neighborhoods and communities rather than overwhelms them—these cities have little choice but to try to do things differently. Similarly, the extreme traffic congestion that afflicts most of California has altered everyone's sense of what's acceptable. The drive required to reach a new single-family subdivision is so long that many residents—affluent and middle class—are willing to live in smaller housing units or different types of neighborhoods if they can avoid commuting.

Furthermore, as discussed in chapter 16, the recent run-up in California housing prices has made some of the "smart growth" ideas more attractive as well. Especially in coastal areas, communities seeking to provide middle-class housing have little choice but to consider alternatives they have never been willing to consider before. The boom in housing prices that began in 1999 has placed the single-family home outside the reach of most middle-class residents—even those who make $100,000 to $150,000 per year in some expensive communities. Small-lot single-family developments—sometimes with lots as small as 2,500 square feet—are becoming common in coastal areas, as are townhomes and condominium projects.

In this context, some of the basic principles of smart growth have gained a kind of traction in California that no one could have foreseen a decade ago. A greater mixture of housing types is not just a lifestyle choice but in many cases an economic necessity. A mixture of housing and other types of development, such as office and retail, is often a way to best use the remaining available land resources. Placing these new developments in existing neighborhoods is almost inevitable—and so it is advisable to use sensitive design and transportation alternatives to lessen the impact. Bus, light-rail, and other public transit choices are not an option in most places yet, but California is gradually gaining neighborhoods and communities where residents can drive shorter distances or use alternatives for some trips.

Emerging Smart Growth Strategies

Smart growth policies and projects in California have been focused mostly on older city and suburban neighborhoods which, by conventional planning standards, are already "built out." This is different than smart growth efforts in many other parts of the country—especially in Florida, where smart growth policies and New Urbanist projects have often focused on greenfield sites. In that sense, smart growth in California truly does represent a "New Urbanism," whereas smart growth in many other parts of the country, including Florida, other Southern states, and the Mid-Atlantic states, often amounts to a kind of "New Suburbanism."

Smart growth policies and projects in California have been focused mostly on older city and suburban neighborhoods which, by conventional planning standards, are already "built out."

Over the past two decades, the character of the postwar suburbs has changed dramatically. Such areas as the San Francisco Peninsula, Silicon Valley, the San Fernando Valley, and northern Orange County were all developed as first-generation suburbs. They were built quickly in the 1950s with inexpensive single-family tract homes and neighboring shopping centers. These suburbs were auto-oriented; the residents lived mostly in nuclear families; in the pre-freeway era they were focused on arterial streets; and most breadwinners drove off to central cities for work.

Today, all that has changed. Older suburbs are increasingly crowded, diverse, and jobs-rich. The single-family homes that sold new for $10,000 in the 1950s now fetch upwards of $700,000. They have spawned their own suburbs because workers drawn to jobs in these locations can't afford to live there. All of this means the market for development in these areas has changed.

Older suburbs are increasingly crowded, diverse, and jobs-rich. The single-family homes that sold new for $10,000 in the 1950s now fetch upwards of $700,000.

So has a developer's definition of land supply. These areas may be out of raw land, but today they are rich with underutilized parcels—some of them zoned for residential use, but many more of them are commercial parcels, either in old downtowns, declining shopping centers, or commercial strip areas from the 1950s and 1960s.

As the state's demographic and economic patterns have changed—and as land costs and traffic congestion have increased—these areas have become much more viable as locations for a second generation of urban growth. Indeed, in many ways California's historic patterns of suburban development have provided the state with a vast and diverse supply of land to be "recycled" for new urban uses.

Most communities developed prior to World War II have small downtowns—often charming and walkable, sometimes in decline. Los Angeles and the Bay Area probably have the richest stock of small suburban downtowns anywhere in the nation. Similarly, the supply of land along postwar commercial strips is vast, especially in areas like southern L.A. County and northern Orange County, which were primarily developed in the '50s. In many cases, this land has been rendered obsolete for retail by more recent trends. Finally, many shopping centers and regional malls developed between the '60s and the '80s are either being redeveloped or renovated with smart growth components.

Old Downtowns

Throughout California, old downtowns are attracting attention—not just from planners, who have always wistfully hoped that they would "come back," but also from developers and investors, who see the opportunity to profit from a large niche market of people who prefer to live and work in compact, mixed-used neighborhoods.

Perhaps the most extraordinary example of downtown revitalization is San Diego, where the redevelopment planning and subsidies of the '70s and '80s have paid off in a big way.

Perhaps the most extraordinary example of downtown revitalization is San Diego, where the redevelopment planning and subsidies of the '70s and '80s have paid off in a big way. In recent years, San Diego has effectively leveraged its considerable urban assets—including the light-rail system that opened in 1981, the Horton Plaza shopping center dating from 1985, and the historic character of the surrounding "Gaslamp District"—into a thriving big-city downtown. Most significant in recent years has been the tremendous increase in condominium construction downtown, which has created a big enough market to support an urban-style Ralphs supermarket. San Jose has undergone a similar, though somewhat more modest, renovation.

More common has been the redevelopment of downtowns in smaller cities that Californians seem to view as more manageable.

The revival of the large-scale downtown is the exception rather than the rule in California. More common has been the redevelopment of downtowns in smaller cities that Californians seem to view as more manageable. Perhaps the most electrifying transformation has been Old Town Pasadena.

Blessed with spectacular civic buildings and a wonderful stock of 1920s commercial structures, Pasadena began reviving its downtown feebly in the 1970s with the construction of sterile office buildings and a conventional suburban-style shopping center, Plaza Pasadena, that cut the Civic Center in two. By the mid-1980s, however, the city had undertaken a new strategy—to revive the old commercial core with entertainment uses, supported by strategically located parking garages just off of Colorado Boulevard.

Within a decade, the decrepit Old Town area had become, essentially, one of Los Angeles's most successful shopping centers—a huge regional draw for entertainment and retail that successfully competed with such nearby attractions as the mammoth Glendale Galleria.

In the late 1990s, however, a second and even more remarkable transformation began to take place: Plans for the Gold Line light-rail system connecting Pasadena to Downtown Los Angeles were nearly complete, and housing developers took a renewed interest in Old Town. By the time the Gold Line opened in 2003, Old Town was experiencing a housing boom. Two housing projects are constructed over the actual Gold Line tracks. Perhaps the most innovative project is the renovation of the Plaza Pasadena shopping mall, which will be discussed below. Remarkably, what begin in the mid-1980s as a retail strategy based on strategic use of parking garages had been transformed, over 20 years, into a transit-based housing effort.

Even some of California's smallest downtown areas have recently been retrofitted to incorporate smart growth principles. Perhaps the best-known example is downtown Brea, near Highway 57 in northern Orange County. Though developed mostly during the postwar era, Brea did have a small old downtown commercial district. Downtown business had eroded in recent decades, however—partly because of the rise of other commercial centers but also partly because the arterial highways that cross-sected the area had been widened to suburban standards. The city worked with a developer to create Brea Town Center, a small renovated downtown area. The arterial highways were narrowed somewhat, but more importantly the new project took advantage of a small "street to nowhere" that runs through the downtown. This renovated Main Street now has housing above the retail stores as well a multiplex movie theater.

Even some of California's smallest downtown areas have recently been retrofitted to incorporate smart growth principles. Perhaps the best-known example is downtown Brea in northern Orange County.

Old Malls

Smart growth principles usually call for a kind of "centeredness"— that is, the use of a district rather than a corridor to create a sense of place around which a mix of uses can be organized. This is why California's old downtowns are prime locations for smart growth policies and projects. But it is also the reason why planners and developers are looking at older malls and shopping centers as "smart sites."

Old malls and shopping centers are virtually the only district-sized chunks of property from the suburban era that are likely to become available for "smart growth" use in the years ahead.

Smart growth principles usually call for a kind of "centeredness"—that is, the use of a district rather than a corridor to create a sense of place around which a mix of uses can be organized.

The State's Role in Promoting Smart Growth

AS CALIFORNIA'S LOCAL Governments and developers face the question of where and how to implement smart growth ideas, the question inevitably arises as to what role the state government should play.

As we stated in previous chapters, California is so big and complex that the state has never passed a comprehensive growth management law, as Oregon, Washington, and Florida have. Except for housing, there are no state policies that are directly imposed on local governments—and, as chapter 16 described, the Housing Element process creates such enormous resentment that it is impossible to imagine a comprehensive state "smart growth" policy being created in Sacramento. Some lobbyists have tried; the Sierra Club and others have, in recent years, floated the idea of a mandatory urban growth boundary, as Oregon has. And when he became president pro tem of the Senate in late 2004, Sen. Don Perata of Alameda County—a former county supervisor—suggested that perhaps the state should reclaim control of all land use decisions.

Realistically, however, further state control of land use is politically unimaginable in California. It is more feasible to imagine the state using its financial resources in the manner that Governor Glendening did in Maryland—as a set of smart growth incentives.

In fact, there actually is a state law that could serve this purpose: AB 857, which was passed by the legislature and signed into law by Governor Gray Davis in 2002. This law requires

Established suburban residential areas, though they could theoretically accept more residential growth, are slow to change, and current residents are often extremely resistant to more density. By contrast, retail properties are quick to change because retailing is so fast-moving and faddish. Yesterday's hot shopping center can easily become today's vacant property, meaning these properties are much more likely to come onto the market. Furthermore, shopping center properties are anywhere from 10 to 100 acres, usually shaped in a rectangle—perfect to manufacturing a pedestrian-oriented district similar to a downtown.

The most extreme case is a "dead mall"—a shopping center that has gone out of business completely and is therefore available for a complete overhaul. Perhaps the most prominent example in California is The Crossings in Mountain View, designed by New Urbanist architect Peter Calthorpe. A dead mall was completely razed and replaced with a fairly high-density housing development that included small-lot single-family homes as well as an attractive park. The property was located adjacent to Caltrain, the San Francisco-to-Silicon Valley commuter rail system, so a new Caltrain stop was built. Dead malls such as The Crossings site are sure to become more and more common in the future, though innovative smart growth projects often have to compete with lucrative big-box retailers to use them.

Another example is an old mall that is still in business but begins to incorporate smart growth principles as part of a renovation. Because retailing is so faddish, malls and shopping centers are always changing, adapting, and renovating in some way. Sometimes the change is as simple as a new store. Other times, however, major physical renovation is required—thus opening the door to housing and other mixed-use activities.

Here again the most dramatic recent example in California is in Pasadena. The city's first effort at downtown renovation included Plaza Pasadena, a traditional enclosed mall that was built right on Colorado Boulevard in 1980. Twenty years later, mall owner Trizec Hahn worked with the city to engineer a dramatic renovation. Much of the renovation focused on the shopping center itself. The mall was converted to open air, and a major chunk of it was removed in order to re-open the axis between the City Hall and the Civic Auditorium that had been cut off by the original mall. The plain brick front on Colorado Boulevard was redesigned to include windows and other interesting elements. An upscale Gelson's Market was included in the new mall.

Most dramatically, four stories of apartments and condos were built on top of the mall. Trizec Hahn sold the air rights to residential developers that built separate but integrated housing projects on either side of the new open-air plaza. The entire mall is, of course, walking distance from the Gold Line. Both the new Paseo Colorado mall and the housing on top of it are among the hottest real estate developments in Southern California.

Not all attempts to introduce a mixed-use element into an expanded mall are politically successful. In 2004, the Mills Corp. attempted to include housing as part of its expansion of Torrance's Del Amo Fashion Center—already the largest mall in the United States. Neighborhood opposition caused Mills to drop the housing part of the expansion.

Commercial Strips

Commercial strips are much more difficult to transform with smart growth principles, but in the long run they may represent California's largest stock of reusable land for future urban growth.

Urban development patterns in California from the 1920s through the 1960s focused on commercial strips along arterial roads. These linear strips accommodated the street-front retail that consumers of the time were accustomed to in downtowns, yet also permitted easy access by cars. Residential neighborhoods of all types were located

all state actions affecting growth to promote three state policy goals:

• Promoting infill development

• Promoting compact development when it occurs on greenfield sites

• Preserving open space and agricultural land

The Davis Administration took this law fairly seriously and was in the final stages of preparing a required implementation plan for AB 857 when Davis was recalled in November 2003. Although housing and transportation have been high priorities for Governor Schwarzenegger, his administration has not pursued implementation of AB 857 aggressively.

Seriously pursued, AB 857 could make a difference. For example, the state's vast open space resources—billions of dollars for acquisition, thanks to recent bond issues—could be targeted to high-priority state conservation areas, just as was done in Maryland. But this is difficult because of the longstanding tradition of "park barrel" politics, in which local conservation groups get their pet projects funded in the bond issues whether or not they are of statewide significance. Similarly, the state could have an enormous impact on growth patterns by targeting the $25 billion in recently passed school bonds to designated growth areas, as Glendening did in Maryland. But the school construction bureaucracy is located in the Department of Education, completely separated from most growth policy in the state government. In both school construction and transportation, attempts to tie state funding to any growth policy—smart or dumb—has never gotten very far. ■

behind the commercial strips. This form of development was overtaken in the '60s by shopping centers and malls.

Today, California's commercial strips are changing dramatically. Some have mid-rise office buildings. Others seek to cram two- and three-story strip commercial centers onto narrow parcels. Those in depressed neighborhoods usually feature vacant lots, junk yards, and swap meets. In many cases, however, these commercial strips struggle to attract the retail businesses that served as their original reason for being.

Many planners have identified strip commercial property as a huge potential source of land for housing.

Many planners have identified strip commercial property as a huge potential source of land for housing. The advantages are many. The land is sure to become available. Especially in today's market, housing is a lucrative alternative to retail land uses, and high-density housing can be introduced into an area without intruding directly on an existing single-family neighborhood.

Some strip housing has been constructed, in both rich and poor neighborhoods. Perhaps the best examples of both are in Los Angeles. In South-Central Los Angeles, a well-designed affordable housing project was constructed on Vermont Avenue after a major neighborhood battle in the 1990s. On the fashionable Westside, massive upscale apartment complexes—developed at densities up to 100 units per acre—have been developed along Third Street and in similar locations. In recent years, almost half of all new housing in the city of Los Angeles has been built on commercial strips.

The commercial strip has lagged behind the old downtown and the shopping center as a focus of smart growth development.

Even so, the commercial strip has lagged behind the old downtown and the shopping center as a focus of smart growth development. Because strips are corridors, it is difficult to make them work as mixed-use districts. The strategy is heavily dependent on easy access up and down the corridor by bus or rail transit—something that few corridors in California have. Furthermore, the arterial streets that form the strips still must carry huge amounts of traffic, making a pedestrian-oriented environment difficult to create. Finally, property owners on urban commercial strips are often not motivated to maximize use of their property—many have owned their land for a long time and have a low tax base—and therefore land assembly can be difficult.

Conclusion

There is little question that infill development will dominate growth patterns in California in the future, especially in the mature urban growth areas like the Bay Area, Los Angeles, Orange County, and

San Diego. In lifestyle terms, infill and smart growth is clearly a strong niche market; beyond that the economics of land and housing prices make it the only alternative for many residents if they do not want to commute long distances.

The biggest concern in these existing urban areas is traffic. It is axiomatic among smart growth advocates that people who live and work in infill areas must have transportation alternatives, so that not every project creates a traffic snarl. And especially in crowded neighborhoods, traffic is usually the biggest obstacle to political support. But California will remain an auto-oriented society for many years to come. Only a few small portions of the state are transit-rich enough that one can live without a car—San Francisco, Berkeley and Oakland, downtown Los Angeles, downtown Pasadena, downtown San Diego. Most old downtowns and commercial strips have bus service that is somewhere between poor and adequate, and of course middle-class residents in California are sometimes intimidated by the idea of riding transit. The smart growth movement is likely to create more and more mixed use centers where people can live, work, and shop in a pleasant pedestrian environment—but most of these centers will continue to be connected by cars.

It is axiomatic among smart growth advocates that people who live and work in infill areas must have transportation alternatives, so that not every project creates a traffic snarl.

Furthermore, it is clear that infill and smart growth projects are most likely to succeed in the marketplace when land and housing prices are high and traffic is extremely congested. It is only then that high-density living in crowded older downtowns and other centers becomes an attractive alternative to suburban living for most people.

It is clear that infill and smart growth projects are most likely to succeed in the marketplace when land and housing prices are high and traffic is extremely congested.

This means that it is extremely unlikely that smart growth and infill will move inland in a significant way over the next 20 years, except in isolated locations such as Sacramento. In the San Joaquin Valley and the Inland Empire, land remains cheap and abundant in comparison with the coastal areas. Indeed polling suggests that the residents of these areas are, to some extent, self-selected in favor of people who don't like an urban lifestyle and are willing to endure a long commute. One recent estimate suggested that, while the San Joaquin Valley will double in population by 2040, urbanization of land will triple or perhaps even quadruple. Thus, the inland areas are likely to continue to sprawl even as smart growth and infill development become more prevalent in the older coastal metropolises.

Chapter 18

Urban and Environmental Design

Planning is not strictly speaking a design profession, in the sense that architecture and landscape architecture are. But the arrangement of buildings, roads, parks, community facilities, and other components of the urban environment across the landscape—in other words, community design—is an important part of the planner's task.

The profession of city planning in the United States originally emerged from landscape architecture, and at least until the 1940s planning was viewed almost entirely as a design art rather than a social science. Although planning has often strayed from design in the succeeding decades—focusing on statistical analysis of demographic and economic forecasting, land use regulation, and so forth—the field always seems to return to design in the end. Design may not always be a major component of what planners do on a daily basis, but it is almost always part of the foundation of who planners are.

Design may not always be a major component of what planners do on a daily basis, but it is almost always part of the foundation of who planners are.

Currently, design-oriented planners are enjoying a renaissance in popularity, both in California and around the country. In the urban realm, a group of planners and architects known as "The New Urbanists" have focused popular attention on the fine-grained details of urban design for the first time in decades. In the environmental realm, skilled site planners are increasingly called upon to translate environmental protection policies into on-the-ground patterns that accommodate new development while preserving essential elements of the natural landscape.

These two areas of concern—one dealing with the natural environment, the other what what is sometimes known as the "built" environment—represent the poles within which planners

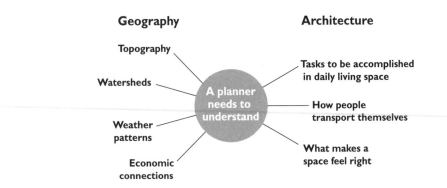

Geography

Topography

Watersheds

Weather patterns

Economic connections

A planner needs to understand

Architecture

Tasks to be accomplished in daily living space

How people transport themselves

What makes a space feel right

must function in order to make two-dimensional plans into three-dimensional reality on the ground.

Whether the subject is the natural or the built environment, however, it is important to understand that planners approach the field of design with an acute sense of the spatial relationships in a community—one that combines the view of the geographer with that of the architect. From the geographer, the planner borrows a large-scale understanding of spatial relationships—such notions as topography, watersheds, weather patterns, economic connections within and between communities. From the architect, the planner borrows a small-scale understanding of how people function within an environment that is designed for their use—what tasks people must accomplish within their daily living space, how they transport themselves from one place to another, and what it takes to make any given place feel right.

Design-oriented planners must work to craft communities that take all of these considerations into account, even though they may be highly constrained by economic limitations and political realities. Even planners who do not do design on an active basis—planners oriented toward policies and regulations, for example—must have an active understanding of design. Because, in most cases, the end result of any policies or regulations will be a network of buildings, roads, parks, farms, and other components of a community's physical landscape.

It is also important to note that design, whether urban or environmental, usually represents an effort to incorporate public or community values into a realm of activity that is usually dominated by private landowners and private goals.

In describing urban design, planners often speak of the need to create a good "public realm." By this, they simply mean that they hope to create a sense of community ownership and heightened

Planners approach the field of design with an acute sense of the spatial relationships in a community—one that combines the view of the geographer with that of the architect.

Even planners who do not do design on an active basis—planners oriented toward policies and regulations, for example—must have an active understanding of design.

activity in the public areas that connect private development projects—whether that space is a courtyard, a park, a sidewalk, or the median strip of a six-lane arterial highway. In environmental design, site planners must often shape private development to accommodate the public goals of environmental protection, as in preserving wetlands and riparian habitats. In truly inspired site design, these two goals can be intertwined—so that the natural areas being protected are also used as (or connected to) public spaces that people can enjoy and claim as theirs. In this sense, of course, design represents the tangible manifestation of planning's abstract policy goals—the melding of public and private goals to create a strong and well-functioning community.

Environmental Design

When older land use planners say that California was at the forefront of the planning movement in the 1960s and '70s, they are often referring to the environmentally sensitive site planning practices developed during that period—many of which still form the basis for land use and site planning around the state.

The concept of site planning with special attention to environmental protection is not exclusively a California idea. It first came to widespread public attention with the publication of Design With Nature, a book written by the Scottish-born planner Ian McHarg, whose practice was based in Philadelphia. In this seminal book, McHarg laid out a site planning process based on an "overlay" system. Planners should draw maps of environmentally sensitive areas—slopes, riparian areas, woodland, and so on—and then overlay them in order to determine which portions should be left in their natural state and which are suitable for development.

Planners should draw maps of environmentally sensitive areas and then overlay them in order to determine which portions should be left in their natural state and which are suitable for development.

McHarg was not the first planner to take topography and the environment into account in laying out development projects. This practice dates back at least as far as Frederick Law Olmstead and his sons, who designed a large number of beautiful suburban subdivisions in the late 19th and early 20th centuries. But while they appreciated the environment's natural attributes, as landscape architects the Olmsteads also manipulated and improved upon nature. Central Park, Olmstead's masterpiece, achieved legendary status as a piece of landscape architecture even while obliterating almost every natural feature contained on the site.

McHarg's revolutionary idea was that, once identified, natural areas should remain natural, and the goal of the site designer

Design Review

ALTHOUGH THE DESIGN OF buildings and neighborhoods typically begins with the artistic judgment of architects and urban designers, in most communities these designs must eventually be approved by the city or county through the bureaucratic—and often arbitrary—process known as "design review."

California courts have clearly stated that a local agency's police power in the land use arena covers aesthetics. (Many of these cases upheld the desire of local governments to restrict billboards. In general, the size and appearance of billboards can be controlled, but the content is protected by the First Amendment.) This line of cases has allowed most cities and counties to adopt regulations governing the design of buildings as part of the zoning ordinance or development code.

But different communities approach design regulations differently. Some communities, such as Santa Barbara, essentially dictate that buildings be designed according to a particular architectural style that fits in with the community. (In fact, Santa Barbara's Mission-style red-tile-roof appearance was created from whole cloth through the imposition of design regulations after a major earthquake in 1925. Santa Barbara was not a predominantly Mission-style city prior to that time.) Other communities do not dictate architectural style, but subject the design of projects to review by an Architectural Review Board or Design Review Committee, often composed of architects and other design professionals.

Both of these approaches to design review bring their own problems. Dictating a particular architectural design inhibits the freedom of architects and urban designers. Beyond this concern, however, a specific architectural theme may simply be inappropriate or may not be executed well.

should be to accommodate the required development project with as little disruption to nature as possible. And although McHarg lived in Philadelphia, California proved to be the great laboratory for his ideas.

Because major developers owned huge tracts of land, it was possible to follow the McHarg model and set aside large portions of environmentally sensitive property in the context of an urban development project. And because environmental sensitivity in California was high, there was considerable public pressure to restrict development and minimize its impact on the natural landscape. Perhaps the crowning achievement of this early '70s site planning was the Sea Ranch project along the coast in northern Sonoma County. A low-density, second-home residential project, Sea Ranch jettisoned the heavy landscaping typical of master-planned communities and, instead, placed the houses far from one another in a natural grassland environment so untainted that residents and visitors constantly run the risk of attracting ticks.

Over time, McHargian site-planning ideas became engrained in California planning practice and even in the regulatory system. Both the National Environmental Policy Act and the California Environmental Quality Act encourage site planning that maximizes the preservation of natural systems. Local governments' power under the Subdivision Map Act allows them leverage over private developers in laying out their subdivisions.

State and federal environmental laws—designed to protect specific natural resources—have forced land developers to pursue McHargian methods. Under the federal Clean Water Act, for example, the Army Corps of Engineers requires landowners to obtain a federal permit—separate from local planning approvals—when intruding upon sizeable wetlands. This has forced site planners to minimize disruption of natural systems in hopes of avoiding the need for a federal permit.

Urban Design

Urban design is a related but somewhat different activity—related because it also deals with site planning, but different in the sense that it focuses mostly on "built" spaces rather than the natural environment. In the same way that architecture focuses on the aesthetics and the functions of an individual building, urban design focuses on the aesthetics and the functions of an urban neighborhood or district. Urban design pays particular attention to what planners and designers often call the "public realm"—the parks, plazas, streets, sidewalks, and other connecting spaces that form the fabric of an urban neighborhood, rather than the individual buildings themselves.

If environmental design is, in some ways, an offshoot of landscape architecture, then urban design is mostly a creation of the profession of architecture. Many of the greatest practitioners of urban design were trained as architects, and have used their architectural training to advantage when working on the broader canvas of an entire urban district.

As an area of interest within the field of planning, however, urban design has had a somewhat checkered history. There was a time—especially in the 1940s and '50s—when planning was largely viewed as an urban design process, especially in large cities. How should the buildings constructed by private developers relate to one another? What public improvements (street trees, pedestrian pathways, public parks) should be constructed in order to make urban neighborhoods more livable? How should the public and private realms mesh in order to create a cohesive urban whole?

At the same time, turning design review over to a board of experts runs the risk of creating an arbitrary process. Aesthetic design is such a subjective topic that thoughtful and well-qualified individuals can have violent disagreements over what's tasteful and acceptable and what's not. And who's to say that the aesthetic judgment of an architect who's on the city's Design Review Committee is more valid than the aesthetic judgment of a different architect who happens to be designing the building in question?

Perhaps the best way to approach design is to focus on what might be called "functional" as opposed to "aesthetic" design. Aesthetic design can be defined as surface, cosmetic items that can be changed easily, such as color. Functional design can be defined as more substantive issues—often dealing with site planning—which, once decided, are essentially unchangeable for decades.

All too often, Design Review Committees find themselves engaged in long arguments about the color of a building, while giving no thought at all to more important questions—for example, the building's mass or its access for pedestrians as opposed to motorists.

In a way, the focus on aesthetics is understandable; the color of a building is the sort of thing that people react to with emotion. But in the end, this focus is misplaced. It's better to concentrate on concrete items that make a difference in how people use a building than on surface emotions, which are open to the charge of arbitrariness.

This kind of design review can be strengthened and made more predictable if the community adopts specific design standards and makes them part of the general plan. Then the job of the Design Review Committee is transformed. Instead of imposing a subjective judgment on the project at hand, this committee's task—similar to the planning commission's task in land use cases—is to apply the general plan's standards. ■

This design-driven view of city planning fell by the wayside in the 1960s with the rise of two related movements, environmentalism and urban social activism. It remained relevant only in large cities, such as New York and San Francisco, where the pedestrian orientation of the neighborhoods required a fine-grained approach to urban design. In general, however, a new generation of urban planners focused on the social and economic structure of cities. It sought to stabilize urban neighborhoods by improving the lives of the urban poor, and often believed that the design focus of architect-planners did not take social and economic needs into account. For some 20 years, it was difficult for design-oriented planners to work effectively in urban neighborhoods for this reason.

At the same time, most of the design creativity in planning focused on new suburban development because of the environmental movement. Unable to make much of a difference in the cities, many design-oriented planners chose to work in the realm of environmental planning or suburban site planning. At its best, this combination has created some outstanding examples of how urban and environmental design can be combined. In a few cases, new suburban neighborhoods have managed to create effective public spaces while at the same time preserving the basic environmental values of the site. But more often, suburban site planners focused on the private realm of individual homeowners and the preservation of environmentally sensitive areas with little concern for the public realm that urban designers had always sought to foster.

New Urbanism

Beginning in the 1980s, a group of architects and urban planners from around the country began to re-introduce traditional—rather than suburban—design ideas into both urban and suburban design patterns.

As we stated in the previous chapter, smart growth is concerned not so much with the quantity of development but, rather, with its form. This emphasis is due in large part to the rise of a related movement arising out of urban design, which has come to be known as New Urbanism.

Beginning in the 1980s, a group of architects and urban planners from around the country began to re-introduce traditional—rather than suburban—design ideas into both urban and suburban design patterns. Whereas suburban-oriented planners in recent decades had favored informal patterns, segregation of land uses, an orientation toward the automobile, and a separation of vehicle traffic and other types of community activities, "neo-traditional" planners favored the reverse: formalistic neighborhood design, integration of land uses, emphasis on pedestrians and transit, and integration of the street into neighborhood design. These neo-traditionalists also argued that their design ideas could curb suburban sprawl by creating more compact neighborhoods and lessen suburbanites' dependence on automobiles.

In the early '90s, the neo-traditional architects and planners coalesced into a full-fledged movement they called The New Urbanism. They began to promote alternative zoning codes and traffic engineering standards that would permit narrower streets, a mix of land uses, and other aspects of neo-traditional planning that conventional suburban standards could not accommodate.

The biggest impact that New Urbanists had in the 1990s was simply to focus attention on the physical design aspects of planning for the first time in a generation or more. At least since the 1970s, it had been unfashionable for most planners to be interested in the on-the-ground, foot-by-foot impact of planning decisions. They were trained to be concerned either with the social impact of growth and change, or with the overarching demographic and economic trends that created change in communities. Now, for the first time in four decades, they are openly discussing the minutiae of urban design as part of the broad public discussion about planning.

For a variety of reasons, New Urbanism took hold more quickly and strongly in other parts of the country, especially Florida. The first New Urbanist project in California was Laguna West in suburban Sacramento, designed by New Urbanist architect Peter Calthorpe for developer Phil Angelides (later elected State Treasurer). The project received national attention but

Form-Based Codes

AS NEW URBANISM AND SMART GROWTH have become more common concepts in California, they have begun to spur a significant change in one of the most important areas of planning implementation—the zoning code. In particular, traditional codes are beginning to be replaced with "form-based codes"—sometimes known as "smart codes."

As we explained in chapter 7, traditional zoning codes focus on a "do-and-don't" set of regulations for each individual parcel of land—what uses are permitted, the bulk of the buildings, and standards such as parking and landscaping that are designed to minimize the "bad" side effects of development.

New Urbanists have often complained that the traditional zoning code not only impedes more traditional-style development but in fact makes it impossible to build. Many of our best-loved cities and neighborhoods, they often point out, would be illegal today. The solution, they often suggest, is a dramatic overhaul of zoning codes. To make this point in dramatic fashion, New Urbanist architect Andres Duany used to ritualistically dump a codebook into the wastebasket as part of his standard speech.

The form-based code is an attempt to overhaul zoning codes by turning the traditional assumptions of zoning codes upside down. Instead of focusing on uses that are permitted or not, form-based codes focus on the buildings. Instead of dealing with each parcel in isolation, form-based codes seek to deal with neighborhoods and districts as a whole. And instead of being written mostly in text by lawyers, form-based codes are often drafted by designers who use many visual images.

At the core of the form-based code is the idea that the form of the buildings is more important than the use, and therefore standards traditionally associated with use—especially parking—are separated from the individual parcels subject to the code. Thus, the zoning code for a particular district might specify and even visualize building size, shape, massing, and relationship to the street, and also provide options for design styles. Within broad categories, virtually any use may occur within the buildings.

Form-based codes represent an exciting approach for downtowns and other dense urban districts—such as an old mall that is being redeveloped into a downtown-like environment. But the separation of standards such as use-based parking from individual parcels suggests that form-based codes cannot succeed on their own. Rather, they must be accompanied by district- or neighborhood-level plans for parking, landscaping, and other "impact" issues that have been traditionally dealt with at the parcel level.

For example, many New Urbanists seek to implement a "park once" philosophy. The idea is that if a district or neighborhood is walkable, with many diverse activities within close proximity to one another, then many people will be able to park their car only once in that district. Thus, fewer parking spaces are needed in each district or neighborhood. By contrast, a traditional zoning ordinance embodies what amounts to a "park one" strategy for each parcel of land. The assumption is that each person traveling between one parcel and another will drive, and therefore their car must be accommodated on each parcel. The eminent urbanist Jane Jacobs used to call this "duplicate" parking.

Therefore, as form-based codes uncouple individual buildings and individual parcels of land from use restrictions and use-based standards such as parking, those issues must be dealt with in another way. Many downtowns and dense commercial districts—including those where form-based codes work well—have reduced or eliminated parking requirements, but only after carefully studying parking issues and ensuring that parking structures or other parking areas are available nearby. It is probably not a good idea to adopt a form-based code without a district-level parking strategy. And the parking issues get trickier when downtowns and other dense districts add housing and become more truly mixed-use—because Californians might leave their cars several blocks away to shop or work, but they are accustomed to having immediate access to their cars at home. ■

floundered at first in the poor development market of the mid-1990s. A number of other projects designed by the Berkeley-based Calthorpe—including Aggie Village in Davis and The Crossings in Mountain View—opened in the late 1990s to considerable success. But large-scale New Urbanist projects were more prominent and more successful in Florida, where both market conditions and political circumstances proved more conducive to large-scale "greenfield" projects with a different urban form. In California, most greenfield development in the Central Valley and Inland Empire remained suburban in form because there was little market or political pressure to do otherwise.

Beginning in the late 1990s, however, a new economic boom led to new levels of traffic congestion as well as a rapid increase in both land and home prices. This set the stage for considerable interest in New Urbanist design ideas—and smart growth policy ideas—in existing urban areas along the coast, where land prices were highest and traffic congestion was worst.

The Future of Urban and Environmental Design

This chapter has presented urban and environmental design as something of a dichotomy. Urban design has been described as a process oriented around built spaces and often focusing on compact or high-density settings, whereas environmental design has been described as a process oriented around protecting the natural environment, often in low-density settings.

This description is not completely accurate, of course. In practice, urban and environmental design are really one process—the process of altering the natural landscape to meet the needs of human settlements. And now that the New Urbanists have put urban design back on the planning agenda, it is reasonable to assume that these two traditions in physical design will continue to work together to shape our communities.

Clearly, some New Urbanist values will be integrated into many development projects that, at the same time, will be seeking to retain the natural environment in which they function. As older communities are retrofitted, it seems likely that environmental design principles will be used to restore and enhance the natural environment in an urban setting, while The New Urbanism will be used to strengthen the urban fabric. The critical question will be the extent to which both of these processes become engrained in the regulatory system of local land use planning in California.

Environmental values will continue to be imposed on the community design process through the California Environmental Quality Act. And New Urbanism may be encouraged through revised zoning ordinances around the state. But how well will the two work together to create a different kind of physical setting for tomorrow's California communities?

Part Five

Infrastructure and
Infrastructure Finance

Chapter 19

Infrastructure and
Infrastructure Finance

Imagine a situation where two virtually identical pieces of farmland, the Jones tract and the Smith tract, lie several miles apart. Let's say both consist of several hundred acres that are still being actively farmed. Let's also say that both lie just beyond the urban fringe and might be ripe for development or, at least, land speculation. As part of its farmland preservation program, the county government has placed both pieces of land in a restrictive agricultural zone—and perhaps even entered into Williamson Act contracts that grant tax breaks to both landowners in exchange for not developing their land.

Now imagine that there is one difference between the two tracts—access. Let's say the Jones tract is several miles from any major road, while the Smith tract has a four-lane freeway running down the middle of it.

It's not too hard to imagine how this planning scenario is likely to play out. Because it is located far from any existing freeway, the Jones tract will probably remain viable farmland for many years to come. But preserving the Smith tract as agricultural land—which is the county's public policy goal—will be much harder. Tempted by the Smith tract's proximity to the freeway, developers will probably start making offers on the land even though it's in a farmland preserve, and they will begin applying political pressure on the local government to open up the tract for development. Once this speculation and political pressure begin, the tract will almost certainly be developed sooner or later.

Once speculation and political pressure begin, a tract will almost certainly be developed sooner or later.

This little scenario illustrates the overwhelming power of capital improvements to control the development process and shape

Plans and regulations may reflect a community's vision of its own future. But major pieces of infrastructure are far more powerful in actually determining patterns of development.

communities. Plans and regulations may reflect a community's vision of its own future. But major pieces of infrastructure, such as highways, water and sewer lines, and airports, are far more powerful in actually determining patterns of development.

Plans and regulations can be changed with a simple majority vote of a planning commission and city council, but once infrastructure is installed, it cannot be moved. And hooking onto existing infrastructure is so much easier and cheaper than building new public works projects that development will almost always follow the infrastructure that's already there. Building a freeway interchange on the Smith tract, for example, would require only a tiny fraction of the time and money needed to build a new freeway to the Jones tract.

Thus, the building of infrastructure—sometimes known as "capital improvements" or "public works projects"—is just as important to a community's future as all the lengthy and complicated planning processes covered earlier in this book. If the infrastructure is not in place, the plans are not likely to become reality. If the infrastructure is built in the wrong location—that is, in conflict with what plans call for—then there is little hope a community will realize the vision of the future it has laid out for itself in its plans.

If the infrastructure is built in the wrong location, then there is little hope a community will realize the vision of the future it has laid out for itself.

Regional vs. Local Infrastructure

The regional versus local dilemma that characterizes economic development generally (*see* chapter 14) also characterizes the world of infrastructure. This should not be surprising; after all, the types of physical infrastructure described in these chapters (roads, sewers, schools, water facilities) are an important piece of economic infrastructure—they are part of the foundation required by any community or any region to ensure prosperity. The Alameda Corridor, featured in chapter 14 as part of the economic development discussion, is a classic piece of regional infrastructure.

Regional infrastructure is generally undertaken by regional, state, or federal agencies as a means of stimulating regional economic growth.

Regional infrastructure is generally undertaken by regional, state, or federal agencies as a means of stimulating regional economic growth. These efforts are usually funded from broad-based revenue sources such as taxes, and they are often undertaken with little regard for the impact they may have on individual communities.

Local infrastructure, by contrast, is generally undertaken by local governments—sometimes to stimulate growth, but more often simply to respond to local needs being created by broader trends in economic growth. They are not always coordinated with regional or broader-based infrastructure efforts, and they are often funded by user fees—charges on new development and so forth—rather than taxes.

The reason that local infrastructure tends to respond to demand rather than driving it is simple: Economic growth is typically a regional process, and growth patterns within a region are usually dictated by the big-ticket infrastructure items like airports, rail lines, and freeways. It is unlikely that any piece of local infrastructure could single-handedly alter the course of regional growth.

Economic growth is typically a regional process, and growth patterns within a region are usually dictated by the big-ticket infrastructure items like airports, rail lines, and freeways.

For example, probably no public agency has had a greater influence on California's current development patterns than Caltrans, the state Department of Transportation. Caltrans almost single-handedly constructed the statewide California freeway system, which is one of the great public works projects of the 20th century and an important element in the state's continuing prosperity.

Even today—more than 30 years after the bulk of the freeway system was built—the freeways provide the spine for growth in California. Communities along important freeway corridors get growth; communities distant from them don't. There is probably nothing that a community along a strategic freeway corridor can do to repel an onslaught of growth (though there are many steps that can be taken to shape or direct it). Likewise, there is probably nothing much that a community far from any freeway corridor can do to attract growth away from freeway communities. Local infrastructure efforts, while they may have a significant impact on specific communities, are really just nibbling at the margins of larger economic forces.

Capital Improvement
Planning and Coordination

Historically, one of the great weaknesses of planning in California has been a lack of coordination among the agencies that build regional infrastructure and the agencies that do local planning. This is not just true for big agencies like Caltrans, which have always had an awkward relationship with local governments. Even in their own local infrastructure planning, communities do not always fit their plans together with their capital improvement programs.

Historically, one of the great weaknesses of planning has been a lack of coordination between the agencies that build regional infrastructure and the agencies that do local planning.

Each city and county in the state is supposed to draw up a capital improvement program (CIP). Usually covering a five-year period, the CIP identifies the capital projects to be undertaken and the source of funds for those projects.

CIP = Capital improvement program

Theoretically, the CIP should be closely tied to the general plan, so that private development projects are coordinated with the construction of the public infrastructure projects needed to support them. In fact, state general plan law requires consistency between the capital improvement plan and the general plan, and a discussion of capital facilities must be included in several general plan elements.

In practice, of course, the relationship is not always close. Coordination between the CIP and the general plan requires a good working relationship between the local planning department, which prepares the general plan, and the public works department, which is usually responsible for the CIP. However, the relationship between the planners in the planning department and the engineers in the public works department can be poor. Very often, the public works department pursues its own construction agenda in response to the needs it perceives, instead of coordinating with planners to take future development patterns into account.

However, as private developers shoulder the cost for more and more capital improvements, this relationship has drawn closer. A few cities have already combined their CIP with their growth-management system, because impact fees or special taxing districts from new development provide the funds for the capital improvements. Though creating a partnership with private developers is not always a good idea, the trend toward linking capital plans with development plans is a good one.

In the future, even regional infrastructure is likely to be driven more by local concerns than in the past. As we will see in chapter 20, local governments and the regional agencies that represent them have much more control over transportation programming and funding than they once had. This, too, is a mixed blessing. On the one hand, infrastructure planning is likely to be more responsive to local concerns. On the other hand, regional goals can sometimes be lost in the thicket of parochial interests that always accompanies more local control.

Paying for Infrastructure

Just as most houses are too expensive for the average person to buy with cash (especially in California!), most infrastructure improvements are too expensive for local governments to pay for "up front" out of the current year's budget. Most of the time, this means infrastructure must be paid for with the municipal equivalent of a mortgage—a bond.

Coordination between the CIP and the general plan requires a good working relationship between the local planning department, which prepares the general plan, and the public works department, which is usually responsible for the CIP.

In the future, even regional infrastructure is likely to be driven more by local concerns than in the past.

However, just as your mortgage must be paid back out of your salary every month, a bond requires an available revenue stream to make the payments to the investors. For infrastructure of statewide importance, the state government has increasingly floated its own bonds, which are paid back out of the general fund. (This is especially true for school construction, as chapter 21 explains.) For local infrastructure, bonds are usually paid off with a stream of revenue that is derived from the increased value of new real estate development itself—either a special tax of some kind or fees on the development.

For local infrastructure, bonds are usually paid off with a stream of revenue derived from the increased value of new real estate development itself.

Since the early 1990s, California has seen a resurgence in bond issues—both state and local—as other sources of infrastructure funds have dried up.

The Changing Federal Role

During most of the postwar period, many California communities relied on the federal government for infrastructure funds and therefore didn't need to rely on bonding. The federal government provided the funds for most of the freeway system and also paid for many local sewer systems and sewage treatment plants under the Clean Water Act, which focused on improving water quality. The federal government has also provided communities with large chunks of money for community infrastructure under the Community Development Block Grant program, which has been a mainstay of local planning and housing efforts for decades.

During most of the postwar period, many California communities relied on the federal government for infrastructure funds and therefore didn't need to rely on bonding.

Localities regarded this federal largesse as free money, permitting them to invest in infrastructure at no cost to the local taxpayer. (What was actually happening, of course, was that federal taxpayers all over the country were subsidizing specific local infrastructure projects.) Sometimes this process permitted the federal government to encourage private investment in depressed areas by building projects that the local or state government could not afford. More often, there was pressure in Congress to distribute the funds in a politically equitable manner, so that even prosperous communities received ample funds.

During the federal budget cutbacks of the 1980s, virtually all of these programs either vanished or were reduced to a fraction of their peak funding, and the money has never really returned. Thus, local governments had to wean themselves off of a lucrative and politically attractive source of funds for infrastructure construction and community development.

How Bonds Work

WHEN FEDERAL AND STATE FUNDS are not available, local governments often pay for capital improvements by issuing tax-exempt bonds.

A bond is similar to a home mortgage. It is a way for a government entity to borrow a large sum of money and pay it back, with interest, over a long period of time—usually 20 to 30 years. Of course, bond issues, like mortgages, are very expensive when compared with cash purchases; in each case, the homeowner or governmental entity can expect to pay approximately three times the actual cost of the home or facility over the 30-year period. But, like mortgages, bonds have the advantage of requiring little up-front cash on the part of the governmental entity. When financing facilities that will last 20 to 30 years, such as buildings, sewers, and other public facilities, bonding is considered a prudent method of financing.

And, just as a homeowner seeking a mortgage goes to the bank, a governmental entity seeking to issue bonds goes to another type of financial institution, a bond underwriter. Bond underwriters, like banks, are really "middlemen" between people who want to lend money and people who want to borrow it. In the case of a traditional savings-and-loan, the bank is the "middleman" between depositors, who essentially lend money to the bank in return for a predetermined interest rate, and borrowers, who pay a higher interest rate to gain access to that same money. In the case of a bond issue, the underwriter is the middleman between Wall Street investors, who want to purchase tax-exempt government bonds as an investment, and the government agencies that want to issue bonds to raise capital funds. In fact, the primary buyer of municipal bonds is the wealthy individual who has considerable funds to invest and is attracted by the stability of municipal bonds and the fact that the interest income he or she receives is not taxable. ▪

State Bonds

The California state government has also played an important role in paying for the infrastructure needed to support urban growth around the state. However, the state's role is ever-changing, depending on economic and political conditions in Sacramento and throughout California.

Unlike the federal government, the state government must balance its budget each year (although recent state budgets have been "balanced" only through semantics, accounting slight of hand and a great deal of borrowing). Rather than appropriating large amounts of money each year for capital programs, the state issues tax-exempt bonds, just like local governments do. Traditionally, these bonds were used to finance the state's own construction programs, though recent state bonds have been used for other purposes, such as school construction, municipal sewer and water projects, and city parks. Bonds have also been used for miscellaneous other state programs, such as providing subsidized mortgages for military veterans who live in the state.

In the Proposition 13 era, however, state bonds have come to play a peculiar—and increasingly important—role in California's land planning and infrastructure finance. On both the state and local level, most financial measures require a two-thirds vote. For example, under Proposition 13, the two-thirds voter-approval requirement applies to a local library bond, which requires an increase in local property taxes to make the bond payments. On the state level, all year-to-year appropriations must be approved as part of the state budget, which does not require an election but does require two-thirds approval of the legislature.

But there are two important exceptions to the two-thirds vote requirement: local school bonds and state bonds. In 2000, state voters amended the state constitution to allow passage of local school bonds with a 55 percent majority vote. State bonds have always needed only majority voter approval because state bonds do not automatically trigger a tax increase.

Since the switch to 55 percent passage, local voters have passed tens of billions of dollars worth of local school bonds (*see* chapter 21). State bonds, which grew in popularity during the 1980s, hit record levels starting in the late 1990s. In less than five years, voters approved three statewide school bonds worth a combined $34 billion. From 1996 trough 2004, voters approved nine other bonds totaling $13.7 billion for a wide variety of purposes, ranging from local infrastructure and libraries to open space acquisition and environmental cleanup to construction to seismic retrofitting of highways to a veterans home. (In that same time frame, voters also approved a $15 billion bond to balance the state budget, a $2.1 billion housing bond, and two bonds totaling $900 million for veterans home loans.)

State bonds, which grew in popularity during the 1980s, hit record levels starting in the late 1990s.

In the recent state bond elections, advocacy groups have found that the everything-but-the-kitchen-sink approach is effective. So, advocates have put something for everyone into bond initiatives. Consider the official title of Proposition 40, a $2.6 billion bond that voters approved: "The California Clean Water, Clean Air, Safe Neighborhood Parks, and Coastal Protection Act of 2002." Who could vote against that?

In the recent state bond elections, advocacy groups have found that the everything-but-the-kitchen-sink approach is effective. So, advocates have put something for everyone into bond initiatives.

The recent state bond elections have been of interest for another reason, and that is the shift in voter preference from jails to schools. During the 1980s, at the urging of Governor George Deukmejian, voters routinely approved prison construction bonds, but the most recent prison bond—Proposition 205 in 1996—failed at the polls and no one has tried a prison bond since then. Instead, state voters have approved three gigantic school construction bonds and made it easier for local voters to approve bonds in their own school districts.

Fiscal conservatives have long warned that the state was "maxing out" its bond capacity. When the percentage of the state budget devoted to bond payments rose from about two percent during the early 1980s to about five percent in the early 1990s, the warnings got louder. Since then, the debt ratio dropped and then increased rapidly so that about seven percent of the state budget now pays off bonds, including bonds used to balance the budget. Despite the state's debt load, financial institutions and investors have been quite willing to buy the state's tax-exempt bonds.

Despite state voters willingness to borrow huge amounts for a wide variety of projects, local and regional infrastructure needs are so great that state bonds alone cannot be more than one of several funding sources. Thus, local shoulders must carry most of the infrastructure finance load.

Local Infrastructure Finance

At the local level, infrastructure can be financed in one of two ways. First, it can be paid for by the entire community—which generally means a tax, or at least a broad-based property assessment. Or it can be paid for by those landowners and other users who will benefit from this infrastructure. This second method can take many forms, but there is no question that it has become important because of the post-Proposition 13 belief in California that growth should pay for itself.

The most basic infrastructure financing tool in local government is the "general obligation bond." This is simply a bond issued by the local government that is payable out of the jurisdiction's general fund, which usually consists mostly of property and sales tax revenue. Prior to Proposition 13, general obligation bonds were commonly used—with voter approval—to finance a wide range of community facilities. Some of this infrastructure was meant to benefit an entire community, while some was designed to facilitate specific new development. In general, the assumption was that the additional debt load would be offset by general growth in the tax base as the result of new development.

By dramatically cutting property tax rates, Proposition 13 gave new meaning to the phrase "growth should pay for itself." With low property tax rates, new growth rarely paid for itself out of general tax revenue. In addition, for some years after Proposition 13's passage, most legal interpretations made it virtually impossible to implement a voter-approved property tax increase for general obligation bonds.

In recent years, general obligation bonds have made something of a comeback on the local level. They are now clearly permitted with two-thirds voter approval. In most cases, however, local jurisdictions do not even attempt to pass such bonds except for the most popular public facilities, such as libraries, parks, and fire stations. (With the lowering of the voter threshold to 55 percent, schools are a different story.)

At the same time, the cost of almost all infrastructure associated with new real estate development has been shifted from the general taxpayer onto the landowners, home buyers, and real estate tenants in these new developments. This make-growth-pay-for-itself philosophy is politically popular because, from the point of view of the average voter, it amounts to a tax on somebody else—either a large landowner, who is in the minority at election time, or else residents or businesses not yet located in the community.

In general, the financing mechanisms used to make growth pay for itself fall into three categories: fees and exactions, assessment districts, and land-secured bonding mechanisms such as Mello-Roos bonds.

Fees and Exactions

Fees and exactions are discussed at length in chapter 10 in the context of the land use regulatory system. In general, fees and exactions can be imposed only in proportion to the infrastructure needs of the real estate development project in question.

From the point of view of a city or county, the tidiest solution to infrastructure problems in new areas is simply to have the developer build the needed infrastructure and then deed it over to the community or to a homeowner association. This is how infrastructure finance typically works for "internal" needs—roads, sewers, parks, and other capital items within a subdivision.

From the point of view of a city or county, the tidiest solution to infrastructure problems in new areas is simply to have the developer build the needed infrastructure and then deed it over to the community or to a homeowner association.

Hemmed in by their ability to raise taxes, cities and counties now seek to obtain money from developers for community infrastructure far beyond a particular subdivision's borders—for new or expanded freeway interchanges, for example. However, it is often difficult to translate these funds into infrastructure improvements quickly. Fee revenue is typically neither large enough to permit the locality to pay cash for infrastructure nor reliable enough to use as a revenue stream for bond payments.

Fee revenue is typically neither large enough to permit the locality to pay cash for infrastructure nor reliable enough to use as a revenue stream for bond payments.

For these reasons, fees are typically used to make minor improvements, or else they sit in the bank until they can be combined with other revenue sources in order to actually construct the needed infrastructure. This delayed project delivery is one of the many reasons why both local governments and developers often prefer assessment districts or taxing districts, such as Mello-Roos districts, to the collection of fees.

Assessment Districts

Assessment districts have been widely used in California since the early part of the 20th century as a means of paying for public infrastructure. Instead of requiring property owners to pay based on the value of their property—as a property tax does—an assessment district typically requires property owners to pay based on the benefit each property receives from the construction of the public infrastructure.

Assessment districts were first authorized by several laws passed during the Progressive era in state government between 1911 and 1915.

Assessment districts were first authorized by several laws passed during the Progressive era in state government from 1911 to 1915. Another important law, the "Landscaping and Lighting Act," was passed in 1972. These laws typically permit cities and counties to establish assessment districts in new or existing neighborhoods to pay for infrastructure within a subdivision or tract, such as streetlights, landscaping, or curbs and gutters. Significantly, many assessment districts can be created without a vote of affected property owners—or at least they could be until the passage of Proposition 218 in 1996.

After the passage of Proposition 13, California localities began to use assessment districts more frequently.

After the passage of Proposition 13, California localities began to use assessment districts more frequently. They covered a wide variety of facilities and services, including libraries, fire protection, and parks. Assessment districts were especially popular because they could be used to fund operation and maintenance of public facilities as well as construction. Their use was stepped up in the early 1990s, after the state transferred about 25 percent of all property tax revenue from cities and counties to school districts.

The net effect of all this activity was to broaden the use of assessment districts to cover construction and operation of facilities that had a broad community benefit, not just a benefit to specific property owners. Perhaps the best example came in the city of Orland, located in Glenn County approximately 90 miles north of Sacramento. Unable to maintain city parks out of the general fund, Orland created an assessment district that included all the property located inside four local school districts and imposed an assessment of $24 per parcel. The city made a finding that all parcels benefited equally from the parks, even though some properties were located as far as 27 miles away from any park.

Several local property owners sued, claiming that the assessments were, in fact, disguised taxes that should have required a public vote. The California Supreme Court upheld the assessment district, concluding that there was no evidence in the record that all properties did not benefit equally from parks. (The Orland story and the Supreme Court's ruling is contained in *Knox v. City of Orland*, 4 Cal. 4th 132 (1994). The *Orland* case was one event that sparked a taxpayer backlash against assessment districts that led to the passage of Proposition 218 in 1996. See below for more information.)

Mello-Roos Districts and Dirt Bonds

Perhaps the most important new method of financing community infrastructure that emerged in the wake of Proposition 13 was the "Mello-Roos bond." Though they are tax-exempt instruments of debt issued by public agencies, these bonds are sometimes called "dirt bonds" because they are backed by the value of the land involved, not by general tax revenue.

Perhaps the most important new method of financing community infrastructure that emerged in the wake of Proposition 13 was the so-called Mello-Roos bond.

The Mello-Roos law was a landmark piece of legislation passed in 1982 under the sponsorship of two then-powerful legislators, Senator Henry Mello of Watsonville and Assemblyman Mike Roos of Los Angeles. It was a blatant—and ultimately successful—attempt to find a narrow constitutional path through the thicket of Proposition 13 that would permit public financing of new infrastructure.

Under the Mello-Roos law, local cities, counties, and school districts may create "community facilities districts" to finance the construction of needed community infrastructure. (The Mello-Roos law is found at Government Code § 55311 *et seq.*) This CFD, as it is typically called, is empowered to levy additional property taxes on land located inside the district, thus creating a dependable revenue stream that can be used in issuing bonds to pay for the new infrastructure. Large new subdivisions—especially in Riverside and Orange counties, which, together, have about one-third of all CFDs—often use Mello-Roos tax levies to finance construction of schools, roads, and sewers.

Under the Mello-Roos law, local cities, counties, and school districts may create community facilities districts to finance the construction of needed community infrastructure.

CFD = Community facilities district

Like most other property taxes, Mello-Roos taxes are subject to approval by a public vote. However, the law contains one important provision that makes it attractive to both local governments and developers. If the proposed district contains fewer than 12 registered voters, then the election takes place not among the voters but among the property owners. This provision permits large developers to create Mello-Roos districts by fiat—or, more accurately, by a vote of 1 to 0.

Typically, a developer and a county create the Mello-Roos district together (called, for example, "Orange County Community Facilities District #5") as part of the initial development approval.[1]

1. Although counties create Mello-Roos districts most frequently, they are also created and administered by cities and school districts.

Oftentimes, the Mello-Roos district is part of a package of approvals that includes a specific plan (which lays out the infrastructure requirements to be financed with Mello-Roos bond proceeds) and a development agreement (which guarantees that the developer will be permitted to build the houses necessary to pay off the bonds). The new district will be administered by the county, which will float the bonds, construct the roads and schools, and then add the Mello-Roos tax to a new homeowner's property tax bill.

In many communities, this additional tax burden has become a controversial political issue. Early on, many homebuyers were shocked when they received their first tax bill and complained that they had not been informed. These complaints led to amendments to the Mello-Roos law requiring disclosure of these additional taxes at the time a home is purchased.

Even today, however, Mello-Roos taxes can be a marketing liability for a developer. It's not uncommon to drive along the freeway in a fast-growing area in Riverside County and see a developer's billboard boast: "No Mello-Roos!"

Mello-Roos taxing districts have caused other problems as well. Chief among these is the simple fact that they usually cannot generate enough bond money to cover the cost of all the infrastructure a community needs. The amount of a Mello-Roos bond issue is usually determined by two financial limitations—one demanded by the Wall Street bond buyers, and one demanded by the home-buyers who will eventually be stuck with the tax bill.

Wall Street investors are a conservative lot, unwilling to take many risks. To be marketable on Wall Street, a Mello-Roos bond must be so financially solid that the bond buyers are unlikely to lose their money no matter what happens to the development project. In practice, this means a Mello-Roos bond must contain a lien-to-value ratio of 1:3—one dollar of bonding for every three dollars of land value. Thus, a property with a value of $30 million prior to development could not support more than $10 million worth of bonds.

Similarly, if Mello-Roos taxes are too high, homebuyers will balk. Unlike regular property taxes, Mello-Roos taxes are not based at all on the property's value. Instead Mello-Roos taxes relate in some fashion to the size of the house. As the price of new homes has shot through the roof in recent years, Mello-Roos taxes have become a smaller part of tax bills than they were during the 1980s and 1990s. Still, even some of the most popular developments appear wary of having Mello-Roos taxes of more than about $2,000 per year.

The end result of these constraints is that local governments and school districts cannot extract all the infrastructure they need out of a Mello-Roos district. Indeed, cities and counties often fight with school districts over who will control the Mello-Roos district and, therefore, the bond proceeds. The loser in this fight will typically have to make up the difference by trying to extract higher up-front fees from the developer, by passing a general obligation bond issue—or by doing without needed infrastructure altogether.

Mello-Roos bonding has been extremely popular and, by most accounts, extraordinarily successful. Administration of Mello-Roos districts is so good that during the recession of the 1990s, when land prices plummeted, almost no Mello-Roos districts collapsed—despite many predictions to the contrary. Although the ease with which schools may now pass bonds has decreased school districts' reliance on Mello-Roos taxes, many cities and counties still rely on Mello-Roos districts to pay for roads, storm drains, parks, water and sewer lines, and other basic infrastructure. Every year, Mello-Roos financing generates approximately $800 million to $1 billion for public facilities.

Mello-Roos bonding has been extremely popular and, by most accounts, extraordinarily successful, even during the recession of the 1990s.

Yet Mello-Roos districts represent everything that is bad about community planning in California as well as everything that is good. Local governments like Mello-Roos bonding because it shifts the cost of community infrastructure from general taxpayers to the "consumers" of new development projects. Developers like it because it represents a cheap source of capital. Because Mello-Roos bonds are tax-exempt, they can provide infrastructure money much more cheaply than if the developers were forced to borrow the money privately.

Mello-Roos districts represent everything that is bad about community planning in California as well as everything that is good.

For this same reason, Mello-Roos districts have put all large development projects in the state on the public dole in a sense—creating the need for a public-private deal even for high-end suburban subdivisions. And yet, paradoxically, they have further accentuated the sense of privatization of communities. Those residents who are paying extra taxes for schools, roads, libraries, and other community facilities understandably develop a sense of ownership about them, and are less likely to view themselves as true members of a broader community. Yet the Mello-Roos game keeps rolling along—for the simple reason that in a highly constrained fiscal environment, there is almost no other game in town.

Proposition 218 and the
Future of Infrastructure Finance

Since the passage of Proposition 13 nearly three decades ago, the trend in California has been toward constraining infrastructure finance options rather than expanding them. This theme was reinforced in 1996, when the state's voters overwhelmingly approved Proposition 218, the Right to Vote on Taxes Act. A citizen initiative supported by a broad range of taxpayer groups, Proposition 218 was widely regarded as the final nail in the coffin of government spending that was first attacked by Proposition 13. As usual, of course, local government officials, clever consultants and judges have found that Proposition 218 is not quite as iron-clad as promised.

Ever since Proposition 13 passed, local governments have sought to finance capital projects and operating expenses through whatever loopholes remained—principally assessment districts, Mello-Roos districts, redevelopment activities, and certain types of taxes, such as utility taxes, that apparently did not require a vote under California law. Especially after the legislature shifted a large portion of property tax revenue away from counties to school districts in 1992 and 1993, counties turned to assessment districts as a way to plug the financial gap.

Proposition 218 was designed to close loopholes that gave local governments the ability to impose new taxes or fees without any kind of a vote.

Proposition 218 was designed to close most of these loopholes—especially loopholes that gave local governments the ability to impose new taxes or fees without any kind of a vote. Among other things, Proposition 218 changed infrastructure finance in the following three important ways:

- Following on a California Supreme Court ruling from 1995, *Guardino v. Santa Clara County Local Transportation Authority,* 11 Cal. 4th 220 (1995), Proposition 218 clarified that all local taxes of any kind, including utility taxes, are not valid unless they are approved by local voters.
- As explained above, Proposition 218 also sought to rein in the profligate use of assessment districts by subjecting them to a protest process very similar to an election.
- Proposition 218 also stated that voters have the right to repeal any tax via initiative at any time.

Early predictions of Proposition 218's effects were dire, especially from government agencies. They claimed that they would never obtain the needed two-thirds vote for utility taxes, hotel occupancy taxes, and the other local taxes still available to them. They feared that voters would use the initiative process to repeal tax revenue streams needed to pay back outstanding bonds, though taxpayer advocates insisted that this was not their intent. They also argued that the assessment provisions were confusing and unfair.

Prior to Proposition 218, assessment districts could be created and property assessments could be levied without anything resembling a vote. If enough property owners protested, an assessment district could be stopped—but the likelihood of rounding up a majority of property owners to file protests was slim. Under Proposition 218, if property owners do not affirmatively state their support for the assessment, then they are assumed to be casting a "no" protest—making it much harder for property assessments to be imposed without an actual election. The assessment provisions of Proposition 218 were squarely designed to repeal the California Supreme Court's expansive ruling in *Knox v. City of Orland.*

Given all these dire predictions, it was not too difficult for local governments to calculate that they would likely lose billions of dollars in needed revenue as a result of Proposition 218's passage. Some local government officials and environmental leaders even talked about suing to overturn portions of the initiative, or placing another initiative on the ballot to give local officials more leeway.

In fact, however, the taxpayer advocates were correct in insisting that they had merely created a logical extension of the right-to-vote-on-taxes principle established by Proposition 13. The sky has not fallen, and, as Proposition 218 lawsuits have gone through the courts during recent years, courts have made clear that the Right to Vote on Taxes Act does not mean people get to vote on all taxes.

The state Supreme Court has issued two Proposition 218 rulings, and in both cases it sided with the government agency. In the first case, the court ruled that the city of Los Angeles's annual apartment inspection fee of $12 per unit (which funded slum abatement, not infrastructure) was not subject to Proposition 218 because the city imposed the fee

The Most Obvious Loophole

ONE OF THE PECULIARITIES of Proposition 13 is that it requires local governments to receive two-thirds voter approval for special taxes. Special taxes are levied for a specific purpose—often for transportation projects—but Proposition 13 appears to allow local governments to increase a general tax with approval of only a simple majority of voters. Revenue from a general tax flows into the government agency's general fund without restrictions on how the money is to be spent.

More than 20 years after Proposition 13's passage, the city of Woodland, a farming town turned Sacramento suburb, exploited this loophole. After years of fairly rapid growth, Woodland was feeling the impact of development and a number of pressing needs were becoming obvious. City leaders explored ways to pay for these things before settling on a half percent sales tax.

First, the city got special state legislation passed allowing Woodland to levy the tax, with voter approval. (Typically, only counties may put a sales tax measure on the ballot.) Then the city crafted Measure H, a half cent sales tax that would expire after six years. Unlike the normal sales tax "override," Measure H did not specify how the city would spend the money. Instead, city officials had conducted a number of public meetings to help determine how the community would like new revenue to be spent. Once they had received input, city officials drafted four advisory measures for inclusion on the same ballot as Measure H. The advisory measures asked, yes or no, if people would like additional revenue from the proposed sales tax to be spent on city road repair and rehabilitation, a new police station, a community/senior center, and softball and soccer fields.

During the March 2000 primary election, 65 percent of Woodland voters approved Measure H. That vote would have fallen short if Measure H was a special tax, but the vote was more than enough for passage of a general tax. City officials had spent months trying to gain the trust of voters—the advisory votes were not legally binding—and the efforts paid off. Voters also approved all four advisory measures, which city leaders took as direction that they should spend the sales tax revenue in all four areas.

The additional sales tax went into effect in July 2000. The city used the new revenue in conjunction with development impact fees, and within four years the city had built a new police station, purchased land for a community/ senior center, and undertaken a major road repair program. Revenues did not arrive as quickly as expected, however, and city officials could ask voters to extend the sales tax for another period.

Other cities and a few counties have tried to copy Woodland's approach, but more often than not voters have rejected these general sales tax increases. In 2004, voters in the nearby city of Davis approved a general purpose half cent sales tax increase with the understanding that the money would pay for basic municipal services, such as police and fire protection.

Somewhat ironically, Woodland voters were given a chance to extend the sales tax from 2006 until 2012, with the money funding a flood protection project. Federal officials had determined that much of the city was within Cache Creek's 100-year floodplain and recommended the city build a new levee. The federal flood control recommendation was very unpopular in town and during an election in 2002, 70 percent of voters rejected the sales tax extension. ■

based on use of the property. *Apartment Owners Association of Los Angeles County, Inc. v. City of Los Angeles*, 24 Cal. 4th 830 (2001). More importantly from an infrastructure finance standpoint, the state Supreme Court has also ruled that a special district's charge for a new home to connect to a water system was not subject to Proposition 218. *Richmond v. Shasta Community Services District*, 32 Cal. 4th 409 (2004). In that case, a community services district in rural Shasta County levied a charge of about $3,000 for a new house to connect with the water system. The charge was based on the estimated cost of future improvements needed to serve new development within the district. Because the district charged only individuals who requested a new water connection, the charge was not an "assessment" under Proposition 218, the court ruled. (Curiously, the court also ruled that the charge was not a development fee because someone could theoretically request a water connection without developing property.)

Thus, whether they are considered loopholes, end-runs, or simply parts of the system, methods for raising infrastructure revenue do exist. It is far from impossible to pass bond issues, hotel taxes, or other tax-related measures, even when they require a two-thirds vote. The more popular the set of items to be funded—roads, fire stations, and parks often top the list—the greater support there is at the ballot box.

The unfortunate side effect of Proposition 218 and other tax limitations is that they do not balance the playing field but, rather, make it even more unbalanced than in the past. Taxpayer advocates claim, with justification, that local governments have abused assessment districts and other revenue-raising mechanisms simply to plug budget holes without obtaining widespread public support. But since Proposition 13, the taxpayer initiatives have been creating a skewed situation, and Proposition 218 is no exception.

More than ever, Proposition 218 promotes the notion that growth must pay for itself. It is no accident that virtually the only infrastructure finance tool left untouched by Proposition 218 is the Mello-Roos district. Mello-Roos taxes meet the taxpayer advocates' technical test of accountability—they are subject to a public vote. But perhaps more important, a Mello-Roos tax imposed in a new development is really a tax on somebody else—a large property owner, or homeowners and businesses who have not yet moved into a community.

Unfortunately, taxpayers often make a mental leap from believing that growth must pay for itself to believing that growth must solve all problems. It is not uncommon for taxpayers who did not pay developer fees when their homes were built to insist that new home buyers pay extra fees to solve traffic or school crowding problems that already exist in the community.

The other long-term impact of Proposition 218 and other tax restrictions is that local governments are likely to look more to the state to pay for infrastructure through statewide bond issues that are easier to pass. Unfortunately, it is often easier for local governments to try to squeeze infrastructure funds out of developers or the state than to persuade their own voters to pony up a few bucks to solve a problem. In this way, taxpayer restrictions on new community taxes sometimes erode a broad sense of community necessary for people to take responsibility for a town's problems. And that's not good for the long-term planning of any community.

The other long-term impact of Proposition 218 and other tax restrictions is that local governments are likely to look more to the state to pay for infrastructure through statewide bond issues that are easier to pass.

Chapter 20

Transportation
Planning and Financing

The transportation system probably does more to shape the physical form—and the daily functioning—of California's communities than any other piece of public infrastructure. There is a kind of chicken-and-egg relationship between land use and transportation planning. Traffic engineers often complain that they must design roadway and transportation systems to accommodate travel needs created by land use patterns both good and bad. Land use planners often complain that the land use demands in any given community are driven as much by the transportation patterns as they are designed by the traffic engineers.

It is hard to know whether the chicken or the egg comes first. But there is little question that transportation plays an important role in community planning, and, together with the pattern of land use, defines the form and function of any community. Furthermore, most of the trends in land use and urban planning in recent years have forced communities to confront transportation planning questions directly. Urban traffic congestion has increased dramatically—not only because the population is increasing, but also because the typical automobile user drives far more miles per year now than 20 or 30 years ago. In addition, as air quality regulations have become more strict, smog regulators have sought to reduce automobile travel demand because two-thirds of all air pollutants in California result from vehicle emissions.

Large-scale transportation projects, such as railroads and freeways, have dictated the patterns of urban growth in California since their inception. Indeed, during the suburban era, the freeway system provided real estate developers quite literally with a road map

There is little question that transportation plays an important role in community planning, and, together with the pattern of land use, defines the form and function of any community.

to promising locations. Even today, California's fastest-growing communities typically sit along well-positioned freeways on the periphery of the state's major metropolitan areas.

At the community planning level, the transportation system typically dictates both the form of a community and its capacity to absorb urban growth. Local roads often provide the focal point for technical analysis about community planning and for political debate over whether and how a community should grow.

As with other aspects of public infrastructure, such as parks and schools, transportation systems should be designed in concert with the communities they are supposed to serve. However, as the introduction above suggests, planning and building transportation infrastructure actually takes place on two levels, the regional and the local, each with a different type of relationship to local land use planning processes.

Regional transportation infrastructure means, simply, large-scale freeway and road systems, railroads, airports, and other transportation projects that transcend community boundaries and serve regional or inter-city needs. The political will for these projects—and their funding—usually comes from a higher level of government. Traditionally, the state and federal governments have been the "drivers" of regional transportation infrastructure, though California's counties are becoming increasingly involved in both planning and funding of big projects.

Local transportation infrastructure is a different story. At the community level, transportation planning is tightly connected to land use planning. In the typical general plan, the transportation and land use elements are well coordinated, with the transportation system sized and financed to fit the land use patterns called for in the general plan. But local plans can typically control only local streets, roads, and transit systems. They have little control over state highways, the freeway systems, regional railroads, and other pieces of transportation infrastructure that extend across jurisdictional lines.

Of course, these two types of transportation infrastructure work together in creating California's communities and linking them together. In some ways, though, they move on separate and somewhat parallel tracks. This planning system allows each type of transportation project to be dealt with at the scale for which it is most appropriate (regional or local). Not surprisingly, it also creates some conflicts and gaps in the system.

At the community planning level, the transportation system typically dictates both the form of a community and its capacity to absorb urban growth.

In the typical general plan, the transportation and land use elements are well coordinated, with the transportation system sized and financed to fit the land use patterns called for in the general plan.

The Big Picture:
Regional Transportation Planning

The construction of large-scale transportation projects has been one of the key success stories in the history of California's ongoing urban development. From the transcontinental railroad of the 1860s to the comprehensive freeway system a century later, high-quality transportation systems providing easy access over long distances have facilitated the development of a state that might otherwise have languished.

This history has been punctuated by a series of upheavals in how transportation projects are planned and paid for. In the railroad era, the federal government subsidized long-distance rail development in order to stimulate economic growth in previously inaccessible locations, such as the Central Valley. In urban areas, streetcar systems were usually built and operated privately, often by the landowners and developers who stood to benefit from them.

During the automobile era, the method of financing large transportation projects changed dramatically. Since the 1920s, state-level roadway construction has been financed by gasoline taxes—essentially, a user fee on cars and trucks that use the roads. The modern freeway era began in 1947, when the Collier-Burns Act increased the gas tax and other fees on motorized transportation and created a statewide funding system adequate to pay for the system of freeways then on the drawing boards. For the next 25 years, the California Department of Transportation—then known as the Division of Highways, now called Caltrans—planned and built the modern California freeway system, which eventually connected almost every community in the state with a population of 15,000 or more. Although overburdened and in poor repair in many places, this freeway system still provides the backbone of auto and truck transportation throughout California, and still helps to shape growth patterns throughout the state. Many parts of the freeway system were built mostly with federal funds—these are the portions of the system designated as interstate highways—but they were largely planned and executed by Caltrans engineers.

Beginning in the 1970s, the financial formula that had built the freeway system in California began to fall apart. Drivers began to buy fuel-efficient cars, meaning they paid less gas tax per mile driven. At the same time, environmental and social mitigation requirements, along with rising labor expenses, made planning and constructing new freeways more expensive. And local opposition to freeways, which had started in San Francisco in the late 1950s,

The construction of large-scale transportation projects has been one of the key success stories in the history of California's ongoing urban development.

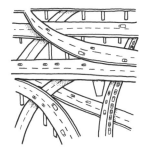

Caltrans = California Department of Transportation

Evolution of Federal Transportation Policy

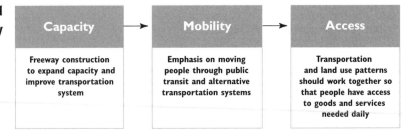

Capacity	Mobility	Access
Freeway construction to expand capacity and improve transportation system	Emphasis on moving people through public transit and alternative transportation systems	Transportation and land use patterns should work together so that people have access to goods and services needed daily

In the last decade, state and federal policies on regional transportation have shifted toward mobility, giving metropolitan areas more power to determine how funds will be spent.

spread to urban areas around the state. Throughout the United States—but especially in California—transportation policy for big-ticket regional projects began to change.

Some transportation historians have divided the history of federal transportation policy into three eras: capacity, mobility, and access. The freeway construction era represented the capacity approach—simply expanding capacity to the highway system in hopes that it will run more smoothly. The anti-freeway revolts led to the mobility approach, which emphasized movement of people over highway capacity and led to greater investment in public transit and other alternative transportation systems. More recently, the concept of access has come to the forefront. This is the notion that transportation and land use patterns should work together to ensure that people have access to the goods and services they need on a daily basis, whether this requires a short walk or a long drive.

At the regional level, transportation planning today frequently struggles to find a balance among all three of these concepts. In the last decade, state and federal policies on regional transportation have shifted dramatically away from capacity and toward mobility, giving metropolitan areas more power to determine how state and federal funds will be spent. In addition, the rise of the "transportation sales tax"—an additional sales tax imposed at the county level and used for transportation purposes—and changes in state law have given county-level officials more control over regional transportation projects.

Planning, Programming, and Funding

The world of transportation planning is a confusing world of overlapping government agencies, pots of money, and acronyms.

The world of transportation planning is a confusing world of overlapping government agencies, pots of money, and acronyms. It is beyond the scope of this book to explain this world in detail, but it is important to understand the broad outlines of how regional transportation planning works.

Transportation policy in California consists of three interrelated parts: planning, programming, and funding.

Planning generally means long-range planning efforts designed to identify and coordinate transportation requirements over a 20- to 30-year period. Programming generally means the creation of short-term (usually 5 to 7 years), financially constrained plans that identify specific transportation projects and their funding sources. Funding is, of course, the allocation of public resources to specific transportation programs and projects.

Until the late 1980s, this world of transportation policy was oriented overwhelmingly toward construction and maintenance of roads, and was controlled largely by Caltrans and the California Transportation Commission, an independent state commission based in Sacramento that prioritizes transportation projects of regional and statewide significance which are paid for with federal and state funds. More detailed regional transportation planning was undertaken by regional agencies such as the Metropolitan Transportation Commission in the Bay Area and SCAG in the Los Angeles area. However, these regional organizations had limited power over programming and funding.

In the late 1980s, however, some local transportation officials—especially in the Bay Area—began to rebel against the highway-oriented transportation decisions made by Caltrans and the CTC. In part, this rebellion represented a desire to spend more money on public transit and alternative transportation and less money on highway construction. However it also represented a growing concern about the relationship between transportation and land use. Why should transportation funds continue to be poured into new highway construction, the argument went, when the reason new highways are needed is because of sprawl-inducing local land use patterns?

During the late 1980s, the MTC increasingly bucked Caltrans's desire to spend money on highways. In addition, in 1988, Contra Costa County—one of the fastest-growing counties in the Bay Area—passed a ballot measure that sought to combine growth management and transportation funding. The measure added a one-half-cent sales tax within the county to pay for transportation improvements—a step many metropolitan counties in California took during the 1980s in order to gain more control over their transportation investments. But the measure also required cities and the county to prepare growth-management plans, showing how their land use patterns would minimize the need for new highway construction. The power to certify these plans and dole

APCD	=	Air Pollution Control District
AQMD	=	Air Quality Management District
CMA	=	Congestion Management Agency
CMP	=	Congestion Management Plan
COG	=	Council of Governments
CTA	=	County Transportation Authority
CTC	=	California Transportation Commission
DOT	=	U.S. Department of Transportation
FHwA	=	Federal Highway Administration
FTA	=	Federal Transit Administration
ISTEA	=	Intermodal Surface Transportation Efficiency Act
MPO	=	Metropolitan Planning Organization
MTA	=	Los Angeles County Metropolitan Transportation Authority
MTC	=	San Francisco Bay Area Metropolitan Transportation Commission
RTIP	=	Regional Transportation Improvement Program
RTPA	=	Regional Transportation Planning Agency
SCAG	=	Southern California Association of Governments
STIP	=	State Transportation Improvement Program
TCRP	=	Traffic Congestion Relief Program
TMA	=	Transportation Management Agency
UZA	=	Urban Zoning Agency

Unraveling the Acronyms

IN REGIONAL TRANSPORTATION PLANNING, there are so many government agencies and planning organizations involved that you can't tell the players without a scorecard. So here's the rundown:

Federal Agencies

Over the last two generations, the federal government has served an important role in developing national transportation policy and in providing the lion's share of funding for transportation projects. The federal role has changed in many ways during recent years, especially because of the new priorities created under ISTEA (the Intermodal Surface Transportation Efficiency Act) and TEA-21 (the Transportation Equity Act for the 21st Century). Nevertheless, the federal government remains a key player.

Most federal transportation functions are consolidated under the U.S. Department of Transportation. Two agencies within DOT are critical to the transportation programming/funding process in California: the Federal Highway Administration and the Federal Transit Administration.

These two agencies work together to administer ISTEA and its transportation programming and funding requirements. In this capacity, they oversee the work of state, regional, and local transportation agencies.

The Federal Highway Administration is responsible for all federally sponsored highway programming and funding. FHwA oversees the preparation of each state's State Transportation Improvement Program, or STIP, which is required under federal transportation law. FHwA also oversees the distribution of ISTEA highway money.

The Federal Transit Administration, formerly the Urban Mass Transit Administration, is in a parallel position: FTA administers all federally sponsored programming and funding for transit-related projects. Historically, FTA has worked more directly with local and regional

out the money was placed in the hands of a countywide transportation commission.

In 1990, the State of California adopted a similar approach in passing the package of transportation funding reforms that included a gradual doubling of the state gasoline tax. Along with the gas tax increase, the state created the "congestion management planning" program. This program was a statewide version of the Contra Costa County approach. It requires a designated countywide agency—often the county transportation commission—to approve growth-management plans from cities and counties before they receive their share of the increased gasoline tax funds.

Many of the California reforms were also contained in the federal transportation reform passed in 1991—the Intermodal Surface Transportation Efficiency Act, commonly known as ISTEA (pronounced "ice tea"). ISTEA authorized expanded funding for federal transportation programs to $155 billion over a six-year period. It was reauthorized, with substantially the same policies, in 1998 with the Transportation Equity Act for the 21st Century, better known as TEA-21. ISTEA and TEA-21 shifted federal transportation policy significantly away from capacity and toward mobility—and even took a few steps in the direction of access.

Among ISTEA's most significant changes were:

- **Emphasis on multi-modalism.** Highway funds may be used for transit projects under certain circumstances and vice-versa.
- **Emphasis on linking** transportation to air quality and land use decisions. Transportation policy decisions made under ISTEA must conform to Clean Air Act documents. (Significant amendments were also made to the federal Clean Air Act in 1990.) ISTEA also incorporates California's congestion management planning provisions.

- **Greater decision-making** power at the regional/metropolitan level. Unlike its predecessors, ISTEA gives metropolitan planning organizations broad discretion in allocating federal transportation funds and encourages the MPOs to engage in a wide-ranging planning process that includes the participation of local governments and other government agencies.

As a consequence of these policy changes, ISTEA created a number of pots of money to fund specific types of activities—many of which have a stronger relationship to local planning than traditional state and federal transportation activities. For example, ISTEA created an environmental enhancement program that has funded bikeways and other community improvements nationwide. Similarly, ISTEA set aside a large chunk of money for transportation projects that supposedly improve congestion and air quality.

All of these changes bring regional transportation decisionmaking into closer alignment—at least theoretically—with local land use and environmental planning policy. Perhaps the biggest change is simply that ISTEA turned transportation decisionmaking upside down. Instead of being initiated from the top, transportation project ideas often bubble up from below—sometimes from cities and counties, sometimes even from advocacy groups such as bicyclists. These ideas are then prioritized not by the state, but by the metropolitan planning organizations such as MTC and SCAG, which are controlled by local officials. MTC officials, for example, may now choose whether to fund a major Caltrans highway improvement, extension of a light rail line or a bike path proposed by a local bicycle club. Even at SCAG, in Los Angeles, the bread-and-butter highway projects of past regional transportation plans have largely given

transportation agencies than has FHwA, which has used Caltrans as an intermediary. This relationship is partly because of the fact that federal transit funds are often used for operations as well as capital projects. However, rail construction projects funded with FTA money must be in the STIP.

State Agencies

In California, two state agencies play important roles in the transportation programming and funding process: The California Transportation Commission and the California Department of Transportation, usually referred to as Caltrans.*

The California Transportation Commission's primary job is to allocate all federal funds and all state funds, including gas tax and sales tax revenue. The CTC's main programming vehicle is the State Transportation Improvement Program. This document includes a seven-year plan for all transportation capital projects to be funded.

Caltrans, one of the state government's largest single agencies, is responsible for engineering and planning, and for the construction and maintenance of all state highways and major arterials and roads. Caltrans also provides funding for a variety of other transportation projects and programs, ranging from intercity rail lines to transportation demand management programs to the landscaping of scenic highways.

Regional and Local Transportation Agencies

The hierarchy of regional and local agencies that engage in transportation planning, programming, and funding can be confusing indeed. State and federal transportation law requires local and/or metropolitan agencies to engage in a wide variety of transportation activities. State and federal laws typically attach a different name (and, hence, a different acronym) to the agency performing each activity.

* Caltrans was known as the Division of Highways, a unit of the Department of Public Works, until 1972.

To make matters even more confusing, several of these functions are often performed by the same local agency. But in each metropolitan area, the array of regional and local transportation functions will be divided differently among the different agencies. Here, then, is a list of the functions performed by local agencies and their acronyms.

The metropolitan planning organization, or MPO, is a regional agency designated by the U.S. Department of Transportation to carry out several functions specifically required under federal transportation law. Among other things, the MPO is charged with preparing a Regional Transportation Plan, the long-range plan for transportation in that particular region.

The Regional Transportation Planning Agency, or RTPA, is an agency designated by the state to carry out certain functions required by state law. In particular, the RTPA must prepare the Regional Transportation Improvement Program, or RTIP, which is a regionwide priority list of transportation projects to be funded in the short term. The RTPA is also charged with administering additional requirements imposed on air quality "nonattainment areas." These areas are designated by ISTEA as either Transportation Management Agencies (TMAs) or Urban Zoning Agencies (UZAs).

The Congestion Management Agency, or CMA, is an agency designated under both state and federal law to prepare each county's Congestion Management Plan, or CMP. The state-mandated congestion management planning was part of the 1990 gasoline tax increase. ISTEA picked up the congestion management provisions the following year.

The County Transportation Commission or County Transportation Authority performs a variety of functions that differ from county to county. Among other things, the CTC/CTA might be charged with administering local transportation funding programs (such as a transportation sales tax) and might also be the operator of the local transit system.

way to carpool lanes, busways, commuter rail, and other projects that emphasize access.

Put together, the county transportation commissions and their sales tax funds, the state congestion management program, and ISTEA/TEA-21 represent a major shift in the way regional transportation projects are planned and built. Local officials are more intimately involved in these decisions than they used to be, and the opportunity exists for more conformance with land use policy.

Of course, because of California's characteristically decentralized decision-making process, these policy changes are not always implemented as effectively as they might be. Most of the new policies (congestion management, Clean Air Act conformance) require county or regional approval for transportation projects affecting local communities. Since the county transportation commissions and regional agencies are typically made up of local officials, however, they are often reluctant to use their power to the fullest extent. After all, if a city council member sitting on a county transportation commission or regional planning agency votes against providing funds to somebody else's city, then representatives of that city may turn around and do the same thing.

At the same time, not everybody believes that the ISTEA revolution has been a good thing. State highway departments and advocates of a highway-oriented transportation policy are bitter about the fact that they have lost power—and they argue, with some validity, that in a nation so dependent on private automobiles and trucks, our transportation policy should enhance the existing system rather than discourage its use. In the pitched congressional battle over the reauthorization of ISTEA, the highway crowd fought ferociously—but unsuccessfully—to reverse ISTEA's policy direction.

It is also fair to say that ISTEA's policy innovations—like so many other planning and environmental policies—are designed to ensure that many bad things don't happen. As it stands, ISTEA appears to discourage new freeway and highway construction and encourage the diversion of funds to bike paths, public transit, and similar projects, but it doesn't really lay out a positive, integrated vision of how community life will function as a result of this shift in funding priorities. That requires the kind of connections to other aspects of planning—land use, finance, parks and open space—that local planning processes are well suited to address.

In recent years, state officials and voters have tried to direct more money to transportation, but a state budget deficit has thwarted those efforts. In 2000, Governor Gray Davis enacted the Traffic Congestion Relief Program. It earmarked surplus state funds for transportation projects and directed that, beginning in 2003, the sales tax on gasoline be devoted to highways, streets and roads, and public transit. In 2002, state voters overwhelmingly approved Proposition 42, which included Davis's plan for the gasoline sales tax, which amounts to approximately $1.5 billion annually. (The state's 6 percent gasoline sales tax is separate from the 18 percent "excise tax" on gasoline and diesel fuel, which is devoted entirely to transportation.) But Proposition 42 went further than Davis's program in emphasizing automobile transportation. The initiative directed that, beginning in 2008, 80 percent of gasoline sales tax revenues go toward state highways (40 percent) and local streets and roads (40 percent). Public transit, under Proposition 42, gets only 20 percent of gasoline sales tax revenue.

There was one catch, though. With a two-thirds vote, the legislature may suspend or modify the provisions of Proposition 42.

The Air Quality Management District or Air Pollution Control District (AQMD or APCD) is responsible for preparing regional air quality plans under the federal Clean Air Act. Under federal law, the Regional Transportation Plan and the air quality plan must be in conformance with one another. Therefore, AQMDs and APCDs have significant interaction with MPOs over Regional Transportation Plans.

In many cases, one local agency will perform most or all these functions. Often this agency is the regional Council of Governments, or COG—an association of local governments that performs many other regional planning functions under state and federal law.

However, the confusion of alphabet soup begins when different types of agencies perform different functions in different parts of the state.

For example, in the five-county region comprising Greater Los Angeles, the MPO is the Southern California Association of Governments, or SCAG, which is the regional COG. However, the RTPA and CMA functions are carried out by individual county transportation commissions. In Los Angeles County, the county transportation commission has been subsumed as part of the giant L.A. County Metropolitan Transportation Authority (MTA), which is also the region's chief transit operator.

The Bay Area has a completely different structure. The Bay Area Metropolitan Transportation Commission, or MTC, serves as both the MPO and the RTPA, thereby combining many transportation-related functions. But the MTC is not the designated CMA for the nine Bay Area counties; that function is filled by county-level entities such as the Santa Clara County CMA.

However, unlike L.A., where SCAG serves as both the COG and the MPO, the MTC is separate from the Bay Area's COG, the Association of Bay Area Governments. The two agencies are housed in the same building and share support services, and recent legislative proposals have called for their merger, but those proposals have continually failed to pass. ∎

The Four-Step Process

LAND USE PLANNERS ARE OFTEN mystified by the fact that traffic engineers seemed to have a black box in their office—a set of computer programs that mysteriously spit out traffic projections based on land use information and other data provided to them. Because of its quantitative nature, the black box has traditionally given traffic engineers considerable bureaucratic power over the planning process that land use planners are hard-pressed to combat.

Though the computerized calculations may be complicated, the underlying concept is far from mysterious. Here, then, is a brief explanation of the four-step process that traffic engineers use to calculate the traffic that will be generated by a development project or a plan. Though the four-step process is standard in the traffic engineering business, this description draws heavily on information provided by Richard Dowling, a prominent Oakland transportation consultant.

"Traffic behavior can be best understood by breaking down people's travel behavior into four sequential decisions," Dowling has written. Those four decisions are:

• Whether to make a trip
• Which destination to visit
• Which mode of transportation to use
• Which route to use

This translates logically into the four sequential steps that computer models are set up to predict:

• Trip generation
• Trip distribution
• Mode choice
• Route choice

All of these predictions are based on the land use data provided by land use planners to traffic

The initiative passed just as the state's budget situation became dire, so lawmakers and both Governors Davis and Schwarzenegger agreed to suspend Proposition 42 so that gasoline sales tax revenue was spent on government programs other than transportation.

The Community Story: Local Transportation Planning

On the community level, land use planning and transportation planning tend to operate much more in unison. In large part, this is because of the general plan requirement that the land use element and the circulation element be devised and implemented in a "correlated" fashion. (*See* chapter 6, General Plans.) In part, however, this better integration is simply a function of the fact that in local communities, as opposed to the region, land use and transportation planning are being conducted by the same organization (the city or county) at the same level of government.

Many of the issues in local transportation planning are similar to regional issues. Planners must estimate (and often try to shape) demand for transportation facilities based on local land use patterns, and then determine the best way to raise and use revenue for those transportation facilities. Local communities, of course, don't have the independent power to plan or build major regional transportation facilities, and they don't usually share in the big pots of state and federal money that have been set up to fund such projects. They do receive a lot of state transportation revenue, though, mostly in the form of pro-rated shares of gasoline tax revenues and sales tax revenues from the sale of gasoline. And they often set up "traffic mitigation programs" and "traffic impact fees" as a way of raising revenue from real estate developers.

The state gasoline tax revenues provide most local communities with the money they use for basic transportation programs. Cities and counties typically use most of the funds to maintain the existing system of local streets and roads, and also to upgrade that system by building key additional roads, restriping lanes, installing new traffic signals, and similar activities.

The revenues from state gas tax are devoted almost entirely to public transit systems, especially bus and rail systems. Half of this money flows to Caltrans, which funds a variety of programs including ride-share programs and inter-city rail subsidies. Most of the rest goes to local transit operators—mostly local bus companies—to subsidize their operations. The *sales* tax on fuel has long been a general purpose revenue that gets split between the state and locals. According to the LAO, only a "small portion" has ever been used for transportation. That's what Davis and Proposition 42 tried to correct. Coordination between local transit operators and local governments is not consistent. In a few communities, the cities actually own the bus companies. More commonly, a local transit operator is a cooperative organization that serves many communities, and coordination with local land use planning is not always strong.

Traffic mitigation programs and traffic impact fees represent the most important growth area for local transportation planning and funding. Cities and counties pursue traffic mitigation for the same reasons they pursue other exactions, most of which are outlined in chapter 10. Most commonly, local governments simply do not have enough general fund money to cover the cost of constructing transportation facilities to serve new development. In addition, local planners and politicians often believe that new growth should pay for itself.

Mitigation usually comes at two levels, and it is often established and calculated as part of the engineers. Perhaps the key assumption in the whole process is the translation used by traffic engineers to convert land use data into trip data. To make this translation, traffic engineers use (or adapt) the trip generation estimates for different land uses— the so-called "trip tables"—which are produced by the Institute of Transportation Engineers. These trip tables provide estimates for different types of land uses, which are then used to calculate overall trip generation.

For example, the ITE trip tables estimate that a single-family home produces nearly 10 trips per day, while a multi-family residence produces three fewer daily trips. A 1,000 square-foot office generates 11 trips per day, while the same sized light industrial building creates 7 trips daily. The traffic generated by retail development depends on the type of store. A drugstore or restaurant will generate about 90 daily trips for every 1,000 square feet of development. A big-box discount store will create about 47 daily trips per 1,000 square feet, a general purpose shopping center 43 tips per 1,000 square feet. (It is important to note that these trip estimates include not only residents, employees, and shoppers coming and going, but also other trips such as deliveries to homes and factories.) Similar estimates are made for morning and afternoon rush hours, as transportation systems are often sized to accommodate peak-hour traffic rather than overall traffic patterns.

The trip tables are updated regularly, and they provide estimates for a variety of contexts (such as urban, suburban, and rural). In addition, good traffic engineers will use their own judgment to determine whether some special situation exists that is not taken into account by the standard trip generation estimates. ■

Riding the Pork Road

CALIFORNIA HAS LONG followed a programmatic—some might say overly bureaucratic—approach to transportation planning. But in 2000, Governor Gray Davis bypassed the bureaucracy when he introduced the Traffic Congestion Relief Program (TCRP).

At the time, the state was swimming in an unexpected wave of revenues, produced largely by the technology boom. Davis's five-year plan called for spending $5 billion—that otherwise would have gone into the state's general fund—on about 140 highway and transit projects across the state.

An infusion of that amount of general fund revenue into transportation projects might ordinarily draw cheers from just about anyone stuck in California's legendary traffic jams. Instead, reaction to the TCRP was decidedly mixed. Why? Because Davis did not select projects based on priorities established by regional transportation planning processes. Nor did he attempt to spread the spending equally across all parts of the state. In fact, the TCRP ignored 33 of California's 58 counties. Rather, the $5 billion spending plan was based on the governor's own notions of how best to relieve congestion, enhance transportation "connectivity" and facilitate the movement of goods. The list also appeared to favor Davis's political backers: Silicon Valley business interests got money for a BART extension to San Jose; an Indian tribe with a casino in Riverside County got funds for a freeway interchange; and transit proponents in Los Angeles got money for express bus routes.

Sure, some of these projects were regional priorities. But some were backburner items and others had been specifically rejected by regional

California Environmental Quality Act review process. At the general plan level, communities predict the large-scale traffic impact of the new growth called for in the plan. They often use this prediction to establish a city- or countywide mitigation program. All developers are typically required to pay traffic mitigation fees based on the traffic demands estimated in the general plan.

But many real estate development projects will get hit with additional traffic mitigation requirements at the project level. Plan-level analyses can predict overall traffic flows, but they are unable to estimate increased traffic levels on specific streets and at specific intersections. (Also, many real estate development projects require a change in the general plan because developers want to build something different from what's called for in the general plan.) At the project level—usually as part of the CEQA analysis—traffic engineers will estimate precise levels of congestion, and additional mitigation may be required.

One common problem is that increased traffic congestion associated with an individual development project spills across city or county lines. In most cases, the traffic analyses prepared under CEQA will clearly identify what these cross-jurisdiction congestion problems are, but the city or county processing the project will pay little attention to mitigating the traffic problems being created outside its boundaries. The result: Jurisdictions file CEQA lawsuits as a means of extracting traffic mitigation funds from an adjoining jurisdiction or the developer just across the city or county line.

Bending the Trend: Shaping Travel Demand Rather Than Responding to It

As the above discussion suggests, most local transportation planning efforts usually assume that almost all travel demand will be met by people driving alone in their cars. Yet there is increasing pressure to craft alternative transportation strategies that will lead to more ridesharing, transit use, and use of nonmotorized modes of transportation such as walking and bicycling.

The increasing cost of building and maintaining roadways—along with the sheer physical space required to accommodate them, and the air quality problems associated with vehicle emissions—has caused many communities to rethink traditional transportation planning strategies. Yet quantifying the alternatives and making them work has proven elusive to many communities.

As the general plan chapter suggested, when additional growth is expected to increase congestion, a community has four options: (1) expand road capacity, (2) shift new development to areas with excess road capacity, (3) reduce the overall amount of development, or (4) try to reduce vehicle trips or shift travelers to other modes.

The first option, road expansion, is often too expensive—and, increasingly, politically unpalatable to local residents. The second option, putting development where excess road capacity exists, is a common solution, though critics argue that it's a formula for suburban sprawl. The third option, reducing the overall amount of development, is probably the most common solution. Like many growth-management techniques, however, this choice may simply bounce growth to a nearby community, making regional problems worse.

The fourth option—bending the trend—is the appealing one to many planners because it permits a community to accommodate necessary growth while minimizing the traffic impact. However, this option is by far the hardest to achieve because trend-bending strategies have met with only mixed success.

Perhaps the most obvious way to bend the trend is to stimulate a shift of modes—that is, encourage more people to walk, bicycle, or take public transit instead of driving alone in their cars.

Public transit—mostly regularly scheduled buses and trains—would seem to be the most obvious way to bend the trend. But despite increased government

transportation experts. Moreover, the TCRP was even more divorced from growth policy than the usual transportation planning system.

Some members of the transportation planning bureaucracy were grateful for the TCRP's extra money, even if the projects were not ideal. After all, could any program that puts money into the movement of people and goods be a bad thing?

But more skeptical people noted that the TCRP, in addition to being pork-barrel spending, cleverly contained just enough money to skew the normal transportation planning process. The TCRP did this by providing only partial funding for projects, meaning that normal transportation revenues would be needed to complete the projects that the governor had selected. It was as if Davis had started driving the transportation bureaucracy from Sacramento to L.A., but he only put $10 worth of gas in the tank. The bureaucracy would either get stranded in Santa Nella, or it could put another $30 in the tank to finish the trip.

As it turned out, the TCRP crashed before it ever got up to speed. At the same time that Davis was rolling out his plan (mid-2000), the state's economy was starting to turn in the wrong direction. The technology profits that were supposed to fuel the TCRP vanished. Right after the 2002 election, the Davis administration had basically abandoned the TCRP because the state budget surplus had evolved into a deficit.

This outcome might have been the worst one possible. Transportation agencies that had started planning, engineering, and even pouring concrete for dozens of projects on the TCRP list were stuck with partially completed projects—which the agencies may not have wanted in the first place—and no money to complete the work. ■

Linking Land Use and Transportation

AS EXPLAINED ELSEWHERE in this chapter, land use planning and transportation planning are often done on parallel tracks, even though they have enormous impacts on one another. But in recent years, the largest regional planning agencies have taken steps to tie land use planning and transportation planning together.

Regional transportation planning agencies in metropolitan Southern California, the Bay Area and Sacramento have all moved toward transportation plans that have at least some relationship to land use planning. No agency has gone further than the San Diego Association of Governments (SANDAG), which covers San Diego County. In fact, SANDAG has even attempted to use transportation funding to influence growth patterns. SANDAG is ahead of other regional bodies partly because it is a metropolitan planning organization and a regional transportation planning agency that also has some powers of a transportation commission, and partly because San Diego County has a longer history of looking at things regionally than anywhere else in the state.

In 2004, SANDAG adopted a regional comprehensive plan (RCP) that tied future investments in transportation to a more urban approach to land use. The RCP tried to tackle two huge problems in San Diego County—housing and traffic congestion. SANDAG planners determined that city and county general plans provided for only 314,000 new housing units by 2030. Demographers, however, estimated the county would need 407,000 new units to accommodate about 1 million new residents. So the RCP sought to add more units by using infill, rezoning, rehabilitation and affordable housing programs in what planners called "smart growth opportunity areas." These areas lie along bus, trolley, light rail and railroad corridors, in and near city centers, and, in unincorporated "rural villages."

spending on public transit since the 1970s, only a tiny fraction of commuters rely on transit. During the 1990s, the state allocated about 9 percent of transportation spending to rail projects. That money augments local sales tax overrides in urban counties, where an even larger percentage was invested in rail. Sacramento, San Jose and Los Angeles all opened significant light rail systems during the 1990s, Los Angeles launched a heavy rail system and opened a subway system, BART extended its reach in the Bay Area, and San Diego expanded its trolley while also introducing heavy rail service to northern suburbs. Still, only about 1 percent of commuters ride the rails to and from work. Buses—which are not nearly as sexy as sleek trains and nostalgic trolleys in planning circles—carry three or four times as many commuters as rail, and do not require the enormous up-front investment that rail does. Still, the vast majority of Californians either drive alone to work (at least 70 percent) or take a carpool (about 15 percent).

In large part, the decline of public transit appears to stem from suburban land use patterns, which are often oriented around automobiles even when neighborhoods are developed at fairly high densities. These denser land use patterns also have not pushed more people to bicycle or walk to work. Those numbers remain fairly constant despite considerable public investment, especially in bikeways.

Still, public agencies and a handful of developers are trying to buck the status quo by building what are known as transit-oriented developments. Typically, these are high-density and mixed-use within a few hundred feet of a light rail or train station. These are often infill developments, so there may be close proximity to existing stores, offices, and public facilities. These developments often contain apartments or condominiums, some retail shops, and maybe a few offices. The idea is that people who live in a transit-oriented development will ride the rails to and from work, and may be able to take care of day-to-day shopping and personal needs by walking within their neighborhood. Depending on the definition of "transit-oriented development," several dozen of the these projects have been built since the mid-1990s. Areas around BART stations are among the most popular.

While many planners and policymakers endorse the theory of transit-oriented developments, the success of individual projects has varied. Studies have found that although residents of transit-oriented developments are far more likely than average to ride public transit, residents do not automatically opt out of their cars. Furthermore, the projects can be extremely difficult to build because banks are leery of the concept, city zoning codes can discourage the projects, and existing residents complain about the high density of the new projects. A study by the state treasurer's office found that nearly all transit-oriented developments of recent vintage would not have gotten built without a public subsidy. Additionally, if a transit station was constructed without a transit-oriented development in mind—if, for example, the station is isolated by rail lines, big parking garages, or highways—it can be nearly impossible to design a good transit-oriented development around the station.

While federal, state, and local government agencies have poured billions of dollars into commuter rail systems during recent decades, one form of "commuting"—other than driving alone—is on the rise with almost no government intervention—telecommuting. At the dawn of the telecommunications age 25 years ago, many estimates suggested that 10 to 15 percent of the workforce could work at home or in a neighborhood work center by 2000. The 2000 Census

Only cities and the county government have authority over the development of land; SANDAG has no land use police power. But SANDAG's plan and the pronouncements of its leaders made clear that SANDAG would use transportation funding to reward local governments that make development decisions compatible with the RCP. Jurisdictions that refuse to go along might find themselves left off SANDAG's list of transportation projects.

The RCP is an attempt to turn San Diego County away from the suburban model of development, which SANDAG officials and many other people said has been responsible for both the county's miserable traffic congestion, and for a shortage of affordable housing. In recent decades, almost all development has been "automobile oriented," while transit opportunities, although they have been growing, remain limited. The RCP has tried to foist a more urban approach to development on the region. Instead of tracks of single-family homes spread across the landscape and accessible only by car, the RCP encourages development of apartments, condominiums and townhouses—all of which are typically cheaper to develop than single-family units—within walking distance of transit stations and city centers. The apparently compatible ideas are to provide housing and to get people out of their cars.

It is too early to tell whether the RCP will be effective. Although they endorsed the RCP, county officials have worried that SANDAG's new approach would reduce money available for roads needed to serve growth in unincorporated areas—a consequence that SANDAG might have favored. Furthermore, city officials who have backed the RCP will have to approve dense developments that are popular among SANDAG planners, but not among local residents. Also, the RCP needs the cooperation of Caltrans and the California Transportation Commission to be truly effective. ■

said the true figure was closer to 4 percent, but other surprising patterns are emerging. One is a dramatic increase in home-based businesses. Another is a rapid increase in the employees who work at home some of the time—but not all of the time.

Both of these trends would seem to bode well for reducing future traffic congestion in urban areas. At the very least, home-based workers will not be traversing city streets and freeways at rush hour. Furthermore, if they live in traditional neighborhoods, they may have access to necessary business services within walking distance of—or perhaps a short drive from—their homes. At the very least, telecommuting provides the opportunity for some workers to alter their travel patterns some of the time.

The other encouraging trend-bender has to do with the interest in building "new" traditional neighborhoods using New Urbanist principles. In recent years, New Urbanist traffic engineers have argued that more traditional neighborhood land use patterns can reduce overall vehicle travel and reduce traffic congestion.

Obviously, some New Urbanist advocates believe that their design ideas will increase walking, bicycling, and transit use. But, interestingly, this is not the core of the New Urbanist transportation argument. Rather, the New Urbanist traffic engineers argue that traditional neighborhood patterns will lead to shorter vehicle trips. Rather than driving two miles on an arterial to get to the store, the argument goes, the resident of a traditional neighborhood might drive only a half mile on a local street—at a lower speed. The New Urbanists also argue that the traditional grid system increases overall transportation capacity because drivers are not forced onto a few huge arterial highways and because there are more left-turn opportunities.

Computer models have estimated that traditional neighborhood design can reduce total vehicle miles traveled measurably.

Computer models have estimated that traditional neighborhood design can reduce total vehicle miles traveled measurably. Though these estimates have been questioned by many critics, nevertheless the New Urbanists raise many useful points about transportation in our communities. Where do we go and why? How far must we travel to fulfill our daily needs? Must we all drive on large arterial highways or is it possible to increase traffic on neighborhood streets without alarming the residents of those neighborhoods? All of these questions point to the need for a stronger connection between transportation and land use—a connection that is gradually emerging, however fitfully, from the current discontent with traffic congestion.

Chapter 21

School Facilities Planning

P ublic schools are undeniably a part of almost every community. They are an asset when they are good and a liability
when they are bad, but residents—especially parents—expect
them to be there, just like roads or parks or libraries.

Like these other pieces of public infrastructure, schools
require land, and they require money to construct—often a lot of
money because California state specifications for school design are
very strict. But there is one important aspect that sets schools apart.
Unlike parks and roads and libraries, schools are owned and
operated not by the local city or county but by a completely different political entity—a local school district that has its own separately
elected board of trustees. This situation creates troublesome problems and also raises the chicken-and-egg question of whether
school construction drives growth, or growth drives schools.

For decades, city and county officials, school district leaders,
developers, and community members wrestled with these problems, which grew increasingly difficult during the 1980s and '90s
because school construction was not keeping pace with population
growth in many places. In recent years, however, everything has
changed. And what has caused the change is, purely and simply,
money. Since 1999, the state and local school districts have raised
and spent tens of billions of dollars on an unprecedented wave of
school construction and rehabilitation. But while the school construction binge has been welcomed by most people, there is one
significant catch—with few exceptions, this enormous investment
in a key piece of infrastructure has been made without any consideration of local or regional land use planning. Thus, while

*Unlike parks and roads and libraries,
schools are owned and operated by a
completely different political entity—a
local school district that has its own
separately elected board of trustees.*

California continues to get more classrooms, they may not be located in the most strategic places.

Shortly after passage of Proposition 13, cities and counties, school districts, and developers began arguing over how to provide new schools, because Proposition 13 prohibited school trustees from raising property taxes. The government entities looked to the developers, while the developers complained that they were being asked to mitigate a problem that was only partly of their making.

The first remedy was the School Facilities Act, which the California legislature passed in 1986. Under that measure, developers would pay their share, school districts would raise some local money, and the state would provide the rest.

But the school mitigation issue did not remain "fixed." The need for new schools grew faster than anyone anticipated. The state's role as a financier of school facilities was disrupted by failed bond issues and other financial problems. Local bond issues were uncertain propositions. The real estate development industry had its ups and down. As a result, the same problems arose again and again in communities all over the state. Who should pay for new schools? How should cities and counties deal with school mitigation in their planning and development approvals? How should school districts get involved in local land use planning efforts? How much money should developers contribute toward the construction of new schools?

All of these questions remained up in the air—and heavily litigated—until November 1998, when California voters approved Proposition 1A, a record-setting $9 billion state bond for school construction. Behind Proposition 1A was a political deal. The homebuilding development industry agreed to support the Proposition 1A bond because the measure also imposed significant new restrictions on the way school districts and local governments could impose development fees.

Only two years later, state voters, possibly without knowing it at the time, revolutionized local school bonds. Approved in November 2000, Proposition 39 lowered the vote threshold needed to pass local school bonds from two-thirds to 55 percent. With the two-thirds requirement, only about 60 percent of local school bonds passed, and many districts did not even try. Since the lower vote threshold has been in place, voters have approved more than 80 percent of local school bonds—even though far more districts than ever are placing bonds on the ballot. These days, it is not

In 1998, California voters approved Proposition 1A, a record-setting $9 billion state bond for school construction, which the homebuilding development industry agreed to support.

Proposition 39 lowered the vote threshold needed to pass local school bonds from two-thirds to 55 percent.

uncommon for voters to decide on 40, 50 or more local school bonds during a statewide election.

But the problem of building schools within a larger planning context remains. California's 1,000 local school districts must educate the students who appear at their doorstep, no matter who they are or where they come from. Naturally, the districts are concerned about rapid community growth that will inevitably affect the schools' abilities to provide a good education for students. But most school officials are inexperienced in land use planning issues and often do not know how to go about influencing the land use decisions that drive every community's growth.

California's 1,000 local school districts must educate the students who appear at their doorstep, no matter who they are or where they come from.

School districts' lack of land use sophistication combined with local governments' zealously guarded power to regulate land use creates a chasm. Falling into this chasm are the state's thousands of land developers and homebuilders, who must answer to both masters and carry a significant financial burden. The enormous flow of money into school construction projects during recent years eased two decades worth of bruising political and legal battles among the schools, cities and counties, and developers. Still, plenty of issues remain—as do the memories of those battles.

The Emergence of School Mitigation as an Issue

Like many current issues in local communities throughout California, the school mitigation problem has its roots in the passage of Proposition 13.

Prior to the passage of Proposition 13 in 1978, local bond issues financed by property taxes were a popular source of funds for constructing new schools. The general assumption was that the increased property values created by new houses and other new real estate development would offset the added cost of bond payments. By dramatically reducing property tax rates, Proposition 13 rendered this equation obsolete.

Prior to the passage of Proposition 13 in 1978, local bond issues financed by property taxes were a popular source of funds for constructing new schools.

In the years after Proposition 13, school districts—like cities and counties—scrambled for community infrastructure funds wherever they could find them. By 1982, several options had emerged, and local school districts began to use to all of them to close the gap. These options included:

- **The state's own school bond program.** These voter-approved bonds provide a 50 percent match for construction of many local schools and rehabilitation of older campuses.

- **Mello-Roos districts,** which were described in chapter 19. After the Mello-Roos law was passed in 1982, many school districts helped developers set up Mello-Roos districts. Even if the Mello-Roos districts are administered by cities or counties, many school districts receive a share of Mello-Roos revenue for school construction.

- **Local school bonds.** In 1986, local school districts regained the power (lost in the Proposition 13 shuffle) to issue bonds for school construction and repay them with an increase in property tax rates, so long as local voters approve the bond issue. Until 2000, a two-thirds vote was required to pass a local school bond.

All of these options put together still did not provide enough money, however. Seeking to close the gap, school districts—like cities and counties—began turning to real estate developers for additional school construction funds. Developers were already paying fees for roads, sewers, and other community facilities. Furthermore, many residential developers view good local schools as an important selling point for their projects. School districts were not specifically authorized by state law to collect these fees, but many began working with cities and counties to add school mitigation to the package of fees imposed on a new development project when it was approved.

The 1986 school fee law expressly authorized school districts to levy fees directly on developers, but restricted school fees to $1.50 per square foot on residential projects and 25 cents per square foot on commercial and industrial projects.

Fearing that they would become the financiers of last resort for new school construction, the state's homebuilders went to the legislature for help. The result was the 1986 school fee law. The law expressly authorized school districts to levy fees directly on developers. Govt. Code § 53080. But the law also restricted school fees to $1.50 per square foot (plus cost-of-living increases) on residential projects and 25 cents per square foot on commercial and industrial projects. (The current figures are $2.24 and 36 cents.) Govt. Code § 65995; Education Code § 17620. The fees were expected to raise about 30 percent of needed construction funds. Local bonds would provide more money, while the state would provide the rest as the true financier of last resort.

By the time the school fee law went into effect, it was already clear that the state would have trouble providing enough funding. Among other things, school enrollment was growing much faster than anyone had anticipated. The law had assumed enrollment would grow by approximately 100,000 students per year. By the late 1980s, enrollment was growing at double that rate.

The *Mira* Line of Cases

Many school districts didn't like the restrictions imposed by the state on their ability to levy impact fees on developers. In particular, school districts in fast-growing suburban areas—for example, Riverside, San Joaquin, and Placer Counties—believed they could get developers to pay more if only they had the legal authority to demand it.

So, immediately after the school facilities law went into effect in 1987, some school districts undertook an aggressive campaign to challenge it in court. They recognized that they were not likely to overturn the state-imposed limits on fees they could charge. So they took a different tack: They argued that the law didn't pre-empt the power of local cities and counties to further mitigate or deny projects based on school capacity issues. In other words, the school districts claimed, they could get more money from developers for school construction if school capacity was identified as an issue in local planning documents.

Immediately after the school facilities law went into effect in 1987, some school districts undertook an aggressive campaign to challenge it in court.

In 1988, the school districts won their first major victory in the *Mira* case from San Diego County. *Mira Development Corporation v. City of San Diego*, 205 Cal. App. 3d 1201 (1988). In that case, an appellate court ruled that pre-emptions of the School Facilities Act applied only to quasi-judicial decisions, such as tentative map approvals under the Subdivision Map Act, and not to legislative decisions, such as general plan amendments and most zone changes.

Three years later, school districts won two more important victories that further undermined the law's pre-emption clauses. *William S. Hart Union High School District v. Regional Planning Commission*, 226 Cal. App. 3d 1612 (1991), reaffirmed *Mira*, and *Murrieta Valley Unified School District v. County of Riverside*, 228 Cal. App. 3d 1212 (1991), clarified the earlier rulings. *Murrieta* said that the law did not prohibit land use planning changes or mitigation measures to lessen the impact of new development on schools.

In 1993, a pair of related court cases further underscored the general principle that more school mitigation can be obtained only if a local government's planning policies recognize school capacity as a potential problem. In *Corona-Norco Unified School District v. City of Corona*, 13 Cal. App. 4th 1577, the Fourth District Court of Appeal ruled that a city or county is not permitted to deny a tract map under the Subdivision Map Act because of school overcrowding. A few months later, in a second case, *Corona-Norco Unified School District v. City of Corona*, 17 Cal. App. 4th 985 (*Corona-Norco II*), the Fourth District clarified that local governments can request additional school mitigation only if their general plan contains specific policies relating to school capacity issues.

Thus, the court cases in the late 1980s and early '90s established a clear rule: Local governments could demand additional school mitigation beyond the school fees permitted under state law, but only if those local governments have strong school mitigation policies contained in their general plans. If a city or county demands additional mitigation but does not have the appropriate general plan policies, that city or county simply doesn't have the legal power to follow through on its demand. Similarly, if a school district shows up at the hearing for tract map approval or some other quasi-judicial permit and demands additional mitigation, the city or county cannot require that mitigation even if the appropriate general plan policies are in place.

The Impact of *Mira*

For cities and counties, the *Mira* line of cases became the most significant point of contact between school districts and the local planning process. By requiring strong general plan policies, the *Mira* line of cases increased the school districts' understanding of why general plans and related policies are important. By giving school districts some leverage over the planning process, *Mira* and its progeny made cities and counties more aware of the need to consider school facilities in their planning and infrastructure policies.

By giving school districts some leverage over the planning process, Mira *and its progeny made cities and counties more aware of the need to consider school facilities in their planning and infrastructure policies.*

After *Mira* and the other cases were handed down, a series of lawsuits and negotiations around the state ensued in which school districts, local governments, and developers attempted to resolve the school mitigation question. In general, most of these disputes were resolved by splitting the difference.

Developers argued that they should not pay more than the fees permitted under state law (somewhere between $1.70 and $1.90 per square foot, depending on the year). School districts demanded full mitigation, usually calculated as somewhere around $5 to $6 per square foot, or about $8,000 for a standard suburban home. Cities and counties were caught in the middle. Most of these situations were resolved when the developers agreed to meet the school district halfway and pay somewhere in the vicinity of $3.75 to $4 per square foot. Cities and counties were, of course, the vehicle for this additional mitigation, because anything beyond the state limit of $1.70 to $1.90 had to be paid to them as a condition of development approval, rather than be paid directly to the school district.

Many statewide surveys suggest that the *Mira* doctrine was not widely used among local school districts. Only about 50 or 60 school districts around the state successfully extracted more money from developers in this way—mostly fast-growing suburban districts. For a decade, though, *Mira* was an important symbol for school districts.

Along with the financial settlement, the *Mira* line of cases often forced cities or counties to broaden the school capacity policies contained in their general plans—or simply take them more seriously. The impact of the *Murrieta* ruling on Riverside County is a good example. In the *Murrieta* case, the court of appeal faulted the county for not dealing with school capacity issues in its the South West Area Plan (SWAP). The county general plan calls for school development to meet capacity needs, as well as cooperation with school districts.

Along with the financial settlement, the Mira *line of cases often forced cities or counties to broaden the school capacity policies contained in their general plans—or simply take them more seriously.*

Subsequent to the court ruling, the county adopted a new school mitigation program, which required each school district to submit districtwide school facility mitigation plans. These plans had to be drawn up according to the county's own criteria regarding demographic projections and construction cost. Once the county certified the mitigation plans, then additional mitigation could be imposed on specific development projects so long as a legislative action (a general plan amendment, a zone change, or a specific plan approval) was required on the county's part. Again, the net financial result appeared to be mitigation in the range of $4 per square foot.

Proposition 1A
Marks a Sea Change

The basic assumption about how school facilities will be financed in California has remained unchanged since the passage of the School Facilities Act in 1986. It's supposed to be a three-legged stool including state bonds, local bonds, and developer fees. For more than a decade, the interest groups—including local governments and the building industry—were stalemated in Sacramento over how to re-calibrate the three-legged stool so that it really worked.

This stalemate was finally broken in 1998, when the California Teachers Association and the California Building Industry Association successfully promoted a repeal of *Mira,* combined with a long-term state commitment to school bonds. The voters readily approved this package as Proposition 1A in 1998.

The Biggest District

PERHAPS NO SCHOOL district in the United States has as great a need for new and rehabilitated facilities as the Los Angeles Unified School District. At the same time, there may be no place more difficult to find new school sites than in the L.A. basin.

For a variety of political and economic reasons, the LAUSD built very few new schools during the 1970s, '80s, and '90s. Yet the number of pupils in the district continued to grow. The district housed those students in increasingly crowded schools and by using staggered schedules that have kids in school year-round.

Finally, in 2000, the school district adopted a new facilities master plan that identified 158 short-term building projects: 79 new schools (including 15 comprehensive high schools), 60 school upgrades and expansions, and 19 playground additions. With political and legal pressure on state officials, the district in 2002 started getting state school bond funds, money that suburban school districts normally would have snapped up. That same year, LAUSD voters also approved a $3.3 billion bond.

However, a good plan and money go only so far. The district must identify sites for its projects. The district covers some of the most densely populated areas of the country, so most of the likely sites for school projects already have homes and businesses. Within two years of adopting the master plan, LAUSD trustees had also adopted eminent domain resolutions to

⇒

The Proposition 1A package included $9.2 billion in state education bonds, to be issued over an eight-year period (although the money was actually spent much faster than that). In exchange for the huge state commitments to bonds, however, local school districts now must cover half of the cost of new schools, and *Mira* has been suspended. With the *Mira* powers gone, a statewide cap on school fees of $2.24 per square-foot for housing and 36 cents per square-foot for commercial and industrial construction is back in force.

The developer-fee provisions allow districts to levy fees to cover 50 percent of land and construction costs—and, therefore, exceed the statewide cap—if they have conducted a needs analysis and are certified by the State Allocation Board as eligible for state funding. In addition, they must meet at least one of four conditions:

- **Have attempted a local school bond** in the last four years that received at least 50 percent of the vote but short of the required two-thirds majority
- **Have passed bonds equal to** 15 percent of bonding capacity
- **Have 30 percent of students** on a multi-track year-round calendar, or
- **Have 20 percent of students** housed in portable classrooms

After January 1, 2000, districts had to meet at least two of those conditions in order to levy these "Level 2 fees," which are above the statewide cap. If the state bond money runs dry, the *Mira* provisions could be reinstated, within limits. But that appears unlikely because teachers, business leaders, and elected officials have joined to help pass large state school bonds, and all of the interest groups realize that keeping money in the system helps prevent the *Mira*-style battles of the past.

Initially after the passage of Proposition 1A, local school districts who were accustomed to using *Mira* complained that the solution was too constraining. But the change in the state constitution to allow passage of local school bonds with a 55 percent vote makes *Mira* seem like ancient history. Easier passage of local bonds combined with the infusion of billions of dollars of state bond money means that even some of the state's poorest school districts have enough money to meet the demands posed by rising enrollments and decades of deferred maintenance. At the same time, the pressure is off developers to serve as the financiers of last resort.

But while the financial aspects of the school issue are under control, there remain questions about school siting, joint-use facilities, and the timing of construction. "Smart growth" advocates would place new schools in and near existing urban areas and put money into upgrades of existing buildings. Many smart growth backers would also have schools serve as joint-use community centers with ball fields, meeting rooms, and learning facilities that are open to the public on evenings and weekends.

School boards, however, remain largely divorced from the smart growth debate. They make many school construction decisions based on the ease of building and the prospect of new subdivisions. An infill site identified by the smart growth crowd is often smaller and more difficult to develop than a "greenfield" site on the edge of town. School officials, understandably at times, are reluctant to throw the doors open to one and all because of concerns about jeopardizing a school's primary mission. Additionally, school officials often feel ignored by city and county planners who undertake long-term planning efforts, while state officials who control bond funds have barely been willing to even enter the discussion.

A related issue concerns densification and gentrification of older areas. During the past decade, young professionals, childless couples, and empty nesters have returned to central cities and inner-ring suburbs. They come largely for a more urban lifestyle and, often, for real estate bargains. These "urban pioneers" are unlikely to have school-age children. But as these pioneers help transform neglected neighborhoods into desirable ones, more and more families are lured to the area. Because these neighborhoods are already heavily developed, however, there is little or no space available for new classrooms. Los Angeles Unified School District faces this problem, as well as simple densification. The city of Los Angeles contains a great deal of land, but nearly all of it is spoken

acquire hundreds of privately owned parcels of land. Thus, some of the school projects became unpopular in the very neighborhoods that were to be served because the new classrooms and playgrounds were eliminating housing and employment sites, often in the city's poorest districts.

To move forward, the district has gotten creative. The district has approved multistory schools, adaptive re-use of existing buildings, and smaller campuses. Working with city officials and community representatives, the district has helped put together joint-use projects that provide the community with access to school facilities and resources during off hours.

The next step will likely be development of school projects that also have housing units, a commercial component, and possibly a transit station—a true mixed-use project. Although the LAUSD has been reluctant to embrace this idea, state lawmakers, city officials, and housing advocates have pushed it. Such projects require very complicated financing, and they raise issues of legal liability.

Still, the LAUSD will have to entertain these once-radical notions of school development. The 158 facilities required by the master plan were for the short-term. The district needs to squeeze an additional 140 to 160 new schools into L.A. during the next two decades, and no one expects real estate to become readily available during that period. ▪

for. So when more people cram into Los Angeles every year, the school district gets more children to educate but not necessarily anyplace new to put them.

Further complicating the suburban situation is the growing willingness of big developers to provide "turn key" facilities for school districts. Developers have come to realize that school quality greatly affects real estate prices. So, for example, in exchange for approval of a 2,800-unit housing development in the city of Oxnard, a developer in 2004 agreed to build two new elementary schools and an intermediate school. One might argue that this sort of arrangement guarantees that a development's impact on schools is mitigated. But one might also argue that dropping schools into new subdivisions begs a larger question of where public facilities are most needed.

Thus, while California has largely caught up with the need for new and modernized schools since 1999, no one has ensured that those schools are located in the most strategic locations for students and parents.

Part Six

Natural Resources Protection

Chapter 22

Structure of Natural Resources Protection

Forty years ago, few people involved in the planning process concerned themselves with the protection of natural resources. Planning was focused on urban development: how to create and maintain urban systems in a way that was fair socially, and efficient geographically and economically. The idea that nature might also have "communities" and "systems" in need of attention was foreign to most planners. Nature was something that humans could engineer and re-engineer for their own convenience.

That mindset has vanished. Concern for natural resources typically plays a central role in planning and development policy. Often the planning process deals with natural resources first and with the needs of human communities only afterward.

Concern for natural resources typically plays a central role in planning and development policy—often with natural resources first and the needs of human communities afterward.

In California, the idea of incorporating natural resource protection into the local government planning process dates back to the 1960s. Nevertheless, the match between local planning and natural resource protection is not always a seamless one.

For one thing, resource protection is most often a state and/or federal responsibility. This means that state and federal agencies are direct players in natural resource protection with considerable leverage, even at the local level. In most areas of land use planning, local governments simply follow the laws and regulations laid out by the state government, knowing that unless a lawsuit is filed, there is likely to be little administrative oversight. By contrast, state and federal resource laws often contain specific criteria and standards for resource protection, and state and federal agencies often require separate permits before natural resources can be disrupted.

Thus, local governments usually adopt one of two approaches. In some cases, local planners work in concert with state and federal agencies to achieve resource protection goals through mutual action—a task that may seem more harmonious but requires a large amount of coordination and staff time. Instead of integrating resource issues into their local planning efforts, other local governments simply abandon resource protection altogether. In these cases, the local governments tell developers and landowners to obtain federal permits first, then to return to the local government for further processing of land use proposals.

Clearly, both cities and counties deal with resource protection issues, but counties are more likely to be concerned with resource protection in their land use planning policies than cities. In general, cities focus on building out the area under their control with urban development. If the property does not show the potential for urban development, in most cases cities are unlikely to be interested in it. (Some exceptions exist, including the cities of San Diego and Los Angeles, which have large resource-sensitive areas within their jurisdictions.) By contrast, as the stewards of all unincorporated land, counties recognize that they will always maintain land use control over large rural areas and therefore tend to focus their planning policies and practices accordingly.

This does not mean that counties are focused on natural resource protection in the same way that state and federal agencies are. Many state and federal agencies are charged with protecting natural systems such as watersheds, wetlands, and timber areas in order to maintain and improve environmental quality. Counties, on

the other hand, must be concerned with creating a stable local economy and a reliable tax base for themselves. This often means that counties must promote the use of natural resources rather than their protection. Until at least the late 1980s, most rural parts of California were economically dependent on resource-oriented industries, primarily agriculture, timber, ranching, and mining. Partly because of stricter state and federal environmental regulations, some of those activities, especially cattle ranching and logging, have declined dramatically. The drop-off in these industries has been difficult for counties to accept, both economically and socially. For a long time, counties were concerned with managing natural resources based on their extractive value. Forests were studied for how many board-feet of timber could be produced; grasslands were valued for how many cows could graze there. This is a different approach than preserving and enhancing natural systems for their own sake, which is often the charge of the state and federal agencies. Some counties, though, have recognized that "the good old days" are gone. Those counties have started considering the value of the flora and fauna for attracting tourists and even business owners seeking a nice place to live and work.

The Regulatory Framework

The regulatory framework for natural resource protection is shaped by a series of state and federal laws designed to protect either specific geographic areas or specific natural resources. In most cases—especially with regard to the laws designed to protect specific natural resources—CEQA is supposed to provide the connection to local land use planning.

BCDC = Bay Conservation and Development Commission

CEQA = California Environmental Quality Act

LCP = Local coastal plan

Protection of Specific Geographic Areas

In four cases, the state has adopted laws to protect specific geographic areas that contain special natural resources. In three of those four cases, the state has also taken some or all power over land use regulation away from the local governments and given it to a special state agency. These special cases are:

San Francisco Bay. In 1965, amid concern that cities around the bay were rapidly reducing its size and natural value by dredging and filling, the state created the Bay Conservation and Development Commission. BCDC has regulatory power over land use in a 100-foot zone all the way around the bay, effectively giving it control over bay fill. Govt. Code §§ 66600–66661. Most of the 27 BCDC commissioners are local or regional public officials in the Bay Area, while seven are appointed by the state. BCDC is widely credited with stabilizing the size and environmental health of the bay.

The California Coast. In 1972, California voters passed the Coastal Act by initiative, creating the Coastal Commission and giving it strong regulatory power. The Coastal Commission has the authority to regulate land use in the coastal zone—an area that varies in size but, on average, covers the first 1,000 feet or so inland from the ocean. Members are appointed by the governor and legislature, not by local governments (though the state is required to appoint some local officials).

In 1972, California voters passed the Coastal Act by initiative, creating the Coastal Commission and giving it strong regulatory power.

Under the Coastal Act (Public Resources Code §§ 30000–30823), a local government could no longer issue development permits in the coastal zone, as it had done in the past. Instead, it was to work—with the help of Coastal Commission staff—on "local coastal plans" (now referred to as "local coastal programs"). These LCPs, as they are often called, would usually be included as an element in the general plan. When the local coastal plan was completed and certified by the Coastal Commission, development permit authority, for the most part, would be returned to the city or county in question.

Although all LCPs were supposed to be done by 1976, approximately one-quarter of them remain incomplete, meaning that the Coastal Commission still carries a heavy load of permit applications from all around the state. Amendments to local coastal plans still must be approved by the commission—and an LCP amendment is often required for a large project to be constructed. Moreover, many LCPs are now 15, 20, or more years old and, some observers say, vastly out of date. Yet major LCP overhauls are rare, partly because of the expense and political difficulty that an update entails.

Many local land use decisions within the coastal zone may be appealed to the Coastal Commission—even by one of the commissioners—and overruled by the commission if the decision is found to be contrary to the LCP or the Coastal Act. The end result of this system is that virtually every major project proposed along the coast, whether it's a hotel in downtown Oceanside or another golf course at Pebble Beach, gets decided by the Coastal Commission, not by the city or county where the project is located.

The constitutionality of the Coastal Commission came into doubt in a lawsuit filed by the proponent of building an artificial reef off the Orange County coast. An appellate court ruled that the legislature's ability to appoint and remove commission members violated the separation of powers doctrine. The legislature responded by passing a law that set fixed, four-year terms for the eight members appointed by the Assembly speaker and the Senate Rules Committee, and that ended lawmakers' ability to remove commissioners at will. The legislature's response satisfied the state Supreme Court, which unanimously ruled that the appointment scheme is constitutional.

Lake Tahoe. The Lake Tahoe area has had, if anything, a more tumultuous history of environmental planning than the Coastal Act. The area's fragile environment, especially its air and water quality, led to a political consensus in the late 1960s that Lake Tahoe deserved special protection, but this consensus has often fallen apart in the face of conflicting interests. The first bi-state compact between California and Nevada failed because they had dramatically different attitudes about development and environmental protection. Subsequently, the two states formed a new Tahoe Regional Planning Agency, or TRPA. Govt. Code § 66801. This agency almost failed as well, but was rescued by a complicated set of negotiations in the late 1980s that restricted the amount of commercial and residential development in the Tahoe basin.

TRPA = Tahoe Regional Planning Agency

Today, TRPA continues to oversee all land use permits in the Tahoe basin. The whole regulatory structure continues to suffer from the political and legal opposition of some commercial property owners and especially some residential lot owners, many of whom are unable to build under current regulations. The long-running dispute reached the U.S. Supreme Court in 2002. In a setback for the property owners, the high court ruled in *Tahoe-Sierra Preservation Council*, 535 U.S. 302, that TRPA had the authority to impose a 32-month building moratorium, which was extended an additional three years, while the agency updated a regional land use plan. Although the litigation over TRPA's plans and authorities appears to be never-ending, the broad political consensus to protect Lake Tahoe remains as strong as ever.

The Sacramento-San Joaquin Delta. In recent years, the Delta has received increased attention from government regulators and environmentalists—as well as from urban developers, who want to exploit the Delta's rich natural environment and its proximity to fast-growing communities in the Bay Area and the Central Valley.

In 1992, the state created the Delta Protection Commission to devise a land use plan for the area. Unlike the earlier regional commissions, the Delta Protection Commission does not have regulatory power. Rather, it is charged purely with a planning function. The commission is composed of supervisors from the five counties in the Delta, city council members, and state representatives. The Delta plan is supposed to be implemented by the local governments, which are expected to incorporate the provisions of the Delta plan into their general plans.

In 1992, the state created the Delta Protection Commission to devise a land use plan for the area. But, unlike earlier regional commissions, the Delta Protection Commission does not have regulatory power.

The Delta Protection Commission represents a different planning and regulatory approach that shows the difference between the 1970s and the 1990s. Although BCDC, the Coastal Commission, and TRPA all enjoy broad public support, the state has not created any regional land use regulation agencies since 1972. (In fact, such an agency for the Santa Monica Mountains was proposed in the late '70s and not approved.) The Delta Protection Commission—the only regional planning body created by the state since that time—is oriented toward planning rather than regulation, and its policy makers are mostly local officials, not state appointees. In recent years, state lawmakers proposed making the Delta Protection Commission more of a regulatory agency, with the intent of preventing development from further encroaching on the Delta. Counties, cities, and landowners, however, successfully fought the regulatory proposals.

The state and federal governments have also taken a big-picture approach to the Delta by creating Cal-Fed, the California Bay-Delta Authority. The idea behind Cal-Fed was to bring together all of the competing interests—farmers, urban water providers, environmentalists, various government agencies—to work on a mutually beneficial plan. Cal-Fed intended to restore rivers and riparian areas to aid fish and improve water quality. Cal-Fed also proposed altering how water is managed and adding water storage outside the Delta. All of these steps were intended to protect the fragile Delta ecosystem while also improving water quality and reliability for the state and federal water systems, both of which draw most of their water from the Delta. Full implementation of Cal-Fed, however, will take tens of billions of dollars, and the largest player in the game—the federal government—has been reluctant to put large sums into the effort.

Although it is far larger than the Delta Protection Commission, Cal-Fed is similar in that it also is not a regulatory entity. Instead, Cal-Fed's role is to plan and fund projects that other entities, such as water districts, implement.

The idea behind Cal-Fed was to bring together all of the competing interests—farmers, urban water providers, environmentalists, various government agencies—to work on a mutually beneficial plan.

Protection of Specific Resources

Instead of focusing on specific geographic areas, the protection of natural resources in California has increasingly focused on specific resources, such as wildlife habitat, wetlands, and air and water quality.

Instead of focusing on specific geographic areas, the protection of natural resources in California (and elsewhere) has increasingly focused on specific resources, such as wildlife habitat, wetlands, and air and water quality. In all of these resource areas, as in still others, state and federal agencies control the process because they have regulatory authority to protect that resource.

The laws protecting these specific resources will be discussed in more detail in the next two chapters, but briefly they include:

- **The state and federal Endangered Species Acts,** which have had the effect of protecting wildlife habitat in private and public land.
- **The state and federal Clean Air Acts,** which have directly affected the siting of industrial operations and indirectly influenced local land use patterns.

- **The federal Clean Water Act,** which has affected land use and growth patterns by requiring that private landowners obtain federal permits to dredge and fill wetlands, and more recently by imposing new standards on quality of stormwater and urban water runoff.

- **The state streambed alteration permit law,** which requires private and public landowners to obtain a permit from the California Department of Fish and Game before altering the natural flow or the natural contours of any river, stream, or lake.

- **The state Forest Practice Act,** which requires private property owners to prepare timber harvest plans approved by the California Department of Forestry and Fire Protection prior to cutting.

- **The state Surface Mining and Reclamation Act,** which requires mining activities generally to follow state policy as laid out by the California Mining and Geology Board, and requires mining companies to prepare surface mining and reclamation plans, which must be adopted by the relevant city or county in accordance with state policy.

Other Resource-Oriented Requirements and Programs

Natural resources are also protected by a series of state requirements and programs that are carried out by local governments in conjunction with state agencies. These requirements include:

- **Wildland fire protection policies,** which must be included in local general plans and generally conform to the wildland fire regulations issued by the California Department of Forestry and Fire Protection.

- **Special study areas** under the Alquist-Priolo Act, which requires local governments to identify and deal with high-risk seismic areas under guidelines prepared by the state Division of Mines and Geology.

- **Farmland preservation policies,** which may be prepared in conjunction with the state's Williamson Act program. The Williamson Act permits lower

The Concept of Mitigation

UNDER CEQA AND THE RESOURCE protection laws, it is almost always possible to obtain approval for urban development or some other activity that disrupts the natural resources in question. But usually, the permitting agency—whether it is local, regional, state, or federal—requires mitigation in return.

"Mitigation" is simply a way of requiring the developer or permit applicant to (1) minimize the resource damage the project will impose, and/or (2) compensate for harm done as a result of the project by enhancing or restoring a similar natural resource elsewhere.

Mitigation as "minimization" is easy to understand and implement. Often, a project is redesigned or resized to avoid (or only slightly intrude upon) the natural resource in question. A housing development, for example, may be redesigned so that no houses are built in a flood plain, wetland, stream corridor, or other sensitive riparian habitat.

In many cases, however, it is impossible to redesign the project to avoid damage to natural resources. In these situations, the permitting agency is likely to require mitigation as "avoidance" for the loss of natural resources. Mitigation as avoidance is a much less well-defined field and has been subject to considerable criticism.

The underlying assumption of mitigation as avoidance is simply that so many natural resources are either degraded or at risk that a developer who disrupts resources can either restore or preserve similar resources in a way that provides a net benefit to the environment and to society. For example, when a fiberglass insulation factory was proposed in the city of Shasta Lake, one mitigation for the factory's air pollution was a requirement that the fiberglass company pave several miles of dirt roads in the area. By paving the dusty roads, the company would avoid further degrading the air with soot emitted by the factory's smokestack.

It has been difficult, however, to apply consistent standards for resource-based mitigations. As resources have become more scarce, for example, many state and federal agencies have required multiple mitigation—for example, requiring three acres of wetlands to be restored for every acre lost. Equivalent resources are not always readily at hand. So few coastal wetlands exist in Southern California that the Port of Los Angeles has been allowed by the Coastal Commission to meet its mitigation requirement by enhancing a lagoon in San Diego County, 100 miles away.

Ad hoc mitigation has been troubling to both landowners and environmentalists. In Shasta Lake, for example, environmentalists and area residents questioned whether dust from rural dirt roads and soot from a heavy industry's 150-foot-tall smokestack were comparable. The controversy begs the question of what methods biologists and other experts should use to determine how much mitigation is enough. How great should the distance be between the resource being disrupted and the resource being restored? Who will do the monitoring to determine whether the efforts have failed? What if restoration or enhancement efforts fail? These questions are frequently asked in the mitigation world—and they represent one of the reasons why state and federal resource agencies have moved toward planning that provides an overall context and framework within which mitigation efforts can take place. ∎

tax assessments on property that may have speculative value but is used for agriculture, and provides a partial reimbursement from the state Department of Conservation to local governments to offset the lost tax revenue.

CEQA as a Gateway to Resource Protection

Ideally, the CEQA process is supposed to work in concert with these other laws to achieve effective conservation of natural resources. The idea is simple—CEQA is a procedural law that identifies potential environmental harm and informs decisionmakers and the public of these consequences. CEQA itself does not contain any standards for resource protection. By contrast, the other laws listed above all contain standards for resource protection—emissions limits for air and water pollution, for example, and standards for the loss of wetlands and wildlife habitat. Therefore, by using the standards contained in resource protection laws as the "significance thresholds" under CEQA, local planners and environmental analysts can use CEQA as a "gateway" to connect land use decisions to resource protection.

In many cases, the CEQA process actually does work this way—especially when the resource protection law contains a clear set of standards that a local government can easily adopt as the threshold. In many other cases, however, CEQA does not serve as an effective gateway—often because the resource protection laws do not or cannot provide sufficient guidance.

For example, the regulatory power of the endangered species acts is triggered only by the listing of a species as endangered or threatened, which occurs only when the species is almost extinct. But the useful time for CEQA-related action comes earlier—prior to listing, when mitigation measures might help maintain wildlife populations and eliminate the need for listing later. Yet the state and federal species laws provide few standards or guidelines that can be used as significance thresholds prior to listing, so local governments usually must rely on the judgment of their environmental consultants.

In some resource areas, protection may be a general goal but no standards exist. The state's broad policy framework calls for protection of agricultural land and provides incentives under the Williamson Act. However, the state has not provided any useful standard to flag the loss of agricultural land, and therefore CEQA has not served as a useful gateway in this arena.

Emerging Issues and Old Habits

As stated at the outset of this chapter, the relationship between local land use planning and state and federal resource protection efforts has not always been harmonious. Local governments are often driven by many considerations other than resource protection, including economic and fiscal needs, and concerns about providing urban services to human settlements. At the same time, state and federal resource agencies are often able to trump local land use planning with superior regulatory power, at least in certain resource areas.

Local governments are often driven by many considerations other than resource protection, including economic and fiscal needs, and concerns about providing urban services to human settlements.

Ironically, both sides see the other as too narrowly focused. Unable to appreciate local land use planning efforts, many state and federal agencies and are frustrated by cities' and counties' parochial views. Local planners and politicians, meanwhile, argue that federal agencies are intent on preservation of natural resources without considering a local community's needs. This wariness can complicate already difficult political and scientific issues, whose numbers continue to increase.

Perhaps foremost among new issues for planners and developers is urban runoff. No longer is it acceptable to assume that runoff from storms and sprinklers will "take care of itself" by flowing downhill and, eventually, into the ocean. Construction activity can clog streams with silt. Petroleum that washes off roads and parking lots can poison waterways and beaches. Pesticides from landscaped areas can do the same. The more impervious surfaces, such as pavement, that cover over dirt and vegetation, the faster that stormwater flows and the less ability the environment itself has to neutralize pollutants. None of these impacts are new, but as concern has grown, so has the pressure for development projects to mitigate the impact of runoff. (Chapter 24 contains a more complete discussion of urban runoff regulation.)

Perhaps foremost among new issues for planners and developers is urban runoff. No longer is it acceptable to assume that runoff from storms and sprinklers will "take care of itself" by flowing downhill and, eventually, into the ocean.

Related to urban runoff is the issue of TMDLs, or total maximum daily loads. The federal Clean Water Act required all states to identify "impaired" water bodies that do not meet water quality standards. The states are then supposed to identify how much of an

TMDL = Total maximum daily load

individual pollutant, such as sediment or a certain pesticide, a water body can handle and still meet standards—the TMDL. Congress passed the Clean Water Act in 1977, but for two decades, almost everyone ignored the TMDL requirement. During the late 1990s, though, TMDLs started to come to the forefront, partly because nearly every major lake and river in California qualifies as "impaired." Meeting a TMDL requirement can mean, once again, that development projects have to mitigate the impact of runoff.

Air pollution has been a problem in Southern California for more than half a century. Although pollution levels have decreased a bit in much of the Los Angeles basin during recent years, the smog in L.A. remains as bad as anywhere in the country. San Bernardino and Riverside frequently top the list of cities with the most polluted skies. Close behind on that list is the San Joaquin Valley, where air pollution has grown steadily worse for decades. For a long time, urban development was absent from the air pollution discussion, as regulators focused on automobiles and industrial operations. In recent years, though, regional air pollution control districts have begun eyeing the location and style of developments for their impact on air quality, as well as the proximity of new development to pollution hot spots. So far, land regulation based on air quality impacts has been minimal. But the approach could change, especially because air pollution continually ranks as the public's biggest environmental concern.

In recent years, regional air pollution control districts have begun eyeing the location and style of developments for their impact on air quality, as well as the proximity of new development to pollution hot spots.

Endangered species continue to be a huge consideration for planners, developers, and landowners in areas that contain habitat for rare plants and animals. It is in the area of endangered species that planning practices have evolved the most, even as attempts to re-write the Endangered Species Act have failed. In fact, the increasingly common approach of addressing endangered species through adoption of a large-scale habitat conservation plan demonstrates how planners help decisionmakers overcome the tension between social practicalities and the needs of the environment—a tension that frequently has surfaced in conflicts between local officials and resources specialists at state and federal agencies.

The increasingly common approach of addressing endangered species through adoption of a large-scale habitat conservation plan demonstrates how planners help decisionmakers overcome the tension between social practicalities and the needs of the environment.

Habitat conservation plans prepared with extensive input from all levels of government and private landowners are largely a political answer to this tension. The growing popularity of these plans could foreshadow greater cooperation among different levels of government, and the increasing use of political compromises as solutions to natural resource questions.

Chapter 23

Endangered Species:
Habitat Protection

Since the late 1980s, no area of natural resource conservation has played a more important—or higher profile—role in California land use planning than the protection of endangered species.

Most of the period has been marked by conflicts over local land use planning efforts and private real estate development projects in places with habitat for endangered species. More recently, though, cooperative efforts among federal, state, and local officials have resulted in long-range conservation plans designed to resolve those disputes and minimize future conflict.

The endangered species story illustrates virtually every important aspect of the relationship between natural resource protection and local land use planning in California today: conflict and cooperation among local, state, and federal officials; a shift from reactive regulation to active planning; an increasing awareness about the potential role of local governments in using their plans to implement natural resource protection efforts; and ongoing uncertainty about whether those efforts will ultimately succeed. Although many of these same issues emerge in wetlands protection and other areas, the species issue has been the crucible for most of them.

The tool that agencies have turned to is the habitat conservation plan (or, under state law, the natural communities conservation plan). These plans, known as HCPs and NCCPs, have become fundamental tools for regional land use planning. A plan covers a large area, often a large chunk of a county. The plan designates where development may occur, and which natural areas should remain undeveloped for the protection of rare species. Typically, the government agencies

The endangered species story illustrates virtually every important aspect of the relationship between natural resource protection and local land use planning in California today.

HCP = Habitat conservation plan
NCCP = Natural communities conservation plan

involved use the plans to guide the purchase of open space and conservation easements that will prevent future development. The plans may be written for only one species or for dozen of species. In some of California's fastest growing areas, such as Riverside and San Diego Counties, habitat plans are shaping regional development patterns. Although the Endangered Species Act has long permitted HCPs, this more comprehensive approach was rare until the mid 1990's, when the Clinton administration Interior Secretary Bruce Babbitt and Wilson administration Resources Secretary Douglas Wheeler encouraged the use of habitat plans. Now, California has more than 100 HCPs adopted or in the planning stages. Increasing skepticism among environmentalists, however, has slowed the adoption of some HCPs and tempered enthusiasm for this approach.

The Federal and State Endangered Species Acts

The Federal Endangered Species Act, and the companion California Endangered Species Act, were drafted to prevent plant and animal species from becoming extinct, not as land use planning laws.

Neither the Federal Endangered Species Act, passed in 1973 (16 U.S.C. §§ 1531), nor the companion California Endangered Species Act, adopted in 1984 (California Fish and Game Code § 2050 *et seq.*), were designed as land use planning laws. Rather, they were drafted to prevent plant and animal species from becoming extinct. They are probably the strongest environmental laws currently on the books, for the simple reason that they are meant to be the safety net of last resort for species that have become extremely rare. A species on the brink of extinction may be declared "endangered" or "threatened" under either law (or both).

Once a species is listed, the state and federal governments have vast regulatory power to protect those species, and few other considerations are allowed to come into play.[1] For example, the government agencies (the U.S. Fish and Wildlife Service and the California Department of Fish and Game) cannot take into account the economic hardship that protecting the species may bring to private individuals, institutions, or companies. The federal agencies, however, must consider the economic consequences of designating "critical habitat," which are areas where federal review of nearly any sort of development is required. The second Bush administration

---

1. The California law is probably stronger, for two reasons. The first is that protection for the species is granted when the species is first considered for listing as endangered or threatened, rather than at the time of the actual listing. The second is that a species may be listed as endangered or threatened even if it thrives in abundance elsewhere, so long as it is rare within the boundaries of the State of California.

has latched onto this economic study requirement as a way to ratchet back critical habitat designations that environmentalists fought for years to get.

Any person who "takes" a specimen that is endangered or threatened—killing or harming it, deliberately or accidentally—could be subject to criminal penalties. Actual prosecution of anyone in the development industry, however, is exceedingly rare.

The reason that the endangered species laws become enmeshed with land use planning is simple: endangered plants and animals live in specific ecological settings—habitats—that occur in specific geographic areas. (Under the federal laws, the Interior Department must identify the "critical habitat" of each endangered or threatened species.) Altering a habitat can harm or even extinguish the species; therefore, this activity is often interpreted as taking an endangered species in violation of the law.[2] Obviously, a wide range of land use activities can alter a habitat—removal of native vegetation, grading, construction, even changing the irrigation or cropping patterns of agricultural land.

A wide range of land use activities can alter a habitat—removal of native vegetation, grading, construction, even changing the irrigation or cropping patterns of agricultural land.

Until the late 1980s, the endangered species laws did not lead to much conflict with local land use planning or private real estate development activities. For the most part, the early disputes over endangered species involved federal activities. The famous snail darter case in the 1970s revolved around the question of whether the federal government should complete Tellico Dam in Tennessee, which would have altered the natural flows of the Little Tennessee River, thus harming the snail darter's chances for survival. Even the incendiary battle over the spotted owl in the Pacific Northwest and Northern California dealt almost exclusively with logging practices on federal land.

During the real estate boom of the 1980s, however, private landowners—and local governments that regulate land use—began to feel the impact of endangered species laws. Because California was a fast-growing state that still had a great deal of biological diversity, it has been the scene of almost all of the disputes over endangered species on private land. California has also been the locale for most innovations in endangered species protection, beginning more than 20 years ago with the habitat conservation plan.

2. The "taking" of an endangered species should not be confused with a "taking" of property under the Fifth Amendment of the U.S. Constitution. They are completely different terms.

Incidental Take Under State Law

WHILE THE FEDERAL ENDANGERED SPECIES ACT specifically permits the incidental take of endangered or threatened species as part of a habitat conservation plan, the state version of the law is not so clear. This has caused some difficulty in implementing species conservation plans under the state law.

Since the late 1980s, the California Department of Fish and Game has routinely pursued an HCP-style approach to endangered species problems on private land—often signing agreements with landowners allowing development to move forward in exchange for the donation of land or payment of fees as mitigation. In policy terms, these permits were important because of the fact that many species—Swainson's hawk, for example—are listed as threatened or endangered under the state law but not the federal law.

As its legal authority, the state used section 2081 of the Fish and Game Code, which authorized incidental take for scientific or management purposes. In 1996, however, environmentalists in the Inland Empire challenged this practice in connection with a section 2081 permit issued for the Moreno Highlands project, a 3,000-acre development in Moreno Valley. Eventually, this argument found its way into a different environmental lawsuit—the environmentalists' challenge to the Department of Fish and Game's decision to issue a section 2081 permit for all agricultural and emergency repair activities required by the Northern California flooding of 1995.

In 1997, the state court of appeal struck down the use of section 2081 in issuing the emergency management permit and raised questions about the use of section 2081 in other situations as well. Simply put, the court questioned whether the law's definition of management could be stretched to include HCP-style mitigation. The court ruling then led to a bruising battle in the legislature over whether to expand the definition. Environmentalists wanted to limit the definition—and therefore limit Fish and Game's ability to engage in such mitigation deals—while homebuilders and the agricultural lobby wanted to expand the definition. In the end, the homebuilders and farmers won. Under SB 879, passed in 1997, Fish and Game has the clear authority to issue incidental take permits. In addition, the mitigation imposed on property owners must be roughly proportional to the impact of those property owners' activities on the status of the species. ■

Habitat Conservation Planning, Multiple-Species Conservation, and NCCPs

Though the federal Endangered Species Act is a strong law, it is not quite air-tight. In principal, the law has always permitted taking of endangered or threatened species if the take is part of an overall effort to improve the condition of the species. In 1982, this concept was expanded in the federal law to permit "incidental take"—and alteration of habitat—on private land as part of a habitat conservation plan, or HCP.

The HCP concept emerged out of a dispute over proposed development on San Bruno Mountain, south of San Francisco. Home construction threatened the habitat of the Mission Blue butterfly, as did an invasion of gorse, a prickly shrub. Under the San Bruno agreement, some home construction on the mountain was permitted. But most of the mountain was preserved, and either sold or donated to the county and the state.

The result was that, in spite of the development, most of the butterfly habitat was preserved. Furthermore, as part of the deal, the developers agreed to fund a maintenance program for the habitat that would help protect it from the encroaching gorse—so that the development actually helped preserve the habitat rather than destroy it.

Once this habitat conservation plan was completed, local officials went to Congress and secured amendments to the Endangered Species

Act creating the HCP option. Since that time, dozens of HCPs have been approved by the U.S. Fish and Wildlife Service—most of them dealing with California situations.

A few years later, the state, which has its own endangered species laws, took the HCP concept one step further. It was real estate development in fast-growing Southern California that forced the state to take a new approach.

When the Fish and Wildlife Service listed the Stephens' kangaroo rat as an endangered species in 1988, Riverside County learned that recently approved development agreements for 100,000 new houses meant zilch. The houses were proposed for "K-rat" habitat, and developers could not alter that habitat without federal approval. The county and the federal government eventually settled on a mitigation plan in which landowners paid a fee that funded a kangaroo rat preserve. However, the mitigation plan was adopted only after a bruising political battle—and after the housing market had cooled dramatically.

This episode served as a wake-up call to local politicians and planners, especially in Southern California. The state and federal governments were preparing to list many more species, meaning the Riverside County scenario could be played out again every time a species was listed—dozens of times in some counties. In response, federal, state, and local officials began to examine ways to engage in long-term conservation planning that would permit urban development to proceed without being subject to delays and surprises under the endangered species laws.

Federal, state, and local officials began to examine ways to engage in long-term conservation planning that would permit urban development to proceed without being subject to delays and surprises under the endangered species laws.

The test case for conservation planning turned out to be the California gnatcatcher, a small songbird that roosts amid the low shrubs common in both the coastal and inland areas of Southern California. In 1991, both the state and federal governments were preparing to list the gnatcatcher as endangered—a move that, like the listing of the K-rat, would have widespread impact. Large areas of Orange, Riverside, and San Diego Counties were covered with the coastal sage scrub ecosystem that the rare insect-eating bird inhabited. It was also clear that, in the years ahead, dozens of other species that relied on the same ecosystem would also be listed as endangered if nothing was done to forestall the problem.

In response, the administration of newly elected Governor Pete Wilson devised an alternative called a natural communities conservation planning program. Instead of listing the gnatcatcher as endangered, the state enlisted the voluntary cooperation of most large landowners and local governments in the coastal sage scrub area and began a process of creating long-term wildlife preserves. The goal was to set aside enough coastal sage scrub land that neither the gnatcatcher nor the dozens of other species would ever have to be listed as endangered in the first place.

Under the NCCP program, the state imposed interim rules permitting development on no more than five percent of the coastal sage scrub land.

Under the NCCP program, the state imposed interim rules permitting development on no more than 5 percent of the coastal sage scrub land. Negotiating with landowners and local officials, the state then divided the coastal sage scrub area into 11 subregions, each of which was charged with devising its own long-term conservation plan that would ensure the preservation of all the species involved.

NCCP = Natural communities conservation planning

The NCCP process has not been easy. Many local governments and small landowners have resisted participation, believing that they would have to pay the cost of setting aside the land. At the same time, some environmental groups have criticized the process, saying the state is permitting too much development to proceed.

The NCCP process has moved forward—aided, among other things, by the real estate bust of the early 1990s and President Clinton's election in 1992.

In general, however, the process has moved forward—aided, among other things, by the real estate bust of the early 1990s, which slowed the short-term demand for development. The NCCP also got a boost when President Clinton took office in 1993. At the time, the federal Endangered Species Act was under considerable pressure from business interests who wanted it rewritten. From his confirmation hearings onward, Interior Secretary Bruce Babbitt pointed to the NCCP as a national model that would prove that endangered species laws could accommodate economic activity without being rewritten. Later in 1993, Babbitt listed the gnatcatcher as threatened under the federal law—but invoked a little-used section of the law permitting landowners to move forward with development so long as they participated in the California NCCP program.

In the years since, more than 100 habitat plans have been proposed and adopted. Many of them serve as both HCPs and NCCPs. The plans can cover huge areas, or relatively small spots. For instance, the Coachella Valley Multiple Species Habitat Conservation Plan, under development since 2000, covers 1.2 million acres and 27 "natural communities" in the desert and mountains. Meanwhile, the Palos Verdes Peninsula Subregional Plan addresses only the incorporated city of Rancho Palos Verdes, about one-quarter of which remains undeveloped. The Natomas Basin Habitat Conservation Plan, which has been the subject of extensive litigation and revision, covers portions of two counties near

Sacramento International Airport, but focuses primarily on two species, the giant garter snake and the Swainson's hawk. An HCP written specifically for the development of a Hyundai test track in California City designates 4,500 acres for development, and 3,400 acres for preservation of the threatened desert tortoise.

The California City HCP, although it covers a small area, is a good example of how these plans permit some amount of private development or resource extraction. In exchange for development approvals, landowners usually agree to preserve, donate, or sell critical pieces of land for wildlife conservation purposes. In a growing number of instances, the landowners also agree to fund land restoration and management activities as well.

Many habitat plans cover areas with multiple landowners, sometimes thousands of them. In those cases, the U.S. Fish and Wildlife Service has permitted a trading or mitigation program. For example, the San Diego Multiple Species Conservation Program, which is considered something of a model habitat plan, permits development on sensitive habitat in the city of La Mesa to be mitigated with the preservation of similar habitat elsewhere in the southwestern part of the county.

Many habitat plans cover areas with multiple landowners, sometimes thousands of them.

Like most things having to do with land use in California, habitat planning is complex. Large regional plans such as San Diego's rely heavily on subregional NCCPs, which require additional approval by federal, state, and local officials. Years after adoption of the San Diego plan, some subregional plans remained only proposals. These sorts of delays can happen because neither local planners nor landowners have much interest in habitat planning. Plus, larger questions remain. Who will bear the actual cost of acquiring and maintaining the preserved land? Who will determine if the amount and location of preserved land is adequate for species survival? If a species continues to decline, what then?

One of the major enticements for landowners to participate in habitat planning under the federal Endangered Species Act is the "no surprises" concept. The idea is that landowners and developers who abide by a habitat plan cannot be surprised in the future by additional endangered species regulations. The rules of the game are decided up front and cannot be changed. Environmentalists and a number of biologists, however, argue that the plans are one-sided, locking into place a system that provides guarantees for the landowner, but not for a species. If, a decade or two down the road, a habitat plan proves to be inadequate for a species' survival, under

The no surprises concept is the idea that that landowners and developers who abide by a habitat plan cannot be surprised in the future by additional endangered species regulations.

the no surprises doctrine, regulators could not demand greater concessions from landowners. Habitat plan detractors insist that this one-sided arrangement is counter to the Endangered Species Act, and they have begun making inroads in court against the no surprises approach.

The other major complaint of environmentalists and biologists is that habitat plans are, at their core, political answers to scientific questions. The plans, detractors say, simply designate some land—much of which is often already protected as parkland or national forest—and say that will be enough for species' survival, without adequate scientific support.

Pragmatists within the environmental movement have been willing to work on and accept habitat plans. But others, notably the Center for Biological Diversity (CBD), have been hesitant to embrace the idea and have fought it in court with moderate success. The CBD is one of the most important players in the endangered species arena. The Tucson-based group has filed dozens of lawsuits against the Fish and Wildlife Service, demanding that the federal government place certain species on the endangered or threatened list, and designate "critical habitat" for species. The CBD's track record in court is impressive. However federal officials counter that the litigation has forced them to spend their resources on courtroom battles, rather than on protecting species.

The habitat plan approach reached its stride during the Clinton administration and has continued during the second Bush administration. The Bush administration also continued to provide funding to acquire lands designated as habitat. What has not continued is the additional listing of species to the endangered and threatened lists. The Bush administration has added species at a slower rate than any previous administration. The hesitancy provides a good example of how Bush has used quiet administrative processes—rather than more public legislative approaches—to alter environmental regulations.

From a land use planning point of view, however, the most important aspect of the HCP and NCCP approach is the mere fact that local governments have worked together with state and federal officials on what amounts to regional land use plans. All habitat plans designate areas where development can occur and areas that should be set aside permanently as wildlife preserves. These conservation plans have, in turn, been incorporated into the general plans of cities and counties—which are required to implement them

CBD = Center for Biological Diversity

The CBD has filed dozens of lawsuits against the Fish & Wildlife Service, demanding that the federal government place certain species on the endangered or threatened list, and designate "critical habitat" for species.

The most important aspect of the HCP and NCCP approach is the mere fact that local governments have worked together with state and federal officials on what amounts to regional land use plans.

in order to satisfy the state and federal officials that have the power to stop development otherwise.

What started as an uneasy truce has, over the course of about 15 years, evolved into common regional and subregional cooperative planning efforts. Planners in nearly every part of the state, including some of the fastest growing regions, are now familiar with the habitat planning process.

Endangered Species and the Future of California Land Use Planning

The endangered species story is a good illustration of how positive results can sometimes come from seemingly arduous circumstances. Local governments do not want higher levels of government interfering with their land use planning prerogatives. This is part of the reason that the state (and, for that matter, the federal government) has never had the political will to adopt any strong regional planning legislation.

Local governments do not want higher levels of government interfering with their land use planning prerogatives. This is part of the reason that the state (and, for that matter, the federal government) has never had the political will to adopt any strong regional planning legislation.

Yet it is clear that most land use planning decisions have an impact on the entire region, not just on the local community. Plants and animals, like so many other issues associated with natural resources, understand neither property lines nor political boundaries. The endangered species issues has provided a vehicle—albeit cumbersome and imperfect—to begin addressing regional issues in land use planning.

From a comprehensive planning viewpoint, it is probably not a good idea to permit one issue, such as endangered species, to take precedence over all others. The state and federal endangered species acts were not designed as tools for regional planning in fast-growing suburban areas. Yet the endangered species question has forced the creation of innovative structures and new partnerships that are required for land use planning to address regional issues. The results may not be perfect—they may not even protect the species whose survival they are trying to ensure—but they have given regional shape and form to land use planning patterns and processes all across the state. Moreover, the habitat plan approach may provide a model for regulators for addressing other sticky resource issues.

The endangered species question has forced the creation of innovative structures and new partnerships that are required for land use planning to address regional issues.

Chapter 24

Other Natural Resources Issues

Although the endangered species issue has dominated land use planning in some parts of the state, it is far from the only natural resource issue that plays an important role in local planning. Many other resource issues also affect local planning—sometimes as a result of direct state or federal intervention and sometimes because state or federal laws require local governments to take these issues seriously. Local political pressures can also be a factor.

Most of these issues do find a home in the typical city or county general plan. Three of the seven required elements of a California general plan deal with resource-oriented issues: the conservation element, the open space element, and the safety element. In addition, many communities also include optional elements dealing with resource protection. Counties in the Central Valley, for example, may include an agriculture element, while cities in Southern California often produce an air quality element.

In general, the other resource issues can be broken down into five categories: water, farmland, air, hazards and resource extraction. This chapter will attempt to deal with each of the five categories, describing how local planning efforts intersect with state and federal law and policy.

Three of the seven required elements of a California general plan deal with resource-oriented issues: the conservation element, the open space element, and the safety element.

Water

Water availability and water quality—separate but related matters—have more of an impact on planning and development in California than any other natural resource issue.

NPDES = National Pollutant Discharge Elimination System

Runoff Makes for an Endless Bummer

A NEW STATE LAW TOOK effect in 1999 requiring public health officials to test the water weekly from April through October at the state's most heavily used beaches. Although public health officials for several years had warned swimmers and surfers to avoid certain coastal waters after storms because of pollution from urban stormwater runoff, most people assumed the same waters were safe during the dry season. The results of the newly mandated tests were stunning—within two months, health officials from Santa Barbara to San Diego had posted warning signs at beaches more than 600 times.

Then, in July of 1999, health officials closed a stretch of Huntington State Beach, one of the most heavily used in California. Huntington Beach is known as "Surf City," and a large chunk of the city's merchants rely on the spending of beachgoers. City officials estimated the beach closure—which was not fully lifted for three months—cost the city more than $100,000 in sales tax, which equates to lost retail sales of more than $10 million. Pollution was no longer something that only environmentalists and beach bums cared about.

Tests identified the most likely source of the pollution as urban runoff, or what some people in the water industry call "urban slobber." Much of the runoff comes from landscape irrigation and from people washing their cars or hosing off sidewalks. It is not uncommon for the runoff to contain animal waste, pesticides, fertilizers, motor oil, and fine metal particles. The solution to the

⇒

Water quality is governed principally by the federal Clean Water Act, although the state also has its own water quality laws. The Clean Water Act, unlike the Endangered Species Act, is aimed at protecting human health. Two aspects of the Clean Water Act's policies affect land use planning. The first is the movement to clean up urban stormwater runoff and nonpoint source pollution, while the second is wetlands regulation.

Urban Stormwater Runoff and Nonpoint Source Pollution

During the 1990s, public health officials began posting warning signs at beaches and lakes. The brightly colored placards said that the water in which children were splashing and surfers were riding waves posed a potential health hazard. Typically, the warning signs started appearing right after a storm, and at some of the state's most popular recreation areas. The postings raised the public's awareness of contaminated runoff from subdivisions, streets, and other developed areas. This water is called "urban stormwater runoff" and "nonpoint source pollution," terms that primarily refer to the water that flows into any general drainage system, rather than water that flows out of a pipe from a sewage treatment plant or industrial facility.

Traditionally, water quality regulation focused on "point sources"—the specific sources that emitted water (and pollutants) from a particular pipe. In recent years, however, the state Water Resources Control Board and its nine Regional Water Quality Control Boards have increased regulation of stormwater runoff and nonpoint source pollution. This trend is partly because the state has made big strides in improving sewer plant and industrial discharges during the last 30 years, and partly because recent studies have concluded that urban runoff is a larger source of water pollution than wastewater treatment plants and industrial outlets.

Increased concern about water quality, as seen in the public health warnings, and stepped-up regulatory efforts have made water quality a regional issue. The regional nature of the matter has spurred the creation of many watershed planning efforts that operate on a regional or subregional level.

The federal Clean Water Act requires cities and counties to obtain permits that set general standards for the water quality of stormwater runoff under the National Pollution Discharge Elimination System. The cities and counties then must issue permits to developers for most construction projects. This regulatory system is overseen by the Regional Water Quality Control Boards, which are arms of the state government.

The NPDES permit program regarding urban stormwater runoff has been met with considerable resistance by local governments, which have viewed it as another unfunded mandate. Additionally, developers argue that the regulations increase construction expenses without having a major impact on water quality, in part because the rules do not affect existing development.

In general, the NPDES permit programs approved by the regional water boards require all but the smallest developments to slow down and filter their runoff. This is most often accomplished with the construction of grassy swales, detention ponds (that can double as parks and ballfields), and infiltration basins. Slowing down runoff reduces flooding, lessens creek, river, and beach erosion, and gives nature an opportunity to break down pollutants. Filtering urban stormwater runoff through grassy areas or wetlands also takes advantages of natural processes that reduce pollution.

The regulations have touched off battles between inland cities that oppose the rules and cities on the coast that experience most of the pollution and flooding because of upstream development. Opponents have argued in court that the regulations exceed what the federal Clean Water Act allows. In an important 2004 decision, however, a state appellate court ruled that the urban runoff regulations adopted by the San Diego Regional Water Quality Control Board—which are similar to rules adopted by other regional boards—were permissible. *Building Industry Association of San Diego County v. State Water Resources Control Board*, 124 Cal. App. 4th. 866 (2004).

Huntington Beach contamination was to divert the contents of several suspect storm drains, which dripped with runoff year-round, to a wastewater treatment plant.

The closure of Huntington State Beach and others, as well as the hundreds of warnings, raised the ire of some people about upstream development. At one point, residents of Laguna Beach demanded that their city council sue inland cities to force a clean up of runoff. The city council declined, but the spotlight had been flicked on. In Orange County, what to do about contamination from urban runoff had become a major issue.

Although Huntington Beach did not repeat the bummer summer of 1999, beach closures have remained common in Orange County. In response, the county has become something of a laboratory for handling urban runoff. Public outreach programs have urged residents not to over-water lawns or wash cars in the driveway. Cities and special districts have diverted more and more dry season runoff to treatment plants. The upscale city of San Clemente started charging homeowners $5 a month to pay for runoff treatment, and agencies elsewhere began considering similar charges to expand runoff treatment. Meanwhile the Irvine Ranch Water District began building a series of wetlands and "natural treatment ponds" to improve the quality of water flowing into Newport Bay. Various other filtration systems and practices that expose the water to sunlight—sunlight breaks down bacteria—were also being tried. ■

The trend of urban stormwater runoff regulation has not necessarily affected growth patterns, unlike the Endangered Species Act, which has in some cases. Rather, the move to clean up runoff has forced changes in how projects are planned and constructed.

The new regulations also reflect a recognition that more than a century of "hardening" canals and rivers so that urban stormwater runoff reaches rivers and the ocean quickly may in fact cause problems. Beginning in the 1990s, the U.S. Army Corps of Engineers began changing its design approach, often under pressure from local environmentalists. Rather than "channelizing" streams and rivers, the Corps has moved toward greener solutions that give rivers wider, more natural berths.

The stormwater and nonpoint source regulations have also led to a rapid increase in watershed-level planning throughout California.

The stormwater and nonpoint source regulations have also led to a rapid increase in watershed-level planning throughout California. Most of these efforts have been led not by cities and counties but by nonprofit organizations and private-sector groups who are stakeholders in the watersheds. These watershed planning efforts represent a de facto, ad hoc form of regional planning because individuals and organizations with financial and environmental interests in a watershed know that they cannot solve their own problem (for example, flooding, erosion, wetland siltation, or contaminated sediments blocking port and marina entrances) without addressing problems caused further up the watershed, usually in different political jurisdictions.

Political support is also growing. In the last several years, Napa County voters have approved a sales tax increase to fund a "green" flood control project, and Los Angeles voters approved a $500 million bond to fund the clean up of urban runoff and rivers.

Wetlands

AQMD = Air Quality Management District
CDF = California Department of Forestry and Fire Protection
CEQA = California Environmental Quality Act
EPA = Environmental Protection Agency

Though the definition varies, the term "wetlands" generally refers to swamps and other lands where water is often present. Once considered unhealthy, wetlands are now regarded as essential components of a viable ecosystem because they provide habitat for wildlife, prevent floods, and help flush pollution out of water supplies.

Section 404 of the federal Clean Water Act prohibits anyone from draining or filling a wetland without a permit from the Army Corps of Engineers. Historically, this process was not a concern for developers, because the Corps was a development-oriented agency. Sometimes the Corps issued the permit without much fuss; on other occasions, the agency chose not to intervene because the staff did not have time to deal with every wetlands matter. As the environment emerged as a front-page issue, however, the Corps of Engineers began to evolve into something of an environmental watchdog. By the 1980s, the Corps had adopted what is known as the "duck's butt" rule, in which the agency exerted its jurisdiction over any springtime puddle large enough for a duck to park its butt in. By the 1990s, getting a Section 404 permit from the Corps had became one the most difficult parts of the land development process.

Wetlands have received extra attention along the Southern California coast and in the Central Valley because the once-plentiful supply of wetlands has dwindled dramatically. The wetlands issue has held up some of the largest development projects in California, such as the huge Playa Vista development near Los Angeles International Airport and the Bolsa Chica project along the coastline in Huntington Beach. In both of those instances, the state ended up buying most of the wetlands to prevent development of sensitive areas.

Generally speaking, however, environmental groups and state agencies such as the Coastal Commission have played a much greater role in pressuring developers to deal with wetlands issues. The Coastal Commission has pursued a "no net loss" policy along the coast. In some cases, the commission has permitted long-distance mitigation of wetlands, as when the Port of Los Angeles was permitted to restore a lagoon in San Diego County. (Some developers have created new wetlands artificially, but there is controversy among environmentalists as to whether artificial wetlands can operate as successfully as restored natural wetlands.) Under the Clean Water Act, the Army Corps does not have exclusive jurisdiction over wetlands issues. The federal Environmental Protection Agency has veto power over Corps decisions. Even during the Reagan and Bush years, the EPA began to use that power more aggressively, and during the Clinton years this trend accelerated.

Water Supply and Land Use Planning

FOR MOST OF CALIFORNIA'S history, the state has been obsessed not with water quality but with water supply. California usually has abundant water sources in Northern California's seasonal rainfall and the snowmelt from the Sierra Nevada Mountains. The great reservoir and canal projects of the 20th century—the Owens Valley Aqueduct, the Central Valley Project, the Colorado River Aqueduct, the Hetch Hetchy Reservoir, the State Water Project—have sought to move the water from where it exists naturally to where people, agriculture, and industry require it in California.

The net effect of all these water projects is that the question of water supply has not been much of an issue in land use planning in California. Local governments approving development projects simply assumed that water departments and water districts would have the necessary water. Recently, these assumptions have faded. Now, the law requires a link between water supplies and land use planning.

The water supply/land use planning link emerged from two situations in the early 1990s. The first was Contra Costa County's approval of the Dougherty Valley project, an 11,000-home development in the fast-growing eastern part of the county. The second was Stanislaus County's approval of the Diablo Grande resort project, located in the dry hills on the eastern slope of the coast range near Interstate 5.

The Dougherty Valley project is located inside the jurisdictional boundaries of the East Bay Municipal Utility District. But at the time the project was approved by Contra Costa County, East Bay MUD had an environmentalist majority on its board. The board refused to commit the agency to providing water for the project. The result was a huge battle on three fronts—in court, in the legislature, and in the next East Bay MUD board election, where the Home Builders Association sought to wrest control of the board from the environmentalists.

The Diablo Grande controversy occurred at about the same time. The proposed project included a high-end resort and 5,000 housing units on a 30,000-acre site. In approving the project, Stanislaus County permitted the developers to move forward with the first phase of the project (including a resort but no homes) with a temporary supply of groundwater obtained from farmland elsewhere in the county that the developer owned. Environmentalists sued and won based on the argument that a long-term development project cannot be approved with only a temporary water supply. *Stanislaus Natural Heritage Project v. County of Stanislaus*, 48 Cal. App. 4th 182 (1996).

The end result of both projects was the passage of SB 901 in 1995, a bill requiring local governments to consult with water agencies when considering approval of residential projects of more than 500 units—thus bringing water agencies into the land use planning arena for the first time. However, cities and counties widely ignored SB 901. So the legislature in 2001 approved two additional laws. One measure, SB 610, addressed the early part of the planning processing by emphasizing the necessity that all water providers have a valid Urban Water Management Plan—an attempt to close loopholes in the 1995 legislation. The second measure,

More recent political and legal developments would appear to have reversed the trend. The second Bush administration directed regulatory agencies to back off, and the U.S. Supreme Court ruled in 2001 that the Corps of Engineers did not have jurisdiction over isolated ponds and wetlands not attached to "navigable waters of the United States," an apparent rejection of the duck's butt rule. *Solid Waste Agency of N. Cook County v. U.S. Army Corps of Eng'rs*, 531 U.S. 159. In response, the Army Corps has eliminated a requirement that individual development projects replace wetlands on a one-for-one basis. But the Army Corps has maintained an overall no-net-loss policy and in general has been slow to reduce its regulatory role. In California, wetlands are further protected by portions of the Coastal Act and the Fish and Game Code.

In practice, the requirement to obtain federal permits to dredge and fill wetlands has led developers and their site-planning consultants to reshape their projects to minimize the impact. Nowadays, a development project is as likely to include the restoration of a creek's natural streambed as it is to include placement of the creek into concrete culverts.

For many years, wetlands regulations had a minimal impact on projects if they disrupted less than 10 acres of wetlands, streams, or water bodies. Landowners who planned to disrupt between one and 10 acres of wetlands merely needed to inform the Corps; landowners planning to disrupt less than one acre did not even need to do that. However, federal officials and environmentalists were concerned that this permitted too much degradation of wetlands, especially in a place like California, where many wetlands are small, seasonal vernal pools and ephemeral streams that escape regulation. So in 1997, the Corps changed its policy to require that any project of more than three acres get an individual federal permit. Any project of more than one-third of an acre must be reported. Three years later, the Corps further tightened the rules to require permits for any project involving one-half an acre of wetlands, and notification for any activity impacting one-tenth of an acre. These changes have substantially increased the federal oversight of development projects.

Air

California has the most polluted air in the nation. And in contrast to other parts of the country, its air pollution is derived mostly from photochemical smog created from vehicle emissions. The state's unusual topography lends itself to this smog problem. California is really a series of large valleys surrounded by mountains—a situation that creates perfect baking conditions for smog during the summer months.

Obviously, California's dependence on cars and trucks for personal transportation and for the movement of goods—a problem created in part by suburban-style land use patterns—increases the smog problem. But only during the last few years have regulators even broached the subject of regulating the use of land as a way of reducing smog. Thus far, regulation has been cursory at most, although this could change in the future.

Air quality is governed by the federal and state Clean Air Acts. Under both laws, principal responsibility for vehicle emissions rests with the California Air Resources Board, which has historically focused on technological solutions such as better catalytic converters on cars and alternative fuels.

California also has a group of regional air pollution regulators, such as the Bay Area and South Coast Air Quality Management Districts and the eight-county San Joaquin Valley Air Pollution Control District. Historically, these agencies, which were created by the state, have focused on "stationary" sources of air pollution, such as factories and other businesses that emit large amounts of pollution into the atmosphere from one source.

Some of these agencies have sought to deal with land use planning issues by establishing a relationship with local governments, but with mixed results. For example, the South Coast AQMD, which covers metropolitan Los Angeles, has never been able to

SB 221, addressed the later part of the planning process by requiring a water agency, city or county to make a specific finding that adequate water is available to serve projects of at least 500 housing units.

Courts have begun to lose patience with local governments that approve development without ensuring the provision of water. Courts, for example, have become disinclined to let slide projects that propose heavy reliance on the State Water Project. This is because the state has signed contracts to deliver far more water than the State Water Project can provide. The Santa Clarita Valley, just north of Los Angeles, has emerged as a battleground for this fight, as slow-growth forces have attempted to fend off huge new subdivisions.

Many water agencies don't want to be in the middle of the land use planning process because they understand that this places them in the middle of divisive political battles over growth. Nevertheless, water supply seems likely to be a more important issue in land use planning in the future. The days of large-scale dam building appear to be over. And officials in the Bush administration have insisted that California not pump more than its legal allocation out of the Colorado River because of growing needs upstream. Thus, new urban growth will have to be served by water that is taken from existing users, such as farmers. In fact, some farmers have found that they can make more money by selling their water to cities than they can by growing crops. Desalination of seawater and brackish groundwater is another option for increasing supplies, but desalination is expensive and large-scale desal projects are many years away. ▪

Farmland

FARMLAND IS NOT STRICTLY SPEAKING a natural resource, but it is often treated as such. Like urban development, farming requires heavy manipulation of the natural environment with the twin goals of benefiting people and reaping economic gain. Nevertheless, both California custom and California law place farmland in a special category—it is a special land resource worthy of protection.

There is no question that California agriculture is big business. Even today, almost 30 million acres of land—almost a third of the entire state—is cultivated. Large landholding patterns and an orientation toward export crops have always given agriculture in California an industrial bent, and the results have been remarkable. With gross receipts of approximately $30 billion a year, agriculture is still one of California's largest industries. California's farming is concentrated in the Central Valley, where agriculture remains by far the most important economic engine.

However, over the past several decades, California's rapid urbanization has meant that agriculture has been forced to compete for land with urban developers, who can typically afford to pay a far higher price for land. For this reason, large-scale agriculture has vanished from Orange County, and from all but small pockets of the Santa Clara Valley and Los Angeles County. Farming, in fact, is receding in most of Southern California and the Bay Area.

Since the 1960s, the state has made several attempts to encourage farmland preservation, but they have met with middling success. The most important such effort is the Williamson Act, which was established in 1965. Govt. Code

impose land use standards on local governments. The best it has been able to do is fund programs highlighting the relationship between land use planning and air quality, and provide money for air quality elements in local general plans.

But this has not fundamentally altered land use practices in Southern California. On most large development projects, degraded air quality is simply identified as a "significant unmitigable impact" under CEQA, triggering the requirement to adopt a statement of overriding considerations.

In the early 1990s, air pollution became a major consideration in both land use and transportation planning when South Coast AQMD and other agencies promoted carpooling and other ridesharing methods as a tool for reducing vehicle emissions. These programs generally imposed carpooling requirements on large employers—including local governments—and these carpooling requirements were often included as conditions of approval for large development projects. Although they did have some impact on traffic and emissions, carpooling requirements were never popular and most were reduced or eliminated within a few years.

While air pollution has been an obvious problem in Southern California since World War II, dirty air has emerged as a major issue in the San Joaquin Valley more recently. Since the 1990s, the valley cities of Bakersfield, Visalia, and Fresno have routinely ranked behind only the Riverside/San Bernardino metro area and Houston, Texas, on most lists of air pollution. To start addressing the situation, the legislature in 2003 passed a bill that requires all cities and counties within the eight-county San Joaquin Valley Air Pollution Control District to place goals, policies, objectives, and implementation measures for improving air quality in their general plans. Additionally, the air district itself has been working on an "indirect source program" that intends to discourage auto-oriented, suburban style development. The idea has been extremely controversial in the valley, a region where large-lot subdivisions remain the rule and where conservative elected officials are reluctant to impose additional development restrictions.

Resource Extraction

Especially in rural parts of California, local governments and local economies were dependent on resource extraction for jobs and tax revenue for many years. Because of economic changes and environmental regulation, these resource-based industries have dwindled. Still, surface mining and timber harvesting remain important activities in pockets of California.

The state has passed laws to regulate surface minerals (including sand and gravel) and timber. These regulations are intended to protect the resource, in part so that the resource may be economically exploited. Indeed, the Surface Mining and Reclamation Act and the Forest Practices Act protect the industries involved from excessive local zoning practices. In both cases, the state's regulatory framework helps guide local planning.

Surface Mining

California has a very active surface mining industry focused on mining aggregate from streambeds and riverbeds. To protect this resource, the state has passed the Surface Mining and Reclamation Act, known as SMARA.

SMARA permits local governments to regulate surface mining but subjects that regulation to state standards and state oversight. But it is important to note that mines of long standing often have property rights that cannot be easily extinguished by local land use regulations. For example, in the landmark case of *Hanson Brothers Enterprises v. Board of Supervisors*, 12 Cal. 4th 533 (1996), the California Supreme Court ruled that a Nevada County mining operation may have the legal ability to expand its operations even though it was a nonconforming use under current zoning. The reason is that gravel is a diminishing asset, and it is impossible to mine all of it at once.

§ 51200. Designed to preserve farmland as well as promote orderly urban growth patterns, the Williamson Act allows counties to assess farmland according to agricultural use rather than the speculative value for urban development. The state reimburses counties for some of the lost property tax revenue. In exchange for lower taxes, agricultural landowners commit their land to farming for 10 years. (Landowners can pay to remove their property from the Williamson Act in less than 10 years under unusual circumstances, but this is rare.) In 1998, the legislature went a step further in approving the Farmland Security Zone, also known as the Super Williamson Act (Revenue and Taxation Code § 423.4). It provides a further 35 percent reduction in assessed value in exchange for a 20-year commitment to farming.

About 15 million acres—half of the state's farmland—is enrolled in Williamson Act contracts. Still, the Williamson Act is probably not as effective as it could be. The state reimbursement does not make up for all of the lost property tax revenue to local governments, and the state has threatened to end the reimbursements entirely. Moreover, the tax break is not nearly enough to offset the temptation for agricultural landowners to sell out to urban developers, who are often willing to pay 5 to 10 times the agricultural value of the land. The history of the Williamson Act has been that farmers use its benefits until they decide it's time to sell to developers—and then they withdraw from the program. Additionally, a 2003 study prepared for the legislature found widespread abuse of the Williamson Act. Many property owners had continued to receive Williamson Act property tax breaks, even though they had developed houses and shopping centers. Lawmakers responded by doubling the penalties for Williamson Act contract breaches.

Local governments have become more aggressive in seeking to protect farmland, a trend that the Davis administration encouraged. In some areas, especially the Bay Area and the Central Coast, local land trusts work with land-owning families to have the land donated or have conservation easements placed on it so that it will not be developed. In the Central Valley and other locations where a development project would convert farmland to urban uses, local governments sometimes require the placement of conservation easements on farmland elsewhere as a project mitigation. These easements not only protect the underlying farmland, but they can be strategically placed to prevent cities from swallowing up surrounding fields and orchards. In other areas, additional requirements have been placed on the conversion of farmland to urban use. In Napa and Ventura Counties, for example, rezoning farmland requires a vote. Other counties may follow suit.

Though California remains a vibrant agricultural state, farmland preservation is growing as an issue of concern. Rapid urban development in the Central Valley has led some forecasters to predict that this breadbasket of the world will actually become a net importer of food by the year 2050. If the current disparity in land values continues, California will probably need stronger planning tools to retain its base of valuable farmland. ■

Timber Harvest

Even more than surface mining, timber harvest has been pre-empted by the state government. Cities and counties can regulate timber harvest on private land, but only under specified conditions.

In general, the arena of timber harvest is controlled by the Z'Berg-Nejedly Forest Practice Act of 1973. Public Resources Code §§ 4511–4684.5. This law requires private owners of timber land to prepare a timber harvest plan for approval by the California Department of Forestry and Fire Protection (CDF) before cutting trees for commercial use. A timber harvest plan is the functional equivalent of an environmental impact report under CEQA, and the two areas of law have many common threads.

The Forest Practice Act permits local governments to enact timber harvest regulations that are stricter than the state law so long as they are reasonable. Exactly how far local governments may extend this authority has been the subject of litigation since the early 1990s, and the answers provided by the courts have not always been clear.

In 2003, the legislature passed a law giving Regional Water Quality Control Boards clear authority over water quality on timber harvest sites. The primary issue is erosion from logging operations clogging streams. The industry fought the change because the water boards are more likely to impose stricter mitigations and monitoring requirements than CDF would.

Natural Hazards

Over the past decade, natural disasters have become a matter of major concern throughout California. Fire, floods, and earthquakes have raised new questions about the role of land use planning in dealing with natural disasters.

In general, two competing philosophies are at work in discussing the role of local planning in dealing with natural disasters. The first is the avoidance theory—the notion that land use regulation should be used to keep human development out of areas where the risk of natural disaster is great. The second is the mitigation theory—the idea that human development can be tolerated in high-risk areas so long as mitigation measures (such as

Planning for Natural Disasters

brush clearance and use of fire-resistant materials in high fire-risk areas) are used.

In the wave of natural disasters that hit California in the 1990s—ranging from the Oakland fire of 1991 to the Northridge earthquake of 1994 to the Central Valley floods of 1995, 1997, and 1998—a distinct pattern of public opinion emerged. At first, people appeared to believe that future problems should be avoided. However, as time went on and news stories about individual tragedies emerged, public opinion shifted toward permitting people to rebuild their homes as they were before.

This shift was clearly at work in the flooding issue. In 1997, when much of the Central Valley flooded for the second time in three years, the state legislature held many hearings geared toward determining the role of land use practices in creating flood hazard situations. The following year, when the flooding patterns repeated themselves, no such public discussion took place.

While the state does not play a major role in dealing with land use issues associated with flooding, state laws and practices do affect the way local governments are supposed to deal with fire and earthquakes in their local planning. Moreover, the obscure state Board of Reclamation, which has flood control responsibility, has become more circumspect about development in flood prone areas. This board's reticence is attributable partly to a 2003 appellate court decision that found the state liable for damage to more than 3,000 properties when the

The Big Buyouts

IN RECENT YEARS, THE STATE has begun spending hundreds of millions of dollars for land, development rights and conservation easements to block high-profile development proposals. Some of the purchases protected important natural resources, namely wetlands and rare species habitat. Other purchases, however, were driven as much by politics as by concern for the flora and fauna.

The four biggest purchases, all consummated since 1998, were at the Headwaters Forest in Humboldt County, the Ballona wetlands on Los Angeles's Westside, Ahmanson Ranch in eastern Ventura County, and the gigantic Hearst Ranch on the central coast. The 1998 Headwaters deal set the precedent.

The state and federal governments paid $480 million for 9,400 acres of the Headwaters Forest. The natural resource was unquestioned: pristine stands of old-growth redwood trees that provide habitat for rare species. But the price of more than $50,000 per acre—for property that had sold for $3,000 an acre during the mid-'80s—was stunning. The landowner, Pacific Lumber, knew that the political momentum was enormous for anything that would prevent logging. U.S. Sen. Dianne Feinstein had already pried loose $250 million of federal money for the acquisition, and even President Clinton had shown personal interest in the forest. So state officials had little choice and even less leverage.

The next two major purchases were consummated at the tail end of the recall-shortened Davis administration. One of these was a $140 million acquisition at the Ballona wetlands in Los Angeles, a deal that put a tight boundary around the always controversial Playa Vista project. The other deal was the $135 million acquisition of the 2,800-acre Ahmanson Ranch, where a 3,000-unit subdivision approved in 1992 had been languishing.

The Playa Vista project, on the site of a former Hughes aircraft factory, had been controversial since the 1970s. Environmentalists contended that the site had been a marsh and should be restored as such, but the city and landowners envisioned thousands of residents and workers in a grand, mixed-use development. The fight evolved into one of the most high profile environmental battles in Southern California. Eventually, the landowner won the right to build thousands of housing units and a large office/industrial complex, but only on a portion of the 1,100-acre site. Under the deal approved by the Davis administration, the state paid $140 million for 193 acres, and the landowner, Playa Capital, agreed to donate (for a substantial tax write-off) another 300 acres. Playa Capital also waived any rights to develop an additional 68 acres. Thus, about half the site was protected from development, although the deal had done nothing about resource restoration or management.

Detractors complained that the state overpaid Playa Capital for swamp land that was essentially unbuildable. But at least the state had acquired the largest recoverable wetlands in Los Angeles County. The Ahmanson Ranch deal was more peculiar.

Ventura County had approved a specific plan for 3,000 housing units on 2,800 acres at Ahmanson Ranch in 1992. As part of the specific plan deal, roughly 10,000 acres of adjacent land gained permanent protection as public open space. Still, wealthy and politically connected opponents of the Ahmanson Ranch development persisted, filing lawsuits and battling over every administrative detail. Towards the end of the fight, HBO executive Chris Albrecht and movie producer Rob Reiner were leading the campaign to save Ahmanson Ranch. So the state ponied up $135 million to the landowner, Washington Mutual.

The rugged Ahmanson Ranch offers great views of the even more rugged Santa Monica Mountains, but the ranch's ecological value is unclear. The land designated for development was not

Linda Levee in Yuba County failed in 1986, a liability that cost the state nearly $500 million.

Fire

Like most western states, California has many fire-driven ecologies—meaning many natural areas must burn from time to time to rejuvenate themselves.

Increasingly, however, local land use planning practices appear to be at odds with this fundamental precept of California's natural systems. As the urban edge reaches farther into the wilderness, and as retirees, "equity refugees," and telecommuters choose to live in rural counties, more and more people reside in what is called the "urban-wildland interface." These are places where wildfires also burn structures.

Ultimate responsibility for fighting wildfires in California falls to the California Department of Forestry and Fire Protection (CDF). As more residential subdivisions are permitted in high fire-risk areas, CDF has had to alter its firefighting strategies to protect people and structures. The agency has issued fire-safe development regulations, which include both avoidance and mitigation strategies. And in counties where the urban-wildland interface has a high fire risk, CDF tries to play an active role in helping local governments shape their land use policies to minimize the fire hazard, although local officials sometimes resist.

During the 1990s, major urban wildfires struck Oakland, Santa Barbara, Malibu, and Orange County. In the fall of 2003, the most destructive wildfires in state history roared through large portions of San Diego, Riverside, San Bernardino, Los Angeles, and Ventura counties, killing 24 people, destroying 3,600 homes and scorching 1,150 square miles of forest, chaparral and grasslands. Those wildfires spurred the creation of numerous commissions and preparation of many studies, but the upshot was mostly stricter building requirements, such as clearing flammable vegetation around structures, sealing eaves, and prohibiting wooden roofs and siding. No broad planning initiatives resulted from the destruction, partly because so many hazardous areas are already developed.

Earthquakes

The major earthquakes of the last two decades have reminded most Californians that they live in a region where the ground is certain to shake and rattle sooner or later. The Alquist-Priolo Act is supposed to ensure that development patterns do not create seismic hazards. Like many other state environmental laws, Alquist-Priolo is designed to work within the context of the general plan process. However, the law also specifies planning standards local governments should follow in areas of significant earthquake hazard—standards that communities do not always enforce with equal vigor.

Under the Alquist-Priolo Act, the state Division of Mines and Geology must identify areas where the risk of earthquakes is high and designate these areas as "special study zones." Upon further study, the agency determines whether the fault is active or not. If the study zone does not contain an active fault, then development may proceed. However, if active faults are found, then no buildings may be constructed within fifty feet of the fault. If the area on top of an active fault is already developed, the local government is encouraged to adopt policies that will lead to the removal of the buildings in question.

In one sense, the Alquist-Priolo Act is a top-down state mandate—cities and counties must abide by the geological findings of the Division of Mines and Geology. However, the law is also designed to interact with local planning processes. State general plan law specifies that seismic safety information should be contained in the safety element, one of the seven required elements of a general plan. If the Division of Mines and Geology has identified study zones or active faults, the safety element should specify those areas, and the other elements of the general plan should not permit development of those areas.

significantly different from the thousands of acres nearby that had already been preserved. And the site abuts the city of Los Angeles, where the busy sprawl of the San Fernando Valley comes to an abrupt halt at the Ahmanson Ranch fence.

Still, at least the state acquired 2,800 acres of land. The next big deal cost even more and resulted in very little real estate coming into public hands. The deal, closed in 2004, concerned the Hearst Ranch—82,000 mostly undeveloped acres, including 18 miles of spectacular coastline. The Hearst family had sought permission to develop portions of the land for decades (an early proposal called for a new town of 60,000 people) but had met stiff opposition at every step. Finally, the Schwarzenegger administration struck a deal. Hearst received $80 million from the state, a $15 million tax credit, and a $140 million tax write-off. In exchange, the state parks department got 13 miles of coastline (about 950 acres) and Caltrans got 500 acres to allow Highway 1 realignment. Additionally, a conservation easement was placed on about 80,000 acres. To be managed by a private land trust, the easement prevented development but provided for no public access and allowed a continuation of cattle ranching and other agriculture. Furthermore, Hearst maintained the right to build a hotel and 27 mansions, and the landowner kept 5 miles of private beaches. The deal received a mixed reception from environmentalists and locals who had fought development proposals.

All four of these deals were ostensibly about preserving natural resources. But what the deals demonstrate more than anything is that the right mixture of politics and landowner aggressiveness can combine with natural resources to force open the government's checkbook. ∎

Part Seven

Conclusion

Chapter 25

Making Planning Work in California

California has more planners than any other state in the country, and it's likely that Californians spend more time debating the future of their communities than anyone else. But all this does not mean that planning "works" in California.

The goal of planning is, or should be, to shape the built environment for the benefit of society—to meet the needs of all people and accommodate a growing economy, while at the same time conserving natural resources and protecting the environment. To put it another way, planning's job should be to assure that people and activities are arranged on the landscape in a rational, efficient, equitable, and environmentally sound manner.

The goal of planning is, or should be, to shape the built environment for the benefit of society.

To be sure, in selected communities and in selected circumstances, planning in California has taken long strides toward achieving this goal. But from a broad perspective—as this book has tried to point out—the state and its communities have fallen short. There are many planning successes in California. But with every success seems to come some kind of failure as well.

California's preference for home rule has given small cities throughout the state a remarkable degree of freedom in shaping their communities, even when those small cities lie in the middle of huge metropolitan areas. Additionally, California—the most diverse state in the country—remains highly segregated by race, ethnicity, and income, partly because local control of land use has sometimes been wielded in the interests of such segregation.

California has been a leader in opening the planning process to participation by all citizens and all interest groups. Yet citizen unrest about growth and development is more intense here than anywhere else in the country, and citizen groups can often hold the entire planning process hostage in order to pursue a narrow agenda that includes little regard for the overall public interest.

These are but a few examples of the broader trend. And as we think about how to make planning in California work in the 21st century, we must revisit the assumptions on which the current system is based.

The modern California planning system began to emerge in the 1950s, when the state first began to grapple with the problems of large-scale postwar growth. Over a period of approximately 25 years—up until the early 1980s—this planning system matured according to what might be called the "suburban growth model."

The suburban growth model assumed that all growth was more or less the same. Population growth and economic expansion would move forward along a parallel track, meaning that the new residents would usually be middle-class families looking for typical suburban lives. This, in turn, meant that growth would translate into a predictable outward expansion of metropolitan areas. The job of planning was to arrange this outward march in an orderly fashion and try to minimize its inevitable impact on the environment.

All of the important planning tools that emerged during this period—general plan law, the California Environmental Quality Act, revisions to the Subdivision Map Act—still reflect these basic assumptions. So too do the biases of the state's planning infrastructure—the vast cadre of planners, consultants, lawyers, developers, designers, economists, and others (including the authors of this book) who make their living by organizing and managing growth in the state.

The Dynamics of Growth and the Limits of Planning

But today we live in the California of the 21st century, not the California of 1960, or 1970, or even 1980. Most of these basic growth assumptions are no longer true. Much of our population growth is not middle-class suburban growth. There is no predictable relationship between population growth and economic expansion. And although there is still an outward expansion of the urban container, this expansion has begun to take a much different form than traditional suburban development.

In rethinking our assumptions, therefore, we must come to a better understanding about what the dynamics of growth in

California are, and how the planning process can best help to shape growth. In the introduction, this book suggested that growth is not a monolith. Rather, it is a complex phenomenon with at least three different dynamics:

- **Population growth,** and changes in the racial and ethnic makeup of that population
- **Economic growth,** along with the changes in economic structure
- **Changes to the built environment** as the result of private real estate development and public works projects

Planning, of course, can only control the third item. But politicians and the public often expect that, in doing so, they will be able to influence the first two as well. This is not usually true.

Despite the major focus on restricting residential development in many communities, the simple fact is that the typical municipality cannot alter basic population trends. Increasingly, in a working-class economy with many large families, basic population growth cannot be changed in any dramatic fashion by any tool available to local government—or even the state—that could be called planning. Affluent communities with existing single-family neighborhoods can usually prevent much growth or change successfully, but lower- and middle-income communities throughout California are seeing their populations grow dramatically even if they don't permit any new housing.

Despite the major focus on restricting residential development in many communities, the simple fact is that the typical municipality cannot alter basic population trends.

It is also questionable whether planning can alter basic economic trends—and, again, this takes us back to the role of economic development, which is clearly part of the planning process. Is economic development supposed to stimulate general economic growth, or is it supposed to focus on distressed areas? Is it supposed to focus on the economic well-being of a particular jurisdiction or municipality, or is it supposed to focus instead on overall economic growth?

Curiously, planning gets blamed for economic decline but rarely praised for economic growth. In bad times, the complicated and cumbersome nature of planning becomes a scapegoat. Inevitably, there are calls both in Sacramento and in communities around the state to streamline the planning and regulatory process. But streamlining regulation in one particular city is not going to solve an overall economic malaise. Planning may be able to nibble at the edges, but it is unlikely to reverse the entire economic cycle.

Curiously, planning gets blamed for economic decline but rarely praised for economic growth. In bad times, the complicated and cumbersome nature of planning becomes a scapegoat.

Thus, the land use planning and permitting process that we have talked about in this book can really influence only the third item on the list—changes in the built environment. Private real estate development and public works projects are most often the result of—not a cause of—population growth and economic change. Yet the power of planning to shape and manage this activity is extremely powerful.

The sum total of all real estate development—plus capital improvements in roads, schools, and other public sector activities—quite literally shapes our world.

The sum total of all real estate development—plus capital improvements in roads, schools, and other public sector activities—quite literally shapes our world. It affects how far we must travel to engage in any daily activities, whether we must drive, how close we live to our neighbors, and how we affect the natural environment. The process of managing this real estate development creates the shape and form of our metropolitan areas. Planning works best when it provides a framework that reflects a well thought-out policy about the public objectives that are associated with real estate development and changes in the physical or built environment.

As we contemplate how to transform planning in California so that it can address the 21st century effectively, we must recognize both the limits and the opportunities of the planning process, and understand how planning can be used effectively to face the challenges ahead. In particular, planning must be used to address three specific challenges that will dominate the growth and development of California during the foreseeable future.

First, it must pay increased attention to replanning maturing urban areas. Second, it must focus on planning to conserve natural resources. And third, it must recognize the increased need to conduct planning on a scale appropriate to the problem being addressed.

Replanning Mature Urban Areas

As we have stated repeatedly throughout this book, the suburban growth model that has dominated California planning for the last half century is fast becoming history—at least in the older metropolitan areas near the coast. The Bay Area, metropolitan Los Angeles, and San Diego are already massive in geographical size. And, by percentage, they are not likely to get much bigger. Although a good deal of growth will occur in the Central Valley and the Inland Empire, it is probably fair to say that most of the state's future growth must be accommodated inside the urban containers we have already created.[1]

It is probably fair to say that most of the state's future growth must be accommodated inside the urban containers we have already created.

To alleviate urban transportation problems, to reduce the pressure on natural resources, and to provide livable and affordable

1. The one place where this probably will NOT be true is in the Central Valley, where outward urban expansion is likely to continue and must be managed carefully according to the suburban growth model.

neighborhoods, California planners will have to focus more and more on replanning and redevelopment of existing urban areas, rather than on the creation of new suburban neighborhoods on the metropolitan fringe. This is a considerable challenge, because many local planners—and even local politicians—are accustomed to thinking in terms of greenfields and wide open spaces. In addition, there is no question that creating new communities on raw land is easier in many respects. Both planners and developers can move forward without thinking about annoyed neighbors, fragmented land ownership patterns, or high land prices.

California planners will have to focus more and more replanning and re-development of existing urban areas, rather than on the creation of new suburban neighborhoods on the metropolitan fringe.

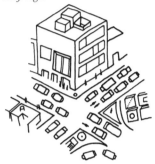

Beyond that, planners dedicated to replanning mature urban areas often have to do so using a planning system that was designed to manage the conversion of raw land to suburbs. But as we have stated throughout this book, older suburban communities are now built-out and both the political will and the technical expertise is beginning to change.

These communities will probably serve as the cutting-edge laboratory for a new kind of planning in California that focuses on replanning urban areas, rather than planning for traditional suburban growth. And the planners who make this transition will be successful in the 21st century—because they will be confronting the core challenge facing the state in the future.

Natural Resources and Urban Form

A focus on replanning existing urban areas will arise not only from population and economic pressures within those areas, but from a renewed focus on protecting natural resources in areas that are just opening up to urban expansion.

As we stated above, greenfield locations were traditionally desirable because they were subject to fewer constraints. Today, this is not so. Increasingly, environmental and natural resources considerations *are* constraining the development of new areas, and natural resources are likely to continue to be a driving force in shaping urban form in California. Simply put, much of the remaining land available for urbanization will be "locked up" in parks and open space preserves.

This is a result of the way the regulatory system at higher levels of government is set up. There are almost no strong state or federal regulations of how to arrange the human environment—i.e., housing. There are strong regulations from higher levels of government on how to arrange the natural environment. The experience of the Endangered Species Act and the Natural Communities Conservation Planning Program is a good example. The conservation plans drawn up under the NCCP effort are large-scale land use plans with the primary aim of maintaining and enhancing the environmental integrity of wildlands and open spaces. Because the creation of these plans has been driven by the Endangered Species Act, their drafters have been under no obligation to consider any other community planning issues, such as housing, transportation, or economic development.

NCCP = Natural communities conservation planning

Yet, clearly, efforts to restore natural resources will have to be linked to efforts to re-plan mature urban areas. In order to effectively preserve natural lands from human intrusion, it will also be necessary to provide habitable built environments—places where people want to live and work—to accommodate a growing population and an expanding economy.

The Problem of Scale

The third consideration has to do with the scale at which planning problems occur and the scale at which they can be addressed.

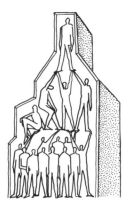

Planning problems tend to occur either at a large regional or subregional level, or at a small neighborhood level. Yet the political power to deal with those problems typically rests somewhere in between—with a local city or county or the state and federal government.

As this book has pointed out, there is often a mismatch between these two concerns. Planning problems tend to occur either at a large regional or subregional level, or at a small neighborhood level. Yet the political power to deal with those problems typically rests somewhere in between—with a city or county—or at an even larger scale, with the state and federal government.

For example, local governments often pursue retail establishments in order to generate more sales tax revenue. But the market area for a large retailer is almost always much bigger than the political boundaries of a particular city. So when cities use the planning process to pursue retailers, they are almost always affecting neighboring communities as well—drawing away their residents and their tax base.

Similarly, transportation problems associated with growth usually occur at a regional level as well. By attracting people from a widespread commuting or shopping shed, large development projects increase traffic and affect transportation patterns over a big geographic area. Again, this geographic area usually crosses city, county, and sometimes regional boundaries.

By the same token, many planning issues are strictly local in nature. Whether a gas station is located on corner A or corner B, for example, makes little difference to the region or even to an entire city. But it can be very important to the residents who live in the immediate vicinity.

Unfortunately, it is rare that these problems can be dealt with at the same scale at which they occur. Cities or counties usually have no obligation to take into account regional problems created by their actions; whereas, if the state attempts to grapple with them, a one-size-fits-all solution may not be appropriate everywhere. By contrast, a city or county that may be too small to deal with regional concerns may well be too big to deal with neighborhood concerns.

It's unlikely that we will see a wholesale realignment of local governments to respond to these concerns. But the political system must find some way to deal with problems at the appropriate scale in order for planning to function more effectively in California.

It's unlikely that we will see a wholesale realignment of local governments to respond to these concerns. But the political system will find some way to deal with problems at the appropriate scale in order for planning to function more effectively in California.

California as a Bounded World

It is perhaps unfashionable these days to say that we live in a world of limits. It is much easier—and more politically palatable—to believe that the sky's the limit, and we have no constraints on ourselves and our daily activities.

The truth of the matter is that most Californians today live, for the most part, in what might be called a "bounded" world. We already know this financially—the state budget is in eternal crisis because of various limitations and commitments. But it is equally true with growth. We have twice as many people today as we did in the 1960s, and we are likely to add another 15 million people at least during the lifetime of most people who read this book. Accommodating this expansion in the future will not be as easy as it was in the past.

The three challenges described above reflect this reality. As they mature, our metropolitan areas are becoming more complicated, more full of political vested interests, and more difficult to reshape in response to changing conditions. At the same time, we have come to realize that the raw land we have always viewed as the solution is not really raw. It is, in fact, filled with important natural systems or with agricultural crops, both of which are important to our future well-being, and are deserving of aggressive protection.

So in the 21st century, we in California must understand that we live in a world where we must make choices. We can no longer have boundless economic growth, endless quarter-acre lots, free-flowing freeways, vast expanses of farmland, and pristine natural settings all at once. We must somehow accommodate all of these things in the bounded space we call our state, and, for better or worse, we must use the planning process to do it.

This may sound like an impossible challenge, but in fact it is an opportunity. Most of the great design solutions in history have emerged from such constrained situations. And planning has always been at its best when it has been able to show people the choices they have in shaping their future.

By responding effectively to maturing urban areas, precious natural resources, and appropriate scale, the planning process can help us make these choices.

In the past, because we in California have not used the planning process effectively, we have often ducked these choices. The results can be seen across the landscape—in the form of blighted inner-city areas, lifeless suburban strips, and squandered natural wonders. Now that it is no longer so easy for us to accommodate our growth, we must make sure that we do not make these mistakes again. By responding effectively to the three concerns listed above—maturing urban areas, precious natural resources, and appropriate scale—the planning process can help us make these choices. And, at the same time, it will help us to maintain California's reputation as a place of opportunity and quality for generations to come.

Glossary

advocacy planning

A view of planning popular in the 1960s that sought to stabilize urban neighborhoods by improving the lives of the urban poor.

affordable housing

Housing that is priced to be affordable to specific segments of the population—usually the poor and working poor, who cannot afford market-created housing.

alternatives

For purposes of CEQA, other feasible projects that meet or substantially meet the stated objectives of the project being reviewed.

assessment district

A financing district that requires property owners to pay based on the benefit each property receives from construction of the public infrastructure.

ballot box zoning

Zoning adopted by initiative rather than by a governing body.

berm

A raised path or mound of earth.

blight

A condition of deterioration of a site, structure, or area that may cause nearby buildings and/or areas to decline in attractiveness and/or utility. Under California Redevelopment law,

a blighted area must be predominantly urbanized, and the blight must cause both a physical and an economic burden to the community, as well as be conducive to ill health, transmission of disease, infant mortality, and juvenile delinquency.

bulk

The height, mass, density, and location of buildings on a piece of land.

capital improvement

The building of infrastructure or public works projects.

capital improvement program (CIP)

A local government's schedule of infrastructure improvements necessary to accommodate existing and anticipated future development. Most such programs include a financing mechanism to fund the cost of the improvements.

California Environmental Quality Act (CEQA)

A state law that (1) defines state environmental goals and the responsibilities of local governments to assist in achieving those goals; and (2) sets forth the requirements for the environmental analysis of proposed public and private projects, including the preparation and/or review of environmental impact reports or issuance of exemptions and negative declarations.

charter city

A city organized under a charter adopted by a majority vote according to provisions of state law. The charter operates as the city's constitution. A city without a charter must follow the general laws of the state in all situations, while charter cities have more discretion within their city charters to establish land use processes.

citizen enforcement

Process by which private citizens and citizen groups use litigation to enforce planning laws.

community facilities district (CFD)

Districts created by cities, counties, and school districts under the Mello-Roos law to finance the construction of needed community infrastructure. The CFD is empowered to levy additional property taxes on land located inside the district, thus creating a dependable revenue stream that can be used in issuing bonds to pay for the new infrastructure.

conditional use permit (CUP)

A mechanism that allows a local government the ability to permit specific uses not otherwise allowed, as long as the landowner or business owner meets certain conditions.

council of governments (COG)

An association of cities and counties that often acts as a regional planning agency with some power under state and federal law.

cumulative impact

Overall effect on the environment of the various projects being considered or that have already been approved. A cumulative impact assessment is a requirement of CEQA.

design

Physical layout of a community or a specific development project, including site planning and urban design.

design review

Process by which a decision-making body considers a project's consistency with the design standards and guidelines established for new development.

detachment

The opposite of annexation.

development agreement

A contract between a city or county and a developer, which may specify conditions, terms, restrictions, and regulations pertaining to all aspects of a development.

development code

The set of rules and regulations that apply generally to all developments of a specific type.

development rights

The speculative value of property for real estate development. Many local land trusts and government agencies choose to buy the development rights of property they wish to protect from development rather than buying the land itself.

direct nexus

Legal term meaning a direct relationship or connection between an exaction and the project on which it is imposed.

dirt bond

Another name for a Mello-Roos bond, so-called because it is backed by the value of the land involved, not by general tax revenue.

discretionary approval

Approval by a decision-making body that has the legal discretion to approve or deny a project.

discretionary review

Process by which a decision-making body considers whether to approve or deny a project.

disposition and development agreement

The agreement between a city and the developer who will be building a project called for in a redevelopment plan.

dissolution

The opposite of incorporation, when an incorporated city ceases to be an independent political entity.

economic development

The task of fueling general economic expansion, often by fostering growth in certain types of jobs and businesses targeted to the needs of a particular community and its labor force.

economic infrastructure

Infrastructure that fosters economic development and growth, such as airports and highways.

element (in general plan)

A chapter or section of the local general plan that addresses a specific topic and sets forth public policies and programs pertaining to that topic. California Planning Law mandates that each city and county prepare and adopt a general plan containing at least seven specified elements (land use, circulation, open space, conservation, noise, safety, and housing).

empowerment zone

A specified area similar to an enterprise zone, in which businesses are given tax breaks as inducement for locating there. Empowerment zones are designated by a federal program providing large sums of federal money targeted for distressed urban areas.

enterprise zone

An area designated by the federal or state government as a distressed area where regulatory and tax burdens are loosened to stimulate private investment.

environmental analysis

Task of assessing the impact of any given plan or development project on the state's environment, an analysis that can range across any number of topics including air pollution, toxics, and impact on wildlife.

environmental design

The process by which site planners shape private development to accommodate the public goals of environmental protection, as in preserving wetlands and riparian habitats.

environmental impact report (EIR)

Detailed informational document prepared by the public agency responsible for carrying out a project as part of the CEQA process that describes and analyzes a project's significant environmental effects and discusses ways to mitigate or avoid those effects.

environmental impact statement (EIS)

The equivalent of an environmental impact report, but prepared under federal law.

essential nexus

Legal term meaning the required connection, either direct or indirect, between a project and an exaction imposed upon it.

exaction

A contribution or payment required as an authorized precondition for receiving a development permit. It usually refers to a mandatory dedication or fee in lieu of dedication requirements found in many subdivision regulations and may apply to land for parks or other public facilities.

exclusive zoning

System of zoning that designates one use to each section of a city.

final map

A map of an approved subdivision filed in the county recorder's office. It shows surveyed lot lines, street rights-of-way, easements, monuments, and distances, angles, and bearings, pertaining to the exact dimensions of all parcels, street lines, and so forth.

findings

A formal and written determination or conclusion based on the evidence presented and prepared by a hearing body in support of its decision. A requirement to produce findings of fact is often found in due process rules of state legislation and in California applies to most discretionary permits.

fire-driven ecology

An ecological system that requires periodic burning to perpetuate and regenerate itself.

fiscalized land use policy

Local land use policy motivated by and focused on revenue generation.

floor-area ratio

A formula set by local ordinance that establishes the maximum permitted building volume as a multiple of the area of the lot.

floor-space control

A growth-management tool that includes numerical restrictions on commercial and residential development.

garden city

The ideal of a planning movement that sought to create new towns on the metropolitan fringe that maintained a village atmosphere, yet accommodated the automobile and incorporated farmland and natural areas into the design.

general control

A method of growth management that is integrated into basic planning policies through the use of a growth-management element in the city's general plan.

general obligation bond

A tax-exempt bond issued by a public agency that must be repaid from general tax revenues rather than from specific revenue sources.

general plan amendment

Change or addition to a community's general plan. General plans can be amended with relative ease up to four times a year.

growth cap

Growth management technique that involves setting numerical limits on new construction over a given period of time.

growth management

The use of a wide range of techniques in combination to permit a community to determine its own amount, type, and rate of growth and to channel that growth into designated areas.

growth-inducing impact

Those effects of a project that are likely to lead to more development. Analysis of growth-inducing effects is a required part of an EIR.

habitat conservation plan (HCP)

Plan prepared under the federal Endangered Species Act that permits development in some areas in exchange for conserving land in other areas where endangered species are likely to be found.

impact analysis

The section of an EIR that analyzes the significant, unavoidable, and irreversible environmental effects of a project.

impact mitigation measure

Action or change to a project that will minimize its environmental effects.

incidental take

Taking of endangered or threatened species if the take is part of an overall effort to improve the condition of the species.

inclusive zoning

System of zoning that creates a hierarchy of use classifications such that each zone may be used for its specific designation or any higher designation, usually with single-family houses as the highest designation and heavy industrial as the lowest.

incorporation

Process by which an area of an existing city or county becomes an independent city.

infrastructure adequacy ordinance

Rule enacted by a city requiring that new development only be permitted if adequate infrastructure exists to service the project.

infrastructure control

A growth-management technique by which new development is only permitted if the project would not have a significant impact on a community's infrastructure.

initial study

Preliminary analysis by a city of a proposed project to determine whether an environmental impact report (EIR) must be prepared or a negative declaration will be sufficient.

initiative

Proposed legislative or constitutional changes that are placed on the ballot by citizen petition, to be approved or rejected by popular vote, thus allowing citizens to enact their own laws, independent of the state legislature or local legislative body.

inverse condemnation

A term used to describe claims by developers that a regulatory taking has occurred and that just compensation is due the landowner by the government under the Fifth Amendment.

LAFCO (local agency formation commission)

A county commission that reviews and evaluates all proposals for formation of special districts, incorporation of cities, annexation to special districts or cities, consolidation of districts, and merger of districts with cities. Each county's LAFCO is empowered to approve, disapprove, or conditionally approve these proposals.

land-secured bonding mechanism

Bonds backed by the value of the land involved, not by tax revenue.

leapfrog subdivision

Development that occurs well beyond the existing limits of urban development and necessary services, leaving intervening vacant land behind.

legislative act

General policy decision by a decision-making body, such as a general plan revision or zoning ordinance.

local coastal plan (LCP)

Plan for coastal development required by the state Coastal Commission before land use permitting power in the coastal zone is returned to local governments.

magic subdivision

Subdivision that predates the original passage of state subdivision legislation.

Master EIR

Document used as the first step in environmental review for broad-based programs where a series of related actions may occur under one project. The Master EIR covers all of the potential environmental impacts that can be feasibly analyzed at the time the overall plan is designed.

master-planned development

Development designed to create an entire self-contained community, rather than an addition to an existing one.

Mello-Roos Bond

Bond issued pursuant to the establishment of a community facilities district created for a new development. The CFD levies additional property taxes on land located inside the district, thus creating a dependable revenue stream that can be used in issuing bonds to pay for the new infrastructure.

metropolitan planning organization (MPO)

The regional agency in each region designated by the federal government to conduct transportation planning under federal law. The MPO is often, but not always, the COG.

mitigated negative declaration

A CEQA document prepared when a project would have significant environmental effects as originally proposed, but the developer can and will eliminate those effects by changing the

project or adopting mitigation measures, meaning that certain steps must be taken but no further environmental review is necessary.

mitigation

Actions or project design features that reduce environmental impacts by avoiding adverse effects, minimizing adverse effects, or compensating for adverse effects.

mitigation money

Fees paid in lieu of other mitigation measures that will be used to mitigate significant environmental effects (often in combination with monies from other projects).

multiple mitigations

Two or more mitigation measures adopted to mitigate the same effect.

naked checklist

A checklist used to assess all the environmental factors and determine if a project may have significant environmental impacts which requires only a "yes," "no," or "maybe" answer with no further explanation. Though widely used in the '70s and '80s for purposes of CEQA analysis, the naked checklist is now illegal.

natural communities conservation planning (NCCP)

Equivalent of habitat conservation planning prepared under state law.

neo-traditional planning

Style of planning that favors formalistic neighborhood design, integration of land uses, emphasis on pedestrians and transit, and integration of the street into neighborhood design.

National Environmental Policy Act (NEPA)

A federal law very similar to CEQA which requires its own environmental review process.

new town

Self-contained community including housing, jobs, and shopping areas located in a newly developing area. Often used to denote a master-planned community.

New Urbanism

A movement in architecture, planning, and urban design that emphasizes a particular set of design principles, including pedestrian- and transit-oriented neighborhood design, and a mix of land uses as a means of creating more cohesive communities.

nexus

Legal term meaning connection.

nexus study

A study, usually produced by a nexus consultant, that documents the connection between an exaction and a development project or class of projects.

NIMBY

"Not in my backyard." Refers to the attitude of residents and homeowners who oppose new development simply because it would be located nearby.

non-conforming use

A structure or use that was legal at its commencement but subsequently forbidden by a change in the zoning ordinance. Most ordinances provide that such a use may be continued but not enlarged.

nonpoint source pollution

Sources of pollution that are difficult to define and that usually cover broad areas of land, such as the carrying of fertilizers from agricultural land by runoff or the carrying of smog from one area to another.

overall plan approval

The first part of a two-step process in approving a large development, where the developer first seeks approval for the basic overall plan, and then seeks approval for individual tracts as the developer is ready to build.

parcel map

A map depicting the establishment of up to four new lots by splitting a recorded lot. Parcel maps are subject to the California Subdivision Map Act and a city's subdivision regulations.

performance standards

Zoning regulations setting specific criteria that limit the operations of certain industries, land uses, and buildings to acceptable levels of noise, air pollution emissions, odors, vibration, dust, dirt, glare, heat, fire hazards, wastes, traffic generation, and visual impact.

Permit Streamlining Act

A law that sets important deadlines for local government action, especially in connection with the Subdivision Map Act.

planned-unit development

A self-contained development, often with a mixture of housing types and densities, in which the subdivision and zoning controls are applied to the project as a whole rather than to individual lots, as in most subdivisions. Densities and lot sizes are calculated for the entire development, usually permitting a trade-off between the clustering of houses and provision of common open space or other amenities.

planning

The process by which public agencies, mostly local governments, determine the intensity and geographical arrangements of various land uses in a community.

point sources

The specific sources that emit water (and pollutants) from a particular pipe.

police power

The inherent right of a government to restrict an individual's conduct or use of one's property in order to protect the health, safety, welfare, and morals of the community.

political control

A form of growth management that requires voter approval or a super-majority of the city council or board of supervisors to expand zoning or increase the amount of development permitted under the general plan.

population control

Growth-management technique where residential construction is limited to minimize population increases.

quasi-judicial act

Decision that applies legislative policy to individual development projects, much as a court might apply legal precedents to a particular case. Quasi-judicial actions merely interpret rather than set policies.

Quimby Fee

An in lieu fee paid to create public parks pursuant to the Quimby Act.

reasonable relationship

The legal standard by which any exaction can be imposed, so long as it furthers the implementation of the city's general plan and bears at least an indirect relationship to the development project being proposed.

redevelopment

The legally-authorized process of rehabilitating or rebuilding a deteriorated section of a city using municipal powers and finances to assemble properties, replace infrastructure, or otherwise assist in creating new facilities and stimulating private development.

redevelopment project area

An area designated by a city to be part of a redevelopment project.

referendum

The process by which citizens elect to vote, approving or disapproving a decision made by a governing body.

regional transportation infrastructure

Transportation facilities that service a region rather than a particular city or county; for instance major highways, freeways, and airports.

regulatory taking

A situation wherein a land use regulation is so restrictive that a landowner is robbed of all economically viable use of his or her land, thereby constituting a "taking" under the Fifth Amendment to the U.S. Constitution.

rough proportionality

The legal requirement that a city make some sort of individualized determination that a required dedication is related both in nature and extent to the impact of the proposed development.

sales tax increment deal

A financing tool by which redevelopment agencies are allowed to keep all additional property taxes generated by their efforts in a redevelopment area.

sequencing

A growth-management technique that identifies the sequence in which specific areas will be developed and then reinforces that sequence with the capital improvement schedule.

significance threshold

Level of an effect on the environment above which the effect must be considered significant for purposes of CEQA.

site planning

The physical layout of building and landscape design.

socioeconomic analysis

The task of assessing the impact of a plan or project on a neighborhood's social structure, on a community's fiscal health, on a region's economic basis, and similar socioeconomic considerations.

special interests

Groups—of citizens, professionals, residents, etc.—who lobby lawmakers about a specific cause or action.

special study zone

Area identified by the state Division of Mines and Geology as high risk for earthquakes that requires special analysis and conditions before considering proposed development.

specific plan

A special set of development standards that apply to a particular geographical area.

sphere of influence

The probable ultimate physical boundaries and service area of a city as determined by the local agency formation commission (LAFCO) of each county.

spot zoning

A practice that essentially grants one parcel of land a designation incompatible with the rest of the neighborhood.

supplemental EIR

A CEQA document that is prepared after a final EIR if there are minor changes to the project.

surface mining and reclamation plan

A plan requiring mining activities to generally follow state policy as laid out by the California Mining and Geology Board and that must be adopted by the relevant city or county in accordance with state policy under the Surface Mining and Reclamation Act.

taking

The appropriation by government of private land.

tax set-aside

A legal requirement that certain tax revenues be set aside for specific purposes, as in housing "set-asides" in redevelopment areas.

tax-exempt bond

A bond issued by a government agency and sold to individuals who do not have to pay taxes on the interest income they receive.

tax-increment financing district

A special district created from a redevelopment area in which the future growth in property tax revenues generated is used to finance the redevelopment program itself. In most cases, redevelopment agencies issue bonds against this property tax increment to pay for public investments inside the redevelopment area.

technical background report

A report created by planning staff, consultants, or other outside experts for the purpose of providing a decision-making body with the facts necessary to make decisions during the CEQA process.

tentative map

Initial map setting forth in detail a proposed land subdivision that must comply with the city's or county's subdivision and zoning regulations and the state Subdivision Map Act. The subdivision of land depicted on the tentative map does not take effect until the Final Map is approved and recorded.

tiered approach

An approach to preparing EIRs whereby a series of EIRs are prepared at different stages of the planning process.

The first-tier EIR covers general issues in a broader program-oriented analysis. Subsequent tiers incorporate by reference the general discussions from the broader EIR, while primarily concentrating on the issues specific to the action being evaluated.

tiering

A method of complying with CEQA used in dealing with very large projects that will be reviewed and built over a long period of time, as with an extensive road-building program.

timber harvest plan (THP)

Plan for harvesting timber required under the Forest Practices Act. A timber harvest plan is considered the functional equivalent of an environmental impact report.

tract map approval

The second part of a two-step process whereby a large development project first receives overall approval, and then individual parts, or tracts, are approved as the developer is ready to build.

traffic impact fee

A fee charged by a local community to mitigate the effects of a development project on traffic conditions.

transfer of development rights

A procedure in which the right to develop one property, a sending site, is transferred to another property, a receiving site. As a result of the transfer, the owner of the sending site receives compensation, even though no additional development occurs at that site. Conversely, the owner of the receiving site can develop that site in a manner that would not otherwise be allowed.

unincorporated territory

The area of a county not within the boundaries of an incorporated city.

urban design

The physical organization of land uses and the creation of their architecturally styled connections into a coherent environment.

urban growth boundary (UGB)

A boundary around a given municipality or developed area beyond

which urban development is prohibited.

urban renewal

A federal program for the physical improvement of primarily urban areas through comprehensive planning and governmental assistance to effect rehabilitation and redevelopment.

urban storm water runoff

The water that flows into any general drainage system, rather than water that flows into a creek, stream, lake, or the ocean from a pipe.

use district

Zoning district that restricts the type of development that may be built there.

use variance

A variance that permits an otherwise unacceptable use on the property without changing the zone.

variance from standards

A variance that permits the landowner to construct a building or open a business without having to comply with the standards required of other landowners in the same zone.

variance

An exemption from compliance with the terms or conditions of a building or zoning regulation by an authorized local board or administrator.

vested right

The irrevocable right of a property owner to develop one's own property that cannot be changed by local government permitting agencies or a slow-growth initiative.

vesting tentative map

A type of tentative subdivision map that, if granted, confers the right to develop the project in accordance with the regulations, standards, and policies in effect at the time that the application for the map was accepted as or deemed complete.

wetlands

Lands that may be covered periodically or permanently with shallow water and include saltwater marshes, freshwater marshes, open or closed brackish water marshes, swamps, mudflats, and fens.

zoning

The division of a city into districts and the application of different regulations in each district.

zoning control

A growth-control scheme whereby open space is downzoned to a restrictive level, and zoning changes are made very difficult to obtain.

zoning envelope

The space in which a project may be built on a piece of land, which is defined by specifying setbacks, height limits, and sometimes limits on the percentage of a site that may be covered by buildings, other structures, and paving.

zoning ordinance

A law dividing all land in the city into zones that specifies uses permitted and standards required in each zone.

zoning tool

Mechanism that landowners, developers, and cities may use to accommodate projects that otherwise would be unacceptable, or to stop projects that otherwise would be allowed.

Acronyms

ABAG	= Association of Bay Area Governments
APCD	= Air Pollution Control District
AQMD	= Air Quality Management District
BCDC	= Bay Conservation and Development Commission
BLM	= Bureau of Land Management
CDBG	= Community Development Block Grant
CDF	= Department of Forestry and Fire Protection
CEQA	= California Environmental Quality Act
CFD	= Community facilities district
CIP	= Capital improvement program
CMA	= Congestion Management Agency
CMP	= Congestion management plan
COG	= Council of governments
CTA	= County Transportation Authority
CTC	= California Transportation Commission
CUP	= Conditional use permit
DOT	= U.S. Department of Transportation
DWR	= Department of Water Resources
EIR	= Environmental impact report
EIS	= Environmental impact statement
EPA	= Environmental Protection Agency
FHwA	= Federal Highway Administration
FTA	= Federal Transit Administration
GSA	= General Services Administration
HCD	= U.S. Department of Housing and Urban Development
HCP	= Habitat conservation plan
ISTEA	= Intermodal Surface Transportation Efficiency Act

LAFCO	= Local agency formation commission
LCP	= Local coastal plan
LUPIN	= Land Use Planning Information Network
MPO	= Metropolitan planning organization
MTA	= L.A. County Metropolitan Transportation Authority
MTC	= Bay Area Metropolitan Transportation Commission
MWD	= Metropolitan Water District of Southern California
NCCP	= Natural communities conservation planning
NEPA	= National Environmental Policy Act
NPDES	= National Pollution Discharge Elimination System
OPR	= Governor's Office of Planning and Research
PAC	= Project Area Committee
RTIP	= Regional Transportation Improvement Program
RTPA	= Regional Transportation Planning Agency
SANDAG	= San Diego Association of Governments
SCAG	= Southern California Association of Governments
SMARA	= Surface Mining and Reclamation Act
SPEA	= Standard City Planning Enabling Act
STIP	= State Transportation Implementation Plan
SZEA	= Standard State Zoning Enabling Act
TEA-21	= Transportation Equity Act for the 21st Century
THP	= Timber harvest plan
TMA	= Transportation Management Agency
TRPA	= Tahoe Regional Planning Agency
UGB	= Urban growth boundary

Suggested Reading

The research that went into this book came from literally hundreds of different sources. Rather than list them all, however, we thought it would be more useful to provide the dozen or so most important and explain a little about what makes them so good. Here, then, are the books we believe must accompany this one on any California planning bookshelf:

Curtin's California Land Use and Planning Law, by Daniel J. Curtin, Jr. and Cecily T. Talbert (Solano Press, updated annually). This book has set the standard as a readable overview of all aspects of planning laws in California. In approximately 500 pages, Curtin and Talbert, who are partners in the respected law firm of Bingham McCutchen, cover every topic from the general plan (on which Curtin is a particular expert) to CEQA, exactions, and initiatives.

The California Planner's Book of Lists (Governor's Office of Planning and Research, updated annually). A good compilation of useful information, including a directory of government planning departments and results of OPR's annual survey of local governments. Available only on the OPR website (www.opr.ca.gov).

Ballot Box Navigator: A Practical and Tactical Guide to Land Use Initiatives and Referenda in California, by Michael Patrick Durkee, Jeffrey A. Walter, David H. Blackwell, and Thomas F. Carey (Solano Press, 2004). A useful overview of the legal aspects of "ballot-box zoning," provided by lawyers with extensive experience in the field.

CEQA Deskbook by Ronald E. Bass, Albert I. Herson, and Kenneth M. Bogdan (Solano Press, updated regularly). Published for the first time in January 1992 as *Successful CEQA Compliance,* this book is the first-ever practical user's guide to explain clearly, yet comprehensively, how to proceed from the beginning to the end of the environmental review process. It summarizes the California Environmental Quality Act and the *CEQA Guidelines,* and focuses on the procedural and substantive requirements of CEQA.

CEQA Guidelines, General Plan Guidelines, and *Planning, Zoning, and Development Laws.* (Governor's Office of Planning and Research, updated periodically). An invaluable trio of documents prepared by California's only state planning office. The *CEQA Guidelines* are, in fact, a set of administrative regulations, but they provide valuable insight into how the CEQA process works. The *General Plan Guidelines* are a detailed and valuable set of recommendations about how local governments should go about preparing general plans. *Planning, Zoning, and Development Laws* outlines the basics of California planning law, including requirements for local governments to establish planning agencies and draw up planning documents. Available from the Governor's Office of

Planning and Research, Administrative Services, P.O. Box 3044, Sacramento, CA 95812-3044. Telephone (916) 445-0613. Some or all of these documents are also available online (www.opr.ca.gov).

Guide to the California Environmental Quality Act, by Michael Remy *et al.* (Solano Press). Like many environmental documents it describes, this book, written by members of the respected Sacramento environmental law firm of Remy, Thomas, Moose and Manley, is thick. But it is also good— a detailed compendium of knowledge about this complicated law.

Land in America: Its Value, Use, and Control, by Peter Wolf (Pantheon Books, 1981). Written for the general reader, this book is a knowing, if now somewhat dated, overview of the importance of land in both the American economy and the American psyche. Covers a broad range of topics, including zoning and land values, land speculation, federal land, and an excellent discussion of the first (1970s) wave of slow-growth sentiment in California. (Out of print.)

Land Use in a Nutshell, by Robert R. Wright and Susan Webber Wright (West Group, third edition, 1994). This small book provides a valuable national overview on all aspects of land use law.

Longtin's California Land Use (Local Government Publications, second edition, 1987, with annual supplements). The ultimate legal reference on all aspects of land use law in California.

The Practice of Local Government Planning by Linda C. Dalton, Charles Hoch, and Frank S. So (New York International City/County Management Association, 2000). The so-called "green book" is designed as the basic reference book for all American urban planners.

Public Choices, Private Resources, by John J. Kirlin and Anne M. Kirlin (CalTax Foundation, 1982). This book, by a public finance expert and a land use lawyer, was one of the first publications to recognize both (1) the fiscalization of land use in California, and (2) the importance of public-private bargaining on development projects and fiscal matters. It remains an important primer on both subjects.

Redevelopment in California, by David F. Beatty *et al.* (Solano Press, updated annually). Like other publications from Solano Press, this is a comprehensive guide, designed to help the reader through the ins and outs of redevelopment in California.

Subdivision Map Act Manual, by Daniel J. Curtin, Jr. and Robert E. Merritt (Solano Press, updated regularly). Like *Curtin's California Land Use and Planning Law,* this book is a readable quick overview of the legal essentials.

Windfalls for Wipeouts: Land Value Capture and Compensation, by Donald Hagman and Dean Misczynski (American Society of Planning Officials, 1978). Dense but vital. This book is a fairly technical discussion of the economic consequences of land use regulation. But both authors are known for a wry and iconoclastic approach to their work. The innovative ideas about how to harness the power of market economics to solve planning problems are still fresh— and still largely unimplemented. (Out of print.)

The Zoning Game, by Richard Babcock. A quarter-century after its publication, *The Zoning Game* remains the most frank and informative explanation of how land use regulation really works in the United States. Less pathbreaking, though still interesting, is *The Zoning Game Revisited,* by Babcock and Charles F. Siemon, a sequel published in 1985. (Both are out of print.)

Index

industrial zone, 131, 133
    See also zoning
industry, 264
infrastructure, 20–21, 338
    See also bonds; highway
        construction; improvements
    capital improvement
        planning, 321–322
    dedications for, 146–147,
        149–150, 185, 222
    finance, 60–61, 184, 322–323
        assessment districts, 327–329
        developer finance,
            61, 222, 327
        fees and exactions, 327
        in general, 326–327
        Mello-Roos district/
            dirt bonds, 327, 329–331
        Proposition 218 and, 332–335
    in general, 319–320
    growth management
        policies and, 202
    public building, 114
    regional vs. local
        infrastructure, 320–321
    transportation infrastructure, 338
Inglewood, Wal-Mart, 253
initial study. *See also* California
    Environmental Quality Act
    CEQA procedures
        for, 157, 163–165
    checklist/"naked
        checklist," 164–165
initiative/referendum
    See also ballot box zoning;
        citizen activism;
        growth control initiative
    application to legislative
        act, 70, 134, 206, 221
    CEQA exemption, 209
    citizen use of, 18, 82, 200
    city-sponsored measure
        is CEQA "project," 160
    definition, 206
    not applicable to
        quasi-judicial act, 71
Inland area. *See also* Inland Empire
    discussed, 31–32
Inland Empire
    development in, 6, 314
    growth in, 16, 290
    interest groups, 9, 12, 23–24
Intermodal Surface Transportation
    Efficiency Act (ISTEA),
    342–343, 344
inverse condemnation, 229–230
    See also takings
investment, 256. *See also* economic
    development; redevelopment
investor, 10, 66, 97, 98
Inyo County, discussed, 39
Irvine, 48
    UC Irvine, 45

Irvine Company, The, 48, 98, 222
Irvine Ranch
    discussed, 48
    Water District, 387
Irwindale, 264
Isenberg, Phil, 262
ISTEA. *See* Intermodal
    Surface Transportation
    Efficiency Act

J

Jacobs, Jane, 314
jobs. *See also* income
    community balance and, 251
    current job total, 3
    labor market, 248
    relation to housing, 209
    relation to population, 243–244
Jost, Kenneth, 235
judicial review. *See also* courts
    CEQA, 159, 178
    "constitutional" case, 83
    exhaustion of administrative
        remedies, 231
    general plan, 120–124
    "statutory" case, 83–84

K

Kelo v. City of New London, 268
Kennard, Joyce, 194
Kern County, discussed, 35–36
King City, 289
Kings County, discussed, 35–36
kit fox, 216
Knox v. City of Orland,
    328–329, 333

L

La Mesa, 381
LAFCO. *See* local agency
    formation commission
Laguna West, 313–314
Lake County, discussed, 34–35
Lake Tahoe, 82
    discussed, 368–369
Tahoe Regional Planning Agency,
    92, 237–238, 369
Tahoe-Sierra Preservation Council
    v. Tahoe Regional Planning
    Agency, 42–43, 237, 238, 369
Lakewood, discussed, 56–57
land. *See also* agricultural
    land; land speculation
    as "an exhaustible resource," 10
    dwindling land supply, 16–17
    "entitled" land, 97
land acquisition
    program, 229–230
Land Park, 45
land speculation,
    10, 145, 146, 209, 319
    city planning, 45–48

land use element, 57
    See also general plan
    circulation element
        and, 109, 113–114
    in general, 108, 110–113
    interaction with other
        elements, 109, 113–114
    land use diagram, 110–111
    noise element and, 114, 119
land use regulation, 13
    history, 41–44, 48–52
    local government
        authority, 66–68
    must be consistent with
        general plan, 151
    must be "reasonably related"
        to public welfare, 67
    "national land use policy," 80
    "subdivision regulations," 103
    voting/non-voting cultures, 207
Landis, John, 17, 201
landowner
    See also property rights
    role in land use, 98
landscaping, 131
Landscaping and
    Lighting Act, 328
large lot subdivision, 38
    See also subdivision
Lassen County, discussed, 39
Lathrop, River Islands project, 176
Latinos, 5–6
Laurel Heights Improvement
    Association v. Regents of
    the University of California,
    172–173, 174
LAUSD. *See* Los Angeles
    Unified School District
law. *See also* common law; state law
    relation to planning, 8, 44–45
Lawndale, 69
lead agency, 162
    See also California
        Environmental Quality Act
League of California Cities, 81
legislation, 81
    "juice" bill, 81
legislative act. *See also* local
    government; ordinance
    discussed, 70
lenders, 98–99
Lesher Communications, Inc. v.
    City of Walnut Creek, 121
level of service (LOS), 202
Levine, Ned, 201, 210
Levittown, 56
    See also suburb
"lifestyle centers," 129
liquor stores, 138–139
litigation, 14
Livermore, 215
lobbying, 9, 11, 81
    See also politics

single-family home
    See also housing; suburb
    as model,
        51–52, 53–54, 56, 128, 280
Siskiyou County, discussed, 39
site planning. *See also* planning
    discussed, 309–311
slaughterhouse, 41–42, 49, 62
SMARA. *See* Surface Mining
    and Reclamation Act
Smart Growth America, 295
smog, 109, 337, 374, 391–393
    See also air quality
smoke detector, allowed as
    development condition, 150
snail darter, 377
social activism, 312
    See also citizen activism
socioeconomic analysis
    See also economic development
    planning process
    consideration of, 8–9
Soderling v. City of Santa Monica, 150
Solano County, discussed, 33–34
Soledad, 289
Solid Waste Agency of N. Cook
    County v. U.S. Army
    Corps of Engineers, 390
Solimar Research Group,
    206, 207, 238
Sonoma County, 26, 153, 207
    discussed, 33–34
    Sea Ranch, 310
    UGB, 209–210
South Carolina, *Lucas*
    decision, 234–235
South Coast Air Quality
    Management District, 109
Southern California, 211, 244
    Gateway Cities, 246–247
Southern California Association
    of Governments (SCAG),
    31, 32, 95, 96, 281, 341, 343
SPEA. *See* Standard City
    Planning Enabling Act
special district, 20, 78
    See also assessment district
    discussed, 66
"special interests," 9
specific plan, 11, 105, 330
    See also general plan
    in general, 211–214
    master-planned development
        discussed, 215–217
        in general, 214
    multi-owner property
        discussed, 217–218
        in general, 214–215
    relation to general plan, 213
    specific urban plan
        discussed, 218–220
        in general, 215
    types of plans, 214–215

Specific Plan Guidelines, 213
spot zoning, 134–135
    See also zoning
spotted owl, 35, 96, 377
    See also endangered species
sprawl, 4, 31–32, 36, 43, 48,
    56–57, 294, 305, 313, 341
    See also suburb
Standard City Planning Enabling
    Act (SPEA), 51, 55, 104
Standard State Zoning Enabling
    Act (SZEA), 51, 54
Stanislaus County
    Diablo Grande, 165, 389, 390
    discussed, 35–36
Stanislaus Natural Heritage Project v.
    County of Stanislaus, 165, 390
Staples, 275
state agency. *See also* federal
    agency; state government
    cooperation with local
        government, 87–89, 373
    coordination among, 321–322
    land use authority, 58, 59, 66
    regional land use agencies, 92–93
    role in planning process, 85–89
    state conservation agencies, 92–93
    state infrastructure and
        development agencies, 89–92
    transportation agencies, 338, 343
State Board of Reclamation, 395
state government
    See also federal government;
        local government; state law
    California legislature, 80–83
    economic development
        activity, 245, 246–247
    grants and financing, 60–61
        state bonds, 324–326
    no state planning model, 257
    public-private deals, 331
state law. *See also* law
    general plan consistency
        with, 122–123
State Water Project,
    89, 151, 389, 391
    EIR invalidation, 175
statement of overriding
    considerations, 151, 176, 392
    See also California
        Environmental Quality Act
Stein, Clarence, 47
Stephens' kangaroo rat, 379
Stevens, John Paul, 238
Stockton, 26
Stolman v. City of Los Angeles, 136
stream. *See also* streambed alteration
    permit; water pollution
    flood control, 388
    public access requirement, 150
streambed alteration permit, 371
streetcar, 46, 339
    See also railroad; transportation

subdivision, 51
    See also Subdivision Map Act
    large lot subdivision, 38
    "magic" subdivision, 146–147
    "paper" subdivision, 146
Subdivision Map Act
    (Map Act), 86, 211, 357, 402
    background, 55, 80–81, 104
    certificate of compliance,
        146–147, 153
    denial and appeal, 150–152
    design and improvement,
        146, 149–150
    in general, 68, 145–147
    judicial review, 152
    lot line adjustment, 153
    map, 147–149, 212
        final map, 147–149
        tentative map,
            147–149, 152
        vesting tentative map,
            152–153, 221
    Permit Streamlining Act
        and, 153–154
"subdivision regulations," 103
    See also land use regulation
subsidies. *See also* economic
    development
    as economic
        development, 256, 323
    for housing, 290, 351
    for retail development, 251, 269
suburb. *See also* housing;
    single-family home; sprawl
    gentrification and, 254
    invention of, 46
    as planning model,
        22, 27–29, 51–52, 99,
        209, 254, 294, 298, 299,
        350, 391, 393, 402, 405
    "slurbs," 57
Suitum v. Tahoe Regional
    Planning Agency, 239
Sundstrom v. County
    of Mendocino, 165
Sunset Strip, 215
    Sunset Boulevard specific
        plan, 215, 218–220
Surface Mining and
    Reclamation Act
    (SMARA), 92, 371, 393
Sutter County, discussed, 36–37
Swainson's hawk, 216, 378, 381
SZEA. *See* Standard State
    Zoning Enabling Act

T

Taft, William Howard, 53
Tahoe Regional Planning
    Agency, 92, 237–238, 369
Tahoe-Sierra Preservation Council
    v. Tahoe Regional Planning
    Agency, 42–43, 237, 238, 369

**Of Related Interest
from Solano Press**

Ballot Box Negotiator:
Land Use Initiatives and
Referenda in California

California Water

CEQA Deskbook

Code Enforcement

Curtin's California Land Use
and Planning Law

Eminent Domain

Exactions and Impact
Fees in California

Guide to the California
Environmental Quality Act

Guide to Hazardous Materials
and Waste Management

The NEPA Book

The Planning Commissioner
and the California Dream

Putting TDRs
to Work in California

Redevelopment in California

Subdivision Map Act Manual

Telecommunications:
The Governmental Role in Managing
the Connected Community

Transportation Law in California

Understanding
Development Regulations

Water and Land Use:
Planning Wisely for California's Future

Wetlands, Streams, and Other Waters

Cover design by Julie Shell

Book design by Solano Press

Illustrations by Ramón León,
Kevin Steadler, and Shinga Shell

Charts by Richard Yee Design

Maps courtesy UC Davis Information
Center for the Environment

Printed by Publishers Book Services

Index by Paul Kish